The Utopian Conceit
And the War on Freedom

Juliana Geran Pilon

The Utopian Conceit
And the War on Freedom

Juliana Geran Pilon

Academica Press
Washington – London

Library of Congress Cataloging-in-Publication Data

Names: Pilon, Juliana Geran, author.
Title: The utopian conceit and the war on freedom / Juliana Geran
Pilon.
Description: Washington : Academica Press, 2019. | Includes
bibliographical
references and index. | Summary: "In The Utopian Conceit and the War
on Freedom, noted political philosopher Juliana Geran Pilon explores the
roots of this malevolent ideology as the common ancestor of both anti
capitalism and anti-Semitism in the contemporary world, where political
and religious freedom is increasingly under assault"--
Provided by publisher.
Identifiers: LCCN 2019027427 | ISBN 9781680531558 (hardcover) |
ISBN
9781680531664 (paperback)
Subjects: LCSH: Utopias--Philosophy. | Capitalism. | Anti-Semitism. |
Liberty.
Classification: LCC HX806 .P48 2019 | DDC 321/.07--dc23
LC record available at https://lccn.loc.gov/2019027427

It is certainly no coincidence that in all three cases, [the political religions of Nazism, Stalinism, and Islamism], a remarkably similar anti-American and anti-Jewish demonology has been manipulated in the cause of destroying Judeo-Christian values, individual freedom, and liberal democracy.... At their very heart we can find the oldest and darkest of ideological obsessions – that of antisemitism....

Robert S. Wistrich (2010)

The fact that German antisemitism and anti-capitalism come from the same root is of great importance for the understanding of what has happened there... [though] it would be a mistake to believe that the specific German rather than the socialist element produced totalitarianism.

F. A. Hayek (1944)

The battle for freedom must be won over and over again.
Milton Friedman (1994)

Contents

Foreword

Visionaries work everlasting evil on earth.
Joseph Conrad, *Under Western Eyes* (1911)

Bad ideas generate bad consequences. An enduring probe into bad ideas is Richard M. Weaver's 1948 classic *Ideas Have Consequences,* that argues for right reason over unthinking, faulty thinking, shibboleths, intellectual fads, and all varieties of secular nostrums perpetually intent on creating an earthly paradise. The horrific human costs of such bad ideas litter the chronicles of human history, whether ancient, medieval, modern, or contemporary "post-modernism." The persistence of certain bad ideas speaks to their perennial attractiveness, notwithstanding their demonstrated fallacies and repeated evil consequences. Dr. Juliana Pilon's *The Utopian Conceit and the War on Freedom* arrives precisely at another of these increasingly repetitive historical points where half-baked ideas gain purchase once again, not merely in the hypertensive arena of the media and academia, but in political parties throughout the west, the US included.

When moral and behavioral norms thousands of years old and when heretofore normal language, to include pronouns, become the target of language police and censorship it is time, once again, for thoughtful adults to stand up and intone, *stop*, in no uncertain terms. Juliana Pilon is one of those thoughtful adults. Her book walks the serious reader through the bad ideas and their socio-political results that have continuously infected human history. She brings her focus to bear on the plagues of the mind that underlie the "isms" of modern history candidly, courageously, and unafraid of touching so-called third-rail issues.

Topics such as the inherent anti-Semitism lodged in Marx's fixation with the capitalist-bourgeois-Jew; the labeling of anyone opposed to the brown-shirt tactics of contemporary leftist/anarcho-revolutionaries (think *antifa*) as fascists, a bit of the supreme irony of projection and the essence of the *tu quoque* logical fallacy; the apocalyptic fixations of both Marxism and Islamic jihadism that predicate the elimination of those who stand in the way of their scriptural tenets designed to produce their respective earthly utopias – in the case of the Islamic variant an earthly prelude to the sensual pleasures of the heavenly one: all come in for trenchant examination and critique. These are just a few of the numerous bad ideas that the author probes with a welcome clarity of language and reasoned argument.

In the absence of classical learning and classical liberal arts curricula based on the solid foundation of the Judeo-Christian ethic/traditions – now exorcised and replaced by intellectual faddism – many in contemporary generations are ill-equipped to think critically through the barrage of truncated propaganda themes flooding high-tech communications that assault the senses. Indeed, critical thought was one of the first victims of utopian conceit dating back to the earliest of religious and intellectual (i.e., right-ordered thinking) heresies.

It should not surprise the reader that even in the intelligence world (the former profession of this writer), one occasionally encounters efforts in intelligence education to address the principles of critical thinking – a stark acknowledgement of the lack of something so basic to and expected of a craft that calls itself *intelligence*. Something absolutely core to reason and ordered thought has been lost. As a related aside, it is no accident that in the intellectually disciplined world of home schooling, critical thinking suffuses the curricula, many home-schoolers using the classical-medieval model of the *Trivium* (grammar, rhetoric, logic). Instead of damning such creative and productive efforts, the educational establishment might consider emulating them.

Closely attending the loss of critical thought in the perennial quest for utopia is the loss of historical instruction and a sense of history. As an example, consider the rediscovery of so-called democratic socialism. Like the unending quest associated with alchemical thinking and hermeticism (utopianism, yet again), the myth of the perfected earthly heaven refuses to die, notwithstanding the mounds of contrary evidence and mountains of corpses, coupled with the still living testaments to the massive operative failures of hair-brained thinking (think Cuba, Venezuela, among many others). But new generations of poorly taught politically-minded utopians argue that the Marxist model just wasn't applied properly. A fitting response might be, "Oh, they didn't kill enough people?"

However, that retort no doubt would be lost on this latest generation of revolutionaries who are unaware of the massive human cost throughout history of such schemes. Lecturing them, for example, on the horrors of Marxist-Leninist-Stalinist Soviet Russia or Communist China, likely is of no avail given the ongoing proof of the implosion of Marxist Venezuela and its attendant horrors seen daily on the evening news. Reality and facts will never compete with utopian theory, especially in its most recent articulation in critical theory and other pseudo-intellectual argot. In short, historical ignorance has profound consequences, since all reference points have been excised and each new untutored generation sees itself as filling in blank slates, as for the first time ever – following, of course, indoctrination by hyper-politicized utopians working on their own blank slates.

We could go back to the intellectual giants of the classics who foresaw where such thinking, or non-thinking, ultimately leads. Socrates paid with his life for addressing some of the very same fallacies of unhinged thought that we face again in this era. But it might be better to save that deeper approach for a later stage in an ongoing effort to recapture reason. Dostoyevsky, himself smitten early with the revolutionary urge to an earthly utopia -- as was Solzhenitsyn -- is worth revisiting. His later reflective conclusion that without God all is permitted is one of the most enduring and prescient single-line critiques of persistent utopian conceit.

More recent figures of similar intellectual and moral depth speak to us in similar voice and whose work prefigures this estimable effort of Juliana Pilon. What comes to mind are Eric von Kuehnelt-Leddihn's *The Menace of the Herd, Liberty or Equality,* and *Leftism Revisited,* which speak from the twentieth century to the same failed thinking that Dr. Pilon necessarily revisits in the twenty-first. So too does the work of the historian-philosopher recently passed from this vale, John Lukacs, whose *Historical Consciousness: The Remembered Past* marks him as another enduring and corrective mentor to help retrieve right reason. It is hardly coincidental that Kuehnelt-Leddihn and Lukacs come from the eastern marches of Western Civilization.

Such figures seem to possess a trait common to deeply thoughtful writers from that part of Europe: a sense of the permanent things outside of and above the self. Juliana Pilon hails originally from Romania. I am not surprised that she produced *The Utopian Conceit and the War on Freedom.*

John J. Dziak
Washington, DC., May 16, 2019

Introduction:
Beyond Left and Right

Waves of anger and fear
Circulate over the bright
And darkened lands of the earth,
Obsessing our private lives;
The unmentionable odor of death
Offends the September night.

The year was 1939. But W.H. Auden's famous lines resonated once again six decades later, when the waves of anger flooded a bright September morning and turned it into night. The waves had been circulating over the land for some time, but when they finally erupted, Americans were completely unprepared. Had the experts not promised that we could all take a permanent vacation from history? That wasn't much of an excuse: in truth, choosing to confuse what should be with what ought to be, and preferring not to know better, was everybody's fault. We wanted to be duped: it's in the Adamic DNA.

After the Soviet Bloc collapsed, Mr. and Mrs. Average Consumer were more than ready to turn swords into the latest equivalent of plowshares. At long last, we could all stop worrying about geopolitics and return to obsessing full time about one another's private lives. Eager to believe that the whole world had finally abandoned ideology for pragmatism, Americans ignored the resentment of Islamist fanatics who despised and rejected everything we took for granted, such as freedom. Anyway, they lived on the other side of the globe. And obviously in another century.

The public hardly noticed Osama bin Laden's call to the Islamic community (*the umma*) on August 31, 1996: "The people of Islam [having] awakened and realized that they are the main target for the aggression of the Zionist-Crusaders alliance... [the] utmost effort should be made to prepare and instigate the Ummah against the enemy, the American-Israeli alliance."[1] It was nothing less than a declaration of war in the form of an official religious ruling (*fatwa*): "The walls of oppression and humiliation cannot be demolished except in a rain of bullets." Bin

Laden pointedly summoned Allah's help with strategic acumen: "Our Lord, shatter their gathering, divide them among themselves, shake the earth under their feet and give us control over them." Quite medieval, we shrugged.

It seemed so utterly preposterous for a lone lanky mystic wearing an ancient white cloak and a turban, ignominiously exiled from his native Saudi Arabia and later Sudan, to threaten the only Superpower on the planet. Had we missed the punchline?

We had not: there wasn't one. The incongruously medieval figure of Bin Laden was The Voice of the latest version of the Apocalypse. As Laurence Wright explains in *The Looming Tower*, "By declaring war on the United States from a cave in Afghanistan, bin Laden assumed the role of an uncorrupted, indomitable primitive standing against the awesome power of the secular, scientific, technological Goliath; he was fighting modernity itself."[2] But modernity wasn't having it. Mesmerized by computer screens cluttered with appetizing ads, Americans – Westerners generally - found such primitive threats oddly quaint, bordering on the ludicrous.

Bin Laden was undaunted. He returned with another *fatwa* in February 1998, this time speaking on behalf of a rebranded World Islamic Front, signaling better organization and still greater resolve. The newly-coined "Jihad Against Jews and Crusaders"[3] was even more explicitly murderous, declaring that "to kill the Americans and their allies - civilians and military - is an individual duty for every Muslim who can do it in any country in which it is possible to do it." This was nothing less than a blanket declaration of war on the Western world.

It should have registered. But it did not, still. The proclamation's arcane, anachronistic religious language, bizarre to Western ears, again elicited little more than condescending shrugs. In any case - what was there to do? Where would this weird *jihad* strike, and how?

An answer came, six months later, on August 7, 1998, as early simultaneous truck bomb explosions took place at U.S. Embassies in two East African cities - Dar es Salaam, Tanzania, and Nairobi, Kenya. Within seconds, 200 civilians, mostly Africans, were dead, and several thousand wounded. The enemy had demonstrated that it meant business. The war having been declared, however, advance notice of future attacks would not be forthcoming. Two years passed. Then, on October 12, 2000, the U.S. Navy destroyer Cole was attacked by two suicide bombers on a small motorboat. Bin Laden had done it again. Yet still America underestimated the threat: the millennium had come and gone – we were home free.

Until, that is, the day when everything changed. Literally out of the blue, the brightest blue ever to grace the New York skyline, came the killer planes. Nothing would be the same again – or so everyone said, as the nation went numb with fury and incomprehension. But what did it mean? Aside from the usual imagination deficit that afflicts the over-satisfied and overfed, Americans lacked the conceptual categories needed to make sense of that sort of threat. For over a decade after the Iron Curtain crumbled, Francis Fukuyama's comforting "end-of-history" narrative had prevailed. Proclaiming "the end point of mankind's ideological evolution," it declared that ideology was finished and the good guys won, the "universalization of Western liberal democracy as the final form of human government"[4] having prevailed over all rival political systems. Those "ideas in the sense of large unifying world views that might best be understood under the rubric of ideology" had presumably been refuted. But evidently, not everyone got the memo.

To be fair, Fukuyama's 1992 book *The End of History and the Last Man* was more nuanced than his essay, notwithstanding the similar title. He did not, for example, rule out the possibility of continued "high and perhaps rising level of ethnic and nationalist violence, since those are impulses incompletely played out, even in parts of the post-historical world." Surely "Palestinians and Kurds, Sikhs and Tamils, Irish Catholics and Walloons, Armenians and Azeris, will continue to have their unresolved grievances. This implies that terrorism and wars of national liberation will continue to be an important item on the international agenda." Tribal warfare is hard if not impossible to eradicate. "But large-scale conflict must involve large states still caught in the grip of history, and they are what appear to be passing from the scene," he assures his readers. Those obsolete little "ethnicities," with their endless "grievances," will keep cluttering the international agenda with "important items" – but that's just diplomatic-speak for "definitely not cataclysmic." (Read: Coffee breaks may safely be taken between Cabinet meeting "agenda items.") With ideology allegedly "passing from the scene" in big states, like China and Russia, the victorious universalist international community shouldn't be overly ruffled.

Ideology and unreason, for Fukuyama, go hand in hand. He blames nationalism and ethnocentrism on the "irrational" desire to feel superior to others, a predilection he calls *megalothymia*[5] (from the Greek "thymos," meaning a sense of self-worth, or "recognition"). He explains that nationalism is "not fully rational because it extends recognition only to members of a given national or ethnic group."[6] Friedrich Nietzsche most famously captured the enormous allure of power over others, the will to conquer and control of the Superman, the *Übermensch*.[7] Not only for Germans, but for men throughout history, "the kind of strength that excites fear was considered preeminently divine: here was the origin of authority; here one interpreted, heard, sought wisdom."[8] Indeed - but hardly irrational, if it achieves the intended effect, as it generally does. The age-long desire to incite fear, the passion for superiority and control, is reprehensible and perhaps short-sighted, but reason can lead to both good and bad; which is why very smart people can, and often do, perform the devil's work. Conversely, not everything that is a-rational is necessarily bad, quite the contrary: love, thoroughly compatible with reason, transcends it.

Fukuyama would have been better served to use a different word from Greek antiquity to designate the yearning for recognition, power, and superiority. That word is hubris: mankind's tragic flaw. Hubris may be perilous, but not irrational: it is evil. Camouflaged in deceptively benevolent and lofty rhetorical garb, it can be seductive. But make no mistake: if modern versions look different from the old, the roots are ancient, the effects nearly always deadly.

"In Greek tradition," writes Luciano Pellicani, "hubris is the excessive arrogance of man in the face of the gods, the desire to be as and more than the gods, the refusal of man's finiteness. On the basis of [Jean-Paul] Sartre's well-known theory that 'man is fundamentally the desire to be God,' hubris is inevitably a natural and constant temptation." Thus "[h]e is condemned to live an insensate life and destined to be the food of time... [Man] aspires with all his might to live in a transfigured world. This is the existential source of all religions of salvation and all metaphysical needs. It is also the source of the revolutionary spirit and its demiurgic project to reshape the totality of being. In other words: *the objective of revolution is the divinization of humanity.*"[9] Indeed, the self-divinization of humanity lies at the heart of modernity as it evolved in the West. It is the species' fatal conceit. Dubbing it merely irrational won't help us either understand or address it head-on.

It certainly lies at the root of the putatively divinely-inspired Salafist-Islamism that gave rise to al-Qaeda, the global jihad responsible for the Apocalypse of 9/11 which continues to threaten civilization, occasional setbacks notwithstanding. "For al-Qaeda, Islam is revolution not just in the sense of an insurgency but an ideological and political sense as well," writes Michael W. S. Ryan, citing al-Qaeda strategist Abu Ubayd al-Qurashi's summons to holy war against the West. Engaging in a sustained, well organized, long-term struggle must be based on classical guerrilla warfare, writes al-Qurashi. Small wonder that he finds inspiration in "Mao Tse-tung [who] in his writings about the revolutionary war focused on the fundamental relationships between war and politics."[10] Just as Mao had been driven by hubris to control the fate of his countrymen – and of others - no matter what the cost in lives and suffering, so his Islamist disciples wage war against the so-called "infidels" convinced of their quasi-divine superiority.

Al-Qaeda and its offshoots have certainly not been defeated despite the trillions spent and lives lost in the effort. Quite the contrary, writes Bruce Hoffman: it is "a movement whose long-term strategy is showing alarming signs of coalescing." Hoffman also agrees with the Worldwide Threat Assessment that the intelligence community presented to Congress on February 13, 2018, that "its affiliates are getting stronger" as well. And "this isn't happening simultaneously, independently or serendipitously – it's part of an overall global strategic plan that al-Qaida is stubbornly pursuing."[11] Yet nearly two decades after that black day in September when the odor of death filled the nation and the world, we have yet to understand what happened, in historical context. For that, however, we need to have a better grasp of the particular ideas, not only the subconscious drives, at the root of global conflict, including our own preconceptions that prevent us from seeing ourselves candidly, with a minimum of wishful thinking. And to appreciate the kind of world that Salafi-jihadists are seeking to establish, we have to understand the utopian temptation.

But that takes words. And considering how the language of public discourse has been twisted and turned to the point that ambiguity now reigns supreme, this is no easy task: more often than not, we end up talking past one another. We still live in a post-Babel world as much as ever, if not more. And failing to understand one another, we hardly understand ourselves. The biblical story needs to be revisited. Once upon a time, though once again....

As recounted in *Genesis*, initially "all the world spoke a single language and used the same words." Having settled in Babel, men[12] sought to construct a great city there, "with a tower that reaches to the heavens," which then and now implied both literal and sacred height. God naturally noticed, and worried that "nothing they plan to do will be impossible for them" should they succeed: it was the same worry He had expressed after the first couple defied His admonition against eating the fruit from the Tree of Knowledge. It was time for another lesson. God thus preemptively dispersed humanity and "made a babble of the language of all the world." Better to babble than to imagine that heaven could be reached by mere humans.

The babble has only worsened since, words routinely being twisted to suit political ends, as inflammatory rhetoric advancing misleading ideologies proliferate. We now have "democratic" nations that hold sham elections; totalitarian theocratic "republics" that are monarchies in modern garb; and "left vs. right" is no clearer than "red vs. black" (or blue, for that matter). So too "green" is the color of both Islam and the environmental movement, a coincidence that should concern them both. This book attempts to elucidate the most common misconceptions behind the dichotomies responsible for so much of the political turmoil roiling our culture today. Even if we never attain the clarity of unison, we can seek to reduce the cacophony - if only to prevent unwittingly self-inflicted injury. Most important, we must prevent the demise of man's most precious gift: individual freedom. For without liberty, man is mere animated clay.

The philosophy based on that principle has traditionally been called liberalism. It originally consisted in the promotion of political and economic *liberty*, referring to the equal protection of life, liberty, and property through limited government. In the early days of the twentieth century, however, the term's meaning was subtly but quite deliberately changed by proponents of Progressivism. When they proclaimed freedom (a term they generally preferred to "liberty"), self-declared "Progressives" had in mind principally an end to economic inequality, soon known as "social justice." The philosopher John Dewey would thus famously write, in *Liberalism and Social Action* (1935), that activist government and social reconstruction had "virtually come to define the meaning of liberal faith."[13] Dewey had turned the concept precisely on its head. Poor Adam Smith must be exasperated as he turns in his grave watching Dewey and his Progressive colleagues obfuscating the concept of "natural liberty." The semantic subversion had begun.

Thereafter, the original liberals would often be called "conservatives," and more recently, "neoliberal." Under siege and in retreat, some of them have tried to resist relinquishing the name that best captured their philosophy by describing themselves as "classical liberal,"[14] or even Whigs; others sought to take refuge in what they call "new conservatism,"[15] and still others thought "libertarian" would be least confusing.[16] The all-too-common accusations of "fascism" by progressive-liberals occasion howls of pain from their unwitting targets. As the current partisan political discourse suffers in almost equal measure from ignorance and venality, the ensuing cacophony delights America's enemies even as it poisons the domestic debate. In the verbal dueling by expletives, the contestants both lose. Meanwhile, the war on freedom is being won by proxy, its foes watching gleefully from the sidelines.

When Jonah Goldberg, for example, sought to recalibrate the debate in his 2009 book *Liberal Fascism*,[17] it was a bridge too far for his opponents. To his credit, David Oshinsky, writing in the *New York Times,* admits that accusations of fascism, especially after the Vietnam war era, "belonged on the political left. It was their verbal weapon, and they used it every chance they got."[18] Yet by describing the book as "less an exposé of left-wing hypocrisy than a chance to exact political revenge," Oshinsky skirts over the rich evidence that bolsters the book's arguments, turning instead to the default tactic of the ideologue: questioning the author's motives. Never mind the deeper truths his book had revealed.

In truth, Goldberg stopped too soon. For despite arguing that modern-day liberalism has more in common with fascism than with John Locke, he nonetheless surrenders the word to its hijackers. For even if too irrevocably ambiguous by now to be worth rescuing, "liberalism" is nonetheless worth defending in its original iteration as "the system of natural liberty," and deny its usurpers the benefit of its use. Conceding it merely in deference to common usage, far from ending the confusion, only deepens it. Perhaps it is best buried, but it should not be relinquished.

It had been a smart, indeed brilliant, move by the Progressives to appropriate the label. For since the Declaration of Independence is the iconic *liberal* document of the American Revolution, its aura implicitly blesses all who supposedly fall under it. Accordingly, today's progressives (having dropped the capitalization during consecutive rebootings) continue to bathe in its radiance, meanwhile relegating conservatism to inertia: "disposed to preserve existing conditions." Deceptively anodyne, "conservatism" is thus indelibly scarred by the ignominious imprint of timidity and opportunism. Consider its synonyms: obscurantism, dogmatism, reaction, illiberalism, opposition. Nor is "traditionalism" much better, for even that is relative: traditions have notoriously checkered pedigrees. Never mind that most "conservatives" in America today are dedicated to the American *revolutionary* tradition and its commitment to liberty.

No wonder the general public is confused when Russian kleptocrats, Chinese censors, Islamist defenders of stoning, and white supremacists are labeled "conservative" alongside the intellectual heirs of John Locke and the Founders. Since "conservative," moreover, is often used interchangeably with "right-wing" - capitalizing on the common reading of that term as equivalent to "racist," "fascist," and "Nazi" - as soon as someone is thus pigeonholed and smeared, the cards are solidly stacked against any kind of sensible discussion. Such profound conceptual squalor cries out for major semantic housecleaning.

In a debased political culture, smearing is bound to become an equal opportunity pastime. Journalists and politicians of various stripes compete for first prize, and both win. Writes Peter S. Goodman, former *New York Times* economics editor, now the editor of the *International Business Times*: "Political hacks trade in the labels of right and left because it allows them to manipulate the public with shortcut phrases."[19] Their enablers are lazy journalists who like pernicious "labels that perpetuate division" because these sell papers, generating "the sort of tension that feeds narrative." Ultimately, charges Goodman, "left and right are the props of the cynical class who use them to convey a sense of sophistication in place of the messy, difficult work of finding things out, uncovering truths and reckoning with social problems in their fullest human dimension." If only more members of the media would share his integrity. To say nothing of politicians.

Goodman opts for "objectivity" in investigative journalism, defined as conducting "a fully open-minded inquiry," meaning that "[w]e do our own reporting, our own independent thinking, ... [unconcerned] with how others may describe our place on the ideological spectrum." This is remarkably refreshing, considering that the very notion of objectivity has long been under attack, giving way to the post-modernist relativism that currently pervades the academy. Goodman is clear: "[N]o ideological position can be counted on to deliver the facts." And without facts, there can be no civilization.

There certainly cannot be dialogue. Crispin Sartwell is right to denounce "the arrangement of positions along the left-right axis... [as] conceptually confused, ideologically tendentious, and historically contingent. And any position anywhere along it is infested by contradictions." In a word, the axis is "bogus."[20] But excommunicating a specific set of words does not resolve conceptual disagreements that are real, and dangerous. To achieve strategic clarity, they must be described with clarity. And if one group of concepts fails, look for better ones.

Sartwell agrees, so he turns next to the familiar opposition between "equality" and "liberty." But that too won't work, he finds, because it "produces another cluster of contradictions" and confusions. Take the position that holds up "equality" as a fundamental value – meaning of equal outcomes rather than merely equal opportunity. "The means leftists propose to increase economic equality almost always increase political inequality," he observes. So if you are for equality across the board, you land in contradiction. This concept too, like liberalism, has been rendered hopelessly ambiguous.

What of the proponents of "liberty" on the other side, what about opponents of marijuana legalization who yet don't mind government surveillance? Are they for liberty in some areas but not others? Sartwell suggests "arrang[ing] political positions according to whether they propose to increase hierarchy or to dismantle it." Does this mean that some people believe in hierarchies while others believe in horizontal leveling? This sounds a little more promising, except that even the "horizontalists" concede that some form of hierarchy is necessary – they only disagree as to its membership. How about the "meritocratic hierarchists" vs. the "populist-redistributionist hierarchists"? If perhaps a tad closer to analytical clarity, such jargon is irritating to the ear of an average English and even American speaker. It won't fly.

Whatever terms we finally settle on, Sartwell concedes, it "is never a matter of simply starting afresh, employing no assumptions; both sides are engaged in interpreting and re-applying existing traditions." True and wise. So where do we begin? As it happens, the current global malaise exhibits some clear patterns: The United States, along with Israel and other Western-style democracies such as Canada, Australia, the United Kingdom, and Japan, plus the nations of Western and East-Central Europe, are usually – in various and complex ways - pitted against Russia, China, North Korea, and Cuba, along with Muslim regimes such as Qatar, Turkey, and above all Iran. All these states either directly or indirectly support non-state actors, including human traffickers and drug lords, whether as their full-fledged proxies or through financial, logistical, and other means. Weak regimes often cooperate as well, for the benefit of elites.

The result is misery for the people, and danger. But what must strike even, or rather especially, the ordinary observer unencumbered by academese is that autocracies of whatever stripe, whether secular or theocratic, tend to promise utopian goals: an end to conflict, to inequality, to sin, venality, etc. – fill in the blank. At the same time, they oppose dialogue and outlaw pluralism and generally demonize democratic self-rule as evil and/or anachronistic, which must be systematically opposed by any means, if not outright destroyed. Meanwhile, their leaders naturally expect unquestioning, whether real or simulated, adulation.

Yet by disingenuously claiming concern for "the little guy" - the underdog, the oppressed, the poor - such regimes are often able to seduce influential segments of the population inside Western democracies who claim to profess similar ideals. It may seem ironic that the same people who consider themselves the most progressive of democrats should often find allies in virulently anti-Western kleptocracies. What they appear to have in common is a yearning for a heaven-on-earth devoid of strife, inequality, antagonism, and above all, selfishness. In other words: a utopian millenarian ideology that defies reality. (At least this is true of the naïve; the disingenuous are another story.) Utopia is like heroin: the euphoria is ephemeral, illusory, and deadly.

In *The Concept of Freedom*, published in 1962, Frank S. Meyer traces the idyllic vision all the way back to Pharaoh Akhenaton who ruled in the 14th century BCE; it was revived in the Hellenic world a few centuries later, then followed by Gnostic sects of early Christianity: "The myth of the Tower of Babel, like the historical record of the reign of the Pharaoh Akhenaton who attempted to reconstruct Egyptian society in a single generation, testifies to so early an existence of the belief that men can create a perfect world.... Always since, it has been endemic as an underground aspect of Western thought, appearing now and again in the Utopianism and millenarianism of some medieval heresies..... Every revolutionary movement of the last two centuries – however much it may have begun by radical criticism of the state it found in being – ends by deifying the state it has captured and theologizing the concept of the state.... [E]ach in its own way has contributed to that immense growth in the power of the state which is the effective condition of totalitarianism." Concludes Meyer: "The dominant ideologies of the 20th century... are the latest forms taken by this Utopian attitude."[21]

Were Meyer alive today, he would add global Salafi-jihadism to the list. Recent studies reveal the full extent of the continuity between the modern version of jihadism and Western millenarian utopian ideologies or political religions. As a result, in the twenty-first century, affinities between otherwise disparate anti-Western states and organizations have led to threads of cooperation that pose exponentially greater danger to civilization and freedom, as suicidal fanatics gain access to the latest technology.[22]

Meyer's insights came from personal reflection. Born to Jewish parents in Newark, New Jersey, he attended Princeton and then Oxford, where he read Karl Marx and became a radical student leader, secretly joining the Communist party in 1932.[23] His epiphany came while serving with the U.S. Army during World War II, when he encountered F. A. Hayek's (1899-1992) *The Road to Serfdom*, which explained how sacrificing individual freedom, in exchange for centralized economic planning, sooner or later spells totalitarian terror. Hayek was even more right than he knew. But even after he became convinced that Marxism was dead wrong, Meyer did not leave the Communist Party: a holistic ideology that explains every conceivable area of life is difficult to abandon. [24] At last, in 1955, he joined William F. Buckley's newly founded magazine *National Review*, having concluded that "[t]he nature of men, firmly rooted in their creation, belies the constructions of the utopians." Men cannot be turned into angels – which does not mean that they should be denied freedom. On the contrary. "The natural habitat of man is freedom and piety towards the constitution of being, not subservience to a man-made utopian plan."[25] This premise lies at the heart of this book, which shares Meyer's insight that the ideology of "[r]evolutionary millenarianism, in fact, is still with us."

While the journey is fascinating in its own right, watching superficially disparate yet fundamentally similar ideologies across many centuries as they revolve around similar yearnings, appealing to similar motives and drives and failing to deliver even a modicum of the promised nirvana, cannot fail to teach some lessons. Surely, we can learn enough to mitigate future iterations, even if error can never be entirely avoided. Considering how much closer technological advances have brought humanity to "nuclear midnight," it is worth a try.

But first, some key definitions are in order, starting with "ideology." At its most general, the term refers to a picture of the world, a narrative, a system of ideas and ideals which include economic or political theories, however inchoate. We all operate with such mental constructs, from the moment we are born, and we constantly revise them based on experience. Few people do not have some notion of an ideal – namely, what they envision as the best possible outcome for themselves, and perhaps their community. But hopes and ideals turn ideological when reality takes the back seat: a utopian ideologue hangs on to his worldview. Or rather, the worldview is articulated in ways that render it evidence-proof.[26] And when applied to an entire society, an ideology that presupposes political power to emanate from a godlike source thereby becomes "sacralized" to become a political religion.

Like their traditional counterparts, political religions both advocate and command behaviors, while their leaders inspire reverence as they "strategically employ sign, symbol, and ritual," writes A. James Gregor. Most important, in both cases "it is faith, not empirical or logical truth, which inspires loyalty, self-abnegation, commitment, and obedience" even when pretending otherwise, as do putatively secular, atheist ideologies like Marxism-Leninism.[27] Political religions advocated by hubristic self-described messiahs, who convince their followers that utopia is bound to arrive after an apocalyptic liquidation of its satanic enemies, "make the contest of ideas and the challenge of arms more ferocious and destructive than they might otherwise have been."

Hubris affects us all in various degrees, and the propensity is deep-seated. *The Utiopian Conceit* recalls Hayek's last book *The Fatal Conceit*, published in 1988, where "conceit" refers to the fallacious presumption that particularly wise or intelligent individuals can know better what is best for others, indeed for society as a whole. What renders it fatal is its propensity to degenerate into totalitarianism. In Chapter 1, we return to the ancient roots of this conceit in the biblical notion of hubris, as illustrated in two seminal stories from *Genesis* - the expulsion from Eden, and God's reaction to the Tower of Babel – whose own ancestral sources are Egyptian. Chapter 2 then defines "Utopia" as did its author, Privy Counsellor (later, Saint) Thomas More (1478-1535), its publication having fatefully coincided with the publication of Martin Luther's denunciation of Catholic dogma in 1515, which precipitated the radical German Peasant Rebellion shortly thereafter. While the egalitarian society described by More assumed its members to be pious, a more secular conception of utopia on earth was not far off. Though God can never disappear from the human imagination, man aspires increasingly to assume god-like attributes, presuming to emulate the heavenly utopia here and now.

The related theological concepts "millenarian," "millennial," "chiliastic," and "apocalyptic," are thus eminently relevant in a political context, as Richard A. Landes, founder of Boston University's Center for Millennial Studies, points out. Landes credits his mentor Arthur Mendel with

trac[ing] the path from "Apocalypse and God" to the secular versions of millennial ideologies, the "new" products of the modern world – Apocalypse and Reason, History, Nature. Secular revolution, often violently antireligious, represents not an abandonment of millennialism but a change of clothing that jettisons the embarrassing commitment to a God who never kept the promises that the prophets attributed to him.... God having been dropped from the equation, agency shifted almost entirely to 'Man.'[28]

God, to paraphrase Nietzsche, is not dead: He has simply been dethroned by man, whose congenital hubris produces suicidal delusions of omniscience and omnipotence. Even jihadists, who presume to kill for Allah, patently usurp the divine mantle for themselves.

In Chapter 3, we come to the modern utopian revolution of 1789. Neither the Romantically-inclined Jean-Jacques Rousseau (1712–1778) who idolized the "natural," pre-civilized man, nor other luminaries of the French Enlightenment whose belief in God was rooted in reason, could be considered altogether secular. But their repudiation of church and tradition created a new political religion bound to degenerate into terror, leading to the subsequent rise of the egomaniacal Napoleon Bonaparte. Calling this period "The Apocalypse of Reason," Mendel credits advances in science and mathematics with boosting mankind's hubris.

Though the word "Communism" was coined by a little-known French revolutionary, it migrated to Germany, where it would become indelibly linked to antisemitism. That one of its most influential perpetrators in modern times was a Jew himself seems difficult to fathom, but it is true: "The God of the Jew is money," a slogan that captured centuries-long prejudice against money-changers and money-lenders, came from a descendant of distinguished rabbis. Karl Marx (1818-1883) turned Jews into the satanic protagonists of *Das Kapital.* Marx based his vision of altruism and universal bliss on the complete abolition of private property and the class it represented: the capitalist-bourgeois-Jew. Once again, the result turned out dystopian in the extreme: the eventual success of Marx's ideology, in the form adopted by Vladimir Lenin (1870–1924) half a century later, confirmed its ineluctably tyrannical implications. Just as Marx did not flinch at condemning his ethnic kin, Lenin slaughtered compatriots with impunity. It took another seven decades for totalitarian central planning to file for bankruptcy, precisely as Hayek had predicted. By then, millions had been murdered, and an entire population lived in slavery. (Alas, the West not only adamantly opposed holding a Nuremberg-style trial for the regime leaders, it bailed them out.[29])

To be sure, Communists manifestly (pun unintended) do not hold a monopoly on radical hubris. At the end of the 19th century and beginning of the 20th, statist utopian schemes had sprouted throughout the West, notably in Germany and the United States – the topic of Chapter 5. Eugenics, and the racism on which it is based, became respectable when defended in the name of progress. The German form of eugenics did not take long to become genocidal – the topic of Chapter 6, titled "Heroic Totalitarianism and the Holocaust." The lethal obsession of antisemitism took on a whole new dimension.

That both Communist and fascist leaders perpetrated apocalyptic genocide was no accident. Though Mendel labels the former as devotees of the "Apocalypse of History" for having replaced God with History and the latter as proponents of the "Apocalypse of Nature," the difference is ultimately negligible, mere variations on the millenarian narrative. "After all," writes Mendel, "what difference does it make to the victims if they are murdered in the name of God or because of the ineluctable laws of dialectic progress"[30] or Nature, or whatever. The ideology of utopia can mask radical hubris only so far.

Which brings us to the present. Rather than end all wars, the 1919 Versailles treaty contributed to Germany's return to the battlefield two decades later. Less well known is how the Prussians also helped rekindle another hate-filled apocalyptic utopia in the Muslim world. As explained in Chapter 7, "The Protocols of Jihadism," key leaders of the Muslim community revived and reinterpreted elements of their tradition to justify jihad against the infidel (*kafir*) by incorporating Western elements, with German and Bolshevik assistance. Israel and not long after, America - dubbed Little Satan and Big Satan, respectively - became the jihadists' main, if by no means sole, target. Anti-capitalism and antisemitism found a common foe in the friends of individual rights.

Chapter 8 continues the update of utopianism to our own day, including post-Cold War Communism, jihadism, and Western progressivism. The latter include pacifism, feminism, the New Left, Marxism and neo-Marxism, internationalism, globalism, and other "isms" characterized by a supposed search for solutions to income inequality by fighting "the one percent" (to which, paradoxically, they often belong). Promotion of global government, for example, has often been accompanied by a call for the redistribution of resources from "North" to "South," newspeak for exploiters and exploited – Marx's dialectical bourgeoisie and proletariat.

Part III, "Brave New World Order," echoes George Orwell's ironic view of a putatively humanist, but necessarily totalitarian, utopianism that seeks order only to sow chaos. Chapter 9 explores the concepts of liberty and equality, and their relation to private property. The limits of romantic utopian ideology were exposed by philosophers of common sense in the Scottish Enlightenment, thinkers of traditional Judaism, and others who focused on the true basis for charity. Liberty as a repudiation of slavery is traced to ancient Greece and Rome, as well as Jerusalem. Re-conceptualized in the Middle Ages, liberty came to be defended as well by John Locke, Adam Smith, and America's Founders. The main rationale was moral, though practical justifications for individual freedom are often easier to defend before a general audience.

The title of Chapter 10, "Capitalism's Discontents," recalls Sigmund Freud's 1930 monograph *Civilization and Its Discontents,* which exposed the subconscious forces responsible for both progress and mass hatred. Freud's insights are relevant to understanding what has been called anti-Americanism, including the homegrown variety. While radical feelings infected the cultural mainstream most virulently during the Vietnam era, Americanophobia reflects a long-developing, profound skepticism about the importance and meaning of liberty.

While anti-Americanism is clearly a form of anti-capitalism, the affinity with Islamism is more recent. The underlying premise is that Western, especially American and Israeli, aggression and greed lie at the root of most if not all evils that plague the world. As Robert S. Wistrich explains in his monumental history of antisemitism aptly called *A Lethal Obsession:*

> Contemporary Marxists and Islamists share a curiously similar apocalyptic agenda of earthly redemption that aspires to the installment of absolute "social justice" through violent means. For both parties, Palestinian martyrdom has become a glowing symbol of "resistance" not only to Israel but also to globalization and the "corrupt" West. At the heart of such radical utopianism, there is the quasi-religious belief that the world will only be 'liberated' by the downfall of America and the defeat of the Jews. This chiliastic [i.e., millenarian] fantasy has today emerged as a notable point of fusion between the radical anti-Zionist left in the West and the global jihad.[31]

Finally, Chapter 11 reminds the reader that since earth is no heaven, a foreign policy for a political system based on freedom should be at once realistic and idealistic: it must consider both facts and ideas. That was indeed the original attitude of America's Founders, who were prepared to die for their principles yet recognized that absent life, there is no liberty, let alone property. It is good to see the recent interest in the national security community in so-called "weaponized narratives" used by insurgent groups, as well as by regimes inimical to democratic freedom, by corrupt elites who promise impossible Edens while demonizing scapegoats to appease crowds.

A standard tactic of semantic sabotage is the cynical use of misleading labels. Hayek wisely advises looking past labels to what is actually being advocated: "What in effect unites the socialists of the Left and the Right is [a] common hostility to competition and their common desire to replace it by a directed economy. Though the terms 'capitalism' and 'socialism' are still generally used to describe the past and the future forms of society, they conceal rather than elucidate the nature of the transition through which we are passing."[32] If this was great advice in 1944, it is even more so today. Beware of anti-isms and pies in the sky.

Utopias have political traction precisely because they are vague, while anti-isms appeal to visceral fears. Hayek explains the logic of demagoguery: "[I]t seems to be almost a law of human nature that it is easier for people to agree on a negative program – on the hatred of an enemy, on the envy of those better off – than on any positive task.... The enemy, whether he be internal, like the 'Jew' or the 'kulak,' or external, seems to be an indispensable requisite in the armory of a totalitarian leader." Such a leader will invariably lure supporters with a rosy utopian future while calling for the Antichrist-enemy to be eliminated - whether by conversion, guillotine, gas, gulag, or jihad. "In Germany and Austria," continues Hayek, "the Jew had come to be regarded as the representative of capitalism because a traditional dislike of large classes of the population for commercial pursuits had left these more readily accessible to a group that was practically excluded from the more highly esteemed occupations." (Never mind that they managed to also become celebrated writers, scientists, musicians; they were still smeared as dirty, lazy, money-grubbers.) He concludes: "The fact that German antisemitism and anti-capitalism come from the same root is of great importance for the understanding of what has happened there,"[33] adding the crucial caveat that "it would be a mistake to believe that the specific German rather than the socialist element produced totalitarianism."[34] This book seeks to explain why.

Antisemitism is obviously not only, sometimes not even primarily, about Jews – it is equally about America, and the ideal of individual liberty which it represents. Write Dennis Prager and Joseph Telushkin: "[A]lmost as consistently as Jew-hatred, America-hatred has become a moral litmus test of nations, regimes, and individuals. America represents freedom, a higher quality of life, and a willingness to fight for its values.... With all its flaws, America alone stands between democracy and the ascent of tyranny throughout the world."[35] May it survive, for God's sake. And man's.

I. GOD-ENVY:
THE ERROR IN THE BONE

For the error bred in the bone
Of each woman and each man
Craves what it cannot have,
Not universal love
But to be loved alone.

W. H. Auden (1940)

If it had been possible to build the Tower of Babel without
ascending it, the work would have been permitted.

Franz Kafka (1935)

1:
Hubris

Patterns of Thought: Myth, Archetype, and Narrative

"Symbols are not lies; symbols contain truth. Allegories and parables are not falsehoods; they convey information: moreover, they can be understood by those who are not as yet prepared to receive the plain truth," wrote Paul Carus in 1900.[36] But he was only half right. Though truth comes in many shades, plain isn't one of them. Certainly not for the kind of truth needed to confront the loneliness of death. To reflect and navigate his world, man names objects by putting them in categories. But in exploring his own soul he resorts to analogy, myth, visions, dream.

Foremost among man's dreams is heaven. An inverted mirror, a photo negative, it is all that this world is not: a place of plenty, where poor, naked, fragile man is cared for by Someone All-Powerful and All-Good. The place could be called Eden. Or Paradise. Or Utopia. The dream straddles time and space, archeologists having uncovered visions of a Perfect Abode in every land. Illusions of idyllic islands, fantasies of fabulous realms where peace reigns supreme, are not a Western monopoly: most of us seem to have been hardwired to crave such an Ideal.

Is it a universal instinct? Perhaps not; yet decades of research have compelled Fritzie and Frank E. Manuel to "presuppose the existence of a utopian propensity in many, [just] as William James in his famous lectures assumed a 'religious propensity' while pointedly refusing to define religion."[37] Aware of its political ramifications, the Manuels seek to understand the function and context of this tantalizing aspect of human nature; but "instead of sitting in pontifical judgment and either approving or condemning"[38] it, they choose to study it. Similarly struck by its ubiquity, Raymond Ruyer, in *L'Utopie et les utopies* (Utopia and utopias), defines the "utopian mentality" as "a mental exercise on lateral possibilities,"[39] deeming it an invaluable human talent that makes possible extraordinary feats of innovation and discovery.

Both the Manuels and Ruyer are right to abstain from quick blame: by no means are all or even most such mental exercises to be condemned – on the contrary. Dreams are as vital to the soul as they are to the body, even if the mechanism is largely unknown. But just as imaginings caused by neurons firing haywire are the stuff of hallucination and nightmare, so utopianism gone amuck from an excess of hubris poses a danger to civilization and freedom. Political utopias advancing various blueprints for a perfect global society, whether largely secular or, as in the case of Salafi-Islamism, fanatically religious, have inspired horrific crimes. In most such cases, a self-proclaimed messianic vanguard opts for coercion over persuasion, and justifies apocalyptic violence by the alleged necessity of its aims.

Admittedly, the Western world is unique in the extraordinary profusion of ideal imagined worlds, and a peculiar obsession with a type of revolutionary utopia modeled on religious narratives. But as the reverberations far exceed the immediate geographic boundaries of their intended targets, the Manuels are right that "the historical longevity of certain mythic themes in utopia that evoke associations remote and deeply rooted in Western consciousness can help us to understand the fascination utopias have exerted over the minds of men"[40] throughout the planet. That fascination is unlikely ever to disappear, its roots deeply entrenched in human nature.

A major reason why a hubristic utopian propensity has been especially dominant in the West is that "the relative unity of Western culture has guaranteed the rapid diffusion of utopian ideas irrespective of the countries in which they originated."[41] The recent revolutionary advance of electronic means of communication has further facilitated the spread of these ideas across the globe with unprecedented effectiveness, posing exponentially greater dangers to fragile societies where hatred and ignorance are easily exploited. The West has sometimes wittingly, though at least as often unwittingly, exported its dreams and nightmares, its hopes and fears, to willing and not-so-willing recipients, with unintended consequences. We are now reaping the sorry harvest.

The prospect of a perfect, just world, free of strife, that would necessarily follow once evil forces have been eradicated in an apocalyptic conflagration, has been made to fit the needs of various epochs and circumstances with relative ease by an articulate self-described messianic elite. Utopian thinkers and activists, who often learned from one another, would adapt the storyline to their intended audiences with breathtaking success. Conclude the Manuels: the twin visions of paradise and the apocalyptic end of the world "have so tenacious a hold on Western consciousness that they are a constant presence – in multiple variations – in all subsequent utopian thought."[42]

Like Paul Carus, so too Carl J. Jung (1875–1961) was convinced that myths hold the key to understanding not only Western consciousness but the spiritual architecture of man's soul. He proposed that humans think and feel according to identifiable "archetypes," which he defined as universal primordial patterns, images, and motifs underlying the species' "collective unconscious." In addition to Jung's countless disciples, students of fairy tales and legends have shared his ingenious methodology. The pejorative connotation of "myth" is actually a relatively recent development: *mythos* originally denoted little more than a sequential ordering of words. Evolved into "mythological narrative," the notion differentiated into two kinds of "histories:" objective, or real, as against imaginary stories.[43] Eventually, myth came to denote mostly the latter, which accounts for the bad rap. But literary critic Northrop Frye warns against underestimating myths, especially those he calls sacred, which are "charged with a special seriousness and importance,"[44] far more powerful than literal truths could ever be.

Scholars reluctant to posit either primordial thought-patterns or inner psychological forces opt for a concept such as *the meme*, defined as an idea, theme, or cultural unit that spreads within social channels across history. Thus Richard Landes refers to the notion of a utopia destined to arrive at the end of time after an explosive Apocalypse as "a meme programmed to spread as rapidly and pervasively as possible."[45] Under the right conditions, "the meme can spread at epidemic speed and breach the public transcript with explosive force. [James C.] Scott calls the same utopian narrative as a 'full throated hidden transcript.'"[46] Such transcripts are all the more potent for being hidden.

"Explosive" is no mere hyperbole. Landes warns against the dangers of "totalistic apocalyptic fantasies, whose adepts so often tend toward inconceivably destructive[,] even self-destructive[,] madness."[47] Intent on minimizing the allure of millennial utopianism, Landes resorts to a repulsive analogy borrowed from epidemiology:

Just as there is a virus that reproduces best in a cow's stomach but keeps getting excreted, and so hasevolved to infect ants with the irresistible urge to climb to the top of the grass blades so that cows can eat them, just so the apocalyptic meme seizes people –

rides them – to destinations and for purposes not theirs, indeed harmful to them. [48]

From the sublime to the ridiculous, eschatology (from the Greek *eskhatos,* meaning last or most remote, and *logos* – concept, plan) becomes scatology.

Unlike programmed insects, however, perpetrators of this virus usually belong to the savvy elite, who assume a messianic mantle which the ancient Greeks identified as an irrepressible desire not merely to emulate but even to become like God. And this not only in knowledge and goodness, which are both commendable aspirations, but in power - and specifically the power to institute utopia on earth and impose it on everyone else (naturally for their own good, whether they know it or not). It is the latter form of hubris that can become fatal in the extreme; the political religion of apocalyptic utopia rests on an ultimate conceit.

Coveting Divinity: Isis, Prometheus, and Satan

The first known instance of a myth about a human being wishing to become divine hails from the shores of the Nile in ancient Egypt - and it was not a man, but a highly intelligent woman by the name of Isis. Having become "weary of the world of men, [she] yearned after the world of the gods,"[49] Sir James Gregor Fraser tells us. But to attain that status, she had to find some way to learn the name of Ra, the great god of the sun – a feat she eventually managed, for she was "mighty in words," impressively cunning. It is notable however that the story of Isis joining the immortals was no exceptional fairy-tale: in ancient Egypt, every magician attempted to appropriate the power of a high god by possessing himself of a sacred name. Thus, writes Sir James,

> religion assumes the operation of conscious or personal agents, superior to man, behind the visible screen of nature...[T]he ancient kings were commonly priests also...[and] revered, in many cases, not merely as priests, that is, as intercessors between man and god, [but] as themselves gods, able to bestow upon their subjects and worshippers those blessing which are commonly supposed to be beyond the reach of mortals. [50]

How could such a presumption fail to become dangerous? The ancient Greeks certainly thought so, as evidenced by a number of myths, especially that of the wily Titan[51] Prometheus (in Greek, "forethinker," or "one who thinks ahead and gains knowledge"). According to Hesiod (7th century BCE), Prometheus was eager to help the hapless humans, whom the gods all but abandoned to their sorry fate soon after their creation. But after managing to steal fire from the father of the Olympian gods, Zeus, Prometheus was punished by being chained to a mountain and condemned to eternal torture as an eagle gnawed at his liver. In the version recounted by Aeschylus (525/4-456/5 BCE), Prometheus is said to have brought not only fire but civilization, the arts and sciences. In Aeschylus's version of story, Zeus's son Hercules resurrects the kind Titan - which led some later scholars to see in Jesus a composite of these mythical two friends of mankind, Hercules and Prometheus.[52] But no matter: angering Greek gods, who did not look kindly upon those who stole their secrets, was very dangerous business.

Which didn't stop even mere humans from trying. Eventually, as nature became increasingly personified in the Greek world, stealing divine secrets gave way to uncovering the mysteries of nature. Mankind could hope to unveil Nature's secrets by tricking them out of her by emulating Prometheus through "tricks," or what later could be called "experiments." Archimedes of Syracuse (c. 287-212 BCE) went a step further, proceeding to design machines based on mathematical models. Yet his untimely death was caused not by any god's wrath, but by a numbskull Roman soldier who defied orders that the scientist should not be harmed. Note this interesting etymology: "tricks" being *mekhane* in Greek, the word evolved into "mechanics."

So then, did the ancients consider the deities mankind's friends or not? The ancient records are frankly ambivalent, especially as some primitive peoples worshipped both God and Satan, both Light and Darkness. According to old Chaldean legends from before the second millennium BCE, the world was thought to have been created from the Deep, or Chaos, called *Tiamtu,* also *Tiamat* in Assyrian. Represented as the Serpent that beats the sea, the Serpent of the night or darkness, the Deep was both wicked and mighty, frightening and strong. Ordinarily associated with the original watery chaos considered the source of all things, representing disorder, *Tiamat* may have been eventually conquered and replaced by the Sun-god, but never completely disappeared from the world.

The Serpent was well known to the biblical authors.[53] "More subtle than all the beasts of the field," *(Genesis* 3: 1) who tempted the first humans, it was often considered a stand-in for the Evil One. While "Satan" is used as a proper name no more than five times in the entire Hebrew Bible, and never in the Pentateuch or Torah (the first five books), in an apparent attempt to avoid myths reminiscent of heathen superstitions, his presence looms large throughout the Abrahamic tradition. Though God was perfect and his world was good, evil is real, and it tempts mankind.

Hubris in the Torah: Eden and the Tower of Babel

Even if the story of Babel had not been told in the nine verses of chapter eleven of *Genesis,* the first book of the Hebrew Bible (the Old Testament), its relevance to 9/11/01 would be inescapable. Both tragedies center on towers built by hubristic humans that dared "to reach the Heavens," with dire consequences. Translated from the traditional Hebrew, the old story's brevity is biblical "zipping" at its finest. Behold:

> [1] Now all the earth was of one language and one speech. [2] And as they journeyed about from the east, they found a plain in Shinar and settled there. [3] And they said each man to his neighbor, "Come, let's bake bricks and burn them thoroughly." And they had brick for stone, and slime for mortar. [4] And then they said, "Come, let us build ourselves a city, with a tower, with its top in the heavens; and let us make for ourselves a name, lest we be scattered over the face of all the earth."[5] But the Lord came down to see the city and the tower, which the children of man were building. [6] And the Lord said, "Behold, it is one people, and they have all one language; and this they begin to do; and now nothing will be restrained from them which they have imagined (or plotted) to do.[7] Come, let us go down and there confound their language that they may not understand each man the language of his neighbor." [8] So the Lord scattered them from thence upon the face of all the earth, and they ceased building the city. [9] Therefore is the name of it Babel, because the Lord did there confound the language of all the earth; and from thence the Lord scattered them upon the face of all the earth. [54]

At first blush, the story's moral is puzzling: what could God have against people understanding one another and building a city where they could finally settle down safely? And how high could that presumably brazen tower really have been anyway, if God had to come *down* in order to see it? Maybe the intention to reach the heavens was a mere figure of speech? Hardly: for in the Bible, figures of speech are never mere. In the first place, explains Leon Kass, Babel itself is not "just any one city but is *the* city, the paradigmatic or universal city, representing a certain universal human aspiration."[55] And it is not just a few inhabitants who share a common "language" but "all the earth" – meaning that humanity shared a common understanding and a common worldview. No dissent, no opposing points of view, observes Kass: consensus reigns.

Wordsmithing had been Adam's first hobby; he labeled everything. Later generations, however, took language-building to the next level, for Babel's architects came to use words not merely to tag objects, but to exhort one another to action, as in: "come, let us build." This expression, explains Kass, comes perilously close to divine speech. For God, to speak and to make or create are intertwined, if not identical: "Let there be X" is to bring X into being. Behold: "In the beginning was the Word," whereupon all else followed. But while for God it may be enough to pronounce something to bring it about, not so for humans: they have to make preliminary plans, later to be adjusted according to contingencies such as conditions on the ground, cost, effort, etc.

So even the most carefully prepared human blueprint will undergo many changes before the projected object becomes material. Like the proverbial distance from lip to cup, the gulf that separates idea from reality is logically unbridgeable. What mortal, imperfect man imagines, and fancies he knows, can only reflect incomplete information, both factual and ethical. An edifice designed for one purpose may prompt its opposite. A dam designed to channel water for irrigation might inadvertently cause a flood. God alone knows all, as He reminded his first children, who refused to believe Him, until it was too late.

But to return to Babel: what is it that most angers God about the tower? True, the desire to "make a name" for oneself is unseemly, but hardly worth so radical an overreaction on the part of a benevolent Creator. Far more disturbing to Him was the stated purpose of the eponymous tower: to enable human settlement, "lest we be scattered over the face of all the earth." Thus, afraid of wandering across a treacherous planet, the mortals of Babel decided to blatantly disregard God's command, upon the exile from Eden, "to be fruitful, and multiply, and replenish the earth, and subdue it." (*Genesis* 1:28) Those goals obviously could not be fulfilled by just settling "safely" in one place. Though fear of the unknown is understandable, indeed natural, it nevertheless demonstrates a lack of faith in God's continuing care for His offspring. Once again, as in Eden, humans defied God's commandment, and substituted their own judgment before His. In a word: they displayed hubris.

No trivial vanity, the wish to "make a name" for oneself is far more serious than it sounds. Though to modern ears it suggests mainly a craving for stardom, the biblical context, explains Kass, implies nothing less than intending "to remake the meaning of one's life so that it deserves a new name. To change the meaning of human being is to remake the content and character of human life. The city seeks to do that: through new modes of independence, laws, and culture, it radically transforms its inhabitants. The children of man (*adam*) remake themselves and thus, their name, *in every respect taking the place of God.*"[56]

As for the ambition to "reach heaven" with their tower, is this not tantamount to "a desire to bring heaven into town, either to control it or, more radically, to efface altogether the distinction between the human and the natural or divine"[57]? As in Eden, God knows where that leads. The Bible quotes Him: "[I]n the end, the men will revere nothing and will look up to nothing not of their own making, to nothing beyond or outside themselves, in part because they will see no eternal horizon." When man comes to worship himself, whatever his rationale – whether intended to deceive others, himself, or both – the horizon will evaporate along with everything else, replaced by an emptiness masquerading as eternity.

There is still God's concern over the oneness of language that requires an explanation, but again Kass's analysis is disarmingly simple: "The much-prized fact of unity, embodied especially in a unique but created 'truth' believed by all, precludes the possibility that one might be in error.... With everyone given over to the one common way, there would be mass identity and mass consciousness but no private identity or true self-consciousness.... The self-sufficient and independent city of man means full estrangement and spiritual death for all its inhabitants."[58] To have the same thoughts, the same ideas, is worse than death; it makes a mockery of imagination and ingenuity, of discovery and surprise, of reason and science.

It may at first seem counterintuitive that aspiring to universal unity would result in alienation. But if such unity means absolute consensus, quite aside from being impossible without totalitarian control, it prevents reaching whatever truth is accessible to ordinary humans. For imperfection - trial and error and trial again - is essential to learning; it forms the core of what would later be known as the scientific method. Moreover, just as there are different languages, different nations, and different cultures, so there are different ways of worshiping the sacred. Diversity, questioning, learning, exploring, are what God intended for human beings.

In Adam, Yahweh did not create a glorified divine pet. If He had wanted to keep the First Parents in Eden, blithely ignorant, self-satisfied and idle, He could easily have done so, being omnipotent - but that was not His purpose. Instead, they were intended to know what it means to choose and thus to be occasionally wrong, thereby becoming humbly mindful of their many limits, while endeavoring as best they could to improve their lot and also the good world that He had created. To do that, they had to seek truth, make mistakes, and try assiduously to better themselves and their offspring, while caring for their habitat. Viewed in that light, pluralism, far from preventing robust and meaningful human dialogue, is a prerequisite to fulfilling God's plan.

Since that requires cooperation, which depends on a certain degree of linguistic unity, God could not have opposed effective human communication. The problem is not whether there is one language or many, "but in the fact that the unified human language stands for and bespeaks merely a humanly constructed vision of the world and carries a purely factitious truth. It lies also in the *pride* human beings take in the plots and projects for 'perfecting' the world that are made possible by an imagination furnished by the shared representations of a uniform language."[59] Improving the world according to human ideals is by no means the same as "perfecting" it in a manner that is God's purview alone.

What God does favor is cultural variety, trial and experiment, but above all, mutual respect based on the awareness that cooperation is necessary for civilization. "The emergence of multiple nations, with their divergent customs and competing interests, challenges the view of human self-sufficiency. Each nation, by its very existence, testifies against the god-like status of every other...."[60] It is just as important for nations to have an appreciation of "the other" as it had been for Adam, when confronted with the presence of his soulmate Eve, to respect her as his equal, for they were both created in the image of God. We all are.

Admittedly, Adam notoriously failed at first: when confronted by his Maker with his transgression, his first reaction was to look out for himself and blame Eve for "making" him eat it, when in fact he was perfectly free to choose for himself. It was the proverbial "error in the bone:" the me-first, me-above-everyone-else syndrome. Yearning to take the next step up from being made in God's image, man indulges in self-apotheosis (from *apo*, Greek for "make," and *theos*, "god") - making oneself divine. By no means restricted to the likes of Louis XIV or Kim-Il Sung, this ultimate conceit afflicts anyone who treats a fellow-human as a means rather than an end – in the extreme, by murder - thereby usurping the divine prerogative over human life and death.

The expulsion from Eden was not only a punishment for insubordination. It was a means of preventing the ultimate blasphemy: the wish to be God. The biblical Creator had long worried about His naughty children's next target: "Behold, the man has become like one of Us, knowing good and evil; and now, he might stretch out his hand, and take also from the Tree of Life, and eat, and live forever." (*Genesis* 3:22) The desire for immorality, however, is only one aspect of self-apotheosis; another, and most disturbing of all, is the presumption of the right to kill the innocent.

Now man was certainly "like" God in the sense of having been created in His image – all good. But after tasting the fruit from the Tree of Knowledge, God expected that he would come to fear death and thus seek immortality – which would effectively render him a god. His expulsion eliminated that danger, for it placed the Tree of Life, the really dangerous one, out of reach. Yet once man's desire to becoming a god himself had been aroused, the temptation of extreme conceit was irrevocably planted in the bone. Hubris would afflict the human race forever.

It flared up in Babel. As Franz Kafka put it: "If it had been possible to build the Tower of Babel without ascending it, the work would have been permitted."[61] But that wasn't an option. Ronald Hendel credits Kafka with this paradoxical insight: "If people had built the Tower of Babel without ascending it, this would have demonstrated that humans have a capacity to restrain our ambitions. But, as *Genesis* observes, we lack this capacity." Hendel agrees with Kafka that the Babel story replicates the dynamics of the Fall. The desire to ascend a tower with its top in heaven "is a biblical image of the monumental ziggurat in Babylon, which the Babylonians called *Etemenanki*, 'House of the Bond of Heaven and Earth.'" This architectural ascent to heaven is a collective assault on God's domain reminiscent of Adam and Eve's effort to cross into the divine world"[62] in Eden.

Most likely conceived in the 8th century BCE by storytellers well aware that their small nation was among the least powerful in the world, Hendel argues that the narrative's original intent was both allegorical and practical. Babylon was sure to symbolize Mesopotamian power, at a time when "people as a whole are filled with hubris and dangerous ambitions, but most particularly so are the powerful men in Babylon." A weak people like the ancient Israelites would be expected to criticize their rulers indirectly, through political parable. Accordingly, the biblical story appears to contain a "hidden transcript."[63] That transcript may change from age to age, taking on new forms of varying lethality, but at bottom the story is about everyone. Concludes Hendel:

The story is a critique of human nature at the same time that it ridicules the pretensions of contemporary Babylon. Perhaps in this sense the story somehow overcomes the boundaries between languages, nations, and cultures. It is not just about the "other," but also about the "self." Both are implicated in the sin of human pride, both pull at the chains of human limitations. Israelites, Jews, Babylonians and every other people are compelled to overreach themselves.

Kafka's parable thus captures the universality of the message with brilliant simplicity. It means, in short, that if we could build the Tower without ascending it, we wouldn't be human. Something better perhaps, but not human.[64] The temptation of conceit becomes fatal to ourselves no less than to others. That said, it is also inescapable. Unable to eat the ultimate fruit, evicted from Eden, man has never stopped yearning for both. He has sought to emulate God in all the wrong ways: seeking immortality through fame, power, and riches; or presuming, whether sincerely or disingenuously, to help his fellow-humans by deciding what is best for them. Most sinister, thanks to modern technology, self-apotheosis could bring an end to all life. "Let there NOT be light" would be man's ultimate revenge on God for not revealing His ultimate fruit.

Revelation

In ancient Greece, *apokálypsis* meant "an uncovering," a disclosure of knowledge, or revelation. In the most common religious context, it refers to heavenly secrets that make sense of earthly realities.[65] The biblical book of *Revelation*, which contains the most widely known version of the revealed truth about the way the world ends, is also known as the book of the *Apocalypse* (and sometimes as the book of *John,* after its presumed author). Occasioned by a great, terrifying conflagration, the final days would allegedly culminate in a Golden Age inaugurated by the messiah.[66] While pivotal to Christianity, this notion predated the birth of Christ. According to Jewish tradition, the messiah will arrive at the end of a thousand days (a metaphorical millennium) to destroy the evil that had infected the whole world, finally bringing bliss on earth forevermore. The earliest known version of this story appears in the book of *Daniel,* composed in the second century BCE, when Jewish Palestine was under Syro-Greek occupation. It was a time of deep divisions among the Jews: while the elite was happily adopting Greek customs, common people stuck to their tradition. The very nature of Judaism and its future was at stake, and questions relating to the final destiny of humanity, or eschatology, were being hotly debated.

The story told in *Daniel* begins as Nebuchadnezzar II, King of Babylon, is tormented by a nightmare featuring four monstrous beasts, symbolizing the empires of Babylon, Medina, Persia, and Greece, which are engaged in deadly combat. When the last beast devours the whole earth, he too is overthrown by the figure of Israel. Personified as "the Son of Man," Israel reportedly "came with the clouds of heaven; He reached the Ancient of Days and was presented to Him. Dominion, glory, and kingship were given to him; all peoples and nations of every language must serve him; his dominion is an everlasting dominion that shall not pass away, and his kingship, one that shall not be destroyed."[67]

Its brevity notwithstanding, this passage contains the essence of all future eschatology, referring to death, judgment, and the End of Time. According to this scenario, the world will eventually be dominated by a beastly Power that causes unbearable suffering to its victims, until God or His messenger (his Son, the Messiah, etc.) rises and overthrows the demon. Whereupon the former victims inherit the whole earth, and history achieves a glorious finale; there will be no successive kingdoms. But beware: only the good will be saved. All those mortals whose names have not been included in the Book of Life are to be cast into a Lake of Fire. The apocalyptic battle against evil was called Armageddon, from the name of its prophesied location - a Greek alliteration of the Hebrew *har magiddô* (הר מגידו), where *har* refers to a mountain or range of hills, and *magiddô* to a place of crowds. But since the name appears in both the Old and New Testament in connection with various battles even without specific reference to the End of Time, further enhancing the figurative connotation of the word, the story led to endless interpretations, controversy, and political manipulation.

Alternative versions of the story proliferated throughout antiquity. In early Jewish tradition, the identity of their savior had originally been God Himself. Later, he was imagined as a wise and powerful warrior. By the time *Daniel* was written, the savior was Israel, or perhaps a superhuman individual.[68] It was but short step to the Christian Apocalypse, envisaged as the complete final destruction of the world, followed by perfect harmony heralded by Jesus's Second Coming. In *Revelation*, Jewish and Christian motifs are intimately intertwined.[69] The Jewish sect that took the Apocalypse most seriously were the Zealots,[70] a first-century political movement that soon died out, in part because of their extreme asceticism. Their influence was minor at best.

By contrast, the millenarian Apocalypse was central to Christianity. From its beginnings, millenarianism had been the official political theory of the Church, even though once Christianity became a state religion, millenarianism began to be frowned upon.[71] The faithful nonetheless continued to believe in the coming of the Messiah, future apocalyptic battles, and eventual absolute peace. These ideas were immensely popular during the Middle Ages, "and much used by preachers, writers and theologians," writes Paul Johnson. "All stressed the coming battle between Christ and Antichrist. The idea could be reinterpreted to fit almost any political situation, and identified with kings and emperors, even popes, whether good or bad."[72] It could, and it was.

Over the course of the ensuing two centuries, self-styled secular messiahs would thereafter adapt the conceptual skeleton of revolutionary millenarianism to offer a blueprint for a heaven-on-earth that was fated to follow once a cataclysmic Armageddon liquidated Evil. In the words of Arthur Mendel, "whether explicitly religious, as were the medieval and early modern messianic movements, or implicitly so, as were their secular revolutionary successors, all apocalyptic movements thereafter *mirrored the original model.*[73]

2:
Egalitarian Christian Utopianism
The Brave New World of King Utopus

The biblical narrative has it that God, who fashioned mankind in His Own Image, placed him in a magnificent garden filled with gold and other precious stones,[74] its trees lovely to behold, their fruit exquisite. All that man had to do was "to till and care for" the bounteous specimens in that idyllic abode, giving him a sense of accomplishment and satisfaction. But God also intended for man to speak and think. And so it was that by labeling the animals, he was implicitly given power over them.[75] Soon came abstract concepts, even without the corresponding words. First was loneliness, which God would alleviate with a helpmate. Together, Adam and Eve had been fashioned in God's image – not in any literal sense but as spiritual beings worthy of respect. Though naked, they felt no shame, since shame implies something bad - a notion still foreign to them. Heedless of danger, without a care in the world, the first humans were wholly innocent, basically clueless. Savoring the formidable fruits of a Garden custom-made, it seemed, for their exclusive enjoyment, their infantile egos became unduly inflated. So when God forbade them to eat the fruit of no more than one tree, it took distressingly little effort by a slimy, slithering reptile to convince them to ignore His commandment.

The price was high: a realization of their own eventual death. Whether the first couple had a word for death, then or later, fully understanding it was another matter altogether. Even if the concept might arise from observing the mortality of animals, no one can fully grasp the meaning of one's own end – least of all the overwhelmingly over-privileged first humans. Snubbing God, Who would obviously discover their guilt given His omniscience, served to underscore not merely their stupidity but the enormity of their hubris. Life as they had known it in Eden's womb would be irrevocably over.

But its memory would haunt the human vision of the ideal forever: a place free of pain and suffering, with plenty to eat, no thought of disease and death, where no one disagreed with anyone and all lived in harmony. Having once known it rendered it all the more tantalizing. Yet so it had to be. Expulsion from Eden taught the first couple to appreciate their own limits, completing the transition from moral infancy to facing responsibility. God at last gave them the gift of freedom and choice, in effect severing their figurative umbilical cord. Only after learning the dangers of hubris could they be born as fallible, imperfect human beings, who had to choose between difficult options, based on necessarily limited knowledge. Thrust into harsh daylight, they would now have to assess evidence, feel pain, know disappointment, make mistakes and then pay for them. Outside of God's evergreen garden, toil was going to be hard, winters cold, and treacherous snakes aplenty.

This did not negate God's love for His children; on the contrary, it reinforced it. For conquering difficulty brought gratitude and joy. Generosity to the less fortunate was rewarded by the satisfaction of philanthropy, beauty became more precious for being ephemeral, each sunrise glorious for being one day closer to the end. That all mankind is created in God's image symbolizes the eternal bond of love between God and humanity; but in addition, it implies that a bond of respect among ourselves had been established. The metaphor amounts to another version of the moral imperative: no one is to treat another as a means to his own ends, but only as an end in himself. Known as the Golden Rule, it became the anchor of Western civilization.[76] But alas, the shores on which it was thrust were often no more than quicksand.

That God had loved his unruly children could be seen from the way he had clothed them with "tunics of skins" (*Genesis* 3: 20) before sending them on their way, concerned for their safety. With the passage of time, however, evidence of His protection seemed increasingly more difficult to discern. Eden gradually morphed into the Western subconscious as a vision of perfection - the place where mankind once thrived, however briefly and metaphorically, unmindful of death, like a child's rosy memory of the idyllic first years. But reality was another matter: when his pain seemed too hard to bear, man would wonder, with Job, whether God had forsaken him. Or indeed if He existed at all.

Even if theological doubt did not lead to outright atheism, the divine presence often eluded the desperate who had hoped Judgment Day would have arrived long ago. The never-ending specter of death was further exacerbated by fear of divine retribution against transgressions, real or imagined, routinely hurled at sinners from thundering pulpits. No amount of perfumed incense could alleviate the awful message. Still worse, as the clergy's often shameful behavior belied their own words, a growing awareness of their hypocrisy angered the flock. Outraged by the increasingly blatant corruption within the Vatican itself, many began to hope that the promised redemption would arrive in their own lifetime. They might have called it "utopia," but the word itself would not be coined for another few centuries.

Not until 1516, to be exact. Its author was the venerable English philosopher and statesman Thomas More, whose book *On the Best Form of a Commonwealth and on the New Island of Utopia* featured it as a proper name. Though not translated from Latin until 1551, the original version was widely read, eliciting immediate interest and considerable consternation. *Utopia,* as it came to be known, was billed as a satire written in the then-popular form of a fictional conversation. But there was nothing especially funny about its discussion of current problems that were widely known to plague England and Europe generally. That raised the question of whether More's ideal island was no mere conceit but a carefully designed source of wisdom, notwithstanding its radicalism. Its ingenious style and cleverly crafted arguments account for the book's continuing influence five centuries later.

More first elucidates "utopia" by revealing its pedigree. A whimsical poem that serves as the book's motto notes that two similar-sounding Latin words may both apply to the island: *utopia* (no-place) sounds remarkably like *eutopia* (good place). Playfully personified as the poem's narrator, the island herself explains that she had been "called once 'No-place' because I stood apart," but having now been acknowledged as "the best in people, wealth, in laws by far the best," she demands a name change: "Good-place" [eutopia] by rights I should be called."[77] While phonetics renders the distinction moot, More subtly reinforces the tantalizing ambiguity concerning the island's existential status through the last name of the story's narrator Raphael: it is Hytholoday, meaning "purveyor of nonsense." Wit reliably succeeds in deflecting heresy.

It worked: most readers seem to have considered More's clever device as reflecting his political savvy.[78] At least as plausible, however, is the conjecture that Moore was genuinely, if rather inscrutably, ambivalent. Stylistic camouflage notwithstanding, *Utopia* changed history, following in the footsteps of Plato's *Republic* two millennia earlier. For Plato too had imagined a well-ordered society which he called Kallipolis, a Greek word meaning "beautiful city" – a transparent precursor to *eutopia*. Plato had used the dialectical style, with his teacher Socrates seeking to teach his students what made a society ideal and also why it could never be found in an imperfect world. Thomas More consciously advances that conversation, as *utopian* now refers to both perfection and impossibility.

The tantalizing ambiguity, however, only enhanced its seductiveness, inflaming many a romantic personality endowed with sufficient hubris to attempt establishing it on this earth.

Ambiguity extends to the conversationalists in the dialogue bearing the names of historic persons - including More himself, his friend and publisher Pieter Giles, and several others - who all engage the fictional narrator Raphael with the disconcerting last name. But there is still another critical historical detail: the fictional island that he describes reflects the extraordinary effect of Christopher Columbus's discovery of the New World in 1492, which in turn was followed by Amerigo Vespucci's voyage in 1499. Two of the latter's widely reprinted letters describing his discoveries, which he allegedly wrote after his return to Italy in 1502, had caused a phenomenal sensation. Portrayed by More as Vespucci's companion, Raphael claims to have stayed on after the famous explorer had left for home, whereupon he, the humble Raphael, stumbled upon the island of Utopia. The narrative in fact mirrors Vespucci's own alleged findings.

Europeans at the time were indeed fascinated by transatlantic stories of natives going around naked, and not simply for prurient reasons. Observes Richard Marius: "The stories of nakedness were more than erotic; Adam and Eve had been naked in the Garden of Eden before the fall, and some minds were naturally stirred with the supposition that these strange new peoples had somehow escaped the corruptions that plagued old Europe."[79] The discovery of a previously unknown continent inspired hope in the possibility of novel and better social arrangements. It was impossible to ignore the enormity of the corruption threatening an imminent collapse of the political order precipitated by a crisis of faith. Many feared total catastrophe and revolution; yet the New World seemed also to offer unexpected hope. Corruption, particularly among the clergy, had been getting worse for a long time, and it was reaching the boiling point.

It was about to explode on the continent. Starting in 1510, Martin Luther had embarked on a vigorous campaign against what he saw as the venality of the papacy and the preposterous system of indulgences that ruined already destitute poor peasants.[80] Less than a year after the publication of *Utopia*, the eloquent professor of theology from Saxony would revolutionize the Christian world with his *Ninety-five Theses,* which denounced the church hierarchy, claiming to demonstrate definitively that the Bible is for everyone. That is, all human beings are capable of understanding the Bible, with no need for priestly intermediaries.

Disseminated first throughout Germany, the Theses would reach all of Europe within two months, thanks to the newly discovered printing press – the world-wide-web of early modernity.

Though the devoutly Catholic More repudiated Luther's radical proposals, he shared the latter's outrage at the appalling corruption that had poisoned the church and indeed society at large. Like his humanist friend Erasmus, whose work he greatly admired, More was desperate for redemption. If only there were some way to create a world where people were unspoiled by greed, lived unselfishly, without concern for money and riches, virtuously and happily. *Utopia* was his attempt at an answer.

The story begins with Raphael and More's friend Giles, along with More's own persona, all bemoaning the depravity all around them, despairing at the depths to which Europe had descended: it was, they agreed, worse than any other place on earth. There follows a lengthy list of wicked practices: widespread executions for theft, which yet did nothing to reduce their proliferation, as women and children were dying of starvation; idle nobles parading with equally idle attendants who turned into vagabonds when their masters died; soldiers who came home from wars that taught them nothing but violence, and then, with no employment prospects, were reduced to crime or starvation.

The litany of horribles ends with Raphael's radical observation that was to become the basis of all revolutionary utopias:

> [W]herever there is private property, where everything is measured in terms of money, it is hardly ever possible for the common good to be served with justice and prosperity, unless you think justice is served when all the best things go to the worst people or that happiness is possible when everything is shared among very few, who themselves are not entirely happy, while the rest are plunged into misery. [81]

He concludes: "I am firmly persuaded that there is no way property can be equitably and justly distributed or the affairs of mortal men managed so as to make them happy unless private property be utterly abolished." [82] If this isn't exactly Communism, it walks and quacks like it. Raphael all but invites revolution.

But remember, this was *not* More's persona talking. As cautious and realistic as the author himself, his namesake More is deeply skeptical of such revolutionary discourse, advising that "if you cannot turn something to good at least make it as little bad as you can." He favors gradual improvements over destroying the whole edifice, given that evil is caused by human beings, whose nature cannot be expected to change radically. He continues: "For everything will not be done well until all men are good, and I do not expect to see that for quite a few years yet."[83] This sounds, and can only be, ironic.

More's namesake clearly seeks to distances himself from Raphael's egalitarianism:

[I]t seems to me that no one can live comfortably when everything is held in common. For how can there be any abundance of goods when everyone stops working because he is no longer motivated by making a profit, and grows lazy because he relies on the labors of others. And then, when people are driven by want and there is no law which enables them to keep their acquisitions for their own use, wouldn't everyone necessarily suffer from continual bloodshed and turmoil?

Pieter Giles,[84] or rather his namesake, echoes More's skepticism: "[Y]ou would surely have a hard time persuading me," he tells Raphael, "that a better governed people can be found in that new world than in the one we know."[85] Admittedly, this implies that such persuasion is not altogether out of the question. Nor does More rule out that human nature might be capable of change, though probably neither quickly nor anytime soon. To these basically empirical objections, Raphael responds with an appropriately factual statement: he has seen the alternative, he says, with his own eyes. No master stylist, his run-on sentence goes as follows:

[W]hen I turn over in my mind the most prudent and holy institutions of the Utopians, who have very few laws and yet manage so well that virtue is rewarded and yet, since everything is equalized, everyone has plenty of everything, and when I contrast their customs with those of other nations, always issuing ordinances but none of them all ever achieving order, where whatever a person can get he calls his own private property, where a mass of laws, enacted day after day, are never enough to ensure that anyone can protect what each calls his own private property or even adequately distinguish it from what belongs to someone else (as can easily be seen from the infinite lawsuits which are always being filed and are never finished), when I consider these things, I say, I have a higher opinion of Plato and I am not surprised that he would not deign to make any laws for people who would not accept laws requiring that all goods be shared equally by all. In his great wisdom he easily foresaw that the one and only path to the welfare of the public is the equal allocation of goods; and I doubt whether such equality can be maintained where every individual has his own property.[86]

That Utopians have "very few laws" yet manage well is due in no small part because "they think happiness consists not in every sort of pleasure but in pleasure that is good and honorable."[87] Hence they never break agreements nor disobey laws "which have either been promulgated by a good ruler or which a people not oppressed by a tyrant or deceived by some trick have laid down by common consent to govern the distribution of vital commodities, that is, the means to pleasure." The entire edifice, moreover, rests on universal piety, "as religion makes clear to true believers, God will repay the loss of brief and paltry pleasures with enormous and never-ending joy."[88]

The inhabitants of Utopians are very different indeed from people living in advanced societies, all but unrecognizably so. They have practically no use for money, see no point in gold and precious stones, and clothing is purely functional. Yet this is far from pure speculation. As R. W. Chambers points out, Vespucci himself claimed he "had found folk holding property in common, and not esteeming gold, pearls, or jewels."[89] Chambers believes Thomas More had been deeply impressed by this account, since "the problem of poverty and unemployment (destined in England to be aggravated by the Dissolution of the Monasteries) was already a European one…. At the root of More's interest in colonization lies his pity for the unemployed laborers."[90]

Whether More believed that Plato had also advocated equality of property (scholars differ), Raphael's discourse endorses that impression, which had been gaining in popularity.[91] Could More have wished to follow in the footsteps of the renowned Greek philosopher with his own, somewhat more realistic ideal society? He does seem to echo the proposal of Gemistus Plethon (1355-1452) "that all the land should be the common property of all its inhabitants, as perhaps it is by nature, and that no man should claim any part as his private property."[92] But while Plethon believed that, as a result, "all the land would be under cultivation and crops," the more skeptical More has Utopia's inhabitants make sure to enforce the edict should observance be lax.

Where Plethon and More do agree is in their condemnation of people, including some of the clergy, who own land yet do not work it –

indeed often waste it. More is especially outraged by "noblemen, gentlemen, and even some abbots (holy men are they)," not merely "thinking it sufficient to live idly and comfortably, contributing nothing to the common good; unless they also undermine it, these drones leave nothing for cultivation."[93]

Yet enforcement crosses a momentous line as Raphael describes the practices of the Utopians in the event of overpopulation:

> [T]hey sign up citizens from each city and send them as colonists to live under their own laws on the nearest part of the continent, wherever the natives have a lot of land left over and uncultivated; they adopt any natives who choose to live with them... The natives who refuse to live under their laws are driven out of the territory the Utopians have marked off for their use; if they resist, the Utopians make war against them. For they think it is quite just to wage war against someone who has land which he himself does not use, leaving it fallow and unproductive, but denying its possession and use to someone else who has a right, by the law of nature, to be maintained by it.[94]

This argument, observes Peter Garnsey, "was to become familiar in contexts of imperialism...[It] appears in More perhaps for the first time."[95] That egalitarianism was perfectly consistent with violence was thus included in the original blueprint.

You didn't have to be a radical revolutionary to pay heed to such radical ideas. By 1516, writes Richard Marius, yearnings for a better society "were fueled not only by the new [transatlantic] discoveries but also by the pervasive conviction in men like More that something had gone terribly wrong with Europe. Gloomy Europeans wanted to believe that somewhere there must be places where the individual and society lived harmoniously together. ... [For that reason,] money and property are frequent topics in nearly everything More wrote."[96]

That said, More was in many ways a conservative, disciplined man, leery of mob rule, schism, and chaos. Devout to the point of excess, he believed perfection had to await Christ's return. Though deeply chagrined by the corruption of the church and the proliferation of vice throughout Europe, More was outraged by Martin Luther's body-blow to Christian unity. Unwilling to betray an order he considered preferable despite serious transgressions among its clergy, More would pay with his life for refusing to recognize King Henry VIII as Supreme Head of the Church of England. He was canonized as a saint in 1935.

Yet his *Utopia* had been more revolutionary than even he realized – or, likely, would have wished it to be. It arrived just in time, as the discovery of America kindled a new appetite for reform. The Renaissance vision of the Greek and Roman world as a Golden Age to be imitated, even worshiped, seemed no longer the panacea it had seemed but a century earlier. More had shown the way to something else. Writes Marius:

> Now the location of the golden age in time began to shift, and increasingly it came to be an age yet to be attained, something glimmering in the future, making all the past of less account. The idea of progress slowly and irrevocably replaced a reverence for tradition. And people were moved, almost unconsciously at first, to renounce all the past as something that should be shaken off, and life began to resound with the tramping feet of a world marching forward into novelty and to what it assumed would be glory.[97]

A pioneer against himself, More's ideas resonated at a moment of great turmoil. Only two things were left to complete the revolutionary scenario: a millenarian apocalyptic narrative and men endowed with radical hubris. That was easy.

Apocalypse Now: Millenarian Utopia

Apocalypse Now, Francis Ford Coppola's epic 1979 film about Vietnam, which portrayed tragic destruction and horror, was an allegorical journey into the soul's ugly abyss.[98] It has since been supplanted by other so-called apocalyptic movies, progressively more gory, superficial, and expensive. *Esquire* magazine chattily explains the genre's appeal: "In a world where each waking day seems to welcome a freshly horrifying news story (usually centered around the increasingly unhinged words of a certain Donald J. Trump), it's really not too ridiculous to start fretting about, y'know, the terrifying spectre of a global Apocalypse."[99] Except that the fretting should have started long ago, when the unhinged words of dictators bent on annihilating freedom and the West were being megaphoned worldwide, reinforced by weapons of mass destruction. By comparison, impolitic tweets and ill-advised remarks pale, no matter how unhinged.

Returning to history, the official status of the church having rendered millenarianism – the expectation of imminent salvation -

politically undesirable, the passage of time further dampened expectations of an imminent Second Coming, and church doctrine was duly adjusted. "[O]nce it had accepted that 'celestial Jerusalem would never come,'" writes Luciano Pellicani, "the only realistic approach was to read the book of *Revelation* as an immense spiritual allegory, to move the soul saving event to another world, to accept to live in, and adapt to, the old world."[100] It was no longer prudent for the church to lead worshipers to believe they would be saved anywhere other than heaven. A compromise had to be found between the egalitarian ideals of Jesus and earthly reality.

That compromise would be articulated by Augustine (later Saint, canonized in 1298), bishop of Hippo (354-430), in *The City of God*, which draws a sharp contrast between the spiritual heavenly city as against the sin-laden politics endemic to the City of Man. The best anyone can expect of the latter, argued St. Augustine, is an attempt to emulate the former. A propertyless society, for example, predicated on perfection, could only be found in Paradise. This does not mean, as Richard Pipes points out, that Christianity championed the abolition of property as an ideal. Especially in the later Middle Ages, the Catholic church defended private property, albeit reluctantly, as a "regrettable but unavoidable reality." It would eventually come to even promote it outright;[101] but the traditional Christian hostility to riches, especially money, remained deeply entrenched, and was never entirely eradicated.

Nor did ordinary folk stop believing in redemptive apocalyptic battles against their enemies, the not-too-distant coming of the messiah and peace in their own lifetimes, but above all, egalitarian ideals. The apocalyptic narrative maintained its popularity throughout this period, being "much used by preachers, writers and theologians. All stressed the coming battle between Christ and Antichrist," writes Paul Johnson. "The idea could be reinterpreted to fit almost any political situation, and identified with kings and emperors, even popes, whether good or bad."[102] In brief, it was tailor-made for ideologists, who galvanized sizeable receptive audiences.

By the fourteenth century, apocalyptic millenarianism was solidly anti-clerical, as well as strongly egalitarian and opposed to all wealth, primarily but by no means exclusively, that of the church. John Wycliffe (cca. 1320–1384), who translated the Bible into Middle English two centuries before Luther did the same for German, was among the first to attack the luxury of local parishes. He inspired the Czech radical Jan Hus (1369-1415) and a slew of followers, who applied Wycliffe's message with the express purpose of unleashing a class war.[103] Luther would later go on to revive many of the Hussite arguments against the Church, though he stopped far short of preaching revolution. Indeed, he became a staunch defender of state power as a bulwark against social disorder and general chaos. But his and other protestant leaders' devastating critiques of Catholicism and the feudal establishment unleashed a pent-up desire for radical, indeed revolutionary, upheaval. And once the dam had been gashed, there was no undoing.

Blood was soon to flow, in rivers. Writes Johnson: "The belief that the millennium was imminent was the signal for an attack on the rich – they were to be dragged to the ground in an earthly Apocalypse before being committed to eternal flames in the next world. Such ideas were expressed in the sermons of John Ball during the Peasants' Revolt [of 1318] in England; they recur constantly in France and Germany during the fourteenth, fifteenth, and sixteenth century. ... There were egalitarian outbreaks in Germany in the 1470s, and again in 1502, 1513 and 1517."[104]

This is how Pellicani describe this tumultuous period: "The flame of expectation of messianic deliverance continued to smolder beneath the ashes and fire spirits every time it became necessary to break away from the oppressive hold of reality. This occurred whenever the impersonal forces of market, competition, and capital set off a mechanism of social mobilization...."[105] In other words, wherever inequality was perceived to be unjust, it had to be eradicated. The result was a powder-keg ready to be ignited by demagogues and idealists alike: "the uprooted masses, already prepared by Christian socialization for the advent of the Redeemer, heeded the words of those preaching the imminent advent of the millennium." Neither for the first nor the last time, religious reformers and the secular revolutionaries (Norman Cohn refers to them all as *prophetae*) had similar ends in mind – and, increasingly, similar means, which included, if not favored, violence.

The original egalitarian and apocalyptic message of the Christian Bible had become deeply entrenched throughout Europe, as the poor thought themselves wronged, and had been growing impatient for some measure of reward sooner rather than later. Posthumous citizenship in the City of God no longer sufficed. They had been paying their dues in sweat and blood all their lives: it was time for payback. Writes Norman Cohn: "The material and moral suffering of the poor and underprivileged was presented as the antechamber of redemption: a completely terrestrial redemption, since the *prophetae* revived the original message of the Bible, with the advent here and now of the Messiah, the bearer of peace and justice."[106] Revolution was in the air, whether Thomas More liked it or not. Thanks to the printing press invented by Johannes Guttenberg around 1440, which by the end of the fifteenth century was mass producing books with what seemed like lightning speed,[107] More's ideas became hot topics of discussion - first, among Latin-speaking theologians, though later, far and wide. But it was not men of More's erudition, temperament, and prudence who would lead the ensuing revolts.

These would often start small, then spread. And suddenly, "there would appear, somewhere on the radical fringe, a *propheta* with his following of paupers, intent on turning [some] one particular upheaval into the apocalyptic battle, the final purification of the world."[108] The situation in Germany at the dawn of the sixteenth century was especially volatile, a veritable tinderbox awaiting arson. As royal power eroded, warring feudal lords set up their own absolutist mini-states, to the consternation of the peasantry, which by 1525 "saw its traditional way of life disrupted and its inherited rights threatened."[109] Ready for radical change, they fell prey to *prophetae* who knew how to capitalize on their anger. Notable among these zealots was Thomas Müntzer (1485-1525), pastor to the town of Mühlhausen, whose role in starting a rebellion with reckless abandon would later immortalize him. For notwithstanding his virtual disappearance from the pages of history for several centuries, he was rediscovered by Karl Marx and Friedrich Engels, who declared him the official martyr of the Peasants War of 1525. They had a point: for though less charismatic than other *prophetae* of his day, what Müntzer was able to do is wed millenarianism to violent revolutionary action designed to abolish private property. He was perhaps the first genuinely apocalyptic, egalitarian revolutionary of note.

Müntzer's career started in the town of Zwickau, where he experienced for the first time the misery of most townspeople, and especially the plight of the unemployed.[110] Revenue from nearby mines had led to some people becoming very rich, and others extremely poor. Equally appalled by the abuses of the Catholic church, he began delivering fiery sermons against the cult of saints, the sale of indulgences, and the general degeneracy of the papists. His rhetoric was extreme to the point that even Luther, who was obviously sympathetic to these criticisms, objected: Müntzer's fury bordered on the hysterical. He became so disruptive that he was repeatedly asked to move: first from the town of Zwickau, and again from Allstedt, where he continued to rant and rave, antagonizing the local Saxon princes. He finally reached the imperial city of Mühlhausen just as the Peasants' War was brewing. Bull's eye: Müntzer would lead his very own Armageddon.

Revolutionary fervor had already been incited there by a former monk, Heinrich Pfeiffer, the leader of the town's poor burghers, who were opposing the monopolistic practices of the oligarchy. A major problem was caused by the abandonment of a long-standing law allowing peasants the common use of certain waters for fishing and woods for hunting. Nobles proceeded to appropriate these lands, writes Roland Bainton; they

> even went so far as to encroach upon cemeteries. Public remonstrances seethed with indignationagainst such foreign innovations. Cries for redress reverberated throughout the letters and tracts of Müntzer as well as in a manifesto of the town of Mühlhausen. In this body of material we find enumerated debasement of the currency, usury, Roman law. The goods of the church should be expropriated and distributed according to the need of the poor.[111]

Passions had reached fever pitch. But Müntzer was only getting started. In April 1525, he unfurled a large white banner featuring a rainbow and the words *Verbum Domini maneat in aeternum* ("The word of God endures forever"), along with the German translation underneath. It was the slogan of the Reformation. Later that month, along with Pfeiffer, Müntzer took part "in a marauding expedition in the course of which a number of monasteries and convents were destroyed."[112] Seeking radical action on a much larger scale, however, he proceeded to write to his friends in Allstedt for help.

In a letter dated either April 26 or 27, he implored them: "Start and fight the Lord's fight! It's high time. Keep all your brethren to it, so that they don't mock the divine testimony, otherwise they must all be destroyed. All Germany, France, and Italy are on the alert." His only concern was that the German peasants "will let themselves be taken in by some treacherous agreement" instead of going all the way. "Don't be moved to pity," raved Müntzer, don't hesitate to destroy the godless. "At them, at them, while the fire is hot! Don't let your sword get cold! Don't let it go lame! Hammer cling, clang on Nimrod's anvil! Throw their tower to the ground!"[113] The letter contains a slew of references to apocalyptic biblical prophecies, including Daniel's dream, and the Day of Wrath, Armageddon. It is hardly a coincidence that, as Kohn points out, Nimrod was seen as "the originator of private property and class distinctions – in fact as the destroyer of the primal egalitarian State of Nature."[114]

It may be that Müntzer's contribution to the evolution of Communism can be, and has been, exaggerated.[115] Kohn explains: "From Engels down to the Communist historians of today – Russian as well as German – Marxists have inflated Müntzer into a giant symbol, a prodigious hero in the history of the 'class war.' This is a naïve view, and one which non-Marxist historians have countered easily enough by pointing to the essential mystical nature of Müntzer's preoccupations, his general indifference to the material welfare of the poor."[116] But that indifference, far from suggesting an exception to the history of millenarian utopianism, secular or otherwise, is typical: the vanguard cares about people in general rather than in particular.

The point of post-apocalyptic nirvana was to render redistribution superfluous since everything would be commonly owned. Karl Marx explained that Müntzer was addressing "the mode of perceiving nature, under the rule of private property and money, [which] is a real contempt for, and a practical degradation of, nature. It is in this sense that Thomas Müntzer declares it intolerable 'that every creature should be transformed into property – the fishes in the water, the birds of the air, the plants of the earth: the creature too should become free.'"[117]

As Marx saw it, Müntzer's crusade against corruption meant freeing nature, and everything in it, from being treated as personal property for selfish purposes. The Revolution-Armageddon would put an end to that "intolerable" situation. Everything was to be transformed back to its "real essence." The context of Müntzer's statement underscores his hostility to the current state. He thus attacks Luther as a "wretched flatterer [who] is silent... about the origin of all theft... [committed by] our lords and princes, [who] take all creatures as their property.... They oppress all people, and shear and shave the poor ploughman and everything that lives – yet if (the ploughman) commits the slightest offence, he must hang." The priest then proceeds to warn Luther, whom he calls a "wily fox," that "things will go with you as with a fox when it is caught. The people will become free and God alone means to be Lord over them."[118]

Müntzer's rants guaranteed his early death. His impact on future political events continues to be hotly debated, resulting in a plethora of "Müntzer legends." But one thing is certain: this strange, unstable man was nonetheless a seminal product of the Reformation, and doubtless contributed to its enormous impact on later revolutionary thought. Though Luther's enemy, Müntzer shared his deep distrust of the Catholic church. True, Luther enshrined respect for the state and opposed social revolt, while Müntzer called for chopping off the head of "any prince, count, or lord" who opposed the principle of "each should be given what he wants and when he needs it." Yet their common attack on the prestige of the clergy was bound to cause an eventual erosion not only of Catholicism but of Christian belief more generally, paving the way to the rise of utopian political religions.

Over the following centuries, Catholicism, known also as the Universal Church, became increasingly subordinate to secular authority, as Holy Roman Emperor Charles V declared in 1519 the primacy of imperial over clerical power. National churches appeared throughout Europe, Luther himself writing an open letter to the Christian nobility of what he called "the German Nation" in 1520,[119] though it would take nearly four centuries for Germany to become unified into something resembling a nation, when Prussian Prime Minister Otto von Bismarck brought together dozens of German-speaking principalities and other political units to form the German Empire in 1871.[120] That significant regional differences persist to this day goes without saying.

No less powerful than his prescient nationalist vision was Luther's virulent hatred of the Jews. "We are at fault in not slaying them,"[121] he had admonished his countrymen. Writes Robert Michael:

> Luther was obsessed with the Jewish "question" throughout his life. Luther saw Jews as "the quintessential *other*" and he placed them far outside his "sacral community." He wrote: "O God, beloved father and creator, have pity on me who, in self-defense, must speak so scandalously . . . against your wicked enemies, the devils and the Jews. Luther's enemies' list changed from time to time but usually included his Protestant and Catholic rivals, unruly German peasants, the pope, the Antichrist, the devil, and the Turks, whom he called "Red Jews." Luther sometimes wrote as if the Jews headed the list, although they were among the most vulnerable and impoverished of his contemporaries. The mere fact of their existence, Luther held, presented a threat to Christians everywhere.[122]

To be fair, Luther was by no means alone in his hatred of Jews. Throughout the Reformation, antisemitism was ubiquitous, as "most blamed the Jews for the plague and the imminent appearance of the Antichrist, an ally of the Jews. Great efforts were made to convert Jews in preparation for the anticipated battle between Antichrist and Christ" at Armageddon.[123] And lest the highly acclaimed humanists of the time be thought untouched by this lethal obsession, even Thomas More's friend, the humanist Erasmus, held that no place existed in Christian society for "the most pernicious plague and bitterest foe of the teachings of Jesus Christ"[124] – i.e., the wretched Jews.

Apocalypse as Revolution

What makes the Apocalypse an especially compelling image is its universality: the millenarian conflagration is expected to engulf the whole earth, affecting believers and nonbelievers alike. Yet that is what renders it especially dangerous, according to Karl Popper. "Utopianism," was quite simply worthless, declared Popper, as was every other similar "social experiment (if there is such a thing)," for it supposedly "could be of value only if carried out on a holistic scale,"[125] which was a practical and even theoretical impossibility. Holistic claims may inspire, but they lack any cognitive currency whatsoever.

At first blush, however, Popper's criticism seems to apply neither to Thomas More nor to Thomas Müntzer: in the case of the former, the setting was a tiny – indeed, mythical - island set in the New World, while the latter's actions were confined to a backwater German province. Undertaking "a social experiment," let alone on a holistic scale, was utterly foreign to their thinking. Yet Popper has a point, for both leave no doubt that their ultimate concern is the future of humanity and the best form of society, which are both universal in scope. Even Thomas More's fictional namesake, who scoffs at the possibility of abolishing property completely, given man's sinful nature, yet confesses that he "would wish" to see "very many [of the Island's] features" applied to "our societies," implicitly sanctioning egalitarian ideals. Similarly, Müntzer justifies the apocalyptic uprising of the poor by predicating a moral, and thus universally valid, right to redistribute their greedy owners' property. Empirical verification withers before faith: the vision of ending social injustice by eradicating superfluous riches was powerful and categorical.

Though long in gestation, utopianism thus came into its own in Europe around the fifteenth and early sixteenth century. Coincident with the broad and rapid dissemination of ideas, both old and new, through the printing press, the catastrophic fall of Constantinople in 1453 at last gave the Ottoman Empire control of the Balkans, which afforded Muslims free passage to the heart of Europe, thereby permanently sealing the fate of the Eastern Roman Empire. Christianity had been seriously, even if not fatally, wounded: a commercial, military, and political disaster for Europe, the Ottoman victory was above all symbolic. It augured the end of an era.

It also prompted a migration wave of scholars in Greek and Roman philosophy, especially to Italy, where they were welcomed warmly. This profound intellectual challenge was bound to cause political and social turmoil. Renaissance humanism had been filtering in gradually for over a century, but the treasure-trove of books and manuscripts brought by the learned migrants were explosive. From the Greek originals, they were promptly translated into Latin and, again thanks to Guttenberg, disseminated widely. Whether or not Columbus himself was part of that migration, his discovery of America in 1492, followed by Vespucci's voyages, in addition to inspiring Thomas More to contemplate alternative societies, also revolutionized European commerce and geopolitics.

The Peasants' War eventually fizzled, but the ideas that inspired revolutionary millenarianism – specifically, the notion that an entirely new political and economic system could eradicate, violently if need be, the pervasive evil on earth – took root. Did that require changing man himself, whose flawed nature is responsible for evil? And was such a notion compatible with the Christian belief that mankind, born sinful, could only find redemption in the afterlife?

Though Thomas Müntzer and Thomas More had both been pastors, they shared a passionate outrage against corruption not only in the church but the society at large. They both rejected the principal opponents of Catholicism in their countries - Müntzer having quarreled with the statist Luther, and More refusing to acknowledge Henry VIII, his nation's political leader, as simultaneously head of the English church. Nonetheless, their common devotion to Christianity as each understood it was unquestionable.

And yet, it is worth noting that More, who had thought of himself a Christian humanist,[126] was undoubtedly familiar with the writings of Epicurus and Lucretius, to whom he obliquely refers in *Utopia*. Vespucci too, whose work as we have seen precipitated the writing of *Utopia*, was part of a humanist circle in which Lucretius's *On the Nature of Things* was being circulated. These pagan Greek philosophers, known as "atomists" because of their materialist vision of the universe as consisting of small particles called "atoms," were also called "Epicureans," after its namesake. Since they reduced ethics essentially to pursuing pleasure, the term has since connoted sensualism; when Raphael describes the island inhabitants as "seem[ing] to be over-inclined to the position which claims that all or most important part of human happiness consists of pleasure,"[127] he seems to intimate the influence of the atomists on the simple natives. All the more reason to make sure there is no excess of property to facilitate debauchery. If Stephen Greenblatt is right that the whole point "of More's celebrated fable is to imagine those conditions that would make it possible for an entire society to make the pursuit of happiness its collective goal," it is easy to see why "[f]or More, those conditions would have to begin with the abolition of private property."[128]

Nor need one fear that there won't be enough to go around. For if "everyone is employed in a useful trade and the trades themselves require less labor, the result is a great abundance of everything... [And sometimes] they publicly decree a shorter workday. ... so that they can devote more time to the freedom and cultivation of the mind. For that, they think, constitutes a happy life."[129] But unlike Lucretius, the islanders "never analyze happiness unless they combine some religious principles with the rational analysis of philosophy, since they think that without such principles reason by itself is too weak and deficient to investigate true happiness."[130] How they imagined God was immaterial; what mattered was to fear Him. And not pursue idle pleasures.

Accordingly, atheism is strictly outlawed by King Utopus, who

> solemnly and strictly forbade that anyone should sink so far below the dignity of human nature as to think that the soul dies with the body or that the world is ruled by mere chance and not by providence. And for this reason they believe that after this life punishments are ordained for vices and rewards for virtues. Anyone who thinks otherwise they do not even include in the category of human beings since he has degraded the lofty nature of his soul to the base level of a beast's wretched body. Still less will they count him as one of their citizens, since he would set no store whatever by all their laws and morality if it were not for fear. For who can doubt that someone who has nothing to fear but the law and no hope of anything beyond bodily existence would strive to evade the public laws of his country by secret chicanery or break them by force in order to satisfy his own personal greed?[131]

More proposes a double safety net: for however altruistic men might become through the abolition of property and universal labor, belief that justice will be met eventually, in an afterlife, is the first and most important law of a society that has even a chance to promote the happiness of its members.

Christianity aside, it is religion itself whose fate More seeks to save from extinction. For insofar as the average man tends to seek "his own personal greed," the most effective antidote is fear. Greenblatt finds here echoes of the infamous Niccolo Machiavelli (1469-1527), More's contemporary:

Even with the full force of Utopian social conditioning, human nature, More believed, would inevitably lead men to resort to force or fraud in order to get whatever they desire. More's belief was conditioned no doubt by his ardent Catholicism, but in this same period Machiavelli, who was considerably less pious than the saintly More, came to the same conclusion. Laws and customs, the author of *The Prince* thought, were worthless without fear. [132]

And who else but God would inspire the ultimate dread? Not only is atheism hard to justify intellectually, being logically unverifiable, it is dangerous on practical grounds. There is no reason to assume that modernity and secularism are antagonistic to religion as such. Instead, they seek to redefine it in political terms. The presumption that many Renaissance disciples of Greek and Roman sages were antagonistic to religion or even professed a stealthy form of atheism, is wrong. On the contrary: like Luther and other Protestants, most of these humanists believed themselves to be offering a deeper, more genuinely Christian, theology. The difference lay in how they viewed man's relationship to God. According to Michael Allen Gillespie, the humanists "suggested in a Promethean fashion that man could lift themselves [sic] to the level of God or even in some respects become God," while the protestant reformers saw God as "omnipotent, and man was nothing without God." [133] What they all believed is that an enlightened mankind could influence the course of history in a positive direction.

Humanists and Protestants alike agreed that God's omnipotence not only did not diminish man's power, it enhanced it, as God was on his children's side. That said, the differences between the two approaches could not but clash: for humanism, explains Gillespie, "put man first and interpreted both God and nature on this basis. The Reformation, by contrast, began with God and viewed man and nature only from this perspective." These irreconcilable differences, which lay at the heart of Christianity from the beginning, "played an important role in the cataclysmic wars of religion that shattered European life in the sixteenth and seventeenth centuries." [134]

The enormity of that cataclysm reverted to some extent the attention of most historians of early Europe from the plight of the Jews, whose pariah status had been pretty much standard fare for centuries. Yet something important had changed. Luther's venom against them reverberated into the following century, when the Viennese Catholic preacher Abraham a Sancta Clara (1644-1709), "like Luther, declared that Jews had changed God Himself into the devil and were themselves devils." With characteristic insight, Robert Wistrich observes that, ironically, "at the intellectual heights of European Christendom, as in its lower depths, Jews ceased to be human beings. They had been ineluctably transformed into a theological abstraction of diabolical perversity and malice."[135]

The ideological underpinnings of modern totalitarian political religion were thus ominously congealing into a satanic lava that would soon shake civilization to its foundations.

3:
Fraternity by Guillotine

Revolution and Modernity

Though revolts and unrest have always been with us, revolution is seen as the quintessential modern form of violent political conflict. In her seminal work on the subject, Hannah Arendt declares unequivocally that "the modern concept of revolution [is] inextricably bound up with the notion that the course of history suddenly begins anew." Her claim that it "was unknown prior to the two great revolutions at the end of the eighteenth century,"[136] however, fails to acknowledge the revolutionary aspects of medieval millenarianism. While conceding that "one may see in the eschatological movements of the Middle Ages the forerunners of modern mass hysterias," she dismisses them as "politically without consequences and historically futile."[137] That so distinguished a political theorist utterly failed to recognize the profound psychological and ideological reverberations of those movements, which rendered then anything but "futile," is at best surprising.

She also assumes that modernity originated no earlier than the eighteenth century, but that is not right. As early as the twelfth century, Joachim of Fiore (1130/35-1201/02) thought of modernity as the final historical stage before the advent of the millennium, which he considered imminent. *Modernitas*, derived from the Latin *modus*, meaning "measure," soon came to be used to differentiate contemporary from past times in vernacular languages as well. In Italian, *moderno* was coined by Dante Alighieri (1265-1321) in *The Divine Comedy*, to indicate how things were done in his day. In a second context, Dante used it to describe the feel of contemporary language.[138] At virtually the same time, Nicholas of Oresme introduced *moderne* in French, while in English, "modern" in the sense of the present, appeared in 1585. "Modernity" itself dates from 1627.

But beyond the linguistic evolution lay a deeper change in attitude toward time, history, man in general. Explains Gillespie: to understand oneself as modern in the sense of new was to understand oneself as self-originating, as free and creative in a radical sense, not merely as determined by a tradition or governed by fate or providence. To be modern is to be self-liberating and self-making, and thus not merely to be in a history but to make history....Being modern at its core is thus something titanic, something Promethean. But what can possibly justify such an astonishing, such a hubristic claim?[139]

Shades of Babel, surely. The answer came in a revolutionary new notion of freedom and progress that accompanied a robust and unprecedented trust in empirical observation. Sir Francis Bacon (1561-1626), who served as Attorney General and later Lord Chancellor of England, argued that modernity was superior to antiquity – a potentially revolutionary attitude. His approach inevitably came to be associated with criticism of the French aristocratic *ancien regime*. François-Marie Arouet (1694–1778), better known as Voltaire, hailed him as the father of the scientific method, who raised Reason to its place of honor. Admittedly, even as Voltaire extoled modernity, his erstwhile comrade and fellow-Encyclopedist Jean-Jacques Rousseau argued against the pernicious effects of civilization. But what they all shared was the conviction that modern times had indeed arrived, and it was time to create an ideal society. Utopia.

By then, the word was quite entrenched. In a rapidly evolving intellectual climate, within a few decades after its coinage, "utopian" came into common usage, no longer connoting a fantasy, located nowhere, but in More's other sense of *eu-topia*: a good place, worth contemplating seriously. Write Frank and Fritzie Manuel: "By the seventeenth century utopia was no longer restricted to a speaking picture [or island] ... [but] came to denote general programs and platforms... that dispensed with the fictional apparatus altogether."[140] The possibility of constructing an ideal, even perfect, society on earth was no longer illusory:

[T]he conception of a millennium as a real society on earth covering a fixed period of time gave rise to speculations about what events would occur in that blessed epoch, what government would be instituted, and what social relationships would prevail. Whenever the vaguely oracular mode of prophecy was set aside in the seventeenth century, the millenarian utopia could respond to concrete, matter-of-fact questions.[141]

It could thereby be amenable to human planning - something like a building, or a tower, of measurable dimensions.

More's Catholic convictions notwithstanding, by seriously intimating the possibility of establishing an ideal human society on earth, *Utopia* was a creature of the Reformation. More had been right to fear that attacks on the papacy would unleash great turmoil: it had been the main reason he opposed Protestantism in all its forms. Britain too succumbed to deeply disruptive sectarian warfare, lasting on and off for well over a century. Except for a relative respite during the felicitous reign of Queen Elizabeth I, religiously-motivated slaughter and fierce feudal fights traumatized the British Isles, as it did other European principalities.

The seeds of modern-style revolution were being sown in English soil in no small measure thanks to John Knox (cca. 1505/1515–1572). A recalcitrant Scottish priest considered by many to have been the founder of Puritanism,[142] Knox had moved to England to escape charges of heresy.[143] Pellicani refers to him, anachronistically though not unfairly, as "a typical ideologue of the proletarian intelligentsia, who had transformed the 'Calvinist concept of saint in an ideal around which men without established social interests could gather'[144] and recognize themselves as an 'elite' separate from society and in conflict with its dominant institutions and values."[145] Before long, the Puritans, argues Pellicani,

> elevated politics to the rank of collective salvation, by identifying it with the methodical reshaping of the existing order according to a design that was intelligible only to the chosen few.... With Puritanism, an absolutely new element was introduced into Western civilization" – or rather, "not so much a new element as the development of an idea that already existed" in the sixteenth century[146] - namely, "(revolutionary) politics as fulfillment of God's will, with the objective of consciously building 'a new human community, that could substitute the lost Eden'[147] and produce a 'prodigious change in human nature.'"[148]

Without resorting to outright Armageddon, the Puritans, certainly many of them, succeeded in wreaking havoc. After the beheading of King Charles I in 1649, during the next decade, the English Civil Wars ravaged England, Scotland and Ireland. Ruled by a republican government with no royal at the helm, these provinces were torn asunder by atrocities. There was plenty of blame to go around.[149] Order did not come to Britain until

1688, with the eponymous "Glorious Revolution," which ended with the ignominious departure of King James II, whose attempts to curtail the powers of Parliament failed miserably, having "miscalculated the country."[150] The contrast with its violent French counterpart a century later could not have been more stark.

True, Britain's system of government had not been changed: it was still a monarchy. But something *was* all but unprecedented: in the soon-to-be Kingdom of Great Britain (so declared in 1707), Parliament's preeminence was now secured – and with it, the principle of popular governance. In sum, the political change across the English Channel, though accompanied by upheavals, had taken place through an evolutionary process rather than emerging from a bloody Apocalypse. Importantly, there had been no serious mass uprising: the wars had been principally a feudal affair, led by nobles, even if the victims, as often happened, were largely rural.

What undeniably did end was any chance of Catholicism becoming re-established in England. The English King as head of the Anglican church had none of the divine authority conferred upon the Bishop of Rome. Theocracy was becoming obsolete as revolutionary winds were blowing - irrevocably.

Catholicism generally, and the power of popes over secular rulers in particular, had been weakening throughout Europe for nearly two centuries, but by the early sixteenth century had reached a crisis from which it never quite recovered. After 1517, Protestantism was established in much of Europe: Lutheranism throughout the German provinces, Scandinavia, and the Baltics; Calvinism in Switzerland, Scotland, France, Transylvania (now in Romania), and the Low Countries (including Belgium and the Netherlands). The most radical Puritans in England, as well as many of the Huguenots in France, would eventually leave the Old World to populate the New.

But the problem wasn't simply sectarian. Alongside Protestantism, anti-clerical sentiment as such was growing. Skepticism flourished in the aftermath of the Renaissance. As already mentioned, this was in part thanks to Epicurus and Lucretius.[151] Their speculations that nature consisted of nothing more than tiny particles they called "atoms," that an afterlife was pure fantasy, and that no divinity could possibly be interested in the vagaries of human existence, increasingly resonated with many a learned scholar who had access to the atomists' newly translated writings. Defying the odds by surviving both physical disasters and censorship, two millennia later the works of these prescient Greek philosophers would help revive a conception of the world in mechanistic terms. While nature had long been believed to be subject to rational laws, empirical investigation and mathematical calculations led to astonishing new discoveries that transformed altogether the archaic, theologically-based view of the universe.

Perhaps the most powerful blow to that worldview was inadvertently delivered by an erudite, diligent and humble Polish mathematician, economist, and astronomer. Well-known among his colleagues, Nicolaus Copernicus (1473-1543) was certainly highly respected, but in no way a superstar. His most important book, fatefully titled *De Revolutionibus*, did not appear until the year of his death, and then only in Latin. Meaning literally "on revolutions," it advanced a highly technical description of planetary trajectories, known as "revolutions" or orbits. In other words, his book was about astronomy, that's all. Or so Copernicus thought. But he was wrong: *De Revolutionibus* had in fact dropped a conceptual hand-grenade. It would ignite what came to be known as *the Scientific Revolution* – followed by social, political, and economic upheavals whose aftershocks are felt to this day.

It took a while. But before long, first the clergy and then the public at large got wind of the stunning ideas hidden behind the Polish astronomer's complicated formulae and astronomical data. The traditional view of the universe based on the Bible was under siege. Consistent with the extensive, entrenched works by Aristotle, who had been the scientific authority embraced by the Church since at least the thirteenth century, that view was geocentric (from *Gaia,* the Earth Goddess of Greek mythology). It assumed the Earth to be at the center of the world surrounded by the divine planets and Sun which all circled it – the circle being a "perfect" trajectory, as befits the Heavens. Unfortunately, empirical observations had consistently failed to confirm the presumed circularity, leading astronomers as far back as Ptolemy (100-168) to resort to adding convoluted little circles on top of circles, like a ghastly mobile, to try to fit the facts to the theory. And it still didn't work very well.

Endowed with a brilliant mathematical mind, Copernicus dared to completely flip the picture: he proposed a heliocentric universe, with the sun (from the Greek god *Helos*) at the center, surrounded by a moving earth and the planets, none in the least divine, all orbiting the sun. This made far better sense of the available data. But in the process, what he also inadvertently turned upside down was man's view of his own place in the universe. The implications could not escape the humble astronomer; yet he could not keep the discovery to himself.

Copernicus's argument was at once empirical and aesthetic: it fit the facts and was simpler than the previous, exceptionally convoluted, system of measuring planetary trajectories, which had astronomers scratching their heads with growing frustration. For the first time in history, Copernicus provided both an accurate method of ordering the planets and a simple formula for calculating the relative distances of the planets from the sun. Not only could these be tested against future observations, they were astoundingly elegant.

Aesthetics was key. In true Renaissance fashion, Copernicus begins his book with an image from Horace's *Ars poetica* (The Art of Poetry). The theories of his predecessors, he writes, were like a human figure in which the arms, legs, and head were put together in the form of a disorderly monster. Not so his own representation of the universe, which formed a harmonious unit: displacement of any part would case disruption of the whole. A far simpler mathematical model, it was also much more consistent with the observations of astronomers, especially the recent measurements of Tycho Brache (1546-1601) and Christoph Clavius (1537-1612).

Though far less bloodless than even the English revolution, the one prompted by Copernicus was cataclysmic. Writes Thomas Kuhn: "The Copernican Revolution was a revolution in ideas, a transformation in man's conception of the universe and of his own relation to it."[152] It had taken nearly two millennia, the delay caused at least in part by the inability to imagine man and his abode anywhere but at the very center of the world. Once the paradigm had shifted, however, a cascade of seemingly miraculous innovations, "unanticipated by-products of Copernicus's astronomical theory,"[153] followed in quick succession, culminating two centuries later in the Newtonian theory of the universe. The Modern Age had officially arrived, and with it a new religion of Science and Reason.

If Copernicus had been its Abraham, Isaac Newton (1643-1727) was its Moses. Hidden inside his massive tome *Principia Mathematica,* a door-stopper published in Latin in 1687, lay a conception of a universe constructed of atoms (with more than a nod to the Epicureans), which move predictably, propelled by forces acting in accordance with a few God-given laws. Most notable among them was Gravity, which pulls all objects to one other. The new model could not but alter many men's image of the Deity Himself.

Whether Gravity acted at a distance through a vacuum or by contact, through some kind of weightless "ether," was hotly debated, but not its demonstrable effects. Hence the mysterious but clearly powerful force of Gravity came to be seen by many as the concrete expression of God's power. Explains Kuhn:

> In the clockwork universe God frequently appeared to be only the clockmaker, the Being who had shaped the atomic parts, established the laws of their motion, set them to work, and then left them to run themselves.... [which led many to see] parallels in the seventeenth-century conception of a smoothly running society.[154]

Unbeknownst to either More or Copernicus, the *De Revolutionibus* had become a veritable addendum to *Utopia*. For if man, with his unaided reason, could grasp the laws of nature so effectively by means of observation and mathematical formulae, why shouldn't he seek to establish a perfect, or at least near-perfect, world?

The conception of a planetary earth orbiting around the sun dealt the most dramatic blow to the traditional view of the world and man's place in history. Though evicted from center stage, man discovered a new self-confidence in his own Reason, reverently capitalized, which had empowered him to understand the mysteries of an incredibly complicated, possibly infinite, universe. But if man could eventually understand the inner logic of God's workmanship, how far could his own mind be from that of the Divine? And if nature's laws obeyed the necessity of logic, would it not be possible to calculate the laws governing a brave new human world as well? Could the wars and corruption that destroyed societies be eliminated through wise planning? Alas, the ominous question inevitably asked itself: had hubris ever been harder to resist?

Purification Through Terror

Independently of Copernicus and his colleagues, alongside the notion of revolution as planetary orbiting, a parallel concept was gaining acceptance in the political realm. Just as a circular object returns to a previous position after a revolution in space, so a society can "return" from a corrupt to a more pristine state of affairs. An Italian work of 1629 on the causes and prevention of "revolution," which found "kingdoms particularly vulnerable because of their monarchs' misconduct,"[155] was among the first to refer to political change. It was followed in 1647 by a treatise concerning an uprising in Naples that year that its author similarly dubbed "revolutionary." Both were symptomatic of what James H. Billington calls "an already well-developed discussion of political revolution"[156] throughout the continent. One English study of the Naples uprising first used the metaphor of a "fire" coming from a small "spark."[157] Aptly, Billington's magisterial 1980 book on revolutions is titled *Fire in the Minds of Men*.

If fire renders a political revolution apocalyptic, the Reformation was doubtless incendiary. The mechanical exactness that the Scientific Revolution assigned to all action in the universe, which extended to human behavior, complemented the religious determinism of millenarianism – an explosive mixture that Emperor Frederick II (the Great) of Prussia (1712-1786) fully understood. Writes Billington: Frederick's "interest in revolution as a spiritual and political event subtly influenced many Germans of his time. He created in Prussia a sense of new Promethean possibilities."[158] For that reason, it seems plausible to infer, as does Billington, that it had been "Germany - not France – [that] gave birth to the sweeping, modern idea of revolution of a secular upheaval more universal in reach and more transforming in scope than any purely political change."[159] Full credit (or blame), however, should probably go to both.

Nor was the upheaval so secular that it dispensed with religion altogether. After all, the principal inspiration behind the first truly modern Revolution, Jean-Jacques Rousseau, was himself at least a nominal believer. Born in Calvinist Geneva in 1712, converted to Catholicism at the urging of a noblewoman at age 16, even training to be a priest, he later returned to Calvinism in 1754, if only to regain citizenship in his native town. Sectarian oscillations aside, Rousseau's theological promiscuity was amply matched by his total indifference to his five legitimate children, who were all deposited to an orphanage after their births. While that alone should have disqualified him as a true Christian, it did not certify him as an atheist; merely as a scoundrel.

In any event, whatever his personal convictions, Rousseau's vision of a perfect state explicitly presupposed allegiance to a Higher Power. Like Thomas More, Rousseau was worried lest no unbeliever could be trusted to obey the laws: religion had, above all, a critical practical function. It was "very important for the State," he writes in the *Social Contract*, "that every citizen should have a religion which may make him delight in his duties."[160] True, he means "the religion of man or Christianity – not the Christianity of today, but that of the Gospel, which is entirely different... [It holds that] all men, being children of one God, recognize one another as brothers, and the society that unites them is not dissolved even in death."[161] Though stripped down to basics, the Gospel is still that good old-time religion, not to be heedlessly discarded.

But was Rousseau's appeal to religion purely political, not to say hypocritical? Perhaps. He does not conceal that his main goal is the survival of the State. "Whoever dares to say 'Outside the Church is no salvation,' ought to be driven from the State, unless the State is the Church, and the prince the pontiff."[162] Realistically speaking, worshiping the state was a far less effective incentive to obeying the laws when compared to fear of a wrathful God and eternal damnation. But Rousseau rejects indisputably the sort of religion that is "occupied solely with heavenly things," which "preaches only servitude and dependence, ... [a] spirit so favorable to tyranny that it always profits by such a regime."[163] The only real source of political legitimacy is "the General Will [that alone] can direct the State according to the object for which it was instituted, i.e., the common good." And the General Will "tends to equality."[164] That in turn implies fraternity, which is all one needs for liberty, is it not? To the barricades, citizens and citizenesses! God's role was merely as Ultimate Enforcer of the General Will: He is the Guillotiner of Last Resort. Man rules.

Rousseau died before the start of the great upheaval that he precipitated, most of whose authors idolized him as its prophet even if they despised him personally. Though he never had a chance to storm the Bastille on July 14, 1789, he shared paternity of that disaster with the *philosophes* of the French Enlightenment, notably Denis Diderot (1713-1784), editor of the *Encyclopédie*, whom he met in 1742. For while the rationalist *philosophes* thought that change could come peacefully and gradually, Rousseau saw a dynamic inevitability in the air that would propel the creation of an entirely new society. That society was eutopian in that it could, if properly instituted, bring lasting peace and equality. What Rousseau provided was the indispensable romantic, millenarian impetus. The *philosophes* idolized Reason and scoffed at base passions - a surefire way to lose the masses, who would have to play the main role in the drama. Rousseau by contrast, though no politician, sought legitimacy in the people as the embodiment of the General Will: and it was this brilliant insight that ultimately carried the day. The *philosophes*, a self-styled enlightened elite, talked to one another and hoped for a *messiah ex machina* who had yet to audition for the role. Without altogether shunning the elite, whom he courted even as he secretly detested them, the quixotic Rousseau addressed the masses – if not quite literally, certainly conceptually. For he knew perfectly well that reason wasn't exactly their strong suit.

If Rousseau's prose won him literary prizes, it was not for clarity. He also badly needed a disciple and friend with savvy and connections. This very thing Providence would provide in Honoré Gabriel Riqueti, Count Mirabeau (1749-1791), a former French ambassador to Berlin. Though a rationalist like Diderot, Mirabeau was mesmerized by Rousseau. Well educated and intelligent, he was also intimately familiar with German thought, and had studied the works of Frederick the Great. Mirabeau, writes Billington, "pioneered the evocative language of traditional religion to the new political institutions of revolutionary France."[165]

Already on May 10, 1789, Mirabeau defined the mission of the Estates-General (the French legislative body called by Louis XVI) as a "regeneration" rather than mere "reform." Later, he would call the Republican National Assembly "the inviolable priesthood of national policy," and the Constitution of 1791 a new religion "for which the people are ready to die."[166] Mirabeau understood that kindling political fires takes considerably more than cold reason, and nothing worked quite as effectively as religious rhetoric to rouse passions. Rousseau was his man.

As chance would have it, the immediate spark that lit the revolutionary pyre was a minor, almost negligible incident: on July 11, king Louis XVI dismissed his reformist Finance Minister. The following day, a lovely Sunday afternoon in the gardens of the Palais-Royal, the radical journalist and politician Camille Desmoulins climbed on a table and cried *Aux Armes!* (To arms!) The drama was worthy of Hollywood. A colleague and composer had provided him with an apt rustic costume, complete with green leaf (perhaps plucked from a nearby tree), meant to contrast with the artificial badges of the aristocracy, and the flamboyant Desmoulins soon attracted an audience. All the theatres of Paris cancelled their performances: it almost seemed orchestrated, and perhaps it was. The atmosphere had been set for assaulting the Bastille two days later. "Take one!" (Take all!)

Felicitously, these developments coincided with the arrival in Paris of the Marquis de Lafayette, who took military command of Paris on July 15th - thereby lending considerably legitimacy to the still inchoate, rather ludicrous, upheaval. He immediately helped draft the Declaration of the Rights of Man and Citizen, which would serve to abolish serfdom and aristocratic privilege. Fresh back from America, the Founders' theories still vivid in his mind, Lafayette was hoping for gradual measures. Unfortunately, his role was short-lived; for he would soon be imprisoned. The political and ideological landscape of France was about to shift, indeed tectonically, its real, terrible, revolution still ahead. Still missing were a call for abolishing private property and a bloody Apocalypse. Popular ire had been kindled by a hubristic avantgarde: the self-styled Gallic messiahs were salivating to decapitate the Antichrists in their midst. Heads would soon roll without their powdered wigs.

Utopian-style Equality

Though Rousseau agreed with the *philosophes'* visceral contempt for hereditary aristocracy, they did not all share his profound distrust of private property. Yet they too were heirs to the traditional Pauline scorn for the love of money as the source of corruption and evil. They made up in intellectual arrogance for what they lacked in political savvy and ignored the inconsistencies in their own thinking. While embracing revolution in the name of universal Reason, they paid scant attention to the practical consequences of regime change. Diderot, for example, complained about gross inequalities in society and decried the plight of the poor, yet he offered no specific proposals for reform.

It was their own reason these elitists trusted, paying little more than lip service to the "universality" of the faculty. Writes Gertrude Himmelfarb: "It is as if the *philosophes* expended so much intellectual capital on the exalted idea of reason that they had little thought left, and even less sympathy, for the common people.... The French idea of reason was not available to the common people and had no such moral or social component."[167]

But it was not merely a matter of feelings – Rousseau was, after all, almost pathologically empathy-challenged. James Boswell, who had visited him in 1764, quotes him as saying: "Sir, I have no liking for the world. I live here in a world of fantasies, and I cannot tolerate the world as it is.... Mankind disgusts me."[168] Comments Richard Pipes: "Ill-tempered but honest; utopias have always served as an outlet for misanthropic emotions."[169] Rousseau loved people only in general, hardly ever in particular. Lack of empathy for the masses would continue to plague future champions of equality-for-everyone-else.

In this regard, Rousseau resembled his rationalist compatriots: few suffered from *philanthropia* (from the Greek *philos*, "love," and *anthropos*, "man"). They would have much preferred an "enlightened despot" - someone like Frederick the Great perhaps, or Diderot's faithful supporter Catherine the Great (who had also been much admired by Voltaire), or some other Whomever the Great. But as an outsider uncomfortable in fashionable Parisian circles, Rousseau fundamentally distrusted rationalism: his rhetoric was pointedly populist. Occasional nods to respect for property were prompted less by conviction than by vacillation; he did end up eventually rejecting inequality of possessions altogether.

Specifically, he famously accused the mythical first man, who allegedly appropriated a piece of ground by declaring it his alone and no one else's, of having originated all other evils – moral, social, and economic. In the *Discourse on the Origin of Inequality* (1754), Rousseau deplores that "[s]uch was, or may well have been, the origin of society and law, which bound new fetters on the poor, and gave new power to the rich... and subjected all mankind to perpetual labor, slavery and wretchedness."[170] Rousseau's original sin took place not in the garden of Eden but outside it: when man attempted to carve out a piece of God's earth. Eutopian theology.

The ensuing decadence that plagued humanity was caused by an artificial "civilization" characterized by money-worship and gross injustice. As he explains in *Discourse on Political Economy* (1755), this must end, to be replaced by an ideal "legitimate government, that is to say, of government whose object is the good of the people, [which must]... follow in everything the General Will." And that requires the protection of *all* the people. If this entails "trespassing on the liberty of others" in some (most) respects, so be it. For how can a government "provide for the public needs, without alienating the individual property of those who are forced to contribute to them?"[171] The establishment of such a eutopian state evidently requires transforming the property arrangements of real societies: people who still have "individual property" have to be "forced to contribute" in order to provide for "the public need." Comments Peter Garnsey: "It is difficult to imagine such a transformation taking place without an element of coercion."[172] Actually, there is no need to imagine: Rousseau says it explicitly.

He dispels any lingering doubt in *The Social Contract*: "Whoever refuses to obey the General Will shall be compelled to do so by the whole body. This means nothing less than that he will be forced to be free; for this is the condition which, by giving each citizen to his country, secures him against all personal dependence."[173] Such language is proto-totalitarian. And in the real world of revolution, words are a prelude to action. Getting rid of Louis XVI and his "*ancien régime*," was the top priority; the king had to be replaced. But The Great Messiah of 1789 had yet to emerge; and what if He did not arrive? That was not an option, though Rousseau had shied away from speculation, and was conveniently dead by the time the dilemma turned real.

Having refrained from practical politics, his rhetoric was flexible, chameleonic - to be blunt, disingenuous. Hannah Arendt observes that "the very attraction of Rousseau's theory for the men of the French Revolution was that he apparently had found a highly ingenious means to put a multitude into the place of a single person; for the General Will was nothing more or less than what bound the many into one."[174] So understood, it seems consistent with Diderot's preference for an elite: "[S]ince of the two wills, the one general and the other particular, the General Will never falls into error, it is not difficult to see on which one, for the happiness of the human race, the legislatures ought to depend, and what veneration we owe the august mortals whose particular wills reunite both the authority and the infallibility of the General Will..."[175]

But Diderot's transparent faith in "august mortals" had drastically curtailed its populist appeal. Rousseau, by contrast, maintained a deliberate ambiguity adaptable to larger constituencies. Writes Pipes: Rousseau's prose "displayed just the right mixture of noble sentiment, lofty rhetoric, muddled thinking, and disregard for reality to attract those intellectuals who, like him, refused to 'tolerate the world as it is.'"[176] Anyone salivating for a fight, intellectual or otherwise, could not resist.

It is thus best to understand Rousseau's General Will as formal and symbolic rather than literal: it wasn't referring to anyone's actual will; its "generality" consciously underscored that it belonged to no one in particular. Yes, it was vague; and yes, it was confusing; but that was all intentional. And it worked. All that Rousseau would say about the source of that mysterious General Will is that it came from "all the people at large as opposed to the monarch or the aristocrats or any other segment." Whether he believed that any "august mortals" had special insight into the people's "true," or "real" interests, all he would say is that "[t]here must be a government, and it may be monarchic, aristocratic, or democratic."

Whatever its form, "since nature and revealed religion have been set aside," explains Alan Bloom, "only the voice of the people can establish law."[177] For they are ultimately the only legitimate law, no matter who speaks with their voice - it could be an enlightened despot, or maybe some kind of General Assembly, Committee, Directorate, or whatever. Rousseau's rhetoric was political dynamite. The General Will had an unmistakably romantic quality: portrayed as a magical spirit, embodied in the people, it inspired a religious zeal in his disciples, fueling their rage, filling them with self-righteous, frenzied self-abnegation.

If this approach had strengths, however, its weaknesses were even more glaring. As even the minimally critical mind can discern, the General

Will is, frankly, meaningless. How exactly could it be detected? How did it differ from the aggregate desires of a multitude? And what if the multitude, or any part of it, refuses to agree with some discrepancy, preferring its own interpretation? These were not mere salon conversations but had obvious real-life implications. In the end it did not matter. Predictably, Reason was shoved aside and murderous frenzy took over.

The *philosophes'* vain hope for democratizing the French system of government without having to resort to regicide or excessive violence proved a mirage. It was another group of wordsmiths, less well-known but politically astute, who would turn Rousseau's most extreme pronouncements into inflammatory crowd-bait. These were the semi-intellectual masters of the tabloid prose, members of a separate constituency known as the Fourth Estate. Writes Billington: "In revolutionary France journalism rapidly arrogated to itself the Church's former role as the propagator of values, models, and symbols for society at large."[178] Alongside academics, artists, and other bohemian characters, these were priests of the secular utopia: self-appointed harbingers of a new world, a "vanguard" eager to lead the masses to their salvation. Nicholas de Bonneville, for example, exalted the "republic of letters" in his newspaper *Le Tribun de Peuple,* rallying intellectuals to lead mankind.[179]

The chaos that reigned throughout the country at the start of the uprisings led many noblemen to flee abroad. Weeks became months, and months became years. At last, in exasperation, worried that French emigres were building counterrevolutionary alliances in Austria and Prussia, the newly elected Legislative Assembly declared war in April 1792. Chaos summarily turned into nightmare, except that the carnage was no ephemeral hallucination.

The dam had broken. The royal residence was attacked by extremist Jacobins, who arrested the king on August 10, 1792 and massacred thousands of accused subversives. The following month, the Legislative Assembly was replaced by a National Convention, which immediately proclaimed the abolition of the monarchy and the establishment of the French republic. On January 21, 1793, the King was guillotined; Marie Antoinette lost her head nine months later. Finally, in June, the hard-core Jacobins took over from their more moderate predecessors, and thousands, suspected enemies of the people, were summarily liquidated. Christianity was abolished, and the fanatical Maximilien Robespierre assumed power. Armageddon had arrived.

Pellicani explains that already in 1792, Georges Danton (1759-1794), the first President of the euphemistically labeled Committee of

Public Safety, had explained "why the Convention had been forced to use terror in enforcing the principle of popular sovereignty: 'The republicans are a minute minority; the rest of the population is attached to the monarchy; it is necessary to terrify the monarchists,' in other words, the vast majority of the French population."[180] It was soon to get worse, as eutopianist revolutions invariably do, after the June coup d'état when "the modus operandi of the revolutionary government became even more paradoxical: not only was it obliged to terrorize the monarchists but also those revolutionaries who refused to accept its programs."[181] So-called "enemies of the people" were feared hiding under the bed of any citizen. The last recourse was inescapable: "All factions must perish at the same time," declared Robespierre on March 15, 1794. That meant his allegedly recalcitrant colleagues, including, of course, Danton.[182]

Far from aberrant, Robespierre's ideology had been deeply influenced by Rousseau. Echoing the Genevan, he contrasted "the people" (singular, abstract, faceless) to mere individuals: "The people is good, patient and generous.... The interest, the desire of the people is that of nature, humanity, and the general welfare.... The people is always worth more than individuals."[183] Like Rousseau, he called for a religious "profession of faith," to which every citizen would be bound in irrevocable allegiance to the state.

It was Rousseau he meant to commemorate above all when proclaiming the Festival of the Supreme Being that supposedly ushered in a "Republic of Virtue." Predictably, in 1792 Robespierre presented a plan for compulsory education in boarding schools to protect children from reactionary ideas they might pick up from their parents – a precursor of the Maoist "re-education camps." Through the Committee of Public Safety and the sinister Jacobin clubs that had proliferated throughout France, he launched a Reign of Terror (*La Terreur*) after issuing a Decree on September 5, 1793. Best known for its gory executions, the Reign also instituted ruinous price-controls, which ultimately turned key artisanal elements of the *sans-culottes* against the regime.

While Paris saw the most blood, terror soon engulfed the whole nation. The Jacobin clubs' relationship with local governments has been described by Michael Kennedy as an "interpenetration," with the former very much in the driving seat.[184] The Committee of Public Safety explicitly asked clubs for names of functionaries "known to be unfaithful and uncivic." The purges were often portrayed as revolutionary social acts. In Lorient, for example, the putative goal was that "the poor shall enjoy the benefits of the revolution which up to now have gone to bankers, big businessmen, and merchants."[185]

It did not take long for Robespierre's drastic actions to enrage his colleagues who feared him, as did the rest of the population. So by the end of July 1794, it became clear that his influence had taken a dive, his popularity all but evaporated. After a failed suicide attempt, he was captured and a few days later, on July 28, guillotined. It was the beginning of the end; yet the Revolution had many acts still to follow before the curtain fell on that appalling spectacle.

For brewing inside the cafes of Paris were a slew of piping hot egalitarian ideas, which continued to gather converts. They found especially receptive audiences among provincial clergy who identified with their rural parishes and the ambitions of the peasants. The Abbe Cournand, for example, proclaimed that "in the state of nature, the domain of man is the entire earth"[186] - a line practically out of the *Social Contract*. Except that he went considerably further, proposing that all land-owners should have plots equal in size, non-hereditary, and non-transferrable.

But even Cournand was outdone by a young rabble-rouser who had been briefly incarcerated for having led a local tax revolt against continued taxes being levied by the National Assembly. Eventually elected administrator of the Somme region in 1792, the hot-headed revolutionary arrived in Paris to pursue "real economic equality" and a new kind of "general happiness unknown throughout the ages."[187] His name was François-Noël Babeuf, a feudal lawyer turned revolutionary journalist, who preferred calling himself Gracchus Babeuf, in memory of the second-century Roman brothers who had sought to redistribute land owned by nobles to the poor. (They had, of course, been assassinated; but Babeuf was undaunted.)

Frustrated by what he saw as half-hearted measures by the republican administration mired in inefficiency, riddled with financial crises and perennial corruption, Babeuf turned to journalism. His prose was Rousseau on steroids. Rejecting the right of property, he argued that society should provide "common happiness" through "perfect equality." In November 1795, he published the *Plebeian Manifesto*, which anticipated its Marxist sequel in performing two functions: first, making "manifest," or explaining, what was needed to bring about "equality in fact" and "the common good," while at the same time inciting violent upheaval, "*une manifestation*," grandly described as "more solemn, more general than has ever been done before."[188]

While the odds against success had been long from the outset, they had since grown significantly. True, Babeuf's small circle of like-minded radicals, the Club of the Pantheon, was summarily shut down by a young general named Napoleon, to whom the floundering French governing body with the unroyal, appropriately bureaucratic label "the Directorate," had outsourced the restoration of order. But that still didn't stop Babeuf and his radical associates, who lost none of their determination. Gone underground, the name of their new group was a deliberate allusion to their hero Robespierre: The Secret Directory of Public Safety.

Secret it was on many counts: its mobilization techniques sophisticated and decentralized, its conspiratorial decisions were reached collectively, announced anonymously. Despite or perhaps because of its radical vision, the Directory's membership soon reached a whopping seventeen thousand.[189] Overconfident in its success, however, it turned to the army as its principal recruiting ground, which soon allowed an informer to infiltrate the organization, leading to the arrest of its entire leadership.

But while the organization could be shut down, its message could not. Robespierre's *Plebeian Manifesto* had sought total equality and, indeed, the end of politics as such. The state itself was the enemy. Defiantly anarchist, he had called for *"bouleversement total"* (total upheaval): "May everything return to chaos, and out of chaos may there emerge a new and regenerated world." There would follow a "great national community" in which all goods were held in common and shared equally.

Billington suggests that "imperceptibly within Babeuf's conspiracy arose the myth of an unfinished revolution."[190] Not that it implied abandoning the millenarian vision of an end to all history. The revolution was not "unfinished" in the sense of being "perpetual" – never-ending strife was precisely what millenarianism was seeking to abolish. Rather, by 1795 it had become quite clear to Babeuf and his associates that they had not yet witnessed the real thing. As his friend Sylvain Marechal explained: "The French Revolution is but the precursor of another revolution, far greater, far more solemn, which will be the last." [191]

If not an outright Communist as defined a few decades later by Karl Marx, when asked "Where does Evil come from?" Robespierre answered: "From the bourgeois." Similarly, his Jacobin colleague, Louis Antoine Léon de St. Just, stated that the objective of Terror was to "overturn the empire of wealth." This, Pellicani observes, came close enough to Communism for "Babeuf [to have] expressed all his admiration for Robespierre's 'regenerating ideas' and proclaimed loud and clear that it was necessary to suppress private property, to materialize the ideal of 'pure equality,' and to purify men, corrupted by 'greed and ambition.'"[192] It certainly quacked, walked, and waddled enough like Communism to count as a close relative.

The revolution may not have been finished, but Babeuf was. He was arrested, and his conspiracy terminated, on May 10, 1796. On May 27, 1797, after a celebrated trial that served to publicize the extent and methods of his activities, Babeuf was hanged. Three years later, on November 9, 1799, Napoleon Bonaparte would stage a coup d'état that put the floundering Directory at last out of its misery, and appointed himself "first consul," thus officially ending the entire French Revolution. Its ideas however were another story: they would migrate far and wide.

Confident of his authority, and contemptuous of the hare-brained egalitarian utopians he had mercilessly crushed, Napoleon rubbed still more salt into their wounds.

In a brazen display of hubris, on December 2, 1804, he arrived for his official coronation already wearing a crown - a golden laurel wreath as an homage to the Roman Empire. Then ostentatiously dispensing with the services of Pope Pius VII, he ceremoniously placed a second one, a replica of Emperor Charlemagne's crown, on the head of his wife Josephine, with his own hands. Adding populist insult to the pontiff's injury, Napoleon's elevation to the lofty throne was reaffirmed by a Stalinist majority (99.93%) of French citizens, through a constitutional referendum held in November 1804. The masses had gladly traded ideological purity for putative stability and gaudy spectacle.

Napoleon's legacy has been mixed, though leaning far toward the negative. Frank McLynn, for example, claims that "he can be viewed as the man who set back European economic life for a generation."[193] Victor Davis Hanson blames him for being "willing to risk the lives of millions for the idea of a pan-European dream."[194] Certainly France's bankruptcy, along with colonial losses, left the nation in bad shape. True, its profligate kings had already squandered their subjects' taxes on overseas adventures, but Napoleon turned out to be little better. This did not prevent the astonishing display of his tomb in the Palais des Invalides, which arguably rivals the pyramids in splendor and surpasses them in popularity, a visible proof that the French still venerate him, and probably always will. It is hard to argue with glories on the battlefield, the restoration of law and order, and above all, imperial theatre. Perhaps more than most, the French love a good show.

From a broader perspective, the aftermath of Napoleon's reign had an enormous impact outside of France as well. It actually did have positive aspects: Alexander Grab suggests that "[b]y building the central state, abolishing the privileges of the Church and nobility and weakening their grip on power, advancing the interests of the bourgeoisie, proclaiming legal equality, and promoting economic unity, Napoleonic rule paved the way for the modernization of Europe."[195] Whether it was worth the death and destruction is quite another question, certainly moot.

To conclude, the French millenarian conflagration became the first real experiment in eutopia. Though unsuccessful at home, it inspired the rise of secret revolutionary organizations throughout Europe, as well as Latin America and the Middle East. Writes Billington: "These groups, although largely unconnected, internationalized the modern revolutionary tradition and the purposes of political power in a post-traditional society."[196] These groups consisted of intellectuals convinced that so long as their utopian vision was still unfulfilled, the revolution could still be just around the corner.

The beauty of millenarianism is its chronological flexibility; "one thousand years" is poetic license, not a train schedule. The true believers decided simply that the *fin-de-siècle* (century's end) calamities had not been horrible enough to prompt the Real Thing – *les sans culottes* had unwisely jumped the gun, so to speak, before conditions had become ripe.

Antagonisms still had to grow, social, political and economic divisions had to worsen. Ideology had to further undermine rational discourse, and group identity take precedence over dialogue and rational skepticism. All of that would be greatly facilitated by an ingenious new contribution to political taxonomy: The Left-Right dichotomy.

Left, Right, and Center

The terms Left and Right were at least as dubious a French contribution to world peace as the guillotine, whose eponymous inventor had actually thought it humane. It all started on May 8, 1789, the Bastille still eight weeks away, with the seating arrangements around the king inside the hall of the National Assembly. Members of the nobility who favored limiting the powers of the monarch decided to sit with the commoners on the left (from the perspective of the presiding officer), letting others flank Louis XVI on his right. The occasion was a vote on opposing proposals: one by Rousseau's disciple Mirabeau, the other by Baron Pierre Victor Malouet (1740-1814). Suddenly, the deputies decided to count heads "by inviting the assembly to divide itself in such a way that those of Malouet's opinion should pass to the right and those favoring Mirabeau should array themselves on the left" – an arrangement, notes Marcel Gauchet,[197] proving cumbersome in the extreme, as it required greater clarity of opinion than many possessed.

It led to pandemonium. People moved around enough as to cause considerable confusion. At the end of August, the Mayor of Nancy Adrien Duquesnoy wrote in his diary, concerning a vote on religious freedom, "that the hall is divided in such a way that in one part sit men who no doubt hold exaggerated opinions at times but who in general hold a very high idea of liberty and equality."[198] Left unsaid was... exactly which part he was talking about! The absurdity of the seating procedure is best described by the Baron de Gauville, who commented after a vote on the issue of royal veto: "I tried to sit in different parts of the hall and not to adopt any marked spot, so as to remain more the master of my opinion, but I was compelled absolutely to abandon the left or else be condemned always to vote alone and thus be subjected to jeers from the galleries."[199]

Needless to say, neither of the two "sides" was homogeneous. As Duquesnoy noted early in 1791, for example, "the left is divided into two quite distinct, quite opposed parties." Meanwhile, wrote the journalist Mathieu Dumas, one of the participants, "a far larger number of enlightened men of moderate opinions, reputed to be wise and almost indifferent observers, hastened to the center, where their mass and packed ranks might, by dint of numerical weight and strength, take on in their own eyes the appearance of an immense majority, comforting them in their timidity."[200] Dusquenoy summarized the position of those in the middle: "They are in favor of everything that is being done, but they would like to see it done more slowly and with less disruption." In sum, instead of facilitating rational discourse, the seating approach to parliamentary debate conflated temperament, expediency, and peer pressure. Ideas were an afterthought.

Among the many issues that cut across ideological lines was the political status of Jews. Whatever the delegates' real feelings, and there are serious doubts about the sincerity of most putative philosemites, Ronald Schechter declares that "any effort to place this group on the right-left political spectrum is doomed to failure."[201] Ideological consistency in the Assembly was all but elusive. The Prince de Broglie, for example, who favored only a future integration of Jews into political life, was a Jacobin, though he fought for American independence[202] Hard to pigeonhole.

The myth that the French Revolution emancipated the Jews is just that: a myth. Noting that a number of deputies to the revolutionary assembly argued over the precise legal status of "Protestants, Jews, actors, and executioners" even as "they were simultaneously establishing general rubrics (e.g., on the basis of wealth, age, and gender) that otherwise determined political rights," Schechter explains why just those groups had been singled out. It's very simple: what they all "had in common was their negligible size." Their symbolic importance however, especially in the case of the Jews, was enormous. "The very difficulty of resolving such notorious problems as the conflict between religion and the state, individual liberty and the common good, and particularism and universalism, assured that the Jews, who as symbols assisted in the articulation of, and apparent solutions to, such dilemmas, would remain a subject of repeated discussion."[203] The French Revolution offered Jews a ray of hope; but it was soon extinguished.

So too, there was a brief moment of relative semantic clarity with regard to ideological affiliation. The 1819-20 session of the French parliament, writes Gauchet, "marks one of the great moments in the history of political vocabulary," as an attempt was made to codify the two terms. It had the predictable effect of pushing those who held their views most stubbornly to gravitate farther from the center. "The logic of the process dictated a policy of isolating the extremes," notes Gauchet. It evidently "created the possibility that the extremes would join forces, a phenomenon with important implications for the coalescence of the semantic system that was beginning to emerge."[204] That allowed radicals, who advocated ultimate victory for their side by making things worse in the short run, to make common cause with their opponents only to defeat them more easily and decisively in the end. This unscrupulous practice muddied the conceptual waters to opacity.

The distinction made a complete U-turn by 1830, when the labels Right and Left continued to be used even as "the political deck was reshuffled."[205] "[t]he division of the National Assembly [no longer] accurately reflected the issue facing the country: to preserve the gains of the Revolution or accede to the counterrevolution," explains Gauchet. The reason? What else: "the scene became more complicated." As one pamphleteer observed in 1842: "a dozen honorable members... have found themselves scattered among deputies of every stripe. As a result, the words right and right side no longer refer to a political party."[206] By 1848, "the right-left language did not spring spontaneously to mind." The banners flown by opposing parties in May 1849 were red and white. Colors would gradually supersede, though not entirely replace, spatial taxonomy. Altogether simplistic, erasing even the illusion of nuance, the key philosophical distinction for the next half-century and beyond were reflected by pigmentation. The side holding out for a possible future utopia, aptly enough, chose the color of blood.

4:
Manifesto Destiny

Marx's Unscientific Materialism

The Age of Reason was not especially reasonable when it came to Jews: even the iconoclastic, witty *philosophe* Voltaire had contemptuously accused that "ignorant and barbarous people," whom he identified as the Hebrews, of having "long united the most sordid avarice with the most detestable superstition."[207] In "The Heaven of the Ancients," for example, Voltaire writes: "their [the Jews'] only science was the trade and usury."[208] (As it happens.....), Voltaire was famously stingy. Writes the historian Paul Johnson: "When the intellectuals of the Enlightenment came to undermine Christianity in the 18th century, they produced the first secular layer of antisemitism: Diderot and still more Voltaire engaged in the most virulent attacks on Judaism, partly as an indirect but safer way of attacking the more dangerous target of Christianity."[209] Not to be outdone, their vituperative German contemporary, Johann Gottlieb Fichte (1762-1814), declared in 1793 that Jews constituted, of all things, "a powerful state . . . continually at war with all the others, and that in certain places terribly oppresses the citizens."[210] If "the Big Lie" had yet to become a major tool of statecraft at the hands of the Politburo (the principal planning committee of the Communist Party, few claims can rival Fichte's for sheer absurdity. But within a few decades, the image of Jews as a nation afflicted with terminal egoism, and obsessed with commerce and business, became commonplace.

The stigma of usury had plagued Jews for centuries, alongside another myth of the vast global Jewish financial conspiracy, adding to such fantasies as using Christian children's blood to make the Passover matzos. Not everyone realizes, too, that the age-long accusation that Jews killed Jesus was not officially repudiated by the Catholic church until the Second Vatican Council in the mid-1960s. With the advent of Protestantism, however, religious anti-judaism took on an additional, secular aspect, which was arguably even more dangerous. By the turn of the nineteenth century, a distinct "anti-Jewish anticapitalist paradigm" (the term is Michele Battini's) had emerged, "constructed on arguments of hostility toward the new market economy and the expression of the reaction by a part of society to the market with finance (and finance with the Jews)."[211] Usury "no longer referred only to money lending, but applied to banking and financial activities generally. In his 1806 pamphlet "On the Jews" (*Sur Les Juifs*), for example, Louis-Gabriel-Ambroise, Viscount de Bonald (1754-1840), blamed the dire straits of peasants in his home region of Alsace on "lenders" whom he identified as Jews no matter what their religious convictions. As such, writes Battini, "*'Sur Les Juifs'* is a paradigmatic document of anti-Jewish anticapitalism and of a traditional defense of rural society from the free market, which was taken up again and reformulated throughout the century."[212]

In 1808, the neighboring Prussians caught up with the French, when Ludwig Borne launched an assault on the Jewish "money-devil." Throughout both France and Germany, observes Robert Wistrich, the practice of linking Jews "with the all-devouring Moloch of Mammon" became increasingly prominent in socialist writings after 1840.[213] In 1843, the German socialist Moses Hess (1812-1875) even identified "the Jewish Jehovah—Moloch," along with the Christian God, with human sacrifice, capitalistic cannibalism, and social parasitism. But it was Karl Marx who brought antisemitism to a whole new level. And it was pure genius.

Marx had an amazing ability to combine ideas to create a powerful, seductive system, whose influence is even stronger today than it had been during his life. By mixing the militant atheism and opposition to private property of Bruno Bauer (1812-1882) with Ludwig Feuerbach's (1804-1872) materialist worldview which reduced all action to economic determinism, Marx's philosophy of "dialectical materialism" gained traction in a way neither of his mentors could ever have accomplished. Nor did Marx actually invent Communism - he did not even coin the word: that honor belongs to the nation that gave us the guillotine.

At the risk of seeming to take a slight detour, the story is worth telling for what it reveals about the ideology. Though nearly lost to history, the first self-described *auteur Communiste* had been a minor player in the French Revolution by the name of Victor d'Hupay (1746-1818), whose *Project for a Philosophical Community,* published in 1779, constitutes arguably the first blueprint for a secular, Communist society in the modern world.[214] Unfortunately for its author, if not for the world, its plan for an egalitarian "community of goods," designed to be enforced through a "community of moral-economic rule" whose citizens would be a sort of master race, left far too many questions unanswered to have made a splash at that time.

Yet it did not vanish. However improbably, Hupay did have one exceptionally ardent disciple. A radical young type-setter, Restif de la Bretonne (1734-1806), published in 1791 a literary fantasy describing an egalitarian society where "all must be common among equals. Each must work for the common good. All must take an identical part in work."[215] Two years later, in February 1793, he introduced "Communism" into the lexicon, to describe a political and economy system that changed the method of ownership to achieve full equality in a way that rendered unnecessary any future redistribution.

The following year, Restif added more details: in a Communist society, all citizens would work (precisely: as in More's Utopia), declaring their annual goals at the beginning of each year - eerily prophetic of Soviet practice. The system would bring an end to the seduction of money, along with the corruption and vice that accompanied it. Not meant for a mere island alone, the plan applied to nothing less than the entire human race. Though not necessarily here on earth. With no trace of irony, Restif suggested... the planet Venus. The choice probably reflected his other, considerably more lucrative, preoccupation: writing pornographic novels.[216]

Restif, like his mentor Hupay virtually unknown during his life, did eventually find an audience – as far as Russia, thus ironically confirming, however belatedly, the global reach of his ideas notwithstanding their stunning lunacy. The first substantive comments on his work came from Alexander Radishchev (1749-1802), a genuinely major figure in the Russian revolutionary intelligentsia. While Radishchev blasted the sexual permissiveness that Restif had in mind for the egalitarian utopia, all but anticipating the rigidity of Soviet life, the model was not dismissed out of hand - its bizarre, indeed embarrassing, choice of extraterrestrial venue apparently irrelevant.

Whether Marx had ever heard of Restif, his own dream of an ideal society was more in keeping with the sensibilities of Paris or Vienna than anything resembling frigid Muscovite puritanism, to say nothing of oxygen-free Venus. In the third of his *Economic and Philosophical Manuscripts* of 1844, Marx opposed the suggestion of J. S. Mill (1806-1873) that workers be encouraged to abstain from pro-creation. "Is this not the moral doctrine of asceticism?" protested Marx.[217] He scoffed too at the faux-enjoyments deplorably "subordinated to capital, and the [way the] pleasure-loving individual is subordinated to the capital-accumulating individual."[218] In a perfect world, by contrast, Marx envisaged man's "relation to the world to be a human one. Then love only can be exchanged for love, trust for trust, etc." – so for example, "if you wish to enjoy art you must be an artistically cultivated person."[219] String quartets would proliferate; opera would flourish. No more NPR fund drives! Now *that*'s paradise. Why bother schlepping over to Venus?

Such musings, however, were rare. Throughout his later writings, Marx showed little interest in speculating about the post-revolutionary world beyond stating that it was both necessary and necessarily ideal. Well, at least eventually. The fundamental fact, from which everything else follows, is that abolishing property, especially in money, eliminates conflict. And since a common definition of socialism at the time included the collective ownership and administration of the means of production and distribution of goods, what Marx advocated was an extreme form of collective ownership, where everything belonged to everyone. At that point, at last, men will no longer regard one another as competitors but as fellow-humans, their individual identity obliterated when they become, at last, true "species-beings." Veritable wingless angels.

In reality, there were more than two forms of socialism in the mid-nineteenth century, with still more in the offing. Each proposed different ways and means of distributing collective goods. What they all shared, however, writes Luciano Pellicani, "was a therapeutic diagnosis of the intellectual and moral anarchy that Europe had fallen into [which showed] a glimpse of opportunity to materialize the Christian dream of universal *renovatio."*[220] But both atheist Communists and secular socialists were heirs to the biblical vision. Explains Antonio Labriola (1843-1904):

> We socialists are going back to the Christian idea of society as an institution of the poor: not providence in the next world but providence in this world. We socialists have the holy audacity to declare ourselves more Christian than the priests, indeed the only Christians of the century. We are the true disciples of Jesus of Nazareth, of Jesus who announced the Kingdom of God who will come in peace and love and will be made thanks to, and by virtue of, our sentiments.[221]

The Kingdom of God had ancient roots which lent it a transcendental plausibility. What united socialists of all stripes was a conviction that evil could be eradicated in their lifetime by abolishing egoism and greed. Leszek Kołakowski, who had once been a Marxist, explains:

Throughout utopian literature [of the nineteenth century] it is assumed that men are intended to live in a state of equality and mutual love, and that exploitation, oppression and conflict of all kinds are contrary to nature's ordinance. The question of course arises: how can it be, in that case, that men have lived for centuries in a manner at variance with their true destiny? [222]

Marx claimed to have the answer. With breathtaking audacity, he and his faithful comrade Friedrich Engels (1820-1895) outlined an entire system of "scientific socialism" or "dialectical materialism," on a par with the natural sciences. Together, they claimed to have discovered the irrefutable Truth.

Though socialism and Communism had often been used roughly interchangeably in the early nineteenth century, by the 1840s [223] Communism took the lead. It became increasingly associated with far-reaching social control beyond the common distribution of goods; and it condoned politically-motivated violence. In 1847, the recently created Communist League provided the two revolutionaries with the chance to outline their ideas in what would become perhaps the most influential pamphlet in history: *The Communist Manifesto*. As Engels explains in his preface to the later, 1888, edition: "[W]hen it was written, we could not have called it a Socialist Manifesto. By socialists, in 1847, were understood, on the one hand, the adherents of various utopian systems... [that were] already dying out; on the other hand, multifarious social quacks, ...men outside the working-class movement." [224] Communism was not utopia but eutopia.

Marx and Engels were sincere in their belief that it was the bona fide working-class, the proletariat, whose movement this had to be. Those members of the vanguard intelligentsia who were gradually but irrevocably becoming convinced of "the insufficiency of mere political revolutions and had proclaimed the necessity of a total social change, that portion called itself Communist." In brief, "socialism was, in 1847, a middle-class movement, Communism was a working-class movement." [225] The *Manifesto*'s authors and their comrades articulated its principles and led the fight on behalf of the proletariat: thus the saviors and the saved were one.

Engels then proceeds to summarize the *Manifesto*'s fundamental proposition, which he attributes to Marx:

That proposition is that in every historical epoch the prevailing mode of economic production and exchange and the social organization necessarily following from it form the basis... of class struggles, contests between exploiting and exploited, ruling and oppressed classes.... [until] nowadays, a stage has been reached where the exploited and oppressed class – the proletariat – cannot attain its emancipation from the sway of the exploited and oppressed class – the bourgeoisie – without, at the same time, and once and for all, emancipating society at large from all exploitation, oppression, class distinctions, and class struggles.[226]

Engels notes too that, in his opinion, this proposition "is destined to do for history what Darwin's theory has done for biology," adding that he had been coming to the same ideas independently. One might say that their intellectual marriage was made in intellectual heaven, which practically guaranteed it would result in real-world hell.

Marx and Engels, of course, never engaged in empirical research to explore optimal ways of improving the lot of the poor. The point was to underscore that the causes of historical change were determined by the concrete, *material* conditions of each social class. Since real economic realities provide the concrete material basis for class struggle, laws of history may be determined with a certainty rivaling the laws of physics. Both govern the universe with the same iron necessity. The argument had already been made by the most famous and influential German philosopher of his time, Georg Wilhelm Friedrich Hegel (1770-1831), author of the dialectical philosophy of history.

Reducing Hegel's nearly impenetrable prose to its essentials, it could be said that his philosophy basically updated the Platonic method of argument into a theory of progress. A Platonic dialogue, a term derived from *dialogos* (*dia* meaning "across," and *legin* – "gather," e.g., words in conversation), consists of a statement, call it "thesis" by a student, which is then confronted, usually by Socrates, who plays the gadfly, by an apparent contradiction ("antithesis"), prompting a revised answer, or "synthesis," only to provoke another antithesis and so forth, all the way to Truth, or at least a close facsimile. "It was this dialectical pattern," explains Arthur Mendel with refreshingly colloquial clarity, "that Hegel transferred from Plato's dialogues to the realms of cosmic, universal, and human history... [where] each cultural period was dominated by a particular religion or set of ideas"[227] that constituted the "thesis." That in turn produced an opposing ideology (antithesis) that eventually would replace both (hence, synthesis), all the way to the End of History –

naturally a realm of Absolute Freedom. Eden on Earth, Heaven reified. Or idealized? Both.

The whole process, then, argue Hegel and his disciples, is as necessary as it is good: what is, should be. For the World Spirit (*Weltgeist* in German), as the driving force of History, is supremely moral, to be judged by a standard that transcends mere individual, personal ethical standards. "What the absolute aim of Spirit requires and accomplishes, what Providence does, [is that it] transcends... the imputation of good and bad motives."[228] In other words, the conflation of the World Spirit and Providence represents a "fusion of the medieval providential God and the rationalists' impersonal God of Reason," concludes Mendel. And that innovation, "together with the dialectical theory, ... laid the foundations for the Apocalypse of History."[229] Hegel had thus merged the Christian Creator with Nature's rational First Mover and history's indomitable Spirit in one seductive Idea. He thus managed to legitimize both the status quo (the "thesis" that defines all stages of history) and revolution (as the necessary "antithesis" required by historical change). Hegel believed that he had not abandoned God, only redefined Him. He was deluding himself.

Most socialists in Hegel's time rejected traditional religion outright; they sought a more secular approach, a political religion. This Marx and Engels eagerly provided, dispensing with the World Spirit: History suffices.[230] All scientific explanations, which they claimed as their own methodology, must be based on concrete, objective – i.e., material – conditions; everything else is bogus. And naturally, what is, must be. Ethical judgements themselves are an illusion. Their own modern capitalist stage in history will eventually ripen to the point that two clashing classes, the bourgeoisie and the proletariat, will collide, and the latter takes charge.

So went the argument. But what about Marx and Engels themselves? How could they be speaking on behalf of the downtrodden - were they not members of the bourgeoisie rather than the proletariat? The *Manifesto*'s answer is to assume what needs proof: in other words, it's circular. The *prophaetae* called "Communists" form "the most advanced and resolute section of the working-class parties of every country, that section which pushes forward all others." They may not be *of* the proletariat, but they are *for* it even more than the proletariat itself. Endowed with special insight and "hav[ing] no interests separate and apart from those of the proletariat as a whole," Communists "have over the great mass of the proletariat the advantage of clearly understanding the line of march, the conditions, and the ultimate general results of the proletarian movement."[231] Case closed.

The line of march is easy to explain, as it must be, so that the uneducated masses may understand: "In short, the Communists everywhere support every revolutionary movement against the existing social and political order of things....They openly declare that their ends can be attained only by the forcible overthrow of all existing social conditions. Let the ruling classes tremble at a Communistic revolution."[232] Forcible though inevitable; go figure.

The "ends" are rather less clear, but they sound catchy. When "class distinctions have disappeared, and all production has been concentrated in the hands of a vast association of the whole nation, the public power will lose its political character.... [For it will be] an association in which the free development of each is the condition for the free development of all."[233] Like Rousseau's General Will, this rhetorical sleight of hand elicited more applause at rallies than intellectual clarity. When the object is to inspire "forcible overthrow" designed to make "ruling classes tremble," fine points of logic are more of a hindrance than an asset.

Marx had provided only a political narrative rather than a genuine, realistic plan of revolutionary action, for a very simple reason: he had none. In a letter dated February 22, 1881, he frankly admitted that "[t]he doctrinaire and necessarily fantastic anticipation of the action for the future revolution is only used as a distraction from the present battle. The dream of the imminent end of the world inspired the early Christians during their struggle against the Roman Empire and gave them faith in their victory" – as it would again and again. It was time to update that narrative: "The scientific understanding of the inevitable degradation before our eyes of the prevailing social order, and the increasing anger the masses are thrown into by the old, now almost spectral, government" - echoes of Apocalypse "while simultaneously one witnesses the positive fact of the incredible progress of means of production – all this guarantees that, at the time of the true proletarian outbreak" - which, remember, is determined - "the conditions for its subsequent *modus operandi* will be given (even though they certainly will not be idyllic)."[234] In other words, writes Pellicani, "capitalism is condemned by history.... Therefore the workers' movement must readily await the final battle, which inevitably will end with the annihilation of bourgeois property and its civilization."[235]

And what exactly is supposed to happen after that "final battle"? Is all Marx can say that the conditions for its *modus operandi* will be given at that time, so let's just wait? Wasn't there going to be a forcible overthrow? What Marx does predict with confidence is that the immediate aftermath of the proletarian "outbreak" will "certainly" not be "idyllic," which must count as the understatement of the century. It did not take much imagination to predict that dispossession would not go unchallenged by those unpersuaded that history demanded their sacrifice.

The quintessential secular ideology, Marxism was a religion in pseudo-scientific garb. According to Domenico Settembrini, the Marxist end of time known as Communism has "exactly the same comforting function as the Christian paradise. Although the advent of the new Jerusalem is awaited literally in time and in space, it is depicted with such characteristics as to virtually disappear in a vanishing future and substantially is no more realistic than paradise."[236] Which is to say, vehement protestations by Marx and Engels notwithstanding, utopian.

Russian dissident Andrei Sinyavsky (1925-1997) agrees: "How is the revolution viewed by its instigators, its true believers? Like the Apocalypse. As if history had ended and 'a new heaven and a new earth' were beginning. The Kingdom of God, Heavenly Jerusalem descending, promising paradise on earth. Yet not by God's will but by man's exertion. This isn't a dream, but a historical law, scientifically proven by Marx, an ineluctable law that will prevail, like it or not."[237]

Marx's appeal to historical necessity, therefore, has a two-fold function. On the one hand, it serves to dispense with ethical reasoning, with all moral or normative questions. And on the other, it invokes a quasi-religious inevitability that is both romantic and inspirational, as well as incontestable. Again, Sinyavsky: "The powers and the laws revealed by Marxism – productive forces and relations of production, determining economic base and class struggle – play the role of divine providence or ineluctable fate. ... [and applies] on the grandest scale, all spheres of human endeavor. The sudden transition from dogma to its generalized application requires violence."[238]

Violence constitutes the ultimate expression of hubris. By deciding who is to live and who is to die, it amounts to taking on the mantle of God: "The violence assumes the guise of an expiatory sacrifice, while the role of Almighty God demanding that sacrifice is played by Historical Necessity. With one innovation: here it is not just a matter of self-sacrifice – held sacred through the ages – but of offering up others, the so-called exploiter classes and much more."[239]

Marx would have blasted any suggestion that his theory had anything whatever in common with religion, which he passionately hated. He fumed against all forms of such superstition, imposed by ruling classes to keep the masses quiet: "the opium of the people." Breaking with Thomas More as well as Rousseau, Marx predicts that "religion" will disappear altogether, because it *must* - along with property, classes, and conflict. Once the new man emerges, the only divinity will be humanity itself. God will have become man. In a grotesque reversal of the Christian creed, the son annihilates the Father. As man returns, omnipotent in his property-less purity, his Creator is worse than dead: He has become irrelevant. Forget religion. Hail *homo*!

The Capitalist/Jew as Antichrist

There was one religious tradition for which Marx had an especially visceral contempt – to wit, his own. Edmund Silberner writes that "in spite of all his other phobias, none was more pronounced than that against the Jews."[240] It never waned; Marx's "aversion to the Jews was deeply rooted in his heart and mind, and lasted to the very end."[241] It predated even his fully articulated Communist ideology, and encompassed all Jews. Nowhere does he distinguish bourgeois Jews from the humble members of the working classes, nor religious Jews from atheists. Though many of his disciples find this deeply unsettling, and many deny it outright, Marx's antisemitism is racist, and as such, pathological. Marx is, admittedly just one of many, the quintessential self-hating Jew.

Paul Johnson argues that "Marx's form of antisemitism was a dress rehearsal for Marxism itself."[242] His ideology is indeed impossible to understand apart from this profound underlying animus. It had been all spelled out in his essay "On the Jewish Question," published in 1844 when Marx was barely twenty-six, in uncommonly plain language:

What, in itself, was the basis of the Jewish religion? Practical need, egoism. Money is the jealous god of Israel, in face of which no other god may exist. Money degrades all the gods of man – and turns them into commodities. Money is the universal self-established value of all things. It has, therefore, robbed the whole world – both the world of men and nature – of its specific value. Money is the estranged essence of man's work and man's existence, and this alien essence dominates him, and he worships it. The god of the Jews has become secularized and has become the god of the world. The bill of exchange is the real god of the Jew. His god is only an illusory bill of exchange.

Marx then delivers the final *coup*:

Once society has succeeded in abolishing the empirical essence of Judaism – huckstering and its preconditions – the Jew will have become impossible, because his consciousness no longer has an object, because the subjective basis of Judaism, practical need, has been humanized, and because the conflict between man's individual-sensuous existence and his species-existence has been abolished. The social emancipation of the Jew is the emancipation of society from Judaism. [243]

Johnson, who refers to this as "almost a classic anti-Semitic tract," writes that it nevertheless "contains, in embryonic form, the essence of his theory of human regeneration: by abolishing private property society would transform human relationships and thus the human personality." In his later writings, Marx "retained the fundamental fallacy that the making of money through trade and finance is essentially a parasitical activity, but he now placed it, not on a basis of race or religion, but of class." The distinction seems to be one without a difference. What Marx wanted to abolish was egoism as such; his was a crusade to create a new man, *homo post-religiosus*.

In effect, Marxism amounted to the ultimate heresy, illustrating what Johnson diagnoses as "Marx's own violence and of the emotional irrationality which expressed itself first as antisemitism and then as generalized anticapitalism. The origins of Marxism in anti-Semitic conspiracy theory can never be wholly erased. Whatever guise Marxism may take, it retains this stigma, like a mark of Cain."[244] The Jews were guilty as a group and had been transformed into a symbol independent of the specific actions of its members, on the ground that they all allegedly "worshipped money" – a charge that Marx had to know was absurd. Like Cain, Marx was prepared, indeed eager, to slay his innocent brother.

Jerry Z. Muller agrees that "On the Jewish Question" is at the root of Marx's entire philosophy, for it "contains, in embryo, most of the subsequent themes of Marx's critique of capitalism."[245] These include: the labor theory of value, which presupposes that all value is the product of labor (not original to Marx), and assumes that capital is unproductive; the salutary elimination of cultural particularity after the abolition of property and of classes, but also the termination of all human communities with particular historical memories. And finally, there was the not-altogether-veiled appeal to violence. Predicting the chaos that would accompany the last stages of capitalism, as "disasters occurring regularly will be repeated on a vaster scale, eventually [they will] lead to the violent fall of capital."

Marx was fully aware of the lethal implication of his language for Jews in particular. The suggestion that society had to be rescued not merely from Judaism but from Jews themselves, predicting that "the Jew will become impossible," came perilously close to endorsing genocide. Concludes Muller: "That would be the theme, with variations, of subsequent anti-Jewish authors from Richard Wagner down to the Nazi ideologist Gottfried Feder."[246]

Anticapitalist antisemitism found no less zealous disciples in France, where the socialist Charles Fourier (1772-1837) identified capitalism with the Jewish elite. So too did his follower Alphonse Toussenel (1803-1885), who penned what "can be considered the first proposal of a socialized economy based on the expropriation of wealth and the redistribution of the capital of Jewish families." This led the infamous Edouard Drumont (1844-1917), founder of the Antisemitic League of France in 1889, to consider Toussenel his "inspired precursor."[247] He was joined by Auguste Chirac (1838-1910) who argued that all capitalists can be considered Jews *without actually being Jewish*, because usury, thievery, social parasitism, and capitalist exploitation are all Jewish practices. Explains Battini:

> All capitalists can therefore be legitimately defined as *"juifs"* [Jews] and treated accordingly: discriminated against, persecuted. The process of generalization and abstraction transforms the *juifs*, as real men, into a symbol of exploitation: *le juif*, and usury at the same time, becomes the figure of speech of all the types of exploitation.[248]

Yet Communism would erupt in none of Europe's most industrially advanced nations. Contrary to the expectation of its founders, who reasoned that Armaggedon would happen in the West, where the class struggle was presumably at its peak, it came instead in backward, feudal Russia. And its Messiah would be the formidable, sinister, Vladimir Iylich Ulyanov, better known as V. I. Lenin (1870-1924). Some called him "the ideologue of the intelligentsia" - the high priest of what has aptly been called "the Jesuit science of the Marxists."[249]

However virulent the antisemitism of French and German anticapitalists certainly was, it was more than matched by to that of Michael Bakunin (1814-1876), leader of the Russian anarchists. Skeptical that the *Manifesto*'s blueprint would really achieve the desired utopia it presumed to prophesy, Bakunin turned Marx's own rhetoric against him. Wasn't he a Jew himself? Why should *he* be trusted? In 1871, Bakunin charged that Marx was no better than the Rothchilds, the legendary banking family who, at the time, possessed the largest fortune in the world.[250] They all belonged to the infamous "Jewish conspiracy." Thundered Bakunin: "The Communism of Marx wants a mighty centralization by the State, and where this exists there must nowadays inevitably be a Central State bank, and where such a bank exists, the parasitical Jewish nation, which speculates on the labor of the people, will always find a means to sustain itself."[251] In one respect he was definitely not wrong: anticipating that central control spells state monopoly.

Bakunin was hardly exceptional in Russia, where antisemitism reached far beyond the aristocracy. Some Russian populists sympathetic to the peasants defended the pogroms[252] of 1881 as a rising of the masses against the tsar. Jews themselves often shared Marx apparent self-hatred, particularly among the younger generation, restless and eager for a better life. Writes Robert Wistrich: "The racist prejudices of Russian and Ukrainian social revolutionaries were sometimes shared by Jews who had rebelled against their traditional Jewish heritage, felt alienated from the Jewish collectivity, and had adopted Russian culture."[253]

The Jews' attitude, observes Vladimir Iokhelson, reflected the hope that "the liberation of the whole of Russia would bring along the liberation of all nations living there." It seems they did not fully grasp that Communism implied eliminating all nations in exchange for a generic "species" identity. Iokhelson concedes "that Russian literature has instilled in us a view that Jewry was not a nation but a parasite class."[254] Evidently affected by the hostility around them, many radical Russian Jews, some perhaps less consciously than others, evidently harbored a secret hope that the new man, who was bound to emerge after the great revolution, will bring about a global metamorphosis of biblical proportions and antisemitism would disappear forever.

Absurd rationalizations aside, self-hatred is essentially pathological. Chaim Zhitlovsky, for example, admitted: "No matter how I felt, from a socialist point of view, I had to pass a death sentence not only on individual Jews but on the entire *Jewish* existence of individual Jews."[255] Comments Wistrich: "This ethnic death wish would continue to characterize generations of Jewish revolutionists who have looked to socialism to bring an end to Jewish tradition, the Jewish people, Jewish identity, and Jewish heritage."[256] Rational explanation eludes us.

But Bakunin had still another objection to German theorists generally, Jews or otherwise: he found them elitists. Mostly urban-based, they treated peasants with condescension. Though not overly fond of such illiterates himself, Bakunin warned that "there is no point in extolling or denigrating the peasants. It is a question of establishing a program of action which will overcome the individualism and conservatism of the peasants."[257] True, those stupid peasants did not grasp the grand design of history, notoriously partial to having their own little plots of land rather than abolishing property altogether; but they were a potent force, not to be ignored. In that last assessment he was spot-on, perhaps more than he knew.

What Bakunin did share with Marx, and even more obviously Lenin, was an unflinching commitment to force. Publishing under a French pseudonym in the *German Yearbook* of 1842, Bakunin called for violent revolution in Germany. Marx's dialectical progression of history had added a quasi-spiritual momentum that served to dispense altogether with the need to morally justify killing. Writes James Billington: "Like earlier metaphysical determinisms (Islam, Calvinism), dialectical materialism provided, paradoxically, an effective call to action."[258] The paradox lay in its simultaneous assertion of hard determinism and moral exhortation to action. If something is necessary, it must be done: the descriptive becomes identical with the moral. The paradox, if not particularly original, was certainly inspired: a hard-headed, masterful rhetorical device cloaked in philosophical jargon, the intellectuals' trademark. By comingling what-is with what-should-be – in the logician's lingo, the is-ought fallacy - the conclusion flowed naturally that since revolution is bound to arrive, therefore it is right.

Logic be damned. Declares Marx in *Theses on Feuerbach* (1888): "Philosophers have only interpreted the world in various ways. The time has come to change it."[259] Determined to be a different sort of philosopher, he sought to raise the consciousness of the cadre. Having provided the terminology and showed the way, it would be Lenin's turn to follow through.

Bolshevik Killing Fields

And Lenin did. His uncanny political horse-sense surpassing even his superlative analytical acumen, he was determined to usher in the Communist utopia no matter what the "material conditions" of his surroundings. Kolakowski believes that even if Lenin failed to fully grasp the nature of the fact-value fallacy, yet he perceived, however "vaguely," that Marxism is neither fully descriptive nor fully normative but both: "theory and application are one."[260] While the vagueness of that belief is debatable, Lenin was certainly quick to appreciate, for example, the importance of Bakunin's insight regarding the peasants. In fact, Lenin's approach to theory came down to the commandment that whatever brings about the revolution is justified. He never wavered from seeing all political alliances as either useful or not, depending on whether they accelerated the arrival of Judgment Day – an approach that Sinyavsky has called "revolutionary utilitarianism."[261] Translation: my end justifies my means. The logic of thugs.

To Bakunin's famous charge that Marx had been disingenuous in pretending to abolish the state while in fact proposing merely to replace bourgeois rule by another, Lenin resorts to his fallback method of argument, the ever-successful *ad hominem*: he accuses Bakunin of "the crudest distortion." Then he turns to sophistry: "[I]n speaking of the state 'withering away,' and the even more graphic and colorful 'ceasing of itself,' Engels refers quite clearly and definitively to the period *after* 'the state has taken possession of the means of production in the name of the whole of society,' that is, *after* the socialist revolution." Crystal-clear, is it not? "Revolution alone can 'abolish' the bourgeois state. The state in general, i.e., the most complete democracy, can only 'wither away.'"[262] Can only; what else could it do?

Lenin's casuistry is impressive. He glosses over the fact that Marx had anticipated that immediately after the revolution there would first be an intermediary stage, soothingly dubbed "complete democracy," which will eventually "wither away." It is that putatively "complete democracy" that Bakunin had the foresight to fear. Lenin knew well that Bakunin had been right; nonetheless, the mantra that abolishing private property and confiscating "the means of production in the name of the whole of society" would eventually eliminate the state was not to be questioned.

So then, what might an "intermediary" stage look like? It cannot mean "a state which recognizes the subordination of the minority to the majority," which entails "the systematic use of violence by one class against another," because if classes no longer exist, neither does violence. Lenin tries to paint a picture of the revolution's immediate aftermath: "We do not expect the advent of an order of society in which the principle of the subordination of the minority to the majority will not be observed." So, if we do NOT "expect" that the principle of subordination will NOT be observed, it obviously *will* be. That double negative twists the brain into silence, defeated by the logic of historical necessity. The majority will, because it must, prevail over the minority (unlike in bourgeois pseudo-democracy), and it won't take too long before even the slightest tiny, quite negligible, remnant of a state disappears altogether.

For, continues Lenin, "in striving for Socialism we are convinced that it will develop into Communism and, hence, that the need for violence against people in general... will vanish altogether since people will become accustomed to observing the elementary conditions of social life without violence and without subordination." He cites Engels' vision of a new generation "reared in new and free social conditions."[263] *We are convinced*? But isn't it determined? A sliver of candor pierces through the ideological carapace. The vanguard knows more than it tells....

So then, Communism will not arrive immediately, because first we have to "strive for Socialism." The striving is bound to take a little while; that's why we'll be calling our country, for now, a Union of just Socialist, rather than full-fledged Communist, Republics. (It's a continuum that starts after Armageddon.) The utopian omelet is still to come, though only after all the required eggs have been broken, the frying pan good and hot. During this transition period, however, people will "become accustomed" to social life "without violence." Well, maybe just an itsy-bitsy little violence to pierce the eggshells, as all private property is completely abolished throughout the vast territory of the USSR. But that will have been it, period. Once true Communism scrambles into socialism - no more eggs. Just leave it to the vanguard - they know omelets.

Lenin's next task was to find ways to sanctify his small cadre of messiah/inquisitors who would manage the details, which mandated the elimination of dissenters. The "scientific" basis of dialectical materialism required that where conditions for revolution did not yet exist, they had to be created – no ifs ands or buts. As Bertrand Russell observed in 1896, "Marx's system is a real religion and it cannot be tolerant of other religions. Just like Christianity, democratic [sic] socialism tends to place itself against all existing faiths; if it did otherwise, it would end up losing much of that formidable emotional impact it owes to the completeness of the system."[264] The job of the Communist Party was to enforce the ideology of eutopia, come what may.

Well, maybe "Party" isn't quite the right word, since its very etymology implies a larger whole, while Lenin conceived of a *single* neo-clergy of the people. As he writes in "What Is To Be Done?" (1902): "History has now confronted us with an immediate task which is the most revolutionary of all the immediate tasks confronting the proletariat of any country. The fulfilment of this task, the destruction of the most powerful bulwark, not only of European, but (it may now be said) of Asiatic reaction, would make the Russian proletariat the vanguard of the international revolutionary proletariat."[265] His vision, like Marx's, was manifestly millennial.

Things became rather more difficult once Bolsheviks actually seized power, with Lenin anointed as the secular Messiah. The Polish-Jewish Marxist Rosa Luxemburg (1871-1919) denounced Lenin's "ruthless centralism" for having instituted a "state of siege psychology."[266] But she was in the minority. Pellicani describes Leninism as a new form of "categorical imperative:"

> [E]very person and thing had to submit to it. The party was simply there to translate its impersonal commands. Every member of the consecrated body had to rid his mind of the ideal of the new man, embodied by Rakhmetov, the main character in Chernyshevsky's *What Is to be Done?*: an individual who was "one with the system," enclosed within it both intellectually and morally, and totally absorbed by the dual mission: "to re-educate himself and to re-educate society according to the spirit of the new science." In other words, a person truly determined to make permanent revolution his mission has to be transformed in a *homo ideologicus*, completely absorbed in the spirit of Marxism and suspicious of the outside world and its spiritual product, which is by definition, corrupt and corrupting.[267]

Rett Ludwikowski's assessment that "the Old Bolsheviks were masters of revolutionary techniques, but they had no experience in running a state" is over-generous. "For them Marxism served as a sort of sacred guide to be followed almost blindly. But ... the tenets of 'genuine Marxism' often proved inapplicable in post-revolutionary Russia." So what was to be done? "The solution hit upon," writes Ludwikowski, was to appear to adhere to the basic dogmas of Marxism, while imposing strictly controlled thought."[268] Except this tactic was not merely "hit upon" but entirely anticipated, and not only by Lenin. Hadn't the Communist prophet Marx himself predicted that the transition, whatever it might look like, depending on "conditions," would be "certainly not idyllic"?

The result of course would be hypocrisy and corruption on a monumental scale, which added a whole new dimension to the violence caused by Soviet-style Communism. As a result, an entire population became complicit in a nation-wide web of lies and immorality. Lenin fully acknowledged, notes Pellicani, that

> his model of revolutionary organization was simply the continuation of an undertaking initiated by the Jacobins, Prudhon's "Jesuits of the revolution." The Jacobins had been the first to actually develop a method for destroying the "empire of wealth" and creating a party that operated like a war machine ... [with] one fundamental goal: the introduction of a "despotism of liberty," a compulsory step in the transition to a purified society.[269]

Like the French Revolution, the most horrific terror did not begin in earnest until after the hard-core thugs took control. The toppling of the Russian monarchy, which took place in February (March, by the newer, Gregorian calendar) 1917, was followed by a brief era of reform, superseded in October (now, November), as the Bolsheviks led by Lenin imposed a Communist dictatorship and proclaimed an open-ended global Apocalypse aimed at annihilating capitalism, imperialism, and of course their economic base: private property.

A veritable explosion of research since 1991 indicates clearly that Lenin's victory had been anything but "inevitable." Writes Sean McMeekin:

> Fueled by German subsidies and his own indomitable will to power, Lenin succeeded in breaking the Russian Imperial Army in 1917 and then reassembled its shards in 1918. Just as Lenin had foretold in his Zimmerwald Left prophesy, the resulting civil war of 1918-1920, which the Bolsheviks fought against a world of foreign and domestic enemies, both real and imagined, turned out to be even bloodier than the "imperialist war" with the Central Powers had been, requiring ever-mounting levels of mass mobilization, state control, and secret-police surveillance and repression.[270]

The prophecy, formulated by Lenin while in Swiss exile as early as 1915, had been predicated on socialists encouraging workers to join the military, who would then turn the armies "red" by promoting mutinies. Most socialists, including Leon Trotsky, who opposed the war, did not support Lenin's idea. It did, however, appeal to the Germans.

As it happens, 1915 was the year that the Germans first learned about Lenin - from two separate sources. The first was Alexander "Parvus" Helphand, a Jewish socialist who had met with the German ambassador to the Ottoman Empire, Baron Hans von Wangeheim, in January of that year and told him that "the interests of the German Imperial Government are identical with those of the Russian revolutionaries."[271] The second, Alexander Keskula, was an Estonian Bolshevik, recently turned nationalist, whose "hatred of Russia" led him to work for German intelligence. Keskula brought Lenin to the attention of the German Consul in Bern, Gisbert von Romberg, who immediately saw Lenin's potential: in September 1915, Romberg started paying Keskula 20,000 marks a month for distribution to Lenin and other Bolsheviks.[272]

The German connection proved invaluable beyond measure. For since Lenin was still in Zurich when Russia erupted in February 1917, he needed help to return: the Germans made that possible. On March 23 (April 1), the German government appropriated 5 million gold marks for Lenin and his entourage of Bolsheviks to travel via Germany back to Russia. (Altogether, it has been estimated that Germany provided Lenin the equivalent of over one billion dollars in today's currency.[273]) Tucked safely inside a sealed train car, the sinister group stopped in Gottmadingen, Berlin, and Sassnitz, where they met several German officers.

After Lenin's return from exile to Finland until October 1917, when he finally managed to slip into Petrograd, the Bolsheviks prepared their seizure of power. Failing to secure victory in the November elections to the Constituent Assembly, they forcibly suppressed the Provisional Government in January 1918, never having received a formal democratic mandate to rule.[274] Yet they did have at least a shred of popular support, based on a promise of peace whose price few understood. Lenin then proceeded to expel the Tsar's supporters and turn his newly reconstituted Russian - now Red – Army against the enemies of Communism.

The old regime refused to die without a fight. Stéphane Courtois describes the situation in his introduction to the magisterial compilation of crimes he co-edited, *The Black Book of Communism*:

> Lenin and his comrades initially found themselves embroiled in a merciless "class war," in which political and ideological adversaries, as well as the more recalcitrant members of the general public, were branded as enemies and marked for destruction. The Bolsheviks had decided to eliminate, by legal and physical means, any challenge of resistance, even if passive,

to their absolute power. This strategy applied not only to groups with opposing political views, but also to such social groups as the nobility, the middle class, the intelligentsia, and the clergy, as well as professional groups such as military officers and the police.[275]

The ensuing civil war that lasted from 1918 till 1920 ended with the victory of Bolshevism, but this only took the conflict to a new stage, with the policy of "de-Cossackization," that was intended to annihilate an entire ethnic group. East Slavic-speaking, the Cossacks were located mainly in Ukraine and several islands in the lower Dnieper, Don, Terek, and Ural river basins. Comparing the Cossacks to French counterrevolutionaries in the Vendee, a region west of France, Lenin subjected them to what his predecessor Gracchus Babeuf had called, in 1794, "populicide."

The Bolsheviks may have prevailed, but the nation's economy unsurprisingly collapsed. Lenin was nevertheless able to convince people to fight on the side of the Communists. The decisive help of peasants was won by a promise that they could help themselves to all the land from the church and crown, without compensation. What they were *not* told was that no promise is sacred when the ends justify the means. The country's economic bankruptcy, not to mention ideological purity, required expropriating grain and eventually punishing peasants who had dared to seize land for themselves. But that would come later.

After Lenin's death in 1924, Joseph Visarionovich Stalin, born Ioseb Besarionis dze Jughashvili (1878-1953) took over the regime after a ruthless campaign eliminating all competitors to the post of messiah-in-chief. The "complete democracy" that Marx had envisioned, and Lenin glossed over, escalated when millions of farmers who opposed Stalin's forced collectivization of Soviet agriculture (i.e., their farms were confiscated by the government) were either shot or exiled. Widespread famine killed millions more. The secret police became the Communist Party's instrument of terror, encouraging people to spy on one another, arresting millions, and turning the country into an enormous prison.

There was, in addition, an actual prison system: the indescribably sadistic Gulag archipelago, an enormous web of detention sites, most located in the frigid steppe of Siberia, filled with a whole slew of people who had dared resist the coming of the egalitarian utopia. (A popular joke was: "You got fifteen years for nothing? That's a lie. For nothing, the maximum sentence is just ten.") The enormity of the crimes committed under the Soviet regime has been amply documented, even if far too little known in the West. What is specifically relevant for purposes of this discussion is the continuity of rationale throughout the life of this anti-human regime: the leveling of society economically and ideologically.

Both Lenin and Stalin were staunch Marxists committed to "the belief that abolishing the private ownership of the means of production will end the exploitation of workers and be a decisive step in the creation of a social-economic system that will not only be just, but also highly productive and infused with a communitarian spirit."[276] So too, the Bolsheviks shared the "ideas [of Marx and Engels] about the necessity and inevitability of the class struggle and the dictatorship of the proletariat [which] were instrumental in the legitimation of coercion and political violence, and the creation of powerful bureaucracies. Probably the major contribution Marxism made to the generous use of political violence with a clear conscience [was] that it assured the rulers that they were engaged in the creation of an exceptionally praiseworthy, morally and historically superior social system, hence they were entitled to use all and any means that promised to bring about this ideal state of affairs."[277]

The Apocalypse had exploded in Eurasia, but it would soon engulf the enormous nation of Asia that had long imagined itself the center of the world: The Middle Kingdom, better known as China.

The Cultural Revolutionary

That Mao (1893-1976) had revolutionary potential became clear as early as 1917 when, as a student in his early twenties, he confessed his contempt for the masses to his best friend: "[T]hey worship hypocrisy, are content with being slaves, and narrow-minded."[278] This made him a fairly typical member of the intelligentsia at the time; what set him apart as a proto-Jacobin Chinese-style Bolshevik, however, was his clear perception of the tactics required by revolution. "Mr. Mao also proposed burning all the collections of prose and poetry after the Tang and Sun dynasties in one go," the startled friend recorded in his diary. "This is the first known occasion when Mao mentioned the one theme that was to typify his rule – the destruction of Chinese culture," writes Jung Chang in *Mao: The Unknown Story*. But the theme that would most accurately reflect his life was mass murder.

We will never know the full story. *The Black Book of Communism* estimates a total of at least 65 million killed, including 10 million "direct victims" of Mao's Communist Party, 20 million who died in the "hidden Gulag" known as the *laogai*; and more than 20 million dead from the "political famine" of the Great Leap Forward of 1959-1960, the "largest famine in history," the result of Mao's insane economics.[279] These numbers do not include the countless traumatized millions who ate their own children, lost their minds, etc etc etc.

How could China's Apocalypse become so enormous? We have a rare glimpse into the satanic nature of its creator's character from his own words. Penned in his student days, Mao's commentaries to a book by German philosopher Friedrich Paulsen (1846-1908), ironically dealing with the subject of ethics, included such candid statements as: "People like me want to... satisfy our hearts to the full, and in doing so we automatically have the most valuable moral codes. Of course, there are people and objects in the world, but they are all there only for me."[280] The world, in other words, existed for Mao's benefit – as if he were a god. Which he was, to himself.

If that wasn't clear enough, he adds: "People like me only have a duty to ourselves; we have no duty to other people." And most ominously "I do not think these [commands like 'do not kill,' 'do not steal,' and 'do not slander'] have to do with conscience. I think they are only out of self-interest for self-preservation." All considerations must "be purely calculation for oneself, and absolutely not for obeying external ethical codes, or for so-called feelings of responsibility...."[281] His hubris was not just extreme, it was absolute.

The future revolutionary praises "Great Heroes [who] give full pay to their impulses, they are magnificently powerful, stormy and invincible" – words that would have been music to the Führer's ears; Mao had beat him to the punch by a few years. It is such Heroes, in Mao's eyes, who can implement the great Armageddon, who are needed for a China full of stupid and slavish people to be reborn strong: "[T]he country must be .... destroyed and then re-formed." So too, the world as a whole: "This applies to the country, to the nation, and to mankind... The destruction of the universe is the same... People like me long for destruction, because when the old universe is destroyed, a new universe will be formed. Isn't that better?"[282] It is hard to argue with that logic. Especially since logic has nothing really to do with it.

Psychopaths who choose revolutionary leadership as a career have an evident genetic advantage. But ruthlessness is only a necessary, not a sufficient condition for success in this peculiar profession. Luckily for Mao, if tragic for China, to say nothing of the rest of the world, the Bolsheviks were determined to expand their millenarian franchise and were turning east. Both Africa and Asia had to join the fold for Communism to become global, as Marx had prophesied.

The Russians lost no time. As early as September 1920, at the First Congress of Oriental Peoples held in Baku, Azerbaijan, Lenin's fellow traveler from Switzerland Grigori Zionoviev told the assembled delegates: "The real revolution will explode when the 800 million people of Asia join us, when the African continent joins us, when we set in motion thousands of millions of men. It is up to us to proclaim a veritable holy war against the British and French capitalists.... We will be able to say that the time is ripe when workers the world over arouse tens and hundreds of millions of peasants, creating a red army in the East and arming and organizing revolts... in Turkey, in Persia, in India, in China."[283] Of the 1,275 delegates, of whom 266 did not declare a nationality, 8 had been Chinese.

It was a modest but important start. As Stalin put it, with the eloquence he honed at the seminary in his youth: "Paraphrasing Luther's famous words, Russia could say: I am at the divide between the old capitalist world and the new socialist world. On this divide I bring together the efforts of the proletarians of the West and the peasants of the East, in order to bring about the collapse of the old world. May the God of History assist me."[284] The narrative works wonders.

Whatever their personal differences, which were countless, Stalin's vision of global Armageddon coincided with Mao's: determined to accelerate the pace of history, neither saw an obstacle in the feudal nature of their countries' economy. At the end of 1918, writes Pellicani,

> in two short but enlightening articles, Stalin illustrated the essential elements of the "Asianization" of Marxism that 10 years later was to find its greatest interpreter in Mao Tse Tung. The future dictator of the Soviet Union stressed that Asia had a decisive role to play in preventing a Eurocentric vision of the revolution. He stressed that the "wave of liberation was advancing from the East to the West" because "the Russian Revolution had been the first to stir up the oppressed peoples against imperialism...." [Thereby] by breaking the chain of imperialism where it was weakest, the Russian Revolution had opened a new historic era, the building of the New World.[285]

Before long, Mao would appropriate the uncopyrighted blueprint for Armageddon-proliferation, to start his own enterprise of exporting revolution beyond his nation's borders. But just on the outside chance that ideology proved insufficient to persuade people to kill in order to change their political system, he resorted to the tried-and-true tools of handing out the usual trio of incentives: arms, money and food. And so, writes Jung Chang, "on 21 January 1960 a new body called the Foreign Economic Liaison Bureau was formed," in order to handle foreign aid to potential liberators. It was most unfortunate that "this spree of gifts by Mao coincided with the worst years of the greatest famine in world history. Over 22 million people died of starvation in 1960 alone."[286] But it was not enough to stop the donations to foreign revolutionaries; Mao wasn't going to be deterred by mere pity from advancing the march of history. Anyway, he felt none.

High on Mao's list of aid recipients was Indochina, which received no less than $20 billion during his lifetime; next came Africa's robust decolonization movement, already bankrolled by the USSR; and the lucky Algerians, whose goody-bags included cash, arms, and other equally nifty stuff in return for fighting the French. As for Latin America, "Peking made a beeline for Cuba after Fidel Castro took power in January 1959. When Castro's colleague Che Guevara came to China in November 1960, Mao doled out US$60m as a 'loan,' which Chou [en Lai] told Guevara 'does not have to be repaid.'"[287] After all, what are comrades-in-arms for?

Not radically different from Russian-style Communism, aside from the identity of its messiah, "Maoism" was officially launched on April 22, 1960, 90 years to the day of Lenin's birth. Despite its disconcertingly un-Chinese title, "Long Live Leninism!" denounced so-called "revisionism," defined as the rejection of violence in the revolutionary cause. Instead, stated the manifesto, "if Communists were to take power they would have to resort to violence." By invoking Lenin, Mao was hoping to out-radicalize Nikita Khruschev (1894-1971), Soviet premier since Stalin's death in 1953, with whom he was not getting along too well. But while the rift between Russia and China would grow over the next several decades, the ideology of terror was similar. With the gory massacres of the Great Proletarian Cultural Revolution that lasted from 1966 until 1971, which made the Taliban's destruction of the ancient Buddhas look like a children's tantrum, Mao seemed determined to outdo even Stalin in wanton cruelty and sheer madness.

Yet, unsurprisingly, the Cultural Revolution was reported at the time by most Western journalists sympathetically. John Gittings is unusual in his remorse over his and his colleagues' bias: "[W]e focused on the idealism without acknowledging the warping effect of violence and the cult of Mao," as in his own article published in the *Guardian*, which had celebrated "the sense of a collective spirit which is perhaps most impressive in education as it is in the rest of Chinese life. ... It is not so much a cult of personality but more a collective way of life, which provides the moral imperatives for the youth of China who will inherit Mao's revolution."[288] Without necessarily seeking to justify this nonsense, he does acknowledge "the attempt some of us made to go by bus into Hangzhou one evening from the hotel where we were staying. We were pursued by our minders who forced the bus to stop while they explained their concern that we might 'get lost.'"[289] The bus turned around; the journalists' naivety was exceeded only by their timidity.

Remorse is a rare quality among Communist sympathizers like Jean-Paul Sartre, who praised the "revolutionary violence" of Mao as "profoundly moral." Chang may be right that "no Maoist party in the West – even the largest one, in Portugal – ever gained more than a minuscule following. Most Western 'Maoists' were fantasists, or freeloaders, and had no appetite for sustained action, least of all if it was physically uncomfortable or dangerous."[290] But the appeal of Mao's ideas, such as they were, was not limited to the fantasists. Couched in disinformation and wishful thinking, they penetrated the West and survive to this day.

After many decades, unfortunately, the system of mendacious state control known as Communism metastasized with sinister logic to afflict society at large. As Vladimir Bukovsky painstakingly demonstrates in *Judgment in Moscow*, "practically the entire leadership of the country was involved, to one degree or another, in 'Stalin's' repressions, starting with the head of the KGB of the time, General Ivan Serov, ... and ending with Khrushchev himself."[291] He despairs at being able "to explain to people who have never lived under this regime that Communism is not a political system and not even so much a crime as a sort of mass illness, like an epidemic of the plague?"[292] Even calling it an ideology doesn't capture the true nature of the disease. The hubris of a few is enough to start the cancer, but stopping it becomes much harder with time, after the vital organs are gradually ravaged. Underestimating, misunderstanding, and especially misrepresenting it, however, threaten others; for this particular cancer spreads beyond its host.

II. MUDDYING THE UTOPIAN WATERS

Analyzed all in his book,
The enlightenment driven away,
The habit-forming pain,
Mismanagement and grief:
We must suffer them all again.

W. H. Auden (1940)

In the socialism of the future… what counts is the whole,
the community of the Volk. The individual and his life play
only a subsidiary role. He can be sacrificed - he is
prepared to Sacrifice himself should the whole demand it,
should the commonweal call for it.

Adolf Hitler to Otto Wagener (February or March 1930)

5:
Progressive State Utopia

Redefining Democracy

The Scientific Revolution dispelled the flattering illusion that the Earth and its human inhabitants were centrally situated in the universe. But paradoxically, evidence of man's all-but-divine intellectual prowess was also music to the hubristic ear. That a special demotion would coincidentally catapult Adam's progeny to heights of self-regard was not a little ironic. For on the one hand, Copernicus, Galileo, and Isaac Newton, amply confirmed the biblical assurance that man had been created in God's image: these were intellectual titans. But was the world just a well-wound, if immensely complex, clock? How could one avoid the chilling suspicion that the Creator had meant His children to fend for themselves? Was the price of scientific knowledge an inescapable sense of unrelenting loneliness? This Faustian pact seemed grossly overpriced.

Though energized by the prospect of understanding how things work, man's discovery that his precious planet was merely one of countless stars also frightened him. Notwithstanding his divinely blessed creation, he had to recognize that he was, after all, a mere speck on the canvas of eternity. The one consolation was the increasingly plausible conviction that, being capable of figuring out the Laws of Nature, he could use them to his advantage. And since those Laws had presumably been issued by a supremely benevolent Being, they governed what had to be a world marching toward outright perfection. Thus mankind, or at least its smartest specimens, could expedite the climax of history. It was an empowering Revelation, pun fully intended.

The Bible had already ushered in a new, linear view of history, each moment being considered unique and unrepeatable, [293] whereas ancient religions had been largely characterized by a cyclical conception of the universe, known as the myth of the Eternal Return. [294] According to this myth – in the sense mentioned earlier, not as a fable but as deeply held belief – the universe is a perpetual cycle of regeneration and death. Each spring sees a rebirth of life, providing an occasion for spiritual rededication. And as ancient divinities were reconnected with humanity through perennial ritual, humans reminded both the Divine and themselves that theirs is an eternal bond. The ultimate purpose of these celebrations was to render each passing a mere prelude to another rebirth, perhaps eternal. Finality was an illusion, death but a semicolon in the sentence of endless time. There may have been commas too, and question marks, but no period.

The advent of linear history subtly inaugurated by the biblical narrative preserved ritual, but having lost its natural cyclical simplicity, spiritual re-connection became far more uncertain. As life felt less like the revolving seasons and more like a nasty, brutish, and short journey from dust to dust, to life ever-after at best perchance, alienation crept in. The ancient cyclical simplicity thus eroded, spirituality became more problematic in an age of growing skepticism and insidious secularism. With modernity, the ancient certainties increasingly gave way to existential anxiety.

While religion continued to console the fortunate faithful, growing numbers needed additional reassurance. Arthur Mendel explains:

> Bit by bit, progress in knowledge about the material world chiseled away at the foundations of the spiritual world. As a result, humanity lost both its divinely rooted self-esteem and its promised city of eternal salvation. New grounds for both the esteem and the promised salvation would have to be found. Denied heaven, man turned back to earth. Deprived of the centrality assigned him in the medieval drama of salvation, he would achieve a comparable self-esteem through temporal achievement.... Most of all, instead of turning to heaven for help in enduring the miseries of earthly existence, he would henceforth devote himself and his labors to the eradication of those miseries.[295]

At least, what comforted both skeptic and devout was the sense that history was marching forward. Writes Mircea Eliade:

> From the seventeenth century on, linearism and the progressivist conception of history assert themselves more and more... [becoming increasingly secularist, until] with Marx, history cast off all transcendental significance.... Yet Marxism preserves a meaning to history. For Marxism, events are not a succession of arbitrary accidents; they exhibit a coherent structure and, above

all, they lead to a definite end – final elimination of the terror of history, "salvation." Thus, at the end of the Marxist philosophy of history, lies the age of gold of the archaic eschatologies [sic].[296]

Thus Eden morphed seamlessly into the endpoint of Progress. But even as it became secularized, proselytes redirecting their deep-seated need for meaning away from the Eternal Beyond to the created world, Progress arrogated the originally spiritual flavor. Whether outsourced to Nature or Nature's Laws, to the *Zeit* (German for "spirit"), *élan vital* ("vital zeal" in French), or Will to Power (in German, *Wille zur Macht*), Progress was meant to be seen as transcendent. As Robert Nisbet observes in *History of the Idea of Progress*, the concept aptly reflects "man's moral or spiritual condition on earth, his happiness, his freedom from torments of nature and society, and above all his serenity or tranquility. The goal of progress or advancement is mankind's eventual achievement, *on earth*, of these spiritual and moral virtues, thus leading toward ever-greater perfection of human nature."[297]

We have seen how Hegel and then Marx adopted the millenarian belief in a final utopian stage as defined by freedom from the torments of nature and society, accompanied by an ever-greater perfection of human nature devoid of selfishness and greed. History saw their ideas take hold in the East. But if their influence is far less dramatic in the West, it is anything but negligible. This is certainly the case in the United States, starting in the late 1800s.

Some Americans encountered Marxist ideas in German schools, while others had German teachers on this side of the Atlantic, notably at the Johns Hopkins University.[298] There was neither widespread nor instant conversion, since the British and Scottish approach to education dominant in the United States from colonial times had been in sharp contrast to the views of pedagogical luminaries from the Continental tradition. The latter's eventual success in late nineteenth century America, though hardly total, was due above all to the extraordinary influence of its highly educated, elite proponents, including two presidents, Theodore Roosevelt (1858-1919) and Thomas Woodrow Wilson (1856-1924). Their differences notwithstanding – in background, temperament, and life experiences – these two men shared a dislike of what they saw as capitalist corruption, and a commitment to what they both called "progressivism."

In Wilson's case, that notion was closely related to a version of socialism which he considered a logical extension of democratic theory. After all, he reasoned, isn't democracy supposed to give all power to the people in their collective capacity, to carry out their common interest through the government? The operative concept, of course, is "in their collective capacity." As he wrote in 1887: "In fundamental theory socialism and democracy are almost if not quite one and the same. They both rest at bottom upon the absolute right of the community to determine its own destiny and that of its members."[299]

The putative *absolute* right of the community to determine "its" destiny is the premise underlying a monistic political system that obliterates genuine differences of opinion and interest. Rousseau found it in the General Will. By Wilson's reckoning, the aim of "genuine" democracy coincides with that of socialism: to abolish inequality. Jane Addams (1860-1935) saw the Progressive Era[300] reform agenda as at bottom consistent with "that true democracy of the early [Christian] Church," for it seeks "to make the entire social organism democratic, to extend democracy beyond its political expression."[301] Also echoing Rousseau, Addams assumes that the "social organism" can operate only on the basis of a common faith - the civic religion of the group.

Like her Swiss-French predecessor, she was not referring to the organized Christian church of her time. But her vision was equally millenarian and eutopian, and fundamentally faith-based. Non-secular, no less than secular, Progressives saw the hand of God in history as did Hegel, who famously described the state as "the Divine Idea as it exists on earth."[302] Presidential candidate Theodore Roosevelt's thunderous proclamation "We stand at Armageddon, and we battle for the Lord!" was a non-sectarian, political summons in religious garb. Though he was addressing the Progressive Party Convention of 1912, he meant to appeal to secularists and believers alike.

By 1912, however, there should have been no confusion as to the nature of the vision being invoked. For starting in 1880, evangelical Protestants who wished to distance themselves from their more traditional brethren initiated a movement that essentially became the religious arm of Progressivism. Called the Social Gospel, it was unabashedly socialist.

"We shall have to resocialize property," wrote its principal spokesman, Baptist minister Walter Rauschenbusch. "Socializing property will mean that instead of serving the welfare of a small group directly, and the public welfare only indirectly, it will be made more directly available to the service of all."[303] But resocializing (it isn't clear how that differs from plain socializing) property was only half the battle. To really affect the political culture, each citizen also had to unlearn the "reactionary state of mind." Translation: re-education had to be undertaken.

Explains Murray N. Rothbard:

The molding of children was of course the key to homogenization and the key in general to the progressive vision of tight social control over the individual via the instrument of the state. The eminent University of Wisconsin sociologist Edward Alsworth Ross, a favorite of Theodore Roosevelt and the veritable epitome of a progressive social scientist, summed it up thus: The role of the public official, and in particular of the public school teacher, is "to collect little plastic lumps of human dough from private households and shape them on the social kneadingboard."[304]

Ross and the other progressives were convinced that the state must take up the task of control and inculcation of moral values once performed by parents and church.[305]

According to the Social Gospel, therefore, progressivism would fulfill Christ's promise *in this life*. Ronald Pestritto and William Atto explain: "Social Gospel theologians asserted that government, because of progress, was now in a position to bring about such an earthly utopia in the form of the modern democratic state."[306] But bringing about an earthly utopia and molding a new *homo progressivus*[307] required proper indoctrination. Championed from the pulpits as well as the schools, the new ideology would involve re-education on a massive scale.

True, a few small obstacles had to be overcome, such as the Constitution of the United States, which inconveniently limited government and permitted a wide variety of views that were sometimes at odds with progressive ideas. The old parchment had placed so many limits on government that it was hard to radically alter society. Lamented Herbert Croly (1869-1930), founder of *The New Republic,* the Progressive movement's principal organ: "[T]he exaggerated value which has been attached to constitutional limitations" on state power, resulting in an "apprehensive and reactionary state of mind, ... [threatens] to undermine the foundations in human nature and human will upon which the whole superstructure of a progressive democratic society must admittedly be built."[308] How irksome that pesky legal niceties should undermine the far-seeing, lofty "human will" of the self-proclaimed elite.

Theodore Roosevelt agreed, incensed at the way the Constitution was practically prohibiting "the whole people of [a] State from adopting methods of regulating the use of property so that human life, particularly the lives of working men, shall be safer, freer, and happier." The judiciary branch had dared to read the text "as if property rights, to the exclusion of human rights, had a first mortgage on the Constitution."[309] Exclusion? The Founders had to be scratching their heads. It could not be that every man's right "to preserve his property – that is, his life, liberty, and estate,"[310] all intertwined, was no longer a self-evident truth in the nation devoted to that principle, could it?

Change was in the air. Writes Roger Pilon (my learned husband):

> [A]s early as 1900 we could find *The Nation*, before it became an instrument of the modern left, lamenting the demise of classical liberalism. In an editorial entitled "The Eclipse of Liberalism," the magazine's editors surveyed the European scene, then wrote that in America, too, "recent events show how much ground has been lost. The Declaration of Independence no longer arouses enthusiasm; it is an embarrassing instrument which requires to be explained away. The Constitution is said to be 'outgrown.'"[311]

A new attitude was being championed by Republicans as well as Democrats. From his political pulpit, Roosevelt stooped to declaring "that each must be his brother's keeper." Whether he was he referring only to American citizens or to the whole world misses the point: this wasn't immigration policy but a homily. The patrician TR was channeling his inner country preacher. Whether the purpose of moral action was presumed to consist in the good of the community or that of the world was beside the point: what it could *not* be was the pursuit of mere individual happiness. To deny being one's brother's keeper would become the essence of anti-Progressivism. Ideological descendants of Cain, they were branded by the swastika of selfishness.

Roosevelt thundered "against the unfair profits of unscrupulous and conscienceless men, or against the greedy exploitation of the helpless by the beneficiaries of privilege,"[312] i.e., the capitalist Antichrist. What it lacked in specificity, the accusation made up in populist demagogy, as Roosevelt proclaimed his "faith in the people." "Our aim," spoke Roosevelt for all champions of the common man, "is to secure the real and not the nominal rule of the people."[313] The Progressives were in favor of Real rather than *ersatz* or nominal – i.e., merely electoral - Democracy. The Spirit of History is far more than the sum of equally myopic little individual components. Wasn't it time for a neo-Catholic unity of purpose? Wasn't the very idea of a "party" pejorative, implying noxious division?[314]

As Richard Hofstadter points out, "the Founding Fathers had inherited a political philosophy which ... denied the usefulness of parties and stressed their dangers... [though] they were rapidly driven, in spite of their theories, to develop a party system."[315] The party system was so obviously flawed, perhaps it was time to rethink it. Roosevelt hoped to create a single political entity to supplant both the Democratic and Republican parties, which he found hopelessly corrupt. In Hegelian-speak, the Progressive Party would constitute a "synthesis," transcending the nefarious antagonistic, antinomial politics of his era.

Progressive representatives, according to this eutopian dream, would seek nothing but the good of the entire society, the whole nation. Unselfish people, exceptional in every way, would presumably hire brilliant specialists, objective professionals who would work out the mundane details of implementation. An administrative state would thereby be set in motion, its apolitical servants devoted to nothing but the latest best information to advance the common good.

As Roosevelt probably knew, however, the one-party General Will model had already been spelled out by his fellow-Progressive, if political rival, Woodrow Wilson, as early as 1886, in an essay with the deceptively innocuous title "The Study of Administration." In an effort to depoliticize the business of government, the study proposed separating administration from politics. Political candidates vying to become the people's representatives could thus promise to enact measures designed to curb the power of the "unscrupulous" and the "greedy," who made "unjust profits," while leaving it to administrators (bureaucrats) to work out the messy details. With administration thus "liberated" from partisan politics, civil servants became the new secular priests, worshipers at the altar of Science.

Insisting on a strict "distinction between constitutional and administrative questions," Wilson admits that "one cannot easily make clear to every one [sic] just where administration resides in the various departments of any practicable government," but dismisses the problem as a mere technicality. Administration is a scientific enterprise, cutting across all branches of government: Congress needs staffers; the judiciary uses clerks; and the executive agencies writes all the statutes. So then, let them work out the specifics. One wonders whether V. I. Lenin had read this essay before writing *State and Revolution* in 1917, where he explains that the Communist plan was simply "to organize the whole national economy on the lines of the postal service."[316] The idea was elementary: once egoism was abolished and everyone pursued the good of all, the business of running a state was mere logistics - like sorting out mail.

We are way behind Europe, warned Wilson. The Old World, though derided by the Founding Fathers for its decadence, had since leapt ahead of the New - thanks in no small measure to strong leaders who knew how to swat away pesky Lilliputian obstacles lacking grander visions of the future. We've lost our edge, New no more. The Continent's allegedly pioneering "governments are now in the lead in administrative practice which had rulers still absolute but also enlightened." Turning Lord Acton's dictum on its head, Wilson suggests that absolute power might be required to un-corrupt absolutely. Those valiant, strong European leaders are to be commended for having bestowed upon future generations an "administration [that] has organized the general weal with the simplicity and effectiveness vouchsafed only to the undertakings of a single will." How else can "the general weal" be expressed if not by "a single will"?

Though Wilson awarded the Gold Medal for technocratic politics to Prussia (Prime Minister Otto von Bismarck, to be exact), "where administration has been most studied and most nearly perfected," Napoleon receives the Silver for excellence in the "perfecting of civil machinery by the single will of an absolute ruler."[317] Such accomplishments are impossible for a committee or an assembly. It takes genius as well as single-minded, messianic determination.

Strong unified leadership appealed to Progressives, who considered a multi-party system inimical to "true" democracy. For when special interests clash, the General Will is lost in the shuffle. At best, a pluralist arrangement is grossly inefficient; at worst, and far more often, argued consensus-lovers, not truly "democratic." Progressives therefore opposed the tiresome balance of powers arrangement outlined in the U.S. Constitution, whereby the legislative, executive, and judiciary powers operated independently of one another as equal branches. This cumbersome system, thought Wilson, both hampers the smooth business of governance and pits one group against another. Can it possibly make any sense for those entrusted with leading the nation, no matter which branch of the government they may serve, to pursue anything *other* than the General Good? If so, the separation can only impede and even undermine the process. James Madison, who had painstakingly explained the rationale for slowing down government action, never imagined that a fellow president, precisely a century later, would so categorically reject them. Then again, Madison had the wise Scottish minister John Witherspoon for a mentor at Princeton; Wilson merely taught there.

Wilson and the Progressives disagreed with the Founders' approach to the problem of special interests (another name for "factions") of pitting them against one another in a system of "checks and balances." The whole selfish, unpatriotic cacophony should be replaced by a single, lovely plainsong: The Voice of the People, its liturgy composed by enlightened, noble leaders, and sung in unison from one sublime score. Wilson cited, approvingly, Hegel's view that concepts evolve as history advances; today's needs are different and call for different rules. The Constitution has passed its expiration date.

If only it were possible to do away with all the electoral hullabaloo, the "nominal" aspects of democracy, things would be so much simpler and more efficient. Real, true, democracy would at last be given a chance. Politics, specifically political parties, only get in the way, distracting the people in different directions, and away from the Common Purpose. Argued Herbert Croly: the multiparty system deflects citizens' zeal away from the national interest. This obsolete political system, that "demands and obtains for a party an amount of loyal service and personal sacrifice which a public-spirited democrat should lavish only on the state,"[318] should be abandoned. He advocated its immediate abolition - the Constitution be damned.

Though he did not go quite as far, Wilson praised the parliamentary electoral model, whereby the prime minister is selected by the majority party, thus effectively uniting the legislative and the executive. In 1912, TR also attacked "both of the old parties" for having turned away from their true purpose as "instruments to promote the general welfare," having become instead "tools of corrupt interests."[319] Given their similar views, far closer than they cared to admit, Wilson could have established the Progressive Party no less than Roosevelt, had the latter not beat him to the punch. They remained bitter political and personal rivals throughout their lives.

The two Progressive presidents both hated big business. Roosevelt's trust-busting campaign that broke up major railroad, oil, and steel was followed by other business restrictions under Wilson's presidency. So too, both men believed in using public education to mold young minds. On November 4, 1916, *The New Republic* ventured to guess that future historians "will interpret the work of President Wilson as a continuation of the work begun by ex-President Roosevelt."[320] This was especially true in domestic policy, opined the editors, who went on to praise Teddy for "his exceptional gifts as an agitator [which] were devoted to concentrating public opinion on the all-important task of democratizing the political system of the country and socializing its economic system." In sum, the Wilson's administration "is clearly a continuation, if not a consummation, of that begun by Mr. Roosevelt. By a skillful use of Presidential initiative and sustained by an aroused public opinion, Mr. Wilson wrote into law the connection between a progressive economic policy and national unity." And so it was.

National Unity

"National unity" is surely the bumper sticker that best captures both these presidents' overarching ideology. It extends even to their most important apparent disagreement, which concerned America's entry in the Great War. At first glance, that disagreement seemed unbridgeable. For while Roosevelt would go on to be remembered for an aggressively military approach to foreign policy – as in "speak softly and carry a big stick,"[321] Wilson gained a reputation for opposing entry into the Great War. But soon the former Princeton professor reversed that policy, leading the dough boys into battle putatively to end all wars forever, to promote his ill-defined version of "democracy" around the world - carrying, as it were, a big stick only to never carry another, while speaking loftily. Yet at bottom these were two sides of the same millenarian coin: a belief in the redemptive power of the Gospel of Equality, made-in-America on a Hegelian pattern pre-emptively sketched out by Rousseau. It turned out to be a wooden nickel, as unintended, if altogether predictable, consequences, once again obeyed their unfathomable laws.

Henry Kissinger prefers to accentuate the differences between the two Presidents instead of their similarities. Roosevelt, argues Kissinger, was the "realist." Though he too would have led the U.S. into the Great War, TR "would almost certainly have expressed America's war aims in political and strategic terms; Wilson, flaunting American disinterest, defined America's war aims in entirely moral categories."[322] Whether the two men sought similar goals, they chose different ways of reaching and justifying them.

Or so it seemed to Kissinger, who writes: "To [Roosevelt], international life meant struggle, and Darwin's theory of the survival of the fittest was a better guide to history than personal morality."[323] Yet Wilson was equally Darwinian. What made him appear less realistic was that he paid less attention to the real world than did TR. Thus Roosevelt's proposal, in 1914, to increase defense spending in order to prepare for potential entry into the war was flatly rejected by Wilson mainly because such a move might signal that "we had lost our self-possession" in the face of a military conflagration "whose causes cannot touch us, whose very existence affords us opportunities for friendship and disinterested service...."[324] His posturing cost soldiers' lives.

Actually, Progressivism did not dictate either entry or abstention in any particular international conflict that did not directly threaten the homeland. The messianic thrust of the ideology nevertheless tilted more in the direction of intervention – of course, in the service of the General Good, whether the nation's or humanity's or, ideally, both. True, Roosevelt had no problem carrying a big stick and flaunting it, while the sanctimonious professor preferred to speak eloquently and inspire the world with "soft power" claiming to end all war. In the end, however, both were moralistic, and neither anticipated the enormous political complexities that transpired after that first apocalyptic bloodbath of the new century. There would soon be others, far bloodier.

Notwithstanding the commander-in-chief-cum-prophet's decision to break his promise to the electorate to stay out of the ill-fated war, America's typical resilience kicked in. Once it had been determined that Germany and Evil had to be defeated, the nation showed remarkable ability to create a respectable fighting force. But military prowess was not matched by negotiating savvy. Europe's top diplomats could not hide their surprise at the ignorance and embarrassing inexperience of the haughty American president. John Maynard Keynes (1883-1946) regretfully notes that "not only was he ill-informed – but his mind was slow and unadaptable. The President's slowness among the Europeans was noteworthy."[325]

The result was devastating: "[T]his blind and deaf Don Quixote was entering a cavern where the swift and glittering blade was in the hands of the adversary."[326] More tragic, this visually and auditorily challenged American wanna-be knight also suffered from an acute case of optimism and arrogance, whose disconcerting effect on his audience was exacerbated by a penchant for obfuscation.

It had started with his War Message, delivered at an extraordinary session of the U.S. Congress on April 2, 1917. Denouncing German submarine attacks against neutral American ships as "unlawful" (leaving unaddressed the debate surrounding the already ongoing, and not exactly neutral, American military support for the Allies), Wilson's declaration of war asserted categorically that "we have no selfish ends to serve." Rather, Americans "fight thus for the ultimate peace of the world and for the liberation of its peoples, the German peoples included: for the rights of nations great and small and the privilege of men everywhere to choose their way of life and of obedience. The world must be made safe for democracy."[327] *Must*: a nice Progressive word.

Less than a year later, he would include these high-minded ideals into the infamous Fourteen Points of America's proposed "Terms of Peace." Incredibly, the document declared: "The program of the world peace, therefore, is our program, and that program [is] the only possible program." Such breathtaking hubris risked instant ridicule; it took a little while for everyone to quite believe what they were hearing. Among the points were the following principles declared indispensable to the establishment of a just peace:

> V. A free, open-minded, and absolutely impartial adjustment of all colonial claims, based upon a strict observance of the principle that in determining all such questions of sovereignty the interests of the populations concerned must have equal weight with the equitable claims of the government whose title is to be determined.
>
> X. The peoples of Austria-Hungary, whose place among the nations we wish to see safeguarded and assured, should be accorded the freest opportunity of autonomous development.
>
> XIV. A general association of nations must be formed under specific covenants for the purpose of affording mutual guarantees of political independence and territorial integrity to great and small states alike.

It is not difficult to imagine the consternation of the jaded, weary diplomats watching the messiah-impersonating Wilson, seemingly so oblivious to his statements' utter lack of clarity. Most appalling, writes Margaret McMillan, the concept of self-determination "was, and has remained, one of the most controversial and opaque. During the Peace Conference, the head of the American mission in Vienna sent repeated requests to Paris and Washington for an explanation of the term. No answer ever came."[328] Maybe because no answer was possible.

What could Wilson have had in mind? Did he mean that every ethnic group had the right to its own government – and if so, did it have to occupy a contiguous area? If some members of that group lived far from others, were they supposed to relocate? Or would a nation consist of several distinct territories, each with its own local leadership? And was a particular kind of political organization more likely to promote self-determination? Specifically, did a new – or, for that matter, old – state have to be "democratic," and if so, what did that mean? One man-one vote? And which electoral system is best, if any? Also: what constitutes the "autonomous development" of an ethnic group? Did ethnicity encompass religion? Language, or language-group? Is autonomy synonymous with self-determination? Which means what, by the way? So too, what is an "impartial" adjustment of colonial claims? Could France and England bear to keep a straight face as they read this? Not likely. These and more questions revealed to all who would dare admit it how mind-bogglingly absurd Wilson's program really was.

It might have helped if the boldness of those commandments had been tempered by some recognition of what the real-world situation actually looked like. But no such luck. In the final paragraph, Wilson boasts without a trace of irony: "We have spoken now, surely, in terms too concrete to admit of any further doubt or question. An evident principle runs through the whole program I outlined. It is the principle of justice to all peoples and nationalities, and their right to live on equal terms of liberty and safety with one another, whether they be strong or weak." Unflinching, the President enlists his entire nation to guarantee this presumed "right": "The people of the United States could act upon no other principle; and to the vindication they are ready to devote their lives, their honor, and everything that they possess."[329]

Such words might be expected from an absolute monarch with an outsized ego; coming from the president of a constitutional republic, whose Founders had pointedly and repeatedly warned against entangling alliances, they were the secular equivalent of blasphemy. His punishment would be the democratic equivalent of burning at the stake, as the Republican-dominated Senate failed to ratify his proposed treaty for the United States to join the League of Nations, which was meant to cement Wilson's legacy, his gift to world peace. Treating his opponents with napoleonic disdain also did not help his cause. Megalomania is a tough disease.

Wilsonianism would henceforth connote naivety and foolish international overreach in the name of goals utterly divorced from reality. McMillan attributes it to a typically American obtuseness, "a tendency to preach at other nations rather than listen to them" - a case of wishful thinking as foreign policy. Not that it ended with Wilson; future presidents succumbed to the temptation as well. In a way, this stance had an endearing quality. McMillan admits that "Wilson kept alive the hope that human society, despite the evidence, was getting better, that nations would one day live in harmony."[330] Keeping hope alive may be commendable, but not by flaunting facts.

Nor when it kills wantonly. When are lovely words worth the price paid in innocent lives and in poorly concluded wars that waste the peace, leading to ever more bloodshed? The devil is in the proverbial details. "Despite the evidence" is quintessential utopianism. Wilsonian foreign policy is the Progressives' version of the Apocalypse: may war bring peace forever. Wilson's off-the-record comments aboard his ship on his way to Paris in 1919 are telling: "I am convinced that if this peace is not made on the highest principles of justice, it will be swept away by the peoples of this world in less than a generation. If it is any other sort of peace then I shall want to run away and hide... for there will follow not mere conflict but cataclysm."[331] He didn't live to run away.

"The highest principles of justice" still need to be applied. Unfortunately, comments David Fromkin, neither Wilson nor his associates "had formulated concrete programs that would translate promises into realities: the President's program was vague and bound to arouse millennial expectations – which made it practically certain that any agreement achieved by politicians would disappoint."[332] That millenarian expectations invariably fail to materialize does little to reduce their use by utopians with a penchant for demagogy; it only leads to new ones.

Racism for the Common Good

Woodrow Wilson's proposal for national self-determination of ethnic groups, or "peoples," was generally understood to refer to relatively homogeneous ethnic communities that had been ruled by foreign princes. It reflected the rapid rise of nationalism in the nineteenth century throughout Europe, which had been predicated on the notion that people who spoke different languages, had different cultural habits, and often belonged to different religious sects, shared an essential, subliminal national ethos. The complex political, if not cynical, undertones of the lofty rhetoric were often neglected.[333] Ethnic, racial, religious and other group identities were bandied about, and it was not uncommon to speak of different human "races" as a vague mixture of genetic and cultural attributes. But Wilson's seemingly inclusive multiculturalism was hiding a dirty little secret. It was called eugenics.

Though claiming to champion the rights of the underprivileged minorities in all the world, Wilson differentiated among more and less "progressive" races, which he identified as the Aryan, Semitic, and

Turanian, in decreasing order of superiority.[334] The self-proclaimed defender of occupied Europeans also minimized alleged "cases of inhuman conduct toward slaves" in the American south, claiming these "were in every sense exceptional." No worries. He even, incredibly, applauded the end of Reconstruction for having cemented "the natural, inevitable ascendancy of the whites, the responsible class"![335] Wilson adopted Hegel's model of historical evolution, whereby certain races, possessed of a modern spirit, supersede earlier ones. Progress involves both winners and losers: the winners advance the General Good, the losers drag it behind.

And Teddy Roosevelt blithely concurred. Explains Pestritto: For Roosevelt,

> equality meant using the power of government to destroy the "special interests" or "special privilege" - defined... as those asserting property rights against the will of the majority. These "special interests" had used the "rules of the game" to benefit themselves and not society as a whole; "I stand," Roosevelt proclaimed, "for having those rules changed so as to work for a more substantial equality of opportunity *and of reward.*"[336] Unlike Madison, who accepted the fact that unequal rewards would result from the equal enforcement of individual property rights, Roosevelt seems to have called for the unequal enforcement of rights (changing the "rules of the game," to use his language) so as to produce more equal results.[337]

Thus both Wilson and Roosevelt put the collective before the individual, the General before the particular Will, high-minded altruism, which is the job of government to enforce, as against greed and egoism. When Roosevelt cautioned Americans about the "base spirit of gain and greed which recognizes commercialism the be-all and end-all,"[338] he was implicitly sending a signal to Jews that, before becoming like other Americans, they would have to expand their interests beyond the business world.[339] In other words, not unlike blacks, Jews had to become more "white," for their own good and that of the nation. Though nothing at all like the lethal strain of European antisemitism, Progressive Era America was yet not overly welcoming to Jews.

Academics set the tone. Adopting the premise of evolutionary racial hierarchy served

To affirm the presumed inherent inferiority of certain nationalities or ethnic groups – especially Southern and Eastern Europeans, Asians, and Blacks. Preexisting prejudices were thus bolstered by "the increasingly systematic use of a biological, deterministic discourse to explain and to remedy, often using racial categories, the root causes of economic problems, especially labor and immigration."[340] Cloaked in a mantle of respectable science, progressive era racial rhetoric was instrumental to "buttress the reformist thought and legislation that was so characteristic of the time." Hostility toward Jewish immigration, mostly from Russia and Poland, was part of this general discourse.[341]

As the Progressive era advanced, "improving the human stock" and reducing the harm to society caused by "defective humans" rose from mild concern to widespread obsession.[342] But which human beings could be properly deemed defective? Did physical disability count as well as psychological? Intellectual ability attracted disproportionate attention; but what techniques could adequately gauge mental "defectiveness"? If assessments made use of questionnaires, were linguistic and other barriers taken into consideration? Could poor results reflect not so much deficient mental ability as insufficient knowledge of English? Also, to what extent did skin color, or any other superficial, merely phenotypical, traits play any role in estimating "defectiveness"? And finally, even assuming it was possible to determine whether someone was somehow "defective," what was to be done with such people? And who would decide?

No one better epitomized the Progressive attitude on this issue than Supreme Court Justice Oliver Wendell Holmes. Ruling in favor of upholding a Virginia law, *Buck v. Bell* (1927), which promoted sterilization of the "feeble-minded," Justice Holmes argued that such impaired human beings would "sap the strength of the State." Frankly speaking, wrote Holmes, sterilization is far and away the most humane course of action. For "[i]t is better for all the world, if instead of waiting to execute degenerate offspring for crime, or to let them starve for their imbecility, society can prevent those who are manifestly unfit from continuing their kind."[343] The measure was all in the name of Progress, and of course for the good of the State. To justify his decision to permit and even encourage sterilization, he then uttered what would become one of the most shameful sentences in American history: "Three generations of imbeciles are enough."

Never mind that the young woman whose case was before the high court for having been sterilized against her will, Carrie Buck, was neither feeble-minded nor otherwise handicapped. It had all been a travesty.[344] And its perpetrators knew it.

"Eugenics," rooted in "well-born" (from the Greek *eu, "good,"* and *genos,* "birth"), refers to the (pseudo)science of improving a human population by controlled breeding, presumably to increase the occurrence of desirable heritable characteristics. While originating in England, it really took off in the United States. Starting with Indiana in 1907, during the following six years eleven additional states would adopt legislation authorizing forced sterilization of "undesirables," especially those of low intelligence. In effect, this meant people "who offended the middle-class sensibilities of judges and social workers."[345]

Measuring "desirability," even if restricted to intellectual prowess alone, is a fool's errand. Which did not stop academics from trying. In a 1914 book titled *Feeble-Mindedness: Its Causes and Consequences,* for example, Henry Goddard gave scientific veneer to "idiots," "imbeciles," and "morons," going on to claim, in all seriousness, that these labels applied to as many as half of all criminals, prostitutes, and almshouse residents in the United States. Three years later, psychologist Robert Yerkes tested no fewer than 1.75 million U.S. Army enlistees, only to find that nearly half of the test takers, all white, also qualified as feebleminded.[346] Was there an epidemic of imbecility in this country?

If so, it likely afflicted not the tested so much as the testers. The eugenicists of the era matched the demographic profile of the reformers. White cites Richard Hosfstadter's "observation that professionals and intellectuals were in the forefront of the reform movements of the era: they were the sort, he noted, who 'see the drift of events' and then 'throw their weight on the side of what they feel is progress and reform.' So it was with eugenics – it appealed, in particular, to academics and professionals, including lawyers, doctors, social workers, and journalists."[347] Salivating at the aroma of a utopian omelet, the elite was determined to facilitate the march of progress, come what may.

A fixation with genetic (racial) perfectibility permeated the academy. No fewer than 376 colleges and universities, including Harvard, Columbia, Cornell, and University of California-Berkeley, taught courses on the subject during the Progressive era. The chairman of Harvard's anthropology department called for a "biological purge," lest Americans sold "their biological birthright for a mess of morons."[348] So too, the same Woodrow Wilson, who in 1917 proclaimed himself the champion of all humanity, and defended the right to self-determination for all the peoples of the world, had only six years earlier, as governor of New Jersey, signed a law authorizing sterilization for "certain categories of adult feeble minds." Far from reluctant, Wilson's support for that law was reputed to have been "enthusiastic."[349] Progress was to be promoted both at home and abroad, and that meant biologically too.

Nor does Theodore Roosevelt lag far behind Wilson in his zeal for biological purification. In a chilling preview of ideologies yet to come, TR's arguments on behalf of eugenics are used to justify not only sterilization but war itself. Certainly "a great war," wrote Roosevelt in 1914, "may do for the whole nation a service that incalculably outweighs all possible evil effects," by purifying it of inferior specimens - at least in principle, though in the real world it doesn't always work out that way. But then goes on to give as a prime example... the American Civil War. Most astonishingly, what he deplores above all is that the *wrong* people had died! Explains Roosevelt:

> That war cost half a million lives. It is certainly a sad and evil thing that timid and weak people, the peace-at-any-price and anti-militarist people who stayed at home, should have left descendants to admire well-meaning, feeble articles against militarism, while their valiant comrades went to the front and perished.... Worthy writers on eugenics must not forget that heroes serve as examples."[350]

And though he commendably counts freeing the slaves as one of the results worth dying for, his jeremiad extoling war as such, along with praising the dead on both sides for their sacrifice, is a disconcerting display of moral equivalence. He ends by bemoaning that timid, weak, "anti-militarist" people went on living and procreating, while the best lay dead. Unabashedly in favor of sterilizing criminals, he regrets that "as yet there is no way possible to devise [a way] which could prevent all undesirable people from breeding." An ardent advocate of "getting desirable people to breed,"[351] Roosevelt proceeds to suggest various effective incentives, in true eugenicist fashion.

These attitudes are shockingly contrary to the general impression that Progressives were champions of all the unfortunate and the weak. In fact, explains Thomas Leonard, "Progressive Era progressives viewed the poor and disenfranchised with great ambivalence. Many clearly believed that defective heredity offered a basis for sorting the worthy poor from the unworthy poor and that uplift of the worthy poor required eugenic control of the unworthy poor."[352] It was egalitarianism with a catch. A sinister catch.

For if different categories of unfortunates are to be treated differently, how does that square with the principle that all men are created equal? Grasping this dilemma is critical to understanding the affinity between Progressive ideology and the monolithic authoritarian nation-state. Ominously, undesirable "defectives" who hinder the march of Progress may be deemed not only unworthy of citizenship but outright expendable. Only after these are expelled, extinct, or eliminated are the remaining members of the community to be treated equally. And once selfishness and greed are eradicated, a superior society will be able to pursue the Common Good.

Art Carden and Steven Horwitz attribute this worldview to the influence of Charles Darwin's *The Origin of Species*:

> The advent and broad acceptance of Darwinism in the late nineteenth century, combined with a more general belief in the power of science and scientific management to solve social problems, led to a fascination with eugenics and the possibility of using public policy to ensure the "survival of the fittest" and the purity and strength of the human race. In the hands of many thinkers at the turn of the twentieth century, Darwinian theory became a rationale for using the power of government....[353]

Once again, what matters is not the individual but the group. If it is in the best interest of the aggregate community to weed out undesirables, so be it. As to who should decide which people fit that description - why, it's the State, ideally through its "technologists." According to a popular textbook from 1923, "[g]overnment and social control are in the hands of expert politicians who have power, instead of expert technologists who have wisdom. There should be technologists in control of every field of human need and desire."[354]

Devoted as Progressives were to the concept of "social control," which reflected a deep commitment to social science and public administration, they categorically opposed free markets. Writes Leonard: "Progressives were drawn to eugenics by the same set of intellectual commitments that drew them to reform legislation. Paramount was the reform idea that laissez-faire was bankrupt. Sidney Webb said flatly, '[N]o consistent eugenicist can be a 'Laissez Faire' individualist unless he throws up the game in despair. He must interfere, interfere, interfere!'"[355]

Expert "interference" was not deemed coercion because it enhanced the forward march of history. Gradual rather than apocalyptic, it was still elite-led: the mindset was pure hubris. To proclaim that sterilizing innocents would render society better off, since it eliminated the intellectually inferior, is morally indefensible. Junky science was used to violate rights and made a mockery of individual freedom. In a classic case of conflating fact and value, American technocrats, both Republican and Democrat, followed in the footsteps the messianic Jacobins and the dialectical Marxists. Pseudo-science in the service of pseudo-morality: some combination!

In Arthur Mendel's words:

> If there is one attribute that more than any other characterizes the modern radical intelligentsia, left and right, it is the conviction that the ideas and ideals they espouse are somehow irrefutably objective and necessary – in a word, scientific. The modern roots of this delusion are … in the period bridging the scientific revolution and the Enlightenment, when the demonstrated discoveries of the first were uncritically converted into the axiomatic assumptions of the second.[356]

The secular Eden was to be expedited by a selfless, non-political elite, armed with the right facts, whose allegiance was to the State alone. A redistribution of resources to a population duly improved: for the eugenicists, this was Progress *über alles.*

The zeal for species-cleansing went far beyond the United States. Writes Edwin Black: "American eugenic evangelists spawned similar movements and practices throughout Europe, Latin America and Asia." And no, it wasn't only the Ku Klux Klan: "A tightly-knit network of mainstream medical and eugenical journals, international meetings and conferences kept the generals and soldiers of eugenics up to date and armed for their nation's next legislative opportunity." Indeed, "eugenics contaminated many otherwise worthy social, medical and educational causes from the birth control movement to the development of psychology to urban sanitation."[357] But he succumbs, alas, to the lure of the sound bite, in claiming to have "discovered that the Nazi principle of Nordic superiority was not hatched in the Third Reich but on Long Island decades earlier – and then actively transplanted to Germany."[358]

While this exaggeration sounds ludicrous, it does contain a grain of truth. Garland E. Allen agrees that Black is "correct that the American and German eugenicists were in close contact with each other, especially after World War I: they were working together in international organizations, following and even reporting on developments in eugenics in each other's countries. The Germans did, in fact, borrow much of their 1933 Law for the Prevention of Hereditarily Defective Offspring (the so-called 'sterilization law') from the model sterilization law drawn up for the various states by Harry H. Laughlin, Superintendent of the ERO [Eugenics Record Office], and a number of American eugenicists were impressed with the Nazi eugenical [sic] laws after 1933."[359] Progressive America, however, the patriotic reader will be pleased to learn, was far behind "Germany [which] had a far more active and virulent pro-Nordic and pro-Aryan tradition than most mainstream American eugenics."[360]

Without doubt. That said, America has much self-searching to do. As Daniel Okrent documents in *The Guarded Gate: Bigotry, Eugenics and the Law That Kept Two Generations of Jews, Italians, and Other European Immigrants Out of America*, the Immigration Act of 1924 reduced the flow of immigrants from the Russian empire from 189,000 in 1921 to a mere 7,300 in 1925. Similarly, around 222,300 Italians entered the U.S. in 1921; by 1925, no more than 2,700.[361] Though no nationalities were singled out in the legislation, everyone knew its intent. Kenneth Roberts of the *Saturday Evening Post,* America's largest and most influential American magazine, spoke for his readers: "If America doesn't keep out the queer, alien, mongrelized people of Southeastern Europe, her crop of citizens will eventually be dwarfed and mongrelized in return."[362] It was an ugly time.

No, blaming America in any way for providing justification to Nazi terror is unwarranted. Yet there is no denying that promoting racial-ethnic self-determination based on racial-ethnic purity provided invaluable support for any identity-group to proceed with whatever type of "cleansing" seemed best for its own vision of "progress," if it presumably enhanced "desirable" traits which putatively "purified" their race.

That an Apocalypse would explode in the very country that had spawned both Hegel and Marx should not surprise. But it came far sooner, and turned out to be immeasurably more horrible, than anyone could ever have imagined.

6:
Heroic Totalitarianism and the Holocaust

Revolutionary Syndicalism

Claiming that fascism would not have been possible without either the French Revolution[363] or the First World War[364] is not to suggest an implacable historical determinism. Trivially true at some level, it does highlight the similarity among varieties of political utopia which has eluded many. A notable exception was Pierre Drieu la Rochelle, who observed in 1939: "[T]he essential traits of Bolshevism, Fascism, and National Socialism all derive from the Jacobin tradition: a ruthless cult of violence, manipulation and mobilization of the masses, with brutal policies, extermination of enemies of the revolution, ideological dictatorship, collectivist economics, war on all fronts, the goal to regenerate the social body through bloody purges and cathartic terror."[365] In a kind of spiritual capitulation, La Rochelle succumbed to fascism during the war. He committed suicide in 1945.

Throughout the world, by the 1930s socialism had evolved. Nationalism had advanced to the ideological forefront among the anti-individualist and anti-capitalist populist groups vying for political power. Detecting a common core to the different anti-liberal European political movements that adopted the "fascist" label in the early twentieth century is thus a major challenge, considering the similarities among otherwise rival neo-Jacobin utopianisms that took root throughout Europe as well as Eurasia. Each claiming to follow a distinct political vision, they deliberately eschewed programmatic consistency for the sake of political expediency. Franz Neumann noted at the time: "National Socialism's ideology is constantly shifting. It has certain magical beliefs – leadership adoration, supremacy of the master race – but [these] are not laid down in a series of categorical and dogmatic pronouncements."[366]

Yet lack of dogmatism does not mean there wasn't a distinct ideological thread, a set of animating principles, shared by the leadership, that underlay the incendiary rhetoric so skillfully wielded to rally mass support. Robert O. Paxton, while not disagreeing with Neumann, contends that at bottom, "fascists knew what they wanted." He suggests defining fascism not only as a political theory but at least as much as a form of "political behavior marked by obsessive preoccupation with community decline, humiliation, or victimhood."[367] Consisting of a "mass-based party of committed nationalist militants," fascism categorically "abandons democratic liberties and pursues with redemptive violence[,] and without ethical or legal restraints[,] goals of internal cleansing and external expansion."[368] He suggests looking at fascist actions to deduce their motivating ideas, instead of the other way around. Though often left unstated, and even unconscious, "mobilizing passions" catapulted megalomaniacal demagogues to power by mobilizing credulous crowds deeply resentful in the aftermath of the 1919 Versailles Treaty. In a rage, Germany flaunted the Treaty and re-armed.

But as often happens with ugly urges that are harnessed to archetypal narratives, visceral resentment was as critical to implementing what George L. Mosse has called "the Fascist revolution" as was military hardware. No less than the French and Russian varieties, the fascist revolution involved "mass mobilization and control and replacing an old with a new elite."[369] While their playbooks were similar, however, each of these movements had its own logic and peculiar utopian leitmotif. The variously pedigreed fascist movements eventually settled on a common theme: a virulent, xenophobic "new nationalism."

The idea was first articulated in France and Italy, though it had gestated for decades inside communities that had long cohabited, if uneasily, within the Hapsburg Empire. Though European ethnic politics are far more diverse than usually assumed,[370] the so-called "new" nationalism proudly proclaimed itself "total." As such, writes Zeeb Sternhell, it claimed "to be a system of ethics, with criteria of behavior dictated by the entire national body, independently of the will of the individual. This new nationalism denied the validity of any absolute and universal moral norms: truth, justice, and law existed only to serve the needs of the collectivity." Sternhell calls this a "truly tribal concept of the nation."[371] Deeming it tribal, however, should obscure neither its fundamentally Marxist origins, nor its universal application.

In a brilliant admixture of Marxism and nationalism, Enrico Corradini (1865-1931) called Italy "a proletarian country" in 1910. Italians, he argued, had to be taught the necessity of international war in the same way that socialism taught workers the principles of class warfare. And "[b]ecause nationalism is by definition national in politics, it cannot fail to be national in the domain of economics, as the two things are interconnected."[372] Observes Sternhell: "In his way, [this] theoretician of

Italian nationalism borrowed the idea of class struggle from Marxism and transposed it onto a higher level, that of war between national groups. The principle remained the same: violence is the motive force of history."[373] An economic system that eschews individual initiative was naturally compatible with a collectivist form of nationalism.

Mosse agrees that the nationalist mystique at the heart of fascism is consistent with a socialist vision. Thus "French socialists of the mid-nineteenth century, and men like Edouard Drumont [founder of the Antisemitic League of France] toward the end of the century, had combined opposition to finance capitalism and the advocacy of greater social equality with an impassioned nationalism."[374]

Among the socialist concepts that evolved from its Marxist context, alongside nationalism, perhaps the most influential was the redefinition of class struggle and its relationship to violence by Corradini's French contemporary, Georges Sorel (1847-1922). In *Reflections on Violence*, published in 1908, Sorel crystallized and clarified the notion of class struggle as the mission of revolutionary trade unions (*sindicats,* in French) through an apocalyptic general strike. It would come to be known as "syndicalism" or, somewhat redundantly, "socialist syndicalism."

He didn't know it then, but Sorel had hit a political homerun. Notoriously poor tacticians, intellectuals often fail to grasp the real-life implications of their words. So too Sorel at first detested his most successful disciple, Lenin. It was not until 1917 that Sorel finally recognized the Russian despot as "the greatest theoretician of socialism since Marx and a statesman whose genius recalls that of Peter the Great."[375] And it was only shortly before his death, in March 1921, that Sorel acknowledged, still grudgingly, that "Mussolini is a man no less extraordinary than Lenin. He, too, is a political genius, of a greater reach than all the statesmen of the day, with the only exception of Lenin."[376] Sorel at last realized that both men, notwithstanding their differences, had adopted his blueprint. They were both devoted to creating a virtuous "new man" devoid of self-interest, and also to violence as the means of energizing the masses to destroy the sclerotic bourgeoisie. Once again, in seeking to understand how socialist utopianism morphed from Marx to Hitler and later, Hugo Chavez and Mahmud Ahmadinejad,[377] the Left-Right dichotomy is practically useless.

Fortunately, history helps throw light on the roots of ideas. "Fascism" (recently degenerated into an all-purpose expletive directed at anyone with the temerity to disagree with the speaker) actually comes from *fasces*, plural *fasci*, an Italian word that, in its sixteenth century Latin version, referred to a bundle of rods. Suggesting strength through unity, *fasci* was first used in Sicily in the late nineteenth century to refer to groups of men organized for political purposes. It was later appropriated by several trade union groups that supported joining the Great War, in opposition to most Italian socialists who preferred neutrality (as had the Bolsheviks in neighboring Russia). At first, the renegade socialists sought to avoid calling themselves a "party," which connoted faction as opposed to common effort and consensus, preferring simply *fascisti.* But symbolism aside, political influence required political action, and patriotic zeal provided a powerful motivator.

Enter political genius Benito Mussolini (1883-1945). Recognizing that fascism had to transition from a mere political association to a modern party, Mussolini finally broke with his fellow socialists, whose neutralism he considered counterproductive, and gathered the three socialist syndicalist leagues into the National Fascist Party. What had changed was not so much ideology as tactics: Italy had to be mobilized whole. Marxism had not been abandoned, merely adapted to evolving circumstances.

The future *Il Duce's* father, a devoted revolutionary blacksmith, had named the boy after the Mexican radical Benito Juarez. The family tradition was proudly maintained as the young Mussolini became a Marxist. He gained status by editing several socialist party journals, including its official publication *Avanti!* (Forward), which underscored his growing influence. But he would soon turn away from the movement's dominant internationalism, shrewdly opting for nationalism. In 1913, he founded a theoretical review aptly, if ironically, called *Utopia,* to give voice to those revolutionary syndicalists who had been ousted by the mainstream socialists. The publication sought to nurture a "genuinely" socialist culture as understood by the syndicalists, based on "reality" rather than wishful-thinking. Most utopians don't believe that's what they are.

Sorel, whom Mussolini had first read in the early 1900s in Switzerland, had made a deep impression on the impressionable young Italian. Sorel too opposes mere "Utopias [which] … direct men's minds toward reforms which can be brought about by patching up the existing system"[378] instead of igniting real revolution. Sorel emphasizes rather the importance of "myths [that] lead men to prepare themselves for a combat which will destroy the existing state of things"[379] – which is to say, Apocalypse. What is more, "a myth cannot be refuted, since it is, at bottom, identical with the convictions of a group, being the expression of these convictions in the language of the moment."[380] It is utopia by another name - genuine and permanent, rather than ephemeral, ersatz utopia. And convictions cannot be refuted because they are not rational.

The conviction of a group is irrefutable insofar as it carries its own truth and justification: "People who are living in this world 'of myths' are secure from all refutation; this has led many to assert that Socialism is a kind of religion."[381] Sorel does not deny it, noting however that "it is not only religion which occupies the profounder region of our mental life; revolutionary myths have their place there equally with religion."[382] To prompt revolutionary change, myths need to be associated with apocalyptic violence, best justified in a religious context. Sorel credits the revolutionary anarchists of his day with having "taught the workers that they need not be ashamed of acts of violence" since they are simply "normal manifestations of the struggle."[383] A faux-utopia, by contrast, directs people toward reform, while "our present myths lead people to prepare themselves for a battle to destroy what exists." They enable the committed, revolutionary vanguard "to explore with profit the whole vast domain of Marxism"[384] - a myth-maker's goldmine. It's a different sort of profit, though in many ways more lucrative.

"Revolutionary syndicalism," gushes Sorel, "might be compared to the Reformation, which wished to prevent Christianity submitting to the influence of the humanists."[385] His understanding of the role played by the imagination and "the psychology of the deeper life" is undoubtedly a major reason for his influence on Mussolini, who grasped the political potency of this insight and, above all, had the acumen to implement it. Having rejected a mechanistic conception of man, Sorel notes the role of emotion in fueling radical action, telling his fellow socialists: "[We must] see ourselves as creating an imaginary world placed ahead of the present world and composed of movements which depend entirely on us."[386] That imaginary world, in turn, consists of what he calls "myths" – specifically, "social myths." Hardly mere descriptions of supranatural events, like cavorting Greek gods, such myths are "expressions of a determination to act" which capture the strongest inclinations of a group of people, a nation, or a class. This was Sorel's most significant contribution to the evolution of Marxism in a fascist direction.

As A. James Gregor points out, Sorel's idea of social myths as "imagined futures," which lent moral dimension to group conflicts, was music to the ears of Italian syndicalists, for "in his work they found all the themes that were to shape their discussion for the next decade." Sternhell also observes that there was a remarkable continuity between their ideas and those of Mussolini in his journal *Utopia*.[387] This new, "mythical conception of politics, or rather this faith in the power of myth as the motive force of history, is the key to the Fascist view of the world."[388]

Notwithstanding Mussolini's eventual break with the syndicalists,[389] he was surely Sorel's most important disciple.[390] For despite a life-long hostility to organized religion,[391] *Il Duce* appreciated the spiritual dimension of all ideology and understood the need for a political religion. As defined by the historian Emilio Gentile, the political variety is "a type of religion which sacralises an ideology, a movement, or a political regime, through the deification of a secular entity transfigured into myth, considering it the primary and indisputable source of the meaning and the ultimate aim of human existence on earth."[392] Fascism, which considered the State to be the source of all meaning, was precisely such a sacralized movement. Understood as an extreme form of civil religion, political religion is all-encompassing: it "denies the autonomy of the individual while affirming the primacy of the community; it sanctifies violence as a legitimate weapon in the struggle against those it considers internal and external enemies; it imposes obligatory observance of its commandments" - in short, it is unequivocally totalitarian.

In its notion of the "conquest of society," which Gentile defines as "an anthropological revolution, the production of a new type of human being" is eerily reminiscent of Marx's projected emergence of the "species-being" – the post-historic Frankenstein. Like Sorel, Gentile describes the fascist vision of the "new State" as a new version of a familiar quasi-religious mythology:

> Fascism defined this myth in terms of a new plan: absolute political supremacy, foreshadowed by the practical experience of the local power groups formed by the fascist squads (*squadrismo*). The organisation [sic] of the armed party (*partito milizia*) was the fundamental structure for the new fascist State.... The mixture of politics and religion, the concept of politics as a lay religious experience, was not a fascist invention, but belongs to the history of nationalism after the French Revolution. The lay religion was, nevertheless, an integral factor in fascism [sic] mass politics.[393]

In effect, the difference between fascism and Communism lay in the substitution of the nation, or nation-state, for class. In its struggle with evil, the unitary nation-state had to be monolithic, and committed to fighting enemies both within and without: *without* were its international opponents, as during the Great War; *within* referred to everyone who did not follow the national leader who single-handedly embodied the spirit of the nation. The utopia they envisaged was naturally a kind of Eden. That very image was used, in fact, by journalists at the time. Writes Charles Burdett:

> In the reported visits to the new towns, one metaphor in particular predominated, that of the discovery of a new land: all observers marveled at how it had taken only a few years for a thriving centre to emerge from a wasteland. In this kind of reporting, the biblical myth of Genesis was replaced by the journey to a Fascist paradise. Littoria was a new Eden, brought into being by the will of the all-powerful Duce, it was a place where every aspect of the life of its inhabitants was rigorously ordered.[394]

The yearning for a quasi-historical Golden Age endowed with mythical qualities is a common feature of nationalism, both old and new. Italian fascism turned it into an engine for future economic and military greatness. Religious overtones allowed it to create an amalgam of pseudo-Christianity and pagan historicism, which the public embraced with alacrity. Burdett continues:

> The success of Fascism in extending the boundaries of the modern state was achieved not only through coercion, but through its ability to encourage mass consensus by propagating a vision of society and history that whole swathes of the Italian public were prepared to appropriate and adapt... At the core of this religious system was the cult of the nation, understood as a sacred community awoken from centuries of decadence first by participation in the First World War ("the Great War") and subsequently the March on Rome. Beyond that lay the veneration for the greatness of the Roman empire, the mystique of leadership, the militarization of the everyday and the celebration of collective action and obedience. This "sacralization" of the nation had a long pre-history, but in an Italian context it was Fascism that took this intellectual or spiritual process to its logical extreme.[395]

Mussolini thought of fascism as transformative, purifying, sanctifying. In a 1926 speech, he boasted that "it is Fascism which has refashioned the character of the Italians, removing impurity from our souls, tempering us to all sacrifices, restoring the true aspect of strength and beauty to our Italian faces."[396] He also grasped that it would take an apocalyptic event such as the Great War for the transformation to occur. As he wrote in 1930: "The war was revolutionary, in the sense that with streams of blood it did away with the century of Democracy, the century of number, the century of majorities and quantities."[397]

The new, lower-case democracy of the fascist State was not about majorities, nor factions, it was transcendent. "Fascism has restored to the State its sovereign functions by claiming its absolute ethical meaning, against the egotism of classes and categories," *Il Duce* told the council of state in December 1928. "It has rescued State administration from the weight of factions and party interests."[398] Fascism was a creed, a faith. As he wrote in the Milanese journal *Diuturna* in 1930, "if Fascism were not a creed, how could it endow its followers with courage and stoicism? Only a creed which has soared to the heights of religion can inspire...." At which point, the consummate secular messiah invokes a Christ-like figure: a recently fallen fellow-revolutionary, hailed as a martyr to the cause.[399] A Verdi requiem would complete the spectacle.

Fully grasping the religious aspect of fascism, the anti-religious, if not atheist, Mussolini does not hesitate invoking God. But in deference to his fellow socialists, he adroitly fudges the allusion: "By saying that God is returning, we mean that spiritual values are returning."[400] Returning, of course, is not to be taken literally; a true radical, he categorically rejects the idea that the Fascist State is reactionary, backward-looking. The past is obviously gone; the return is to be achieved through a rebirth, through revolution. He elaborates:

> If liberalism spells individualism, Fascism spells government. The Fascist State is, however, a unique and original creation. It is not reactionary but revolutionary, for it anticipates the solution of certain universal problems which have been raised elsewhere, in the political field by the splitting up of parties, the usurpation of power by parliaments, the irresponsibility of assemblies; in the economic field by the increasingly numerous and important functions discharged by trade unions and trade associations with their disputes and ententes, affecting both capital and labor; in the ethical field by the need felt for order, discipline, obedience to the moral dictates of patriotism.[401]

Mussolini also does not hesitate to claim, coining a cacophonic word in the process, that "a party governing a nation 'totalitarianly' is a new departure in history" – which indeed it was, although Lenin's Russia had already had a head start, and Nazi Germany was fast catching up. He goes on to boast: "[T]he Fascist conception of the State is all embracing; outside of it no human or spiritual values can exist, much less have value. Thus understood, Fascism is totalitarian, and the Fascist State - a synthesis and a unit inclusive of all values - interprets, develops, and potentates the whole life of a people."[402] Though originally coined by an anti-fascist journalist named Giovanni Amendola, in 1923, "totalitarian" had yet to acquire its pejorative connotation.

The new ideology was nothing if not heroic, utterly selfless: "Fascism believes now and always in sanctity and heroism, that is to say in acts in which no economic motive - remote or immediate - is at work."[403] However un-Marxist in some other respects, Mussolini's intent is to obliterate all egoism, synonymous with those ugly "economic motives" which define capitalism. The fascist new man resembles his Communist brother in that both repudiate *homo sapiens* as we know him. *Homo sovieticus* seems little more than a Russian-speaking *homo fascistus.*

But what about the final triumph of peace that is usually associated with post-apocalyptic Christian millennial eschatology? Fascism extols not peace but war, glorious war: "War alone keys up all human energies to their maximum tension and sets the seal of nobility on those peoples who have the courage to face it.... All other tests are substitutes which never place a man face to face with himself before the alternative of life or death. Therefore, all doctrines which postulate peace at all costs are incompatible with Fascism."[404] But the fascists did not wish to fight forever – they wanted to win wars and implement their vision of utopia. War was only a means to a much loftier end. What they opposed is the faux-peace of defeat and subordination.

Mussolini explains that the utopian myth of fascism conceives "of life as a struggle in which it behooves a man to win for himself a really worthy place," a place winnable by courage and faith to the nation. It is indeed that peace, and not eternal struggle, that represents the real victory of fascism. But man must be willing to engage in such a struggle – "first of all by fitting himself (physically, morally, intellectually) to become the implement required for winning it. As for the individual, so for the nation, and so for mankind." Nor is it only a few individuals, the professional soldiers, but the entire society who must do so - that is why fascism places such "high value of culture in all its forms (artistic, religious, scientific) and the outstanding importance of education. Hence also the essential value of work, by which man subjugates nature and creates the human world (economic, political, ethical, and intellectual)."[405]

Mussolini's – and all his fellow fascists' - first priority was Armageddon, the classic prerequisite for national rebirth. It was how they planned to achieve political power, what their rhetoric addressed above all. Their political religion provided the leitmotif for the unison chant of a cleansed, reborn monolithic perfect society.

The myth of a national rebirth through revolution, writes Gentile, "which already contains a religious matrix and is deeply imbued with religious meaning, contributes by conferring upon fascism the characteristics typical of a political religion with a strong and markedly modern messianic (but not necessarily millenarian) component, because it derives, not from the revival of pre-modern traditions, but from an apocalyptic interpretation of modernity assigning the mission of regeneration to politics."[406] He deems it "not necessarily millenarian" because it does not appeal to pre-modern traditions; but he is wrong. Mussolini's architectural revival of Roman antiquity would find an echo in Hitler's Arian pseudo-prehistory, myth and utopia subliminally intertwined.

Burdett agrees that Mussolini's ideology is a form of utopianism:

The concept of utopia does not simply link Fascism, as a political movement, with the ideological core of an established religion like Roman Catholicism. Initially within the movement itself and subsequently within the propaganda sponsored by the state, the notion of an ideal society served important mobilizing and anticipatory functions. By presenting Fascism as the path towards military might, empire, order and prosperity, Mussolini could allow his followers to enjoy the dream of a magnificent future while enlisting their active support in the creation of that future. The myth of a new beginning for the Italian civilization could be enjoyed as a fantastic projection, while working in the Sorelian sense of an impulse towards radical change.[407]

Mussolini's imminent ignominious demise, along with his unpopular (though, to be fair, reluctant) alliance with Hitler, deflated the appeal of his ideology among his countrymen. But not before it had spread beyond Italy's borders, with predictably disastrous consequences. His

Teutonic rival, the Nazi messiah, would take the next step, unleashing an Apocalypse of truly biblical proportions.

The Führer as Messiah

Like Italian fascism, national socialism did not emerge *ex nihilo*. It took the mad genius of Adolph Hitler (1889-1945) to transform the fetid cauldron of resentment that pervaded the German-speaking world[408] into a vile rhetoric capable of mobilizing mass support for his dream of Aryan supremacy destined to save the world. Like Mussolini, Hitler and his followers used the vocabulary of blood and soil filled with Christian liturgical references, like "martyrdom" and "incarnation." George L. Mosse notes that "historians have recently found that in the past, millenarianism was not simply a protest by the poor against the rich, but a belief shared by most classes."[409] The same was true of interwar Germany, as it had been of Italy.

A cross-national, inclusive appeal was even more politically and ideologically central to the way Hitler described the nature of the fascist struggle than it had been to *Il Duce*. Hitler grasped the potency of the pent-up fury following the Paris armistice which ended the Great War. It raged throughout Germany, notably but by no means exclusively among the workers. Clever electoral maneuvers, ruthless tactics, including lying with a straight face, and a bit of luck, all eventually helped to catapult the Nazi party to power. Writes Mosse:

> [T]he fascist revolution built upon a deep bedrock of popular piety and, especially in Germany, upon a   millenarianism that was apt to come to the fore in times of crisis.... The myths and symbols of nationalism were superimposed upon those of Christianity – not only in the rhythms of public rites and ceremonies (even the Duce's famed dialogues with the masses from his balcony are related to Christian "responses") - but also in the appeal to apocalyptic and millenarian thought.[410]

By no means was pragmatism incompatible with a quasi-religious fervor, the most potent of political instruments, as Sorel had famously noted. Indeed, Nazism was defined as "a religion in the most mystic and profound sense of the word" by none other than Hitler's right-hand man, Joseph Goebbels. Adriano Tilgher also observed, in 1935, that Nazism "presents itself as a religion, which in fact it is, since Race is for it not a scientific concept, not a philosophical abstraction, but an experience lived out on the level of religious adoration."[411] The object of adoration was the Führer and the State, which he was able to control completely.

The Apocalyptic narrative provided the perfect vision for the times. Hitler's great accomplishment was to identify the Antichrist. Based in part on Hitler's own pathology, the ultimate justification for unprovoked war and the torture of innocent victims was based on neither evidence nor logic but on visceral, murderous, racist hatred. Serving as the satanic glue of German unity, even as it nearly erased, with astounding efficacy, centuries of that nation's civilizational advances, that hatred could be none other than antisemitism.

Its origins are ancient. The "lethal obsession," as Wistrich called it, first appeared in the Hellenistic world in the fourth century BCE, when Jews represented more than ten percent of that society, the first pogrom having been recorded in Alexandria as early as the first century.[412] But outright "demonization as distinct from common or garden-variety prejudice or hostility, began with the advent of Christianity and the special role assigned to the Jews in the crucifixion of Christ as related in the Gospels,"[413] writes Bernard Lewis. After the twelfth century, Jews in medieval Christian Europe were increasingly being accused of ritualistic murder, until they "gradually metamorphosed into a *demonic abstraction* more real than any of its individual components."[414] Gavin Langmuir describes the medieval view of Jews as "fantasies, figments of the imagination.... [in effect,] projections of mental processes unconnected with the real people of the outgroup."[415]

Wistrich finds "echoes of such medieval delusions... in Nazi antisemitism." He writes: "Hitler's boundless Jew hatred represented an apocalyptic convergence of anti-Judaism with anti-Christian *Volkisch* (ethnic-racist) nationalism."[416] Citing Hermann Rauschning's record of his conversations with his friend the Führer, Wistrich notes that "Hitler raised antisemitism to a new level of either-or totalitarian politics. The war against the Jews now became an existential issue of 'victory or downfall' (*Sieg oder Untergang*), a vengeful, apocalyptic reckoning to determine the future of civilization. It was a bellicose call to the Last Judgment.[417] ... [Thus] by physically destroying the 'satanic Jews,' the road would finally be paved for the liberation of mankind."[418] According to a 1936 SS indoctrination leaflet, "the Jew is the main obstacle for the fulfillment [*Vollendung*] of our global and historical mission."[419] The Antichrist thus identified, the self-anointed messiah barked at the blood-smelling audience, hypnotizing it into a trance.

Antisemitism was the perfect unifier, as it cut across factions that were otherwise disparate, if not diametrically opposed. Under its umbrella, bigoted reactionaries made common cause with self-styled rationalists. Scapegoating can cross national, religious, and philosophical boundaries with remarkable ease. Notwithstanding their general antipathy to Christianity, philosophers of the French Enlightenment adopted the age-old accusation of usury hurled by Christians against Jews. In addition to the notorious Voltaire, the literature of the Enlightenment is replete with references to Jews as avaricious usurers and economic parasites.[420] But it was not until the nineteenth century that anti-judaism based on the practice of usury, notably egoism and the love of money, became fully weaponized.

Even before Karl Marx, Friedrich Engels had spelled out the notion of selfishness as the organizing principle of capitalism in his 1844 essay, "Outlines of a Critique of Political Economy." "Political economy," writes Engels, "came into being as a natural result of the expansion of trade, and with its appearance elementary, unscientific huckstering was replaced by a developed system of licensed fraud, an entire science of enrichment. This political economy or science of enrichment born of the merchants' mutual envy and greed, bears on its brow the mark of the most detestable selfishness."[421] As Jerry Muller points out, Engels condemned trade primarily for the impurity of motivation that lay behind it. According to Engels, morality - *by definition* - could not be based on self-interest.[422] Never mind that later "materialist dialectic" abolished such idealist, subjective concepts as motivation; Marx also said that the point of philosophy is not to interpret the world but to change it,[423] which implies volition. Contradictory? Sure. But whatever works.

Though every significant ideology of the nineteenth century had its own brand of antisemitism,[424] concern with the status of Jews had become a virtual obsession among German political writers of the time, both Jewish and non-Jewish. According to one estimate, some 2,500 works were published on this topic in Germany between 1815 and 1850 alone.[425] Bruno Bauer, for instance, characterized Judaism as a religion of egoism; but Marx objected that he wasn't radical enough. Writes Mueller: not only does Marx embrace "all of the traditional negative characterization of the Jew repeated by Bauer, and for good measure adds a few of his own" – indeed, "he does so in order to stigmatize market activity as such." All self-interest must be eliminated, come what may.

The Jew as capitalist was the perfect satanic scapegoat at a time when massive technological changes were causing social, political, and economic dislocations throughout the world, especially but by no means exclusively in Europe. The German-born historian and Holocaust survivor Walter Zwi Bacharach notes that the so-called Jewish question

> was a modern phenomenon that became widespread after the 1842 publication of Bruno Bauer's brochure *Die Judenfrage*. It was no longer attributed to a particular nation or state but now reflected a world problem, as Alex Bein has postulated in *Die Judenfrage: Biographie eines Weltproblems*. Antisemitism and the *Judenfrage* became one in modern times. Antisemitism underwent a process of universalization.[426]

In sum, the Jew, who already for centuries had been turned into an abstraction concocted from falsehoods, inchoate fears, and prejudice,[427] was being irrevocably depersonalized, de-humanized. Solving the Jewish question at first sounded like a puzzle, not a call for genocide. But the formulation was deceptive, and Hitler saw its vast lethal potential in a flash. Despite constant rantings against Communism, Hitler himself acknowledges in *Mein Kampf* his profound debt on this topic to Karl Marx.

In his largely incoherent but revealing tome, Hitler writes that he had originally started to gather information about Marxism "with a view to studying the principles of the movement. The fact that I attained my object sooner than I could have anticipated was due to the deeper insight into the Jewish question which I then gained, my knowledge of this question being hitherto rather superficial."[428] Hitler thereby discloses that understanding the Jewish question provided the key to those principles.

He continues by lavishing high praise on Marx's ability to diagnose the cause of the current malaise: "In reality what distinguished Karl Marx from the millions who were affected in the same way was that, in a world already in a state of gradual decomposition, he used his keen powers of prognosis to detect the essential poisons, so as to extract them and concentrate them,"[429] and then proceed, with the sly dissembling to be expected from a filthy Jew, to recommend, "with the art of a necromancer,... a solution which would bring about the rapid destruction of the independent nations on the globe,"[430] namely, the proletarian revolution. But Hitler wasn't going to be fooled – he knew how to distinguish between diagnosis and treatment. Immensely satisfied with his own acuity, Hitler then makes an extraordinary confession: "This knowledge was the occasion of the greatest inner revolution that I had yet experienced. From being a soft-hearted cosmopolitan, I became an out-and-out anti-Semite."[431]

Imagining Hitler to be "soft-hearted" about anything connected to Jews strains credulity to the breaking point, as is the claim that he was impressed by a philosophical insight. What he unquestionably *did* recognize was the extraordinary power of antisemitism as a myth in the Sorelian sense of the word. Hitler's political shrewdness is clearly revealed in this passage about the French and Russian revolutions:

> It is out of the question to think that the French Revolution could have been carried into effect by philosophizing theories if they had not found an army of agitators led by demagogues of the grand style. These demagogues inflamed popular passion that had been already aroused, until that volcanic eruption finally broke out and convulsed the whole of Europe. And the same happened in the case of the gigantic Bolshevik revolution which recently took place in Russia. It was not due to the writers on Lenin's side but to the oratorical activities of those who preached the doctrine of hatred and that of the innumerable small and great orators who took part in the agitation. The masses of illiterate Russians were not fired to Communist revolutionary enthusiasm by reading the theories of Karl Marx but by the promises of paradise made to the people by thousands of agitators in the service of an idea. It was always so, and it will always be so.[432]

No ordinary political windbag, Hitler does not shirk from describing himself as the savior of mankind: "[T]oday, I believe that I am acting in accordance with the will of the Almighty Creator: by defending myself against the Jew, I am fighting for the work of the Lord." The war against the Jews is a holy war of self-defense. Eberhard Jackel thus credits Hitler with adding to traditional antisemitism "a new universal-missionary element," which became central to his foreign policy.[433] Considering the enormity of the Apocalypse he was about to unleash upon the world, nothing less than self-divinization would suffice. He may also have believed it.

"International Jewish domination [was] substituted for religious Messianism,"[434] observes Bachrach. Hitler's racist ideas were welcomed by German academics with shameful and unworthy enthusiasm. The first Nazi rector of the University of Berlin, Eugen Fischer, for example, proclaimed that the Führer, "for the first time in the history of mankind, translated the recognition of the biological foundation of a race-nation, heredity, and natural selection into deeds.... German science placed the tools in the politician's hands."[435]

From a witches' brew that consisted of Marxist anti-capitalist determinism, the pseudo-scientific racism of the academics, the romantic ideal of the Volk, and the Christian dream of mankind's redemption from the satanic Jew, antisemitism provided Hitler with the perfect narrative to mobilize his various constituents. None of these components taken alone provided quite sufficient justification for genocide – nor, indeed, did they all taken together. Admittedly, Hitler needed no excuses; like all would-be messiahs, he considered himself the very embodiment of morality. But he did grasp the power of the Volkish vision to mobilize the masses.

George Mosse defined *Volk* as "the union of a group of people with a transcendental 'essence' ... [which] might be called 'nature' or 'cosmos' or 'mythos' but in each instance it was fused to man's innermost nature."[436] That essence, for the Nazis, was what Hitler called Aryan nationalism, which allowed him to seamlessly gloss over from a geographically confined ethnicity to a transnational, potentially universal, racial identity. Clearly utopian and quasi-religious, a "Germanic faith," the Volkish movement had not been antisemitic from the outset.

Its first prophet, the German orientalist Paul Bottischer, better known as Paul de Lagarde (1827-1891), believed that history was the expression of a religious spirit that could be manifested not through the individual but a community, or *Volk*. Of all the *Volks* in the world, argued Lagarde, the German was "endowed with a particular vital spiritual revelation" capable of culminating in the unity of the nation, which would come about as a result of "the concrete expression of the common spiritual, emotional, and mystical qualities of the German people."[437]

And where did Lagarde find inspiration? Naturally, the mythical past. "Oh, what a delightful time the Middle Ages were," he mused nostalgic. Explains Mosse: "the Volkish thinkers tended to contrast the idyllic medieval Volk with the actual modern present.... [a process of thought that] answered the problem of alienation from society [characteristic of modernity] by positing a suprasocial unity to which it was vital to belong."[438] But it did not take long for this utopian longing to became murderous.

Lagarde tended to use "nation" and Volk more or less interchangeably, though he did distinguish between nation and state. Once the latter was suitably upgraded from a mere political concept to include the spiritual elements of the Volk, it could more easily inspire social upheaval. "As in revolution, so here: the license to use physical force was determined solely by the needs of the Volkish movement. According to Lagarde," writes Mosse, "man was a creature of the will. And once that will was revitalized through the religious inspiration of the Volkish soul, it would ruthlessly seek out victory." The enemy was evil modernity which, in turn, "was epitomized by the Jews." [439]

Late in his life, Lagarde added one more crucial element to his antisemitism by calling for the extermination of the Jews who were "like bacilli."[440] His direct appeals to violence against Jews became more vocal and common, until finally demanding, after 1918, to settle the "Jewish question" once and for all. It had been this accelerated frenzy that, according to Mosse, more than anything else, "contributed to the shaping of a state of mind that either apathetically acquiesced in or actively supported the final verdict."[441]

But "it was the genius of Adolph Hitler to wed the Volkish flight from reality to political discipline and efficient political organization."[442] All he needed was Karl Marx's verdict that "in the final analysis, the *emancipation of the Jews* is the emancipation of mankind from *Judaism*. [For]… emancipation from *huckstering* and *money*, consequently from practical, real Judaism, would be the self-emancipation of our time."[443] The words were custom-made for the Führer. The notion of a Jew-less utopia as millenarian salvation was to be the Nazis' satanic bequest to the world. The Holocaust sought to obliterate all traces of the Hebrew civilization by systematic murder. That it came so close to succeeding must never be forgotten.

Racist Socialism and the Cult of Nature

Small wonder that "Nazi" would soon be synonymous with evil incarnate, beside its near-equivalent "fascism." That both would later come to be identified with capitalism cannot have been due to Hitler's opposition to Bolshevism alone, especially as the USSR had signed a pact with Nazi Germany in 1939. (When Hitler broke it, Stalin was reportedly first unbelieving, then devastated.) It is a tribute to the effectiveness of Soviet and more broadly, Marxist, historiography and propaganda, including its Western enablers, that few students learn about that episode. Instead, the conflation of fascism/Nazism with capitalism "underlies all Marxist interpretations of fascism," as Pellicani points out. After all, the ghoulish horror elicited by the skeletons rescued from extermination camps, the gas chambers, had been too enormous, too universal, not to appropriate and turn into shameless propaganda against the system of natural liberty. A narrative was duly manufactured, the Lie sufficiently Big and audacious to work wonders.

The version of that narrative, articulated by the German-born Jewish philosopher Herbert Marcuse as early as 1934, goes as follows: "[I]t is liberalism itself that generates the totalitarian and authoritarian state, which is the perfection of the liberal state in an advanced stage of its development." He cites no statistics or any other kind of evidence, merely asserting as self-evident the existence of a historically predetermined "line of development that marks the transition from the commercial and industrial society, based on the free competition between autonomous individual entrepreneurs, to the modern monopolistic state, in which changed productive relations demand a strong state equipped with all the instruments of power."[444] In brief, capitalism evolves into totalitarianism, *a.k.a.*, fascism. The line from Adam Smith to Adolf Eichmann is straight.

Straight nonsense, however ubiquitous. As Austrian economist Ludwig von Misses (1881-1973) observed in 1944: "In this age of fanatical anticapitalism and enthusiastic support of socialism, no reproach seems to discredit a government more thoroughly in the eyes of fashionable opinion than the qualification pro-capitalistic. But this is one charge against the Nazis that is unfounded. [The Nazis']... *Zwangswirtschaft* [totally controlled economy] is a socialist system of all-round government control of business."[445] Describing the policies of Hitler's regime at the time, Mises readily concedes: "It is true that there are still profits in Germany. Some enterprises even make much higher profits than in the last years of the Weimar regime." But that doesn't make it capitalist. For there is more to the story: In the first place, "[t]here is strict control of private spending. No German capitalist or entrepreneur (shop manager) or anyone else is free to spend money on his consumption than the government considers adequate to his rank and position in the service of the nation. .... Nobody is free to buy more food and clothing than the allotted ration. Rents are frozen; furniture and all other goods are unattainable."[446]

Hitler's notion of the state bore no resemblance to its liberal republican and democratic counterpart: the "modern state, both secular and liberal," was the enemy. "[B]oth Fascism and Nazism opposed [it] with all their energies," writes Pellicani; "they fought [it] with a program of revolutionary transformation whose aim was to abolish 'any distinction between the individual and the state' on the assumption that 'the will of the state was a divine will.'"[447] The dynamic of fascism and Nazism, "like Bolshevism, posited a total solution to the problems of the modern state, a mythic, fanatical and deeply un-capitalist diagnosis which identified as the premise to a healthy society the purging of 'decadent', 'parasitic' elements, no matter how differently these were conceived."[448] Despite receiving hefty financial contributions from wealthy businessmen who imagined Hitler to be sympathetic to their interests, the Führer had no more use for the free market than did his Communist foe - if sometime ally - to the east.

The notion that German capitalists had "hoisted Hitler into power," that his regime "ruled Germany in the name and for the benefit of big business interests," and facilitated "the robber wars of German imperialism,"[449] has been convincingly refuted in the copiously researched study of Nazi economics by Avraham Barkai. Nazism deified the state – the very opposite of Adam Smith.

> Ideologically, [the Nazi] system proclaimed the rejection of liberalism, that is, free competition and regulation of the economy by market mechanisms; these were to be replaced by the dictum of state supremacy and the state's duty to intervene in all spheres of life, including the economy.[450]

Germany's economic crisis played a major role in Hitler's rise, and the drastic reduction of unemployment during the four years prior to his becoming Chancellor strengthened the Nazi party. This had been partly the result of massive deficit spending, as well as colossal preparations for war; but it was all in the service of establishing a "new order." In the end, concludes Barkai, "it can be stated with certainty that a continuation of the economic system introduced by the Nazis would have been possible only under a permanent and increasingly severe dictatorship."[451]

However erratic, there was indeed a Nazi economic system. Though Hitler famously said different things to different groups, one of the clearest articulations of his own economic views dates from August 1920. Speaking to an assembly of the National Socialist German Workers Party, Hitler describes "[s]ocialism as the final concept of duty, the ethical duty of work, not just for oneself but also for one's fellow man's sake, and above all the principle: Common good before own good, a struggle against all parasitism and especially against easy and unearned income. And we were aware that in this fight we can rely on no one but our own people."[452] He means Germans, or more precisely, Aryans, who for him embody the very ethos of socialism: "Aryanism means ethical perception of work and that which we today so often hear – socialism, community spirit, common good before own good."

By contrast, "Jewry means egoistic attitude to work and thereby mammonism and materialism, the opposite of socialism." Like Marx, Hitler took Judaism to mean the worship of money, or mammonism – i.e., capitalism. This made antisemitism a logical extension of socialism: "How can you not be an antisemite, being a socialist!" hollered Hitler – to whom the audience is recorded to have responded: "Hear, hear!"[453]

Economics, politics, and culture were all intertwined in his eyes. "We are convinced that socialism in the right sense will only be possible in nations and races that are Aryan, and there in the first place we hope for our own people and are convinced that socialism is inseparable from nationalism."[454] In this, Hitler showed considerably more acumen than did the Bolsheviks. A decade later, he would tell Otto Wagener what was "the problem we have set out to solve: to convert the German Volk to socialism without simply killing off the old individualists, without destruction of property and values, without extermination of culture and morality and the ethics that distinguish us Europeans from Asians or from other races."[455]

In other words, he did not want to destroy incentive but tried to use its fruits, controlling the economy instead of gutting it completely, as had happened in the USSR. He did, however, fully endorse the Russians' liquidation policy against undesirable human specimens: "It's understandable why bolshevism simply removed such creatures. They were worthless to humanity, nothing but an encumbrance to their Volk."[456] An even worse mistake, in his mind, was the failure to kill all the Jews. "There comes a time when it will be obvious that socialism can only be carried out accompanied by nationalism and antisemitism. The three concepts are inseparably connected. They are the foundations of our program and therefore we call ourselves National Socialists."[457] Eventually, Stalin came around to Hitler's views. His death alone saved Soviet Jews from potential annihilation.

Whatever else they may have differed about, hatred of both capitalism and of Jews was the one thing all Nazis had in common. Writes Theodor Heuss, the first President of West Germany after the war: "If you are looking for a common denominator in the mentality of the social groups and individuals who join Hitler's party, it can be said that they are linked by an anti-capitalist mentality.'"[458]

How so many ordinary Germans could have been seduced by Hitler's uncanny, demonic charisma and seized with a passion of pathological proportions will never be fully understood. But the millenarian narrative surely contributed to mesmerizing them. Writes

Austrian psychologist Wilhelm Reich in *The Mass Psychology of Fascism* (1933):

> The "salvation of the nation" by an omnipotent, God-sent Führer corresponded exactly to the longing of the masses for salvation. Incapable of thinking of themselves differently, the enslaved masses avidly absorbed the theory of the unalterable nature of man, of the "natural division of humanity into the few who lead and the many who are led," for now the responsibility was in the hands of a strong man. This Führer ideology, whether met with in fascism or anywhere else, is based on the mystic hereditarian concept of the unalterable nature of man and on the helplessness, craving for authority, and incapacity for freedom of the masses. [459]

Not that the God-sent Führer cared about the masses' salvation, or anyone else's but his own.

Michael Burleigh, summarizes perfectly the ignominious legacy of "this tawdry Nazi anti-civilization [which] left nothing of any worth behind, except perhaps its contemporary function as a secular synonym for human evil.... Nazism was literally 'from nothing to nothing,' with its powerful imaginative afterlife curiously disembodied from its pitiful achievements. Rarely can an empire have existed about which nothing positive could be said...."[460] Except, perhaps, that it painted an uncommonly vivid picture of Evil incarnate that we ignore, misunderstand, or misrepresent at our peril.

7:
The Protocols of Jihadism

The Oldest Obsession Refurbished

If only antisemitism were a problem just for Jews; but it's not, warn Dennis Prager and Joseph Telushkin: "Non-Jews make a most self-destructive error when they dismiss it as only the Jews' problem." The reason is simple enough: "[T]reatment of the Jews has served as one of humanity's moral barometers. Watch how a nation, religion, or political movement treats Jews, and you have an early and deadly accurate picture of that group's intention toward others."[461] As the saying goes: "First they came for the Jews, and I said nothing. Then they came for the [fill in the blank] and I said nothing. Finally, they came for me." Whoever you might be. The Antichrist has many faces.

If not the sentiment, the word itself, "antisemitism," is recent, having been coined by Wilhelm Marr (1819–1904),[462] founder of the Anti-Semites League, for the express purpose of differentiating hatred of Jews based on racist political ideology, as distinct from other forms of anti-Judaism. In his 1879 rant *Victory of Jewry over Germandom*, Marr denounced the Jews' "eighteen-hundred-year war" as a racial conspiracy. (Never mind that "Germandom" itself did not identify as such until the end of the 12th century, but who's counting.) Theodor Fritsch (1852-1933) took up the job of conspiracy-mongering where Marr left off. In 1885, he started a discussion forum called "Antisemitic Correspondence," followed eight years later by the *Handbook of the Jewish Question*, also known as *The Anti-Semitic Catechism,* which rose to become a bestseller.

But Fritsch definitively earned a place of prominence in the Genocide Hall of Infamy through his translation of the scurrilous *Protocols of the Elders of Zion* into German in 1920. Purportedly the "minutes" of a secret speech (in some versions, preposterously attributed to Theodore Herzl, the father of Zionism) before the Elders, or Sages, of Zion, the document purports to reveal a two-millennia-old conspiracy, directed by a cabal of (anonymous) bloodthirsty Jews, who by the way already run the world, on the cusp of imminent total victory. The image of the Jew who emerges from this travesty embodies the Antichrist.[463]

The *Protocols* was recently revealed to have been most likely written by the main perpetrator of the notorious Kishinev pogrom of 1903, Pavel Krushevan, possibly together with his equally antisemitic friend G. Butmi.[464] Krushevan was the first to publish it that year, followed by Butmi in 1906; then the two men disappeared in the fog of history. Not so their forgery, which became the most widely quoted antisemitic text of all time.

Its propaganda-value did not escape the notorious Okhrana, the tsarist secret police also known as the "guard department." Though it proved too crude and shoddy[465] for Tsar Nicholas II, who reportedly said that "it is impossible to defend something sacred [Imperial Russia] by dirty methods,"[466] his scruples were not widely shared, and the nefarious document soon got out. The *Protocols* was going to be used, permission be damned. The Tsar had been half right: in little over a decade, Imperial Russia was gone, dirty methods having failed to save his reign. But he was wrong to disparage dirty methods: they could work wonders.

Then the whole damn broke. The end of the Great War, along with the Bolshevik Revolution, transformed Europe. Conspiracies offered ready answers, hatred lubricated the ubiquitous despair, and Jews resumed once again their star role as go-to scapegoats. In a few years, publications of the *Protocols* appeared in all the major languages. Though widely exposed as a forgery and a hoax by Phillip Graves in a series of articles published by the London *Times* in 1921,[467] it continues to be read - and believed - throughout the world.

But nowhere did it resonate more profoundly than in Germany, which had long perpetrated its calumnies as fact. Writes Nora Levin:

> Despite conclusive proof that the *Protocols* were a gross forgery, they had sensational popularity and large sales in the 1920s and 1930s. They were translated into every language of Europe and sold widely in Arab lands, the US, and England. But it was in Germany after World War I that they had their greatest success. There they were used to explain all of the disasters that had befallen the country: the defeat in the war, the hunger, the destructive inflation.[468]

It served a similar purpose elsewhere, with disasters aplenty awaiting assignation of blame. America took on a major shameful role, as Henry Ford's advocacy of the *Protocols* increased both its circulation and its prestige. Starting in 1920, Ford financed an enormous international campaign to publicize the preposterous rag, along with sympathetic commentaries, in a compilation called *International Jew*, which he had translated into sixteen languages. Though Ford at last recanted his views in 1927, grudgingly acknowledging the *Protocols'* fraudulent origin, enormous harm had already been done. Contenders for inclusion in the genocide gallery of notables proliferated.

If the car maker's most notorious admirer was Adolf Hitler, who kept a photograph of the "heroic American, Heinrich Ford" on his desk,[469] another infamous devotee was Baldur von Schirach, leader of the Hitler Youth, who credited *International Jew* for his conversion to antisemitism at seventeen. Alfred Rosenberg, the "official" philosopher of the Nazi party, published his own commentary on the *Protocols* in 1923. When the Nazis took power in 1933, some version of the forgery was easily available for popular consumption. It was only a matter of time before it ignited fire in the minds of Islamists already hard-wired to hate all non-Muslims.

Hard as it may be to believe today, Muslims did not always feel that way. Muhammad had considered not only his own followers but all "the people of the Book," as special. Writes Richard Landes: "Like most apocalyptic prophets ... Muhammad began with no coercive authority....[But] his initially capacious attitude toward Judaism and Christianity, whose eschatological vision – the resurrection of the dead and the Day of Judgment – formed the basic grand narrative around which [he] wove his particular set of prophecies of imminence,"[470] was to change as the Apocalypse failed to arrive during the prophet's lifetime. He also resented, as Luther did, later the Jews' refusal to convert.

Forced to leave Mecca, Muhammad adopted far more belligerent tactics after moving to Medina. The Muslim "martyrs" who died in battle against the infidels were promised heaven. Proclaims one often-cited *hadith* (meaning a saying attributed to Muhammad): "Behold! God sent me [the Prophet] with a sword, just before the Hour [of Judgment], and placed my daily sustenance beneath the shadow of my spear, and humiliation and contempt upon those who oppose me."[471] His apocalyptic warriors fought mercilessly on behalf of Good as against Evil, with great success. Within a few years after Muhammad's death, they had conquered the Sassanian and most of the Byzantine empire. Hardly a century had passed before the so-called *Dar al Islam* – the Realm, or House, of Submission, or Peace – would tower over all others. Total victory seemed imminent.

But *Dar al Harb*, the House of War, persisted. Before long, it would overtake Islam, defying Allah's promise of victory to his faithful followers. As Muslims came in contact with new ideologies and technology, their Quranic worldview was bound to be challenged. By the beginning of the twentieth century, Allah's flock felt utterly lost. Repeatedly joining the losing side in global conflicts did not help. Nor did the cavalier insouciance, bordering on contempt, with which victorious European powers treated their lands. But who was ultimately to blame?

During centuries of hostilities with the Holy Roman Empire, the Jews had not been the Muslims' principal target. Rather, as Landes points out, "most Muslim apocalyptic literature concerns the major military enemy of early Islam, the Christians." Indeed, in modern times, when antisemitism took center stage alongside modernity in its various guises, Muslim "writers had to search for apocalyptic material on the Jews in the hadith and found few."[472] They did find this zinger: "The time will come until Muslims will fight the Jews; until the Jews hide behind rocks and trees, which will cry: 'O Muslim! O servant of Allah! There is a Jew hiding behind me, come and kill him!'" Who needed more?

It has since been endlessly invoked, and gruesomely implemented. This despite the wise caution in the Quran against the lethal Edenic hubris: "[I]t may be that you dislike a thing that is good for you and like a thing that is bad for you, Allah knows but you do not know." Killing another human being is also proscribed, except for special cases when the community is deemed to be in danger, at which point a *fatwa* must be issued. And even then, specific reference must be made to relevant precedents, since no human after the Prophet may presume to transmit the will of Allah. This is particularly true for the Sunni tradition, where only a scholar eminently well versed in the Quran and Islamic tradition may issue *fatwas*.[473]

In reality, however, *fatwas* had been issued throughout history to justify any number of insurgencies and violent actions against foreign domination and perceived heresy, without requiring a declaration of offensive jihad (*Jihad Al-talab waal-ibtida*) in the sense of sanctioned total war that obliges every Muslim to participate on pain of eternal damnation.[474] But legitimization by religious leaders, whose edicts are deemed mandatory by divine fiat, makes the modified quranic approach to warfare particularly effective as a mobilizing and motivating force. At the beginning of the twentieth century, as Mohammad's dream of a global community of Muslims lay in virtual shambles. The political timber was bone-dry; a spark would suffice.

Fatwa Blessed by the Kaiser

The idea of a pan-Islamic alliance, roughly equivalent to the idea of the traditional *ummah*, emerged over the course of history now and again, but at the end of the nineteenth century, as Martin Kramer describes it, "Muslims, separated by distance, language, and history, first thought to make their world whole by assembling in congress."[475] In 1877 or 1878, for example, Jamal Al-Din Al-Afghani (1838/9-1897) recommended to the caliph, who was the chief Muslim leader in Istanbul, that he unite the Ottoman Empire with India and Afghanistan, so as to eventually prevail worldwide. Though his plan did not materialize, the seeds of a new Islamism for the modern age were being sewn. Incorporating reason and science, it was nonetheless predicated on returning to Islam's "basic principles" so as to "shake the entire world with its force."[476]

After the Ottoman Empire fell into the hands of an officers' junta in the early twentieth century, these ideas, paradoxically, resonated again, albeit in a quasi-secular fashion, at least initially. Modernization of sorts ensued when a number of groups took charge of a fragmented society that sought a modicum of unity in what they called "Ottomanism" or "Pan-Islamism." The junta, known as the Young Turks, was a secret society originally established in 1889 by young cadets. After deposing the Sultan in 1908, they enthroned a puppet in his place who would have little or no power. The group inevitably splintered among warring factions and soon brought the country to its knees. In 1913, a coup by one of the factions led by the so-called "Three Pashas" Talaat, Jemal, and Enver, inaugurated a military dictatorship. The economy did not improve, having all but collapsed on the eve of 1914. Desperate to modernize Turkey's communications and transportation networks, after being rebuffed by the other European powers, the Pashas decided to ally the Ottoman Empire with Germany. Though during the war the Turks performed much better than anticipated,[477] Germany still called the shots, and would eventually doom the Empire's political fate. But the Kaiser would also try to enlist pan-Islamism and jihad; religion would be used for political ends again, and once again with unforeseen consequences.

Germany's goal was to win, by any means possible, the war it had done so much to ignite. In an extraordinary 1918 memoir that records his days as America's envoy to Turkey at the onset of the Great War, Ambassador Henry Morgenthau, Sr., records his astonishment at the casual way in which German Ambassador to Turkey, Baron Hans Freiherr von Wangenheim (1889-1981), disclosed why the Kaiser wanted to push Turkey into the conflagration that was about to erupt.

[Q]uietly and nonchalantly, as though it had been quite the most ordinary matter in the world... puffing away at his big black German cigar, he unfolded Germany's scheme to arouse the whole fanatical Moslem world against the Christians. Germany had planned a real "holy war" as one means of destroying English and French influence in the world. [478]

Given Turkey's limited military arsenal, its army was not expected to contribute decisively to the war effort. "But the big thing is the Moslem world," acknowledged von Wangenheim. What he "evidently meant by the 'Big thing' became apparent on November 13 [1914], when the Sultan issued his declaration of war," writes Morgenthau. "This declaration was really an appeal for Jihad, or a 'Holy War' against the infidel. Soon afterward the Sheik-ul-Islam published his proclamation, summoning the whole Moslem world to arise and massacre their Christian oppressors." Almost simultaneously, a secret pamphlet was also "distributed stealthily in all Mohammedan countries.... It described a detailed plan of operations for the assassination and extermination of all Christians – except those of German nationality."[479]

Specific instructions for carrying out the plan included a "heart war," which required every follower of the Prophet to actively and consistently hate the infidel; a "speech war" through words, spoken and written, to spread hatred wherever they live, anywhere on earth; but above all, a war of "deed" – fighting and killing the infidel everywhere. Morgenthau describes the plan:

The latter conflict, says the pamphlet, "is the true war." There is to be a "little holy war" and a "great holy war" – the first local, the second global. There are three tiers: first, war carried out by individuals, second, by organized "bands" or terrorist groups, and finally, by "organized campaigns" – i.e., trained armies.... In all parts of this incentive to murder and assassination there are indications that a German hand has exercised an editorial supervision. [480]

That few outside the academy today remember this *fatwa* is unsurprising. The Sultan's call to jihad fell on deaf ears – and not only because most Muslims could not fathom why they should engage in a Holy War against Christians while being allied with two Christian nations, Germany and Austria. But Morgenthau grasped immediately the real import of what had just happened:

Only one definite result did the Kaiser accomplish by spreading this inciting literature. It aroused in the Mohammedan soul all that animosity toward the Christian which is the fundamental fact in his strange emotional nature, and thus started passions aflame that afterward spent themselves in the massacres of the Armenians and other subject peoples.[481]

The German-Ottoman partnership had begun. Its architect was not von Wangenheim, the Kaiser's loose-lipped envoy to Turkey, but the brilliant Max von Oppenheim, who had persistently promoted it for over two decades. He believed in it passionately; as he put it in 1898, he was convinced it would unleash "Muslim fanaticism that borders on insanity."[482] When the Kaiser finally adopted the plan on July 30, 1914, he laid out the intent: "[O]ur consuls and agents in Turkey, India and Egypt are supposed to inflame the Muslim regions to wild revolts against the British." He hoped that as a result, "England shall lose at least India,"[483] maybe more. Winning the war was to be the prelude to Germany's impending imperial ascendance.

The Oppenheim operation began in August 1914, when the Chief of the German General Staff General Helmuth von Moltke – according to Ottoman War Minister Enver Pasha's himself[484] - asked the Turks to invade Egypt and help trigger sympathetic pan-Islamic revolts. With the help of a boyhood friend, Hans Human, who was also, coincidentally, the German naval attaché, the wily Pasha created an organization alongside a Bureau for Revolutionizing Middle Eastern Lands designed to spread jihad throughout the Caucasus. In late October, the Ottomans duly attacked Russia, which reciprocated on November 2, followed by Britain and France. War had escalated.

But military action was supplemented by a strategy spelled out in a comprehensive 136-page plan on "The Revolutionizing of the Islamic Territories of our Enemies." Oppenheim's plan identified the enemy as not only the Allied powers but "Christians and Jews who supported the allies." This amounted to "Germany's endorsement of a war against civilians and spreading religious hatred," note Barry Rubin and Wolfgang G. Schwanitz. "Thus, German strategy would be intimately involved in the Ottomans' mass murder of Armenians"[485] - confirming Morgenthau's suspicion all along. "Genocide" would not be coined for another three decades, in 1944, by Raphael Lemkin; but Irving Louis Horowitz observes: "The fate of the Armenians is the essential prototype of genocide in the twentieth century."[486] For even if race was not explicitly invoked by way of justification for genocide, religion surely was, providing one more excuse for mass murder based on group identity. If not quite in scale, certainly in ideology, observes Horowitz, "the declaration of war on the Jews was roughly matched by the earlier war of the Muslims against the Christian Armenians."[487]

What Morgenthau could not have known was that Germany had another operation going on, which proved even more successful in changing the map of the world. Equally masterminded by Oppenheim, and also involving von Wangenheim, it had all the makings of an implausible script for a B-rated movie,

As the camera zooms in, it is 1915. The savvy, if excessively loquacious, German ambassador meets a wealthy arms merchant and advisor to the three Pashas who by that time ran Turkey, named Alexander Parvus. Born Israel Lazarevich Gelfhand (1867-1924) in an Odessa *stetl* (Jewish settlement), Parvus had become a Marxist, befriended Vladimir Lenin, and joined the Bolsheviks. In 1910, he moved to Istanbul to make his fortune, but continued his revolutionary activities. His clever articles would soon earn him a considerable reputation. It was his proposal that revolutionaries could ally with the tsar's enemies in an international war to destroy the Russian regime that brought him to German attention as early as 1905, a full decade before von Wangeheim was to make his acquaintance.

The fact that Parvus was Jewish was no obstacle: Germany was perfectly happy to work with anyone to achieve its strategic goals. The Kaiser's own attitude toward the Jews was not especially hostile; mainly, he wanted to solve Germany's "Jewish problem" by getting Germany rid of them. Like many Germans at the time, he was open to encouraging Jewish emigration to Palestine – at least so long as it did not antagonize the Arabs. For this reason, many Jews who had emigrated to Turkey and Patestine hoped for the Sultan's as well as the Germans' support in creating a Jewish state.[488]

As soon as von Wangenheim learned about Parvus, he instantly grasped the man's importance and dispatched the financier to Berlin in March 1915 with a proposal to use German funds to pay off Bolsheviks. Parvus's plan to bring down the tsarist government by subterfuge was adopted immediately. "Soon, through Parvus's networks in Denmark and Istanbul, money started flowing to Lenin."[489] German and Bolshevik collaboration would change history more radically than any of them could ever have anticipated.

Simultaneously, von Oppenheim was busy working on the Islamic front. He proceeded to hire a Middle East expert on the German General Staff, Otto von Wesendonk (1885-1933), along with another dozen German experts, as well as more than two dozen who were mostly Muslim. It was an impressive think-tank: by war's end, a veritably army of some sixty specialists. The Muslims included Tatars, Indians, Persians, Tunisians, Algerians, and Egyptians, notably Abd Al-Aziz Jawish (1876-1929), who, unbeknown to Ambassador Morgenthau, had been the actual author of the infamous secret version of the Sultan's *fatwa* in November 1914.

Though it soon became apparent that the immediate effect of that *fatwa* was negligible,[490] that didn't make it irrelevant. Its real impact was to come later, when conditions had become ripe. Many, if not most, Muslims throughout the Middle East were seething at the way the disastrous Versailles Treaty of 1919 divided the world among the victorious Allies on the basis of Allied interests alone, with no regard to local sensibilities. The *coup de grace* came on October 29, 1923, when the Turkish National Assembly declared Turkey a republic, followed by the abolition of the caliphate on March 3, 1924. Though its role had long been mostly nominal, the caliphate's symbolic presence had postponed having to face the reality of Islam's eclipse. Many took its abolition to mean that the *ummah* was on life-support. Was Islam itself already dead? Unthinkable.

To its zealous and passionate followers, renewed efforts to resuscitate a moribund faith by whatever means necessary seemed long overdue. Organization was key, as was ideological acumen. The re-radicalized Muslims' German training came in handy; it was hardly coincidental that the key advisor to Hasan Al-Banna (1906–1959), founder of the Muslim Brotherhood, was the same Abd Al-Aziz Jawish who had ghost-written the Sultan's proclamation. Jihad could now be lifted to the next level – from mere *fatwa* to tactical implementation. Though few could grasp its full import at the time, it is widely acknowledged that establishing the Brotherhood "marked the start of the modern Islamist movement."[491]

Assistance from the emerging Soviet state was also no accident. One of Lenin's first Muslim comrades was the same Enver Pasha who had done the Germans' bidding in World War I; they had a common friend in Parvus. In the aftermath of its defeat in 1918, a Germany reeling from its wounds temporarily suspended geopolitical intrigue. The baton reverted to the USSR. (Though Parvus, repudiated by the Bolsheviks, died in Berlin in 1924, at least one of his sons is reputed to have become a Soviet diplomat.[492]) "During the early 1920s," write Rubin and Schwanitz, "the leading role in fomenting revolutionary movements in the Muslim world had passed from Germany to the Soviets, who urged Muslims to overthrow their European rulers."[493] Enver proved eager to cooperate with the Soviet regime, and with Lenin's personal support, he was immediately hired to direct its Asian department. Before long, "Enver would persuade Lenin to support an Islamic religious revolt based on a plan drawn up for the Kaiser."[494]

To compound the irony, and further justifying this strange movie script's low rating, the principal organizer of the 1920 Soviet conference designed to rally the "people of the east," held in the Azerbaijani capital Baku, was none other than one of Lenin's fellow passengers on the train from Zurich, Grigory Zinoviev, born Hirsch Apfelbaum (1883-1936). With him in Baku was also another train rider, who had since become leader of the Communist International: Zinoviev's friend Karl Radek, born Karol Sobelsohn (1885-1939). Radek's meetings with members of the German elite eventually led to the April 1922 Treaty of Rapallo under which Germany and the Communist state renounced all territorial and financial claims to one another's territory, and "out of these talks also grew the Bolshevik Jihad."[495] Notwithstanding their contribution to Islamist awakening, the fate of these two Jews was no Hollywood story. The script followed the typical Politburo plot. The always antisemitic Stalin, increasingly paranoid, had Zinoviev executed in 1936, while Radek perished in captivity on no less trumped-up charges three years later.

Progress on mobilizing Muslims was anything but smooth. At first, Enver promised Zinoviev to enlist Afghanistan's ruler King Amanullah, who had been involved in the German-Ottoman strategy, along with one of Enver's old collaborators, the Hindu-born Manbendra Nath Roy (1887–1954). Member of a Brahmin caste, Roy was a great asset: he admired Islamism as an apocalyptic revolutionary ideology, perfectly in line with Soviet thinking. "The phenomenal success of Islam," he wrote, "was primarily due to its revolutionary significance and its ability to lead the masses out of the hopeless situation created by the decay of antique civilizations.... The miraculous performance of the 'Army of God' usually dazzles the vision... Godliness, for them, was not a veil for greediness."[496] But in the end, Enver was undone by his own powerful ambition. After fighting alongside Red Army troops in the Caucasus, he defected to the opposing Islamic forces, only to be caught by the Russians and summarily executed.

It took a while for the USSR's Islamic outreach to bear fruit. For one thing, it was hard for Muslims to forget tsarist imperial ambitions; for another, militant atheism held no appeal for them. But the powerful "Manifesto of the Congress of the People of the East," issued at the 1920 Baku conference, provided a ringing endorsement of jihad that complemented perfectly the Sultan's secret message of six years earlier. It read:

> Into the holy war for the liberation of all mankind from the yoke of capitalist and imperialist slavery, for the ending of all forms of oppression of one people by another and all forms of exploitation of man by man!...In this holy war all the revolutionary workers and all the oppressed peasants of the East will be with you...May the holy war of the peoples of the East and the toilers of the whole world against imperial Britain burn with unquenchable fire! [497]

The conference would be only the first of many venues of cooperation between the USSR and the Islamic world. Over the ensuing decades, the Soviet regime provided assistance - logistical, financial, military and ideological - to Palestinian organizations, undemocratic regimes, and assorted anti-Western groups dedicated to the Islamist cause. Above all, however, it helped fine-tune the narrative of Islamist jihad, which advanced the Soviet regime's global strategic agenda by undermining Western democracy.

The fearless Russian dissident Vladimir Bukovsky's research into the Politburo's secret papers shows the widespread Soviet meddling throughout the Middle East from its inception. Documents obtained after the Gulf War on Iraq reveal its long-term support for Saddam Hussein. Supply of arms to Lebanese insurgents, "usually channeled through Syria, goes back to at least 1970, and by 1975 had grown... immense..."[498] so that "[b]y the mid-1980s, the Soviet Union was training at least two hundred Lebanese thugs per annum, of whom 170 were activists of the Lebanese Communist party and thirty of the Progressive Socialist Party."[499]

The USSR fanned the flames of hatred toward Zionism and Jews generally over Palestine. The theme resonated throughout a Muslim world seething from what they saw as British duplicity regarding the territory,[500] though blaming, of course, mainly the Jews. The "Manifesto" that emerged from Baku had denounced British policy, charging that by "acting for the benefit of Anglo-Jewish capitalists, it drove Arabs from the land in order to give the latter to Jewish settlers. Then, trying to appease the discontent of the Arabs, it incited them against these same Jewish settlers." Its inaccuracy notwithstanding, that narrative worked, allowing the Soviet Union to position itself as an ally of the Muslim world. If in 1920 the USSR was not, as yet, a chief champion of antisemitism, that too would come.

Antisemitism Takes Front Stage

It was only fitting that Germany, cradle of the millenarian utopia culminating in the Reformation, home of Martin Luther, should keep rekindling the scorching torch of antisemitism. Though tolerant at first, Luther had become virulently antisemitic after failing to convert Jews to Christianity. In his German-language tract of 1543 titled "Concerning the Jews and Their Lies," he piled on the most outrageous accusations that had long been hurled against Jews, as poisoners, ritual murderers, devils, and parasites. Writes Robert Wistrich:

> Luther called for setting synagogues on fire, breaking down Jewish homes, [and worse]… Indeed, Jews and Judaism, for the aging Luther, were nothing less than storm troops of the Antichrist, whose demise would bring about the end of time. Not surprisingly, at the Nuremberg trials of 1946, the Third Reich's arch-anti-Semite Julius Streicher was able to claim that he had invented nothing not previously asserted by the German founder of the Protestant Reformation. [501]

But if the Kaiser's willingness to collaborate with the Muslims against the Allies was altogether understandable geopolitically, the same cannot be said for Adolph Hitler, whose worldview was predicated on a visceral antipathy to everyone plagued by dark pigmentation. He saw Arabs and Muslims as just a notch above Jews, thus borderline human. What changed his mind, aside from pragmatic considerations, was a pseudo-historical belief that the people of ancient Egypt and India had been a part of the Aryan culture. [502] Above all, however, he applauded the Islamist war spirit. It was, after all, his own.

Among his most devoted Muslim acolytes was the Syrian-born Mufti of Jerusalem, Haj Amin Al-Hussaini (1895–1974). [503] The Mufti owed his rise to power to the disastrous misjudgment of the British first high commissioner in Palestine, Herbert Samuels, who in 1921 elevated the militantly pro-Palestinian Hussaini to Mufti, imagining him to be malleable. Samuels naively underestimated Hussaini's ability to change sides more quickly than his clothes. (As a Jew, moreover, Samuels might have wished to demonstrate his even-handedness.) After fighting along the Ottomans against Arab nationalists, Hussaini turned against his former friends, then decided to spy for Britain and help Syrian Arabs against the French, only to switch once more and join the French. It would not be the consummate chameleonic survivor's last incarnation.

Though odious in the extreme, Hussaini's moral acrobatics reflected not worldly opportunism so much as its repudiation. A devoted Muslim, he was prepared to do whatever seemed to him necessary to recapture Islam's lost greatness. A learned, capable, shrewd, and sincerely religious man, if rabidly antisemitic, Hussaini had been convinced early on that everything, even elements of modernity, had to be used to resist and eventually defeat the West. Drawing his inspiration from fellow-Syrian Rashid Rida (1865-1935), Hussaini rejected his own father's antipathy to politicizing Islam, and joined the battle. Arguably the founder of modern Islamist politics, he turned out to be a formidable organizer, fundraiser, and spokesman for the cause of jihad in its various permutations.

That meant making common cause with both Hitler and Lenin, for Hussaini understood that Communism and fascism had the same national enemies as the Muslims. Both pseudo-egalitarian monistic ideologies which permitted no dissent, they were thoroughly totalitarian and thus fully consistent with an Islamist politico-religious vision. Writes Laurent Murawiec:

> Starting in the 1920s and 1930s, the Communist Party of Palestine (CPP) was the great instructor of the Pan-Islamist nationalist movement led by the Grand Mufti Al-Husayni in the fine arts of Communist agitprop, the conveyor of crucial Marxist-Leninist concepts, such as "imperialism" and "colonialism." Most of the ugly repertoire of modern Arab and Muslim antisemitism came from the Soviet Union (with only the racial-biological component added by the Nazis). The CPP taught the Arab extremists the use of Bolshevik rhetorical devices previously unknown. The "anti-imperialism" so imported by the Communists was remarkably ingested by the Muslim extremists, to the point of becoming integral to their conceptions and expression.[504]

While Berlin served as the perfect venue for Islamist networking between the two world wars, a similar effort was taking place simultaneously in Moscow. The 1920 Baku conference had been but the first salvo. In 1927, the USSR started bringing Muslim leaders to the Communist International Academy's International Lenin School for a three-year course that targeted future party leaders and influencers. Observed Walter Laqueur in 1956: "It cannot be mere coincidence that the main proponents of fascism in Egypt, Syria and Iraq cooperate nowadays with the Communists in the framework of sundry national, anti-imperialist and 'peace' fronts."[505] Coincidence it was not.

Egypt had already become home to the radical Muslim Brotherhood, established by Hasan Al-Banna in 1928, with Jawish's help. Like Hussaini, Al-Banna was also a faithful disciple of Rashid Rida, having adopted his concept of *salafiyya* which meant a "return of the ways of the ancestors." The charismatic and pious Al-Banna articulated the violent vision that would thereafter define the jihadist movement, in an address to the Fifth General Conference of the Muslim Brotherhood in 1938:

> At the time there will be ready, O ye Muslim Brothers, 300 battalions, each one equipped spiritually with faith and belief, intellectually with [Islamic] science and learning, and physically with training andathletics, at that time you can demand me to plunge with you through the turbulent oceans and to rend the skies with you and to conquer with you every obstinate tyrant.[506]

It is hard to imagine a more apocalyptic scenario. The call to arms is categorical. With populist overtones reminiscent of the millenarian rebels of the Reformation, Al-Banna argues here that Islam can be understood by everyone, "thus transferring Islam to the realm of lay religion."[507] Like Judaism and Christianity, moreover, this creed transcends individual nation-states, eternally true across space and time, meant for all humanity. "Its prescriptions regulate all matters of man in this world and hereafter... Islam is dogma and ritual, homeland and nationality, religion and state, spirituality and practice, Quran and sword." Since Islam means "submission," totalitarianism is its fraternal, even if not identical, twin brother. Explains Murawiec:

> When the world stage was dominated by the rivalry between the "Anglo-Saxon" culture of pluralist democracy and Prussian-inspired authoritarianism, the heart of the Arab elites throbbed

for the latter. When this was vanquished, its tyrannical successors, Soviet Bolshevism, Italian fascism, and German national socialism became the rage of the Arab and much of the Muslim world.[508]

Al-Banna grasps all these similarities with ease.

This newly energized, super-belligerent Islam ambitiously addressed the entire world, guaranteeing that once it had all become Muslim, it would reach a perfect harmony predicated on an essentially egalitarian distribution of resources. Though Al-Banna's economic vision has been described as "neither capitalism nor socialism," he regularly invokes the principle of "social justice." Ivessa Lubben summarizes Al-Banna's economic recommendations as follows: "He wanted to reorganize the collection and distribution of obligatory alms [*zakat*] in a modern social institution. He asked for the prohibition of interest-based loans and the restriction of monopolies... [as well as] a redistribution of income by raising low salaries and capping higher ones."[509]

In a letter written in 1947, "Economic Order" [*Al-nidham Al-islami*], Al-Banna concedes that he had taken "the concept of social justice from socialism and freedom from the Western world." Adding that Muslim Brothers "detest deeply any kind of class antagonism," the freedom to which he refers, however, is implicitly neo-Marxist. Explains Lubben: "The projected Islamic economic order can be understood as the utopia of a 'moral economy' in which ethical values and attitudes dictate labour relations, direct investment, and prioritise the spending of profits on socially useful aims. The same ethical motivation is supposed to guide workers to perform accurately and reliably." If he took "freedom from the Western world," it was only the word.

Al-Banna's hostility to anyone who values money is vintage Marxism. Believing that "work is the worthiest form of service to God," he is referring to manual, by which he means productive, work. Money is intrinsically evil: "Know that heaven will rain neither silver nor gold," he warns. Any profits that "exceed the natural needs," which he assumed to be modest, should be invested in the national economy or donated to support the needy. The central tenets of Al-Banna's Islamist economics thus proved perfectly acceptable to the Communists, whose plans for abolishing all private property from the planet had to be postponed a tad anyway. Defeating the West came first; one war at a time sufficed. With Utopia on track, the precise hour of its arrival could be finessed.

For several decades, the Brotherhood was broadly accepted in Egypt, until the government sequestered most of the organization's assets in 1948. It probably did not help that one of its publications implicitly threatened regime overthrow. Its author, Al-Bahi Al-Khuli, had complained that the rich and idle "systematically oppressed workers," blaming "exploitative monopoly companies and big landowners, while [another of his comrades,] a young labor lawyer, Muhammad Al-Fuli, dared to urge workers to unite and fight against the ruling capitalists.[510] For more than a decade, members of the Brotherhood had been growing increasingly restless and radical. Amidst the political turmoil that engulfed Egypt, after the assassination of Prime Minister Mahmud Fahmi Al-Nuqrashi in December 1948, the troublesome Al-Banna was assassinated at last. But the Brotherhood was not finished – quite the contrary.[511]

The man who took over the leadership of the Brotherhood was the austere Sayyid Qutb (1906–1966), whom most Islamic scholars consider to be the intellectual father of modern Islamist terrorism. Writes Malise Ruthven: "[M]ore than any other recent Muslim writer, he is the inspiration behind September 11."[512] Karen Armstrong also considers him "the real founder of Islamic fundamentalism in the Sunni world."[513] Qutb's seminal work *Milestones* (*Ma'ālim fī t-tarīq*), an Islamist cross between the *Communist Manifesto* and *Mein Kampf,* is essentially a clarion call to Armageddon.

Qutb first redefines Jihad not as a "defensive war" in the narrow, Western sense, but broadly as a "defensive movement" whose aim is "to wipe out tyranny, and to introduce true freedom to mankind, using whatever resources are practically available in a given human situation." He has in mind "the end of man's arrogance and selfishness, the establishment of the sovereignty of Allah and the rule of the divine *Shari'a* [Islamic law] in human affairs." The victory of the realm of peace, *Dar al Islam,* "means that *din* [the law of the society, or human law] should be purified for Allah, that all people should obey Allah alone, and every system that permits some people to rule over others be abolished."[514] This is revolution in an Islamic key, the leitmotif of the Muslim Marseillaise.

Ruthven notes that the "message of revolutionary anarchism implicit in the phrase that 'every system that permits some people to rule over others be abolished' owes more to radical European ideas going back to the Jacobins than to classical or traditional ideas about Islamic governance." He adds:

Similarly, the revolutionary vanguard Qutb advocates does not have an Islamic pedigree, though historically there have always been tribal forces that sought to "purify" Islam from religiously improper accretions. The vanguard is a concept imported from Europe, through a lineage that also stretches back to the Jacobins, through the Bolsheviks and latter-day Marxist guerillas such as the Baader-Meinhof gang.[515]

Citing additional passages from *Milestones* which describe Islam's message as "a call to free the whole of humankind," while simultaneously threatening that if "obstacles and practical difficulties are put in its way, it has no recourse but to remove them by force," Rueven concludes: The implicit "totalitarian menace is clear....The argument is not dissimilar to that deployed by Communists during the 1930s. Qutbism is distinctly modern, both in its adoption of the revolutionary vanguard and in the way it addresses a contemporary phenomenon, the modern crisis of faith."[516] Qutb refurbished the ideology, upgrading its message to fit new circumstances.

An equal opportunity totalitarian, like Al-Hussaini and Al-Banna before him, Qutb cooperated with both the Nazis and the Communists. Revolution, to him, is "the only credible instrument of attaining social justice and of applying the *shar'ia* as "the only proper remedy for decaying societies. *Zalzalah* (shaking) or revolution is the word used to describe the first step in the process of building a new society."[517] But was this an acceptable Muslim concept?

Not exactly. Violence is as old as mankind, and is certainly consistent with the Quran, particularly the later sections concerning Muhammad's sojourn in Medina. But the modern concept of revolution in the sense of creating something entirely new, as opposed to going back to a previous state of affairs, cannot be found in Islam before the twentieth century. The Quran was the word of Allah: once it has been revealed to mankind there is nothing new to be brought about. To Laurent Murawiec, this meant that "revolution in the Islamic polity is a theoretical impossibility."[518] But modern challenges mandated linguistic updates.

European concepts did not translate perfectly into an Islamic context. The idea of *tawhid,* meaning "the unity of God" reflected by unity on earth under *shari'a*, was a monist vision, a culture of One, but it was not equivalent to "totalitarianism," a word first used in a specifically Italian context. Similarly, the closest to Western-style political "revolution" meaning the violent replacement of one type of regime by another, was *thawra*, meaning simply rising, excitement, rebellion. Though hardly ideal, it was conveniently refurbished by Muslims eager for a major shake-up. They realized that, to be effective in the twentieth century, modern Islamism had to become a genuinely political religion and emulate the tactics used by Western-style secular movements.

It finally happened, though in rather unexpected circumstances. For notwithstanding Qutb's considerable success in overhauling Islamism, the Islamist Revolution that turned the tide and appropriated the name would be waged not by his Sunni brothers, but by their Iranian rivals.

Revolutionary Theocracy

Their sectarian differences aside, Sayyid Qutb and Ruholla Khomeini (1902-1989) had both been disciples of Abul Ala Maududi (1903–1979), a Pakistani philosopher who came to believe in an Islamic Revolution of millenarian proportions. According to Maududi, the Prophet Muhammad had been "the greatest Revolutionary of all," nowhere in the same league with "the general, run-of-the-mill worldly revolutionaries." A true "'Muslim," writes Maududi, belongs to "that 'International Revolutionary Party' organized by Islam to carry out its revolutionary program."[519] To be Muslim is tantamount to *fighting* under the banner of Muhammad. These words were music to the ears of Qutb and Khomeini in equal measure: fighting, they both agreed, is mandatory if Islam is to survive.

Maududi's principal contribution to modern Jihadism was to thoroughly weaponize it by reconciling secular and religious ideals and language in ways that could appeal to young and old alike, to the pious and the iconoclasts, utopians of all stripes. To him, Islam is more than a religion; it is "a revolutionary ideology and programme which seeks to alter the social order of the whole world and rebuild it in conformity with its own tenets and ideals." "Jihad," wrote Maududi, "refers to that revolutionary struggle and utmost exertion which the Islamic Party brings into play to achieve this objective."[520] It was magic.

Qutb was thoroughly mesmerized. Michael W. S. Ryan explains:

> Qutb agrees with Maududi's formulation, although Qutb is naturally more Arab-centric and focused on Egypt first. Both men rely to a great degree on passages in the Qur'an and their own views of history. Their ideology can be termed revolutionary Salafism because it goes far beyond the classic understanding of Jihad as primarily defensive and aims at

overturning the modern Muslim social order on a global scale. Qutb thought of Islam as a global revolution that would replace Western capitalism and Eastern Communism. When Qutb spoke of the early Muslim *ummah* going to war against the Arabs of the Arabian Peninsula, he used the word *harb* (war), not Jihad. Jihad includes war but is an all-inclusive struggle.[521]

This became the centerpiece ideology for Al-Qaeda. As Qutb defines it, Islam's enemies include not only America and Israel, but also the secular leaders of Muslim countries such as Egypt, Iran, and Iraq. This renders the war far more ideological than "civilizational," as pious Muslims were now considered under attack even by fellow-Muslims, who were deemed apostates for allegedly sabotaging the *ummah* from within, thus constituting a cancerous obstacle that had to be excised. It is thus up to zealous jihadist visionaries to outline the true path of God, which in turn is destined to become the true path for the entire world. In the final chapter of his book, summarizes Ryan, Qutb "delineates the milestones for his reader to be the 'vanguard' that will lead the way for Islam to take its proper role as leader of the world. The concept of vanguard, a term adopted by Lenin from Marx's *Communist Manifesto*, was one of the key terms with which al-Qaeda strategists were to identify its members."[522] Some words simply have to be appropriated.

But just as the Communist revolution first succeeded in Russia, defying its German architects who had expected it to erupt in the West, so the ideology that seemed ripe to explode in a majority Sunni country would end up overturning a Shiia kingdom instead. To nearly everyone's surprise, the cataclysmic upheaval that changed the Middle East eventually came not to Egypt but to Iran. The self-proclaimed Muslim messiah, the opportunistic Ayatollah Khomeini, turned out to be a skillful practitioner of *taqiyya* (deception). As the Iranian-born scholar Amir Taheri points out, "originally, the Khomeinist leadership itself had hesitated to use the 'Islamic' label, speaking instead of a 'popular uprising' (*qiyaim mardomi*) so as to attract leftist groups and reassure the middle classes that feared religious rule. Soon, however, they realized that they needed Islam to mobilize the muscle required to neutralize the shah's armed forces."[523]

Khomeini had inherited his mentor Maududi's belief in the messianic superiority of Islam. But his self-apotheosis exceeded even that of his totalitarian predecessors, seeing himself as a second Muhammad with a mission to save a dying *ummah*. He virtually anointed himself as God's spokesman. In *Islam and Revolution*, published in 1971, Khomeini explains that in a true Islamic state, "the existence of a holder of authority, a ruler who acts as trustee an maintains the institutions and laws of Islam, is a necessity." After all, "did not the caliphate of the Commander of the Faithful serve this purpose? The same necessity that led Him to become holy Imam still exist," even if no one has specifically been designated to fulfill that function. There is no getting around it: a righteous government "is needed, one presided over by a ruler who will be a trustworthy and righteous trustee."[524] That ruler was, of course, Khomeini. Who knew.

The Shia tradition was especially prone to such millenarian mysticism. As Shmuel Bar points out, "[w]hereas Sunni Islam leaves room for renewing the offensive Jihad if and when the Muslims choose a caliph, traditional Shiite Islam defers it to an apocalyptic era when the Hidden Imam (the twelfth Imam, who is in occultation (*ghayba* [hidden]) and will appear at the end of days as the *Mahdi* [messiah]) will take revenge on the enemies of Allah and bring justice to the world...."[525] Some Shiia scholars hold that at least certain powers of the Imam may be delegated to ordinary mortals, which explains at least in part Khomeini's hubristic aspirations.

Like Lenin, Stalin, and Hitler, Khomeini saw no reason not to assume complete control of the state for the good of the "people," with no intention to consult them. Affectionally, if condescendingly, referring to the masses as *mustazafeen* (the feeble oncs) fully accorded with Islamic tradition, which placed the power of interpreting the Holy Word in the hands of religious luminaries entitled to issue *fatwas* considered binding on all Muslims everywhere.

In his *Solution to Problems (Hal Al-Masa'el),* Khomeini outlines "the right way of doing things" for everything: from cutting one's nails, to sexual conduct, to waging war, the wise leader had all the answers, inferred from the Quran. If freedom in its ordinary sense was lost in the polemical shuffle, Khomeini's totalist handbook replaced it with blissful, utopian security. By his own testimony divinely ordained, the Ayatollah's judgment could not be doubted without risking blasphemy. Explains Mehdi Bazargan, the first prime minister of Khomeini's government after 1979: "[J]ust as an immature child has no right to dismiss his guardian, people, too, have no right to raise questions about the decisions of the Supreme Guide."[526]

Khomeini's paternalistic notion of freedom echoed Qutb's. Rather than individual liberty, what mattered was the Common Good as interpreted by an all-knowing messianic leader. After taking root in one or a few nations, the ultimate aim was to rule mankind as a whole. This required eliminating, "liquidating," in a word, murdering, whatever satanic power stood in the way. It was tailor-made for what Ruthven has called "Islamofascism" – a term that, far from implying Islamophobia, implicitly distinguishes the murderous strain from the peaceful mainstream.[527]

One of the Iranian regime's main theorists, the mullah Morteza Motahhari (1919-1979), who was eventually assassinated by political opponents, explained that Islam rejects "Western freedoms" designed primarily to promote sexual license.[528] Comments Taheri: "If Allah granted man any freedoms, according to Khomeinism, it was not on an individual basis. The human individual has no meaning outside the *ummah*, which is a theatrical device – like 'the people' or 'Das Volk.' This is perhaps why Khomeini and his successors have spoken of 'the *ummah* that is always present on the stage to play the role required of it.'"[529]

Despite massive proof of the regime's anti-Americanism, however, the U.S. has consistently hoped for dialogue. Barack Obama even preferred to overlook evidence indicating the existence of an al-Qaeda-Iran pact, which CIA director Mike Pompeo revealed to have been an "open secret" at that time.[530] Thwarting hopes of an unbridgeable sectarian divide, Shiia Iran pragmatically decided to engage its Sunni fellow jihadists whose ideological roots were similarly Salafi-Islamist, prompting Adrian Levy and Cathy Scott-Clark to declare in 2017 that "al-Qaeda has rebuilt itself – with Iran's help." For the sake of power, ideology can trump sectarianism.

Documents obtained during the 2011 raid that killed Osama bin Laden, only recently declassified, reveal that al-Qaeda and covert Iranian agents had in fact first attempted to broker an unlikely agreement more than two decades earlier. The effort had followed Saddam Hussein's blanket rejection of al-Qaeda's request for military assistance. Once the agreement was in place, Iran provided a veritable life-line for the severely wounded terrorist organization: starting with wives and volunteers, soon the most

> high-ranking al-Qaeda leaders arrived in Iran intending to stay and galvanize the outfit. They were marshaled by Abu Musab Al-Zarqawi, the Jordanian thug who would form Al-Qaeda in Iraq, the forerunner to ISIS. [Others] included Abu-Mihammed Al-Masri ... wanted by the FBI for involvement in the 1998 embassy attacks ... [and] Abu Musab Al-Suri, one of the most important strategic voices in the movement. Immediately, a re-formed al-Qaeda military council planned its first attack from

within Iran, according to Mahfouz, striking three residential compounds in Saudi Arabia, killing more than 35 people (including nine Americans) in 2003.[531]

Al-Suri's importance to the movement cannot be overestimated. A student of Osama bin Laden's co-leader and al-Qaeda ideologist Ayman Al-Zawahiri, Al-Suri adopted most of his mentor's ideas. As Ryan points out, the most important of those ideas is the constant message is that Jihad is the only "solution" and that Jihadist *aqidah* (ideology) is revolutionary and requires uncompromising guerrilla warfare against the West. In addition, Al-Zawahiri clearly states the strategic conclusion that Jihad cannot be regionally based but must be global in nature because of the global nature of the Western threat. Jihadist leadership, moreover, must never compromise with local governments or participate in elections. None of these rules is tactical. They are strategic; they define Al-Qaeda. Equally strategic is the definition of the enemy: Israel and the United States, forever and without any compromise.[532]

Since "Al-Zawahiri had traveled to Iran to find out how they made their revolution work," he borrowed a few ideas. For example, "Iran identified its 'great Satan' as the United States and used it as the external force needed to unify Iran; Al-Zawahiri adopted the term 'great master' for approximately the same purposes." But Ryan believes that "the challenge for al-Qaeda is much greater [than Iran's] because it needs to unify an entire religion spread across the globe instead of just one country."[533] If so, the difference seems tactical rather than strategic, given Iran's persistent geopolitical expansion through proxies such as Hezbollah and alliances with such seemingly unlikely ideological bedfellows as Russia and North Korea. Or are they?

What seems to have gone practically unnoticed in most media discussions of al-Qaeda's ideology is the contribution (which its own strategists readily acknowledge) of radical Western writings and experience. Among the first to explicitly recommend a form of guerrilla war rooted in both ancient and modern Chinese, as well as Communist insurgencies, was Abu Ubayd Al-Qurashi. Though hardly original, he wrote a slew of highly influential articles that turned for guidance to none other than Mao Tse Tung, whom he credits with understanding that "all operations that the revolutionary army undertakes, especially military operations, must serve a political goal."[534]

But Mao is not Al-Qurashi's only source of inspiration. Like Lenin, and later Mao and Castro, he expanded Marx's notion of the proletariat to include the rural poor. Explains Ryan:

In introducing the example of rural revolutionary forces, Al-Qurashi is thinking of the Cuban revolution and the writings of [Cuban Marxist] Che Guevara and [French Marxist philosopher and former Che associate] Regis Debray. Al-Qurashi finds no consensus among theoreticians and practitioners of revolutionary or guerrilla warfare concerning the separation of political cadres from the fighters themselves. He points out that Che and Regis Debray and those who participated in the Cuban Revolution "combined political and military authority in one man, Fidel Castro." For Al-Qurashi, another such man was Osama Bin Laden. [535]

Al-Qurashi's work reveals a remarkably comprehensive study of history, military strategy – including counterinsurgency and counterintelligence – as well as propaganda techniques. He acknowledges, for example,

that to gain the people's support and achieve what [Brazilian Marxist Carlos] Marighella [author of the *Mini-Manual of the Urban Guerrilla*] refers to as the climate of collapse it is necessary to ignite social and economic unrest within a society, claiming that most theorists agree this is a key dimension to revolution. Revolutionaries must exploit social and economic injustice, or at least bad conditions, to gain the people's support for revolution. [536]

Al-Quarashi took to heart Che Guevarra's conviction that the revolution could create the necessary social and economic conditions for apocalyptic revolt. He thus

gives the example of Castro basing his operations in the richest coffee area of Cuba and benefitting from the revenue of what was formerly state property. Other revolutionaries could emulate such an approach and take advantage of conditions as they find them, [and writes:]"Similarly, revolutionaries often target economic facilities for attack with the intention of undermining the economic power of their enemies." [537]

This, after all, is what happened to America in Vietnam: "Producing chaos (*fawda*) in the enemies' ranks was key to victory in Vietnam, according to Al-Qurashi."[538] He has it about right.

To this millenarian concept is added another: a reference to the ubiquitous "oppressed of the earth," rooted in both the Bible and the Quran. Ryan underscores, however, that it reflects "also al-Qaeda's inheritance of leftist rhetoric both from the Palestinian movement and from the books of Communist revolutionaries like Che Guevara"[539] – to say nothing of their predecessors. The narrative is tailor-made for both.

But it was Al-Qurashi's influential disciple Abu Musab Al-Suri who took al-Qaeda's ideology to the next level. A U.S. State Department announcement of a $5 million award for his head described him as "an Al-Qaida member and former trainer at the Derunta and Al-Ghuraba terrorist camps in Afghanistan where he trained terrorists in poisons and chemicals... [and] a Syrian with dual Spanish Nationality."[540] Though eventually killed in a suicide operation in 2014, Al-Suri had time to become the author of al-Qaeda's current tactical approach to global Jihad. That approach follows in Al-Qurashi's footsteps, as it looks not so much to Islam as to the Marxist legacy. Explains Ryan:

The key political factors that produce a climate for revolution, according to Al-Suri, amount to what Communist ideologues of the twentieth century recognized, but without the class analysis. The conditions for revolution or Jihad are generally those that arouse the local inhabitants, although there are a few universal touchstones, such as non-Muslim, foreign invasions. "The best of these conditions which give rise to resistance are foreign invasion and the proliferation of politico-religious, economic, and social causes of revolution and Jihad. This is what is termed in books about guerrilla warfare 'the climate for revolution,' while we use the term 'the climate for Jihad' in our literature."[541]

Though not much of a religious scholar, Al-Suri was a traditional revolutionary. He appealed to the masses in ways similar to apocalyptic utopians centuries earlier. One of his signature slogans, "echoing Al-Zawahiri and Lenin before him," writes Ryan, was "The Resistance is a battle of the *ummah* and not a struggle of the elite."[542]

The self-proclaimed Islamist elite had a problem. For no matter how privileged, they were not a vanguard in either the Marxist or the traditional Islamic sense, not being deeply religious scholars. Membership in the *ummah*, in turn, required both (the right) piety and being duly oppressed. To mobilize them, the leadership needed a suffering underdog. No one else could better fill that role than the hapless Palestinians. Victimized by the Jew – the capitalist Antichrist, anti-Allah incarnation of Satan – they fit the bill perfectly. Antisemitism to the rescue.

Palestinians as Proletarians

Though dejected by Hitler's inability to "finish the job" during the Holocaust, Al-Hussaini quickly took up the mantle of antisemitism with panache. Despite his role in innumerable war crimes of which the Allies, including the United States, were well aware, the wily Haj "was allowed to reestablish himself as the unchallengeable leader of the Palestinian Arabs," presumably to appease the Arabs. Acquiescing to extremism would become a default Western tactic, bound to fail. Instead, it "insured that no compromise or two-state solution would be considered."[543] In addition to his own "liberation" movement, "most of the other forces pushing for intransigence and war over the Palestine issue also came from the same radical Arab and Islamist faction that had cooperated with the Nazis," especially in Egypt, Syria, Iraq. But the Mufti of Jerusalem remained the principal Palestinian Arab and Islamist leader until the mantle was transferred to Yassir Arafat (1929-2004) at a meeting in Al-Hussaini's Beirut home, on December 29, 1968, thanks to Egypt's President Abdul Nasser (1918-1970).

From the outset, Nasser had displayed almost total disinterest in establishing a Palestinian state. Writes Michael Sharnoff: "Nasser commonly deemphasized a distinct Palestinian identity by addressing them as 'Arabs of Palestine' or even more broadly as 'the people of Palestine.'"[544] How little he cared for them is demonstrated by Nasser's continuation of his predecessor's policy of Egyptian control over Gaza, home to more than a quarter of a million Palestinians. Under Nasser's rule, these hapless people "were denied Egyptian citizenship and were harshly ruled by a string of Egyptian governors, who severely restricted their freedom of movement and expression."[545] On March 29, 1955, Nasser stressed to a crowd in Gaza the broader concept of Arab nationalism at the expense of Palestinian nationalism: "We will never forget the conspiracies hatched to eliminate Arab nationalism in Palestine."[546] Their well-being was subsumed to Nasser's pan-Arab designs; Palestinians were being held hostage. Jews forced to leave Arab countries, numbering in the hundreds of thousands,[547] emigrated to Israel and elsewhere; Palestinians were not so lucky.

Al-Qaeda's attitude was no different: these unfortunates served as a political tool, not suffering people. Writes Ryan: "One thing is certain: Al-Qaeda does not care that Palestinians want to have a voice in the way they are governed, frame their own laws, and set up their own system of government. The essence of *hakimiyyah* (according to the way al-Qaeda interprets Islamic law) is that governing belongs to Allah alone."[548] In other words, self-government is anti-Islamic, polytheistic. But if that means using nationalist rhetoric, so be it: like previous revolutionaries, al-Qaeda's leadership uses the downtrodden to advance their own agenda. Antisemitism, however, required no compromise. Though far more virulent in Christian lands, hatred of the Jews is easy to arouse among Muslims. In addition to the usual theologically-based antagonism, Russian-fabricated *Protocols*, and British double-dealing in promising Palestine to both Jews and Arabs,[549] German racist propaganda added fuel to an already smoldering fire.

By the time of al-Qaeda's rise in the 1990s, the Muslim world seemed to have reached a political dead-end. The war of independence in 1947-48 was followed by United Nations recognition of Israel. Repeated Jewish successes, its growing economy, and international reach, were increasingly traumatic. By far the most humiliating, however, was the Arab armies' overwhelming defeat in June 1967, that took a mere six days. The shame seemed unbearable. However powerful the lethal obsession of antisemitism may have been in the past, after that catastrophe, it rallied the entire Middle East as never before.[550]

The growing closeness between the United States and Israel contributed to the perception of a world-wide conspiracy, a sinister plot of capitalist exploitation allegedly concocted inside the lofty towers of New York City. It is only the latest expression of the millennial dualism that concentrates "evil" in order to oppose it with violence. Writes Robert Wistrich: "The 'Jewish question' in radical Islam (as with its Western Christian, Nazi, and Marxist predecessors) is not centered primarily on Palestine – at least not as a territorial or national issue amenable to rational bargaining. The mythical thinking that animates Islamist ideology"[551] is expressed neither in geopolitical nor economic terms. Bar agrees that the narrative is a-rational: "The contemporary doctrine of Jihad is permeated by apocalyptical and eschatological ideas and fueled by texts and concepts that had fallen into desuetude and then been recycled."[552]

Nothing came as close to a confirmation of Islamists' millenarian hopes as 9/11. Shortly thereafter, Muslim Brotherhood cleric Yusuf Al-Qaradawi, chairman of the International Union of Muslim Scholars and trustee of the Oxford Centre for Islamic Studies, currently residing in Qatar, declared that "[t]he signs of salvation are absolute, numerous, and as plain as day, indicating that the future belongs to Islam and that Allah's religion will defeat all other religions... [T]he conquest of Rome and the spread of Islam till it includes all that is in night and day... are prelude to the return of the Caliphate."[553]

His overseas residences notwithstanding, Al-Qaradawi, a disciple of Hasan Al-Banna, is no stranger to America. In 1995, when addressing the Muslim Arab Youth Association in Toledo, Ohio, in 1995, he fulminated: "We will conquer Europe, we will conquer America! Not through sword but through Da'wa [proselytizing]." Which is not to say that he opposes the sword. After citing the infamous antisemitic hadith "You shall continue to fight the Jews and they will fight you, until the Muslims will kill them," he concludes by alluding to the Apocalypse: "The resurrection will not come before this happens."[554]

For condoning Palestinian suicide bombings against Israelis, in 2008 he was refused an entry visa to the United Kingdom, and was barred from entering France in 2012. In December 2014, Interpol issued a bulletin seeking his arrest "to serve a sentence" for crimes including "incitement and assistance to commit intentional murder."[555] That summons was retracted in September 2017, allowing Al-Qaradawi to continue promoting the ultimate victory of Islam unimpeded. Less than a month later, on November 7, 2017, he told the International Union of Muslim Scholars' Board of Trustees, at their fifth meeting in Istanbul, Turkey, that now "is our duty to restore the glory of the nation of Islam back to the level of those days, back to the days where the Muslims were rulers of the world."[556] As of May, 2019, he is happily ensconced in Qatar where, as in Saudi Arabia, the extremist ideology of Wahhabism dominates, and the government provides the Taliban with office space, while also supporting Islamist networks in Turkey, Bangladesh, and elsewhere.[557]

8:
Utopia Update

Citizens of the World Unite

A bumper sticker display of a whimsical "Whirled Peas" and a virtue-signaling "Egalitarian World Government" may raise a chuckle or two in rush-hour traffic. But to President Woodrow Wilson it was no laughing matter. He envisaged the League of Nations as the means to achieve global harmony and justice. Wilson's supra-national League, writes Trygve Thorntveit, had been predicated on "a deliberative, remarkably egalitarian polity, requiring significant concessions of sovereignty from members in order to facilitate cooperative change."[558] The humility-challenged Wilson had undertaken to "develop the nation's first genuinely internationalist foreign policy,"[559] with nary a nod to reality. But he had admitted himself that for peace to last, the "balance of power" had to give way to "'a community of power,' promoting cooperative striving for the global good."[560] Such rhetoric might have worked in Bolshevik post-tsarist Russia, but not in a Europe torn to pieces, let alone in America, whose people had fought for their own community but a few decades earlier, at a staggeringly bloody price. No wonder that when the politically tone-deaf president preached to his countrymen "[w]e are provincials no longer" but "citizens of the world," his millenarian globalism fell mostly flat.

Mostly, but not entirely. Some recognized that his "radical vision entailed radical means to achieve it," and assistance soon arrived, predictably from the radical halls of the academy and the no less radical editorial offices of *The New Republic*. With their help, notes Thorntveit, "Wilson embraced a drastically transformed world order, anchored by a body combining deliberative, legislative, judicial, and enforcement organs, and charged with improving human life, not just responding to crises that threatened it."[561] The chattering classes repackaged, duplicated, and dutifully disseminated the message, applauding the League as a panacea.

The contribution of Wilson's intellectual colleagues notwithstanding, Townsend Hoopes and Douglas Brinkley give the

President most of the credit for the initiative: "[T]he Covenant of the League was mainly the creation of Woodrow Wilson and reflected a soaring idealism rooted in the philosophical premise that there could and must be genuine equality in relations among the sovereign nations of the world."[562] The plan seemed too good to be true: Should any nation wage war, the League required all its members to impose financial and trade sanctions immediately. If that failed, the League's governing Council would have to unanimously "recommend" that governments contribute military forces to carry out "enforcement by common action of international obligation." Idealism had soared indeed, its rocket headed straight into the heavens. It was bound to encounter the fate of its pre-technological prototype, the hapless Icarus.[563]

It is unlikely that additional prudence could have compensated for the fatal design flaws, of which allowing an aggressor nation to veto proposed sanctions against itself was but the most ludicrous. The U.S. Senate, reflecting the common sense of its constituents, rejected United States participation on November 19, 1919. But the 1920 Democratic vice-presidential nominee, Franklin Delano Roosevelt, continued to support the idea of a League, as convinced as Wilson had been of the need for international governance. Three years later, by then a private citizen, FDR developed a Plan to Preserve World Peace that eliminated the unanimity requirement. His main objection to the earlier versions had been merely practical, not philosophical. Writing to his friend George Marvin on January 29, 1924, FDR described his plan "to kill the existing League and set up something in its place that would have allowed countless thousands … [to save] face, honor, and all other fool things they think have to be saved."[564] Among those "fool things," presumably, was national sovereignty. And among those countless thousands so manifestly blind to their own interests were the ignorant American masses.

Two decades later, as president, he was able to take up the torch of internationalism in earnest, as the handsome United Nations (UN) building was being raised on Turtle Bay in Manhattan, with the help of John D. Rockefeller and his son Nelson. Unlike the League, the UN was established not at the end of hostilities but during the very heat of battle. The occasion was the arrival of Winston Churchill in the U.S. on December 22, 1941, primarily to cement the Anglo-American partnership and create a combined general staff to coordinate military strategy. The outcome of that meeting was a Declaration of United Nations, signed on January 1, 1942, promising to create a future peacekeeping organization dedicated to ensuring "life, liberty, independence, and religious freedom, and to preserve the rights of man and justice."[565] ("Religious freedom" had been added at Roosevelt's insistence, over Stalin's objections.) It is noteworthy that all these freedoms are variations on the right to pursue one's life without government interference. But that was about to change.

The Declaration had been drafted by FDR's closest advisor, Harry Hopkins,[566] and affirmed the determination of its signatories – initially 26, with 21 more added by the end of 1945 - to defeat "Hitlerism." The enemy, then, was not the armies of the Axis, nor a coalition of aggressor states, but an "ism," an ideology. Declaring "that [the Allies] are now engaged in a common struggle against savage and brutal forces seeking to subjugate the world," the signatories considered themselves players in an apocalyptic war against the Antichrist of "Hitlerism." The institution's purpose, therefore, was to wage a war of ideas. No wonder it turned out to favor the shrewdest, most devious practitioners of that art. These were clearly not the Western powers.

FDR did not live to see the birth of the UN. But he, as much as his uncle Teddy, to say nothing of Wilson, would have undoubtedly loved the outdoor sculpture whose title was "Let Us Beat Swords into Plowshares." The words come from *Isaiah* 2.4: "And He shall judge among the nations and shall rebuke many people: and they shall beat their swords into plowshares, and their spears into pruninghooks: nation shall not lift up sword against nation, neither shall they learn war any more." One cannot help wondering if not learning it is why they couldn't avoid waging it. But that topic is the subject of another book.[567]

Ironically, the statue of an enormous godlike figure holding a huge hammer and bending a sword into a stone had been a gift from Stalin. Since the symbolism was far from unequivocal, it could have been a subtle joke. Did the hammer symbolize socialism and the sword capitalism? Was a verse about Apocalypse a warning to the West? Perhaps both. What is hard to deny is the UN's value to the USSR as both a propaganda platform and a perfect site for conducting espionage.

Could the UN have promoted anything even vaguely resembling world governance? Its structure alone made that unlikely. Since the Security Council was empowered to authorize military action against an aggressor state *only* in the event of a consensus among its five permanent members, their incompatible worldviews and interests guaranteed its paralysis. The red fox, who had never harbored any illusions, was contentedly ensconced inside the chicken coop.

Literally. For since the UN Secretariat provided a fine opportunity for spies to be hired as "international civil servants," its headquarters in the heart of New York served as a major intelligence outpost.[568] It was ideally suited for the Russians, along with their satellites, and once it joined the Security Council, the People's Republic of China. In 1974, the Palestinian Liberation Organization (PLO) was officially invited to establish its own quasi-national Mission, to be staffed by members of the PLO, while others could be hired to work in the Secretariat.[569] It was a double whammy: not only was the UN conferring legitimacy on an organization that took pride in committing terrorist acts, it also gave them shelter on U.S. soil. Thus, when in 1987, after the attack on the cruise ship Achile Lauro, Congress sought to close the New York Mission along with the PLO's Washington office by denying visas to its members, the Federal District Court of New York declared the attempt a violation of the Headquarters Agreement. Couldn't be done.

Seven decades after its creation, the United Nations' ability to influence public opinion has since grown exponentially. To be sure, the organization is taken less seriously as a prototype for world government, but the utopian idea that inspired Western globalists continues to appeal. Notable among its enthusiastic proponents is the President of the International Studies Association, Thomas G. Weiss, who rhetorically questioned its members, at their 2009 annual convention: "Will it take a calamity on the scale of World War II ... to catalyze a transformation of the current feeble system ... into something with at least some attributes of a world federal government?" – a concept, he regretfully recalls, that had "once been a staple of informed debate on international affairs." He deplores its "replacement by 'global governance'"[570] as something of a sellout.

While conceding that "there are numerous ways to think about an eventual supra-national entity, and human agency is an essential element in every one," the bottom line for Weiss is that "global government rather than [mere] global governance is the missing component of future analytical perspectives." A rose by any other name smells as sweet only if it's still a rose; to him, global governance is more thorns than petals, and no inebriating fragrance. Weiss persists, accusing his fellow "analysts of international organizations [of having] strayed away from paradigmatic rethinking. We have lost our appetite for big and idealistic plans because so many previous ones have failed."[571] OK, maybe all. But failure is no reason to abandon utopia, is it.

He warns against opponents: "The market will not graciously provide global institutions to ensure human survival with dignity." He laments that currently, "at the international level, we have governance minus government, which means virtually no capacity to ensure compliance with collective decisions."[572] In other words, it's merely voluntary – oh that contemptible *market!* - when outright coercion is really called for, in the name of global justice of course. *Pace* cartographers, Weiss applauds Oscar Wilde for saying: "A map of the world that does not include Utopia is not worth looking at." The irony clearly eluded him; if only he had heeded Wilde's other admission: "I am so clever that sometimes I don't understand a single word of what I am saying."

The Apocalypse that was World War II should have been impetus enough, in Weiss's opinion, to create a world government as envisaged by Woodrow Wilson and the three Roosevelts, including Eleanor. Weiss still firmly believes that "human beings can organize themselves to solve global problems," it is only a question of when. He shares Peter Singer's optimism that "[o]ver time, there will be voluntary actions by governments and peoples – akin to what is happening in the European Union – and this gradual process could eventually result in important elements of a world federal government."[573] In the meantime, says Weiss, the UN has to be made to work; indeed, more than that, "it must be seen to work for all." Must be *seen*. Whether it does or not.

The "all" to whom he refers, also loftily called "the world community," is hyperbolic, the populist rhetoric used by the academic clerisy. John Fonte cuts to the chase: "[T]he global governance project" is essentially "a grand ideological and institutional enterprise that promises to be of world-historical significance – an attempt to create new political forms above and beyond the liberal democratic nation-state."[574] True to form, those empowered to speak for "all" are the infamous vanguard, the intellectual elite, who know the real interests of the "countless thousands." These are the *bien-pensants*,[575] who take it as a given that Public International Organizations (PIOs) such as the World Bank, the International Monetary Fund, all the specialized UN agencies, the European Union, and a slew of others, represent the "international community." It goes without saying that anyone in opposition is a troglodyte (caveperson).

Besides inter-governmental groups, however, the international nongovernmental organizations (NGOs), also reverently referred to as the "international civil society," have gradually been promoted to the vanguard of "the international community," becoming increasingly influential. John Fonte refers to both PIOs and NGOs as "the party of global governance," since they all share the hubristic presumption of entitlement to speak for the entire globe. What they also share is a relative indifference to the ballot box, for they act with remarkable independence from control by democratically elected constituencies. The elite "epistemic communities"[576] include academics, diplomats, and international bureaucrats, which all presume to speak "for the interests of the world's poor," the good of "the people." But the presumption they share, sometimes called "internationalism," has come under scathing criticism by American University law professor Kenneth Anderson.

Its proponents' intellectual pretensions notwithstanding (he calls international public law "less academic discipline than club of the like-minded[577]), "internationalism is a faith... like any other," writes Anderson. It assumes that "the highest forms of power and legitimacy be[ing] fused in international organizations, establishing the constitutional supremacy of international law over all national law, as though the world were a unitary society... is morally desirable, good, and right. Internationalism presupposes that moral as well as historical progress, or 'globalism,' is evolving..." In plainer English, "internationalism is progress, and progress is good." End of story.

The same hideous Medusa whose heads instantly regenerate upon decapitation, we have here utopian millenarianism in modern garb. Anderson recognizes the pedigree: "The contemporary claims of internationalism are in many ways merely a secularization of ancient Catholic thought as it was drawn from Biblical texts and then given a specifically medieval Christian cast." Outside this context, those wild claims sound courageous, idealistic. But "they are comprehensible only upon the religious worldview that boldly proclaims the good news of international organizations, differing from the view of the Psalmist – the 'earth is the Lord's, and the fullness thereof' the world, and they that shall dwell therein'" as goes the passage from *Isaiah*. Except this time, scoffs Anderson, it is "the UN, that duly noted steward of the Lord, [who will] inherit the earth."[578] From the sublime to the subliminally subversive.

He attacks more generally "the very idea of a 'world order' as a disturbing remnant of Judeo-Christian eschatology ... that is, if anything, stronger even than its Biblical antecedents... because it imagines that it will be carried out in historical time and not merely in the City of God. It is more frightening, at least to those of us who are frightened by all dreams of political and social totality...." He recognizes, of course, that "the order of 'all nations,' flowing together to a central place, receiving the law from a city and a mountain ... is an ancient and powerful dream." An all-too familiar dream: "This," he notes, "is hubris." Amen.

Another important aspect of the millenarian utopian mindset is pitting the rich against the poor people of the world, insisting that the latter's human rights are *ipso facto* violated by the former, their poverty an accusation in itself. Most NGOs, reflexively, congenitally, progressive, are especially prone to this form of reasoning when they claim to speak in the name of the "public" interest, ambassadors-without-portfolio for "the poor." In an unpublished essay titled "After Seattle," written in 2000, Anderson writes that the "elite media," such as the *Economist*, have only exacerbated the problem by implicitly conferring special moral approval to this putative "international civil society." Such bombast only reinforces the self-righteousness of organizations that are in no way accountable to anyone but their funders, whether government agencies or private donors with individual agendas, however well intentioned.

Anderson charges that the "human rights movement is as a kind of secular religion... increasingly assuming the tone of (prosecutorial) authority and taking its international structures as grounds for the reform of recalcitrant nation-states within what might be thought of [as] the Holy Human Rights Empire."[579] Were it not so disinterested in historical precedent, laments Anderson, this secular religious movement might be more reluctant to formulate "ever-new human rights that have, as their core aim, not just the protection of human beings from what the state might do to them, and not even just the moral improvement of human beings, but their purification."[580] Yet purification is precisely what the crusade requires.

Holy Human Rights Empire

That human rights have been taken hostage by nations fundamentally hostile to traditional freedom as understood by America's Founders should not come as a surprise: The United Nations was an ideological trojan horse from the outset. The UN Declaration of Human Rights, adopted by the General Assembly on December 10, 1948, glorified so-called "economic and social rights" – including health, education, housing, decent work – in addition to traditional civil and political liberties.[581] Write Gillian MacNaughton and Mariah McGill:

> From the initial draft of the then-labeled "International Bill of Human Rights" by John Humphrey, which was based largely upon the constitutions of the members of the United Nations at

the time, to the final Declaration adopted on December 10, 1948, the United States supported this holistic human rights framework encompassing a full spectrum of economic, social, cultural, civil, and political rights.[582]

It wasn't the Kremlin's doing alone: FDR had included all those non-traditional "rights" among his famous Four Freedoms under the umbrella of the alleged "freedom from want," where "want" is left to the discretion and appetite of the listener. Updating his old Plan to Preserve World Peace drafted two decades earlier, Franklin told Congress in his 1944 State of the Union address: "We have come to a clear realization of the fact that true individual freedom cannot exist without economic security and independence."[583] Channeling Jefferson, he declared that "certain economic truths have become accepted as self-evident. We have accepted, so to speak, a second Bill of Rights under which a new basis of security and prosperity can be established for all regardless of station, race, or creed."[584] Among those rights he lists, among others, earning enough to provide *adequate* food and clothing and recreation, along with the right of every family to a *decent* home. Claiming that "we" have accepted "so to speak" all these rights is, as they say, rich.

Unsurprisingly, neither of the two Bills of Rights went anywhere in the Congress at the time of their proposal. But the erosion of constitutionally guaranteed freedoms was well on its way. Explains Aaron Rhodes: "[T]he progressive movement deepened a rupture in American politics about the classical liberalism of the Founders." FDR's proclamation that "true individual freedom cannot exist without economic security and independence .... [manifestly] contradicted the traditional American view that the real threat to freedom is coercion."[585]

A brief definitional interlude is in order, with a more thorough discussion to follow later. Freedom from coercion is sometimes known as *negative* because it consists only in *refraining*, rather than requiring a *positive* action, such as *providing* goods or services. The term is Isaiah Berlin's, who defines negative freedom as "[e]quality of liberty; not to treat others as I should not wish them to treat me; repayment of my debt to those who alone have made possible my liberty or prosperity or enlightenment; justice, in its simplest and most universal sense," which he identifies as "the foundations of liberal morality."[586] These are the rights of the Golden Rule, to which everyone may subscribe without violating anyone else's freedom, as they require only abstention. The same cannot be said of positive freedom, or liberty, which requires positive action. And if that involves coercion, negative freedom is violated. Fortunately, helping the less fortunate happens with commendable frequency; and it is admired precisely because it is not obligatory.

The UN Declaration's ominous proliferation of rights which imply mandatory obligation inevitably "opened a moral and legal space to justify discrimination in the name of an engineered equality," writes Rhodes.[587] This bodes ill for freedom. As Berlin points out, those so-called "economic and social rights" lie "at the heart of many of the nationalist, Communist, authoritarian and totalitarian creeds of our day."[588] While proponents of negative rights "want to curb authority as such," those who champion positive so-called rights "want it placed in their own hands. These are not two different interpretations of a single concept, but two profoundly divergent and irreconcilable attitudes to the ends of life." In fact, continues Berlin, "they have led in the end to the great clash of ideologies that dominates our world." And it is the "positive" conception of liberty" that is, "at times, no better than a specious disguise for brutal tyranny."[589] It's a terrific disguise though; it continues to fool the naïve while protecting the hypocrite.

By calling the latter "rights," indeed of a "positive" variety, its utopian proponents manage to obfuscate their contempt for negative, or traditional, liberty by appropriating its aura while obliterating its true meaning. It was a brilliant semantic coup. By mixing together "the political values both of states committed to individual liberty and of Stalin's totalitarian regime, which, it can be argued, had less respect for individual freedom than had Hitler's Germany,"[590] the latter scored a stunning propaganda victory. Promoting positive "rights" has resulted in "placing economic burdens on governments, imposing themselves on democratic political processes, and reaching toward a coercive, bureaucratic, regulatory utopia."[591] Those burdens do not bother centrally planned regimes for which truth is optional so much as market democracies, whose political practices are being dismissed as superseded by "international norms."

Some of these putative positive "rights" included in the UN Declaration border on the absurd. Article 24, for example, states: "Everyone has the right to rest and leisure, including reasonable limitation of working 72 hours and periodic holidays with pay."[592] Read that in light of Article 2: "Everyone is entitled to all the rights and freedoms set forth in this Declaration... [specifically,] no distinction shall be made on the basis of the political, jurisdictional or international status of the country or territory to which a person belongs, whether it be independent, trust, non-self-governing or under any other limitation of sovereignty." So *everyone* is entitled to *all* the "rights" included in this document – every citizen of the world. And who pays?

Funny you should ask. The UN Declaration must be read together with the UN Charter, signed three years earlier, in 1945, which states as one of its four purposes: "To achieve international cooperation in solving international problems of an economic, social, cultural, or humanitarian character, and in promoting and encouraging respect for human rights and for fundamental freedoms for all without distinction as to race, sex, language, or religion."[593] The UN Declaration duly proceeded to spell them out. For as its Progressive authors knew full well, the United Nations was set up to promote what would later be called, only slightly more candidly, "social justice."

This is further confirmed by the International Forum for Social Development Report titled "Social Justice in an Open World," published by the UN's Department of Economic and Social Affairs in 2006. The Report claims that "[t]he Charter and the Universal Declaration provided the United Nations and its Secretariat with a solid foundation for contributing to the propagation of justice in the world."[594] Hadn't the war-time document preceding the Charter pledged all the states fighting "Hitlerism" to defending "justice"? It was a wolf dialectically clad in sheep's clothing.

Two decades later, the concept would morph more or less seamlessly into its progressive counterpart which stood the classical meaning on its proverbial head. At last ready for prime time,

> social justice first appeared in United Nations texts during the second half of the 1960s. At the initiative of the Soviet Union, and with the support of developing countries, the term was used in the "Declaration on Social Progress and Development," adopted in 1969.[595] Five years later, it appeared in the Charter of the Economic Rights and Duties of States.... By the time [it] came out, social justice was a familiar concept... [True,] social justice, equality and equity were sometimes defined as distinct concepts but were more often used loosely and interchangeably.[596]

And correctly. Thereafter, safely out of the closet, "in spite of the various challenges faced over the years," the Report assures its readers, "the fundamental commitment to achieving global equality and justice has not wavered."[597] This does not imply just focusing on poverty; for "only when it constitutes part of an overall economic and social policy aimed at achieving growth and equality" will it make a difference – in other words, by changing the political structure in a roughly socialist direction. Not that the "s" word need be used when euphemisms will do.

The Report was the culmination of more than two decades of particularly aggressive agitprop for which the UN provided venues, publication facilities, and trained propagandists. Writes Rhodes:

> The early 1990s saw a worldwide resurgence of left-wing politics under a range of slogans providing cosmetic dissociation from Communism and state socialism. Various movements presented themselves as countering "globalization," "neoliberalism," transnational business enterprises and free trade, and campaigning for redistributive policies, including the seizure of property and land.[598]

In the forefront were the self-styled "'human rights' campaigns, promoting social and economic rights and asserting that civil and political rights by themselves are a recipe for exploitative, even racist capitalism. But these were (and are) movements essentially advocating coercion in the name of human rights."[599]

In many ways, however, the change in language evinced a deeper radicalism. The Report readily admits being predicated on the increasingly widespread assumption that "the State is no longer the main actor on the international scene, and its relevance will continue to diminish as the process of globalization gains momentum." Ergo, the principal concern for egalitarian internationalists is no longer seeking a "balance" between rich and poor countries. Instead, the problem of inequality is transnational: everyone is included in the equation. Watch out, developed countries: it is you who are responsible for the world's poor.

The practical implication of treating all human beings as citizens of the world is that *everyone* is held responsible for inequality, thus conveniently circumventing such quaint concepts as divergent national interests, not to mention the responsibility of specific individuals and government officials for corruption, fraud, and mismanagement. Inequality is now understood in the aggregate. We in the West are all our brothers' keepers; our enemies are usually just, well, poor; we need to help, not hurt them. The Report urges that all "[t]hose interested in the pursuit of international justice should work on developing processes and institutions that could regulate and balance the interplay of transnational forces rather than remaining preoccupied with inequalities among entities that are destined to be marginalized and ultimately disappear...." [600] The dialectic of the ruling bourgeoisie vs. a destitute proletariat has been replaced by the developed (capitalist) as against the developing (exploited) countries. Declares the Report: "For the countries of the world, the distance between the rich and the poor, the powerful and the weak, and the self-sufficient and the dependent, is now often characterized as an abyss." [601] Ah yes: apocalyptic.

Describing the distance between these two classes as an abyss leaves little room for nuance. Welcome to the new class struggle, not so different from the old class struggle. The international vanguard is stepping up to the challenge by using all the tools of political warfare at its disposal to achieve its goal of erasing "contradictions," thereby fulfilling the promise of peace on earth. This blatant debasement of standards is due to a corrosive "lack of regard for moral distinctions – between cultures or ideas or principles" to the point of obscenity, charges Rhodes. "International human rights," he concludes, "has become an ideology that, under the guise of protecting human dignity, paints mankind as a species with little more individual autonomy than insects." [602]

You guessed the diagnosis. "Hubris has dragged international human rights law and institutions in political directions, and consequently, political division is weakening the commitment to human rights in Western societies." [603] It explains, though hardly justifies, the repeated failure by Western democracies to speak up as they watch repulsive double standards prostitute the most elementary norms of decency and common sense. Consider, for example, that the Human Rights Council passed a resolution in 2010 for "promoting the rights of everyone to the enjoyment of the highest attainable standard of physical and mental health through enhancing capacity-building in public health" sponsored by the model democracies of Algeria, Brazil, China, Egypt, Iran, Pakistan and South Africa. In a recent *Wall Street Journal* interview with James Taranto, Rhodes describes the Council as "'controlled' by 'Islamic theocracies' and 'heavily under the influence of China.' Those unfree countries [advocate]... human rights without freedom.'" [604]

Of the countless absurdities coming out of the UN system, however, none is more outrageous than the United Nations' condemnation of Zionism as racism in 1975, followed by relentless accusations against the Jewish state as the modern-day incarnation of Nazi Germany.

Down with the Infidel Zionist Bourgeoisie

The infamous Human Rights Council had replaced, in 2006, the Commission on Human Rights, which had been established in 1946 to fulfill the pledge to promote respect for human rights "without distinction as to race, sex, language, or religion." Though during the first two decades the Commission did little more than assist in drafting human rights treaties, that all changed after 1967. The principal impetus, the result of massive and rapid UN-orchestrated decolonization, was a plethora of new kleptocracies ripe for manipulation by the KGB (Soviet secret police).[605]

From the original 51 states, by 1968, UN membership had reached 126. The Commission's membership swelled as well. At that point, the Commission began its campaign against the country it had voted into existence two decades earlier. Writes Hillel Neuer, executive director of the Geneva-based organization UN Watch:

> An alien observing the United Nations' debates, reading its resolutions, and walking its halls would conclude that a principal purpose of the world body is to censure a tiny country called Israel. ... The campaign to demonize and delegitimize Israel at every opportunity and in every forum was initiated by the Arab states together with the former Soviet Union and supported by what has become known as an 'automatic majority' of Third World UN member states. The result today is that the UN's political organs, specialized agencies, and bureaucratic divisions have been subverted in the name of a relentless propaganda war against the Jewish state."[606]

This was written in 2005, but this is what Eric Rozenman writes in October 2018:

> The United Nations, which initially welcomed Israel as a member state in 1949, would become perhaps the most influential purveyor and certifier of anti-Zionist antisemitism. UN agencies, including UNESCO, the General Assembly, at times even the Security Council and virtually always the UN Human Rights Commission – and when that body became too noxious, its barely remodeled successor, the UN Human Rights Council - produced innumerable resolutions condemning Israel for all sorts of non-existent crimes....Israel, the Jewish state, functions in the revival of open, widespread antisemitism as the

individual Jew did in pre-Holocaust Jew-hatred. So at the United Nations it is old business renewed as usual.[607]

In sheer volume, the time and resources spent demonizing Israel is staggering. The UN Watch reports that there are three special UN entities dedicated to the Palestinian cause. The oldest is the Special Committee to Investigate Israeli Practices Affecting the Human Rights of the Palestinian People and Other Arabs of the Occupied Territories, created in 1968. In 1975, the General Assembly added the Committee on the Exercise of the Inalienable Rights of the Palestinian People. Supporting its work is the Division for Palestinian Rights, established in 1977, inside the UN Secretariat, with a large staff and a budget of millions, which it devotes to the constant promotion of anti-Israel propaganda throughout the world.[608]

The General Assembly is the engine driving the Israel-bashing machinery. According to Eugene Kontorovich and Penny Grunseid,

> Israel is referred to as the 'occupying power' 530 times in UN General Assembly (UNGA) resolutions. Yet, in seven major instances of past or present prolonged military occupation – Indonesia in East Timor, Turkey in northern Cyprus, Russia in areas of Georgia, Morocco in Western Sahara, Vietnam in Cambodia, Armenia in Azerbaijan, and Russia in Ukraine's Crimea – the number is zero. The UNGA has not called any of these countries an 'occupying power.' Not even once.[609]

Laments Rozenman: "That imbalance would be striking if the tilt undermined any other country." The title of his book captures it best: *Jews Make the Best Demons*.

The official launch of the UN's war to delegitimize Israel took place on November 13, 1974, when PLO Chairman Yasser Arafat addressed the 138 delegates gathered inside the great hall of the General Assembly. This is how *The New York Times* described the event: "In what a sounded like a threat of intensified guerrilla activity if the Palestine Liberation Organization's proposal for a multi-faith Palestinian state was not accepted, Mr. Arafat said toward the end of his speech: 'I have come bearing an olive branch and freedom fighter's gun.'"[610] Only the olive branch was meant figuratively; under his windbreaker, he was wearing a real holster. A more insolent affront to the putatively peace-seeking organization is hard to fathom.

The anti-Zionist campaign was on, full-speed ahead. First came a proclamation adopted at the World Conference of the International Women's Year in Mexico City on July 2, 1975, demanding "the elimination of colonialism and neo-colonialism, foreign occupation, zionism, apartheid and racial discrimination in all its forms."[611] Not to be outdone, the Organization of African Unity explicitly declared, a month later, that "the racist regime in occupied Palestine and the racist regime in Zimbabwe and South Africa have a common imperialist origin, forming a whole and having the same racist structure and being organically linked in their policy aimed at repression of the dignity and integrity of the human being." On August 30, ministers for foreign affairs of Non-Aligned Countries unable to contain their outrage any longer, decided to "most severely condemn zionism as a threat to world peace and security and call upon all countries to oppose this racist and imperialist ideology."

By November 10 the stage had been set for the UN General Assembly to adopt Resolution 3379 by a vote of 72 to 35 (with 32 abstentions), which announced that the whole world, by majority vote, thereby "determines that Zionism is a form of racism and racial discrimination."[612] This was UN-speak for the Antichrist.

Speaking on behalf of six million murdered Jews, millions more evicted from hostile Arab nations, and his countrymen who had never opposed the creation of a Palestinian state alongside Israel, Israeli ambassador to the UN Chaim Herzog delivered what Simon Sebag Montefiore described as "one of the great speeches of the 20th century." In his address, Herzog mentioned the Arab ministers who have served in his government, the Arab deputy speaker of parliament, Arab officers who voluntarily joined Israel's police forces, "frequently commanding Jewish troops," the thousands of Arabs who come for medical treatment to Israel, and so on.[613] Ironically, noted Herzog, the infamous Resolution had fallen on the 37th anniversary of Kristallnacht, when Nazi stormtroopers attacked the Jewish community in Germany, burning synagogues in all the cities, killing ordinary civilians. He noted that this resolution was "the first organized attack on an established religion since the Middle Ages," and denounced the two great evils of our times: hatred and ignorance.

The ignorance of which he spoke was not merely absence of knowledge but deliberate efforts at disinformation, chiefly instigated by the USSR. Former Romanian chief of foreign intelligence General Ion Mihai Pacepa, who defected to the U.S. in 1978, reports that Soviet General Aleksandr Sakharovsky in 1949 identified the Soviet Union's principal enemy as America's "Zionist bourgeoisie." Sakharovsky, founder of Romania's secret police, the infamous Securitate, explained to Pacepa and his fellow spies that World War III would be waged without weapons: it would be a war of ideas, an intelligence war. The Russians would fight it by disseminating falsehoods that nevertheless looked credible, spreading them throughout the world – and the Securitate would be on the front lines, fueling hatred of the super-Jew.

"The Securitate's first major *dezinformatsiya* task in the new World War III," writes Pacepa, "was to help Moscow reignite antisemitism in Western Europe by spreading thousands of copies of an old Russian forgery, *The Protocols of the Elders of Zion*, in that part of the world. It had to be done secretly, so no one would know that the publications came from the Soviet bloc."[614] Accordingly, in 1951, Sakharovsky brought a copy of the *Protocols* to Bucharest and ordered it to be translated, multiplied and surreptitiously disseminated. It was not long before "the Securitate was spreading the *Protocols* around the Middle East as well."[615]

It had been an exceptionally effective campaign, providing anti-Zionists of all stripes with ammunition for attacking the Jews that confirmed all their worst fears: there was a worldwide conspiracy, which had to be fought at all cost. In addition to Osama bin Laden and his ideological father Sayyid Qutb, along with their Jihadist followers, belief in the fantasies of the *Protocols* is as strong as ever: "To this day," writes Robert Wistrich, "it remains absolutely mainstream in the Muslim world."[616]

By the time Resolution 3379 was finally repealed in 1991, after the Soviet Bloc had disintegrated, it was far too late to undo the damage. UN resolutions never die, they only seep into the political culture to do their slow, lethal damage. In his comprehensive account of the gradual infiltration by the PLO into the United Nations, Harris O. Schoenberg tells a sorry tale of a "strange and frightening transformation," as each passing year, hatred of Israel was increasingly being accepted "as natural and inevitable."[617] The PLO scored its greatest success upon being admitted, on October 31, 2011 as a "member state" of UNESCO (the UN Educational, Scientific, and Cultural Organization). Though praised on occasion for its "moderation" in comparison with its rival Hamas, currently on the State Department's list of terrorist organizations, the PLO has never abandoned its goal to annihilate the state of Israel.

Hatred of the Jewish state must be understood as intimately linked to a rabid anti-Americanism that grew exponentially after 1967. As Robert Wistrich explains, "Israel increasingly became a surrogate target for those reluctant to take on the might of the United States," resulting in "a growing convergence in the demonization of both nations."[618] "In the minds of their adversaries," he continues, the United States and Israel have come to symbolize in recent years a whole cluster of threats – including globalization, neoliberal capitalist exploitation of the Third World, ethnic intolerance" and all the other familiar faces of the Antichrist.

Josef Joffe summarizes the sinister narrative: "Indeed, the United States is an anti-Semitic fantasy come true, the *Protocols of the Elders of Zion* in living color. Don't Jews, their first loyalty to Israel, control the Congress, the Pentagon, the banks, the universities, and the media? This time the conspirator is not 'World Jewry,' but Israel. Having captured the 'hyperpower,' Jews qua Israelis finally do rule the world. It is Israel as the Über-Jew, and America as its slave."[619]

Both Americans and Jews are seen as self-righteous crusaders, on a "divine mission" to liberate the world. They fit perfectly the prototype of money-grubbing profiteers, whose influence – financial, cultural, technological – seems to grow daily. The United States is handled a tad more gingerly than Israel if only because it pays the lion's share of the UN's bills, more than 180 other UN member states combined. But there are many ways to fight against the Antichrist.

The clearest expression of the anti-Zionist ideology has long been available courtesy of U.S. taxpayer-funded textbooks produced by the Palestinian Authority for the UN Relief and Works Agency (UNRWA), taught throughout its refugee camps, in all schools in the West Bank and Gaza.[620] Never mind that UNRWA is supposed to be committed to the UN principles of peaceful resolution of conflicts, and must not represent a member state as illegitimate; this is what eleventh-graders were taught in 2017: "Colonization constitutes the main point in the idea and a practical implementation of Zionism.... That is based on the denial and uprooting of the 'other' rather than on co-existence with it or the acceptance of its existence."[621] Does it matter that Israel voted on November 29, 1947, in favor of the UN General Assembly Resolution 181 calling for the partition of the British-ruled Palestinian Mandate into a Jewish state and an Arab State? Never mentioned; by contrast, "the partition ... was rejected by the Arabs who unanimously agreed to oppose and overthrow it, even by force."[622]

The land that the Palestinians claim as their own, according to the textbooks, happens to coincide with the current state of Israel. The Jews do not deserve a state. According to a comprehensive critical study of the UNRWA textbooks titled "Schoolbooks of the Palestinian Authority (PA):

The Attitude to the Jews, to Israel and to Peace," the Jews are denied "recognition as a modern nation entitled to national rights... They are rather described as citizens of various states."[623] Zionism itself is "described as a tool in the hands of Western Imperialism for the consolidation of its control over the Arab world. At a further stage of the narrative creation, Zionism is actually transformed into a European imperialist invention that later took root among the European Jews themselves."[624]

The textbooks invoke Jihad and martyrdom (*Shahadah*), with a view to giving the violence a religious character. Palestinian terrorists are called "the ones who sacrifice themselves," and if killed are called "martyrs," if imprisoned, "prisoners-of-war." Meanwhile, demonizing Zionism as "a form of racism," an instance of "apartheid" and tool of worldwide "imperialism," goes far beyond stigmatizing Israel the state. It is the latest incarnation of antisemitism.

As Robert Fine and Philip Spencer point out, "in contemporary antizionism... Israel, Zionism and the Jewish state are treated as symbolic representations of all that is illegitimate in the present-day international community."[625] Self-described Marxists, albeit not antizionist, Fine and Spencer explain how this works: "The Jewish question is not just an attitude of hostility to Jews or to those who invoke the sign of 'the Jews' but a theory designed to explain the winners and losers of capitalist society. It is formulated in terms of dichotomies - the modern and the backward, the people and its enemies, the civic and the ethnic, the postnational and the national, imperialism and anti-imperialism, power and resistance, the West and the rest."[626] Vague and ambiguous, these labels rehash the dialectic of struggle as the old millenarian leitmotif.

Their book is aptly titled *Antisemitism and the Left: On the Return of the Jewish Question*. For the Jewish "question" has indeed returned, after having just barely missed being "solved" by the Nazis. In the new version, the Jews are once again the enemies of the people, along with "imperialist" America at the helm of the venomous capitalist West. The "elect" who will prevail after the Apocalypse and inherit the earth are "the rest," the "backward," the "resistance," the victims. Beware their ire. For their ultimate target is not just one country; it is freedom itself.

Post-Communist Communism

To paraphrase Mark Twain's comments on the publication of his obituary, reports of the death of Communism have been grossly exaggerated. But if Twain didn't think the exaggeration altogether absurd in his own case - a mere case of mistaken identity - no such excuse absolves the pundits who assume ideologies can be toppled as easily as walls. Consider *The Washington Post*'s autopsy report, released on the one-hundredth anniversary of the Bolshevik Revolution:

> It [Communism] was done in by cynicism, exhaustion and the inevitable comparisons with the prosperous market economies of the West. Worldwide Communism was America's most fearsome enemy in the middle decades of the 20th century. But since 1989 one country after another has either thrown off Communism entirely, or pushed it discreetly aside in the pursuit of business. Today it lives on in only the most attenuated forms. North Korea is the one ferocious holdout among the remaining Communist nations, but even there markets have been changing the nature of the economy. [627]

The *Post* goes on to describe North Korea as still "more of a monarchy than a truly Communist nation. The introduction of market reforms — though on a smaller scale than in China or Vietnam — has helped the economy...."[628] *Post* readers will need to learn elsewhere the details of daily drudgery and famine. The outlook is upbeat: "[i]nternational organisations [which] have been collecting data in the country for more than two decades... [have found] small but significant improvements in the economy since the 1990s..." Note however that at the time, "the country was ravaged by a catastrophic famine that took the lives of an estimated one million people, out of a population of around 23 million."[629] Under the circumstances, any improvements would be "significant;" far more telling is that they were *small*. It's like saying that the patient is feeling a great deal better than he did when in a coma: he can now open his eyes and pray.

Greater insight may be gained from a recent report by the Institute for Science and International Security,[630] which concludes that what has been keeping North Koreans from starving is, mostly, China, "North Korea's lifeline to the world, providing it with the vast majority of its food and energy, and is the source of 90 % of North Korea's foreign trade."[631] Kim's so-called "free market reforms" are droplets in a vast, hopeless desert. Kim prefers making weapons.

Seemingly to justify Kim's choice of guns over butter, the *Post* notes that "North Korea views nuclear arms as the only means by which it can maintain its sovereignty in the face of what it calls American aggression." Once again more accurately, an article in *The New Yorker* concedes that "[e]xperts can't say definitively why Kim wants nuclear weapons.... Deterrence relies, at bottom, on the assumption that an adversary is not suicidal, but this Administration suspects that Kim's recklessness could trigger his own destruction."[632] That of his own people has been triggered long ago.

To its credit, the *Post* ran a rather more accurate assessment of North Korea's economy a few weeks later, based on gruesome data collected from intestinal contents of a North Korean defector who had run across the demilitarized zone, surviving five gunshot wounds. It writes:

> Doctors repairing the unidentified soldier's digestive tract found dozens of parasites in his intestines. One of the suspected roundworms was nearly a foot long.... According to a report by the United Nations, 2 in 5 people in North Korea are undernourished. Seventy percent of people require food assistance to survive, including 1.3 million children below the age of 5.... And the food they have access to can sicken or kill them. According to the *New York Times*, many North Korean defectors to the South have shown up infected with parasites.[633]

Though less murderous, the other countries the *Post* describes as "attenuated" versions of Communism are one-party "republics," which have all found some cynical euphemism for their autocracies: "Democratic" (Laos and North Korea), "Socialist" (Vietnam), "People's" (China), and "Bolivarian[634]" (Venezuela). All are run by leaders who enjoy *de facto* or even *de jure* lifelong tenure. All restrict political and civil rights to their rights-deprived citizens. And while none invokes a divine right to rule, none fools any observer with a modicum of respect for the evidence on the ground: they are all dictators without a shred of concern for their putative "people." The acknowledged bankruptcy of their ideology, however, does not amount to its complete disappearance; the platitudes continue to serve a purpose, if only to confuse the gullible, the ideologically blinded, and the just plain ignorant.

That said, the Republic of Cuba and the Russian Federation should certainly be commended for at least dropping Orwellian qualifiers from their names. But make no mistake: the voting that takes place inside their borders is a sham. This is how Freedom House describes Cuba: "Cuba is a one-party Communist state that outlaws political pluralism, represses dissent, and severely restricts freedoms of the press, assembly, speech, and association. The government of Raúl Castro, who succeeded his brother Fidel as president in 2008, monopolizes the bulk of economic activity within centralized and inefficient state enterprises."[635]

Russia provides a rather more complex example of post-Communist Communism. And it has been given a name: *putinism*. Considered coined on September 20th, 2007, by Richard Rahn, it means: "a Russian nationalistic authoritarian form of government that pretends to be a free market democracy."[636] Rahn presciently predicted at the time that "[a]s Russia's economic fortunes change, Putinism is likely to become more repressive. Authoritarian regimes, unlike true free-market democracies, are inherently unstable and rarely end happily." So it did. And with the decline of Russia's economy, especially after the steep fall in oil prices, Putinism became predictably more repressive. Regime critics, let alone opponents, have been silenced, with assassination the technique of choice.

While some saw Putin as a savvy pragmatist,[637] Richard C. Longworth detected a new strategy, writing in 2016 that

[a]t the moment, Putin seems to be promoting a philosophy of Eurasianism, based partly on Russia's geographical sprawl across two continents and partly on the Third Rome concept of Russia as the spiritual link between East and West.... Putin seems to [be] a Slavophile. Onto this, he has grafted nationalism and authoritarianism, both with roots in the Russian past. There may be the seed of a new Russian national identity in all this. Russia's past identities, both tsarist and Communist, were top-down ideologies, imposed by the tsars or commissars who ran the country. Putin is in charge now.[638]

"At the moment" captures nicely the chameleonic nature of Putin's ideology. Two years later, that ideology appears to persist. Stay tuned; but don't hold your breath.

Some describe putinism as sheer "mafia-style" opportunism - a term pioneered by Hungarian politician Balint Magyar to describe a system where the state leader is not unlike a godfather, who "doesn't govern [but]... disposes – of positions, wealth, statuses, persons."[639] In the words of Masha Gessen, "[v]iolence and ideology—the pillars of a totalitarian state—become, in the hands of a mafia state, mere instruments. The distinction is particularly meaningful because all the states the model describes are post-Communist."[640] Former economic advisor to Putin, now Cato Institute scholar, Andrei Illarionov agrees that under Putin, Russia's "economic system is based on mafia-style relations."[641]

But cronyism by any other name does not necessarily imply a lack of a deeper ideology; Illarionov, for example, recognizes that "Putin's ultimate goal is clear – it is to change the world according to his vision." Though admittedly "a vision of the Sicilian world, a world that is ruled by the mighty and the powerful," it is much more than that. It is ultimately imperialist. "The Sicilian model by itself is not imperialist" – yet imperialism is at bottom what appeals to Russians. Argues Illarionov: "Putin's increase in support is not for mafia-like rule, but for imperialism, and the imperial syndrome in Russia has not yet been healed." Invoking visions of Russia's former glory, when tsars ruled over a vast empire, works every time: throughout Russia, *pax slavonika* is remembered fondly. A utopia of the future is thus wedded to a utopia of a golden age.

So it had been when the USSR led the Communist world: Tsarism and Bolshevism had similar global ambitions, equally cloaked in lofty, spiritual rhetoric. Notes Walter Laqueur: "Under the tsars, Russia saw itself as the 'third Rome,' the successor to Rome and Byzantium and the divinely inspired seat of an eternal civilization. 'Two Romes have fallen,' said the 16th century monk, Filofey, 'the third stands, and there shall be no fourth.' The Soviet Union inherited this messianic mission and saw itself as the new pinnacle of mankind's striving."[642]

The atheistic Communists' unabashedly messianic agenda was not especially strange to the Russians, who have traditionally idolized their Caesars as demigods. The Russian tsar could fairly declare not only *"L'état c'est moi,"* as had Louis XIV (aka the Sun King – echoes of the Egyptian sun-god Ra) but *"toute la nation c'est moi."* Thus it is impossible to understand Bolshevism, and now Putinism, without appreciating the enormous power of the centuries-old absolutism at the heart of Russian culture. Putin's genius consists in brilliantly manipulating information to his own purposes perhaps better than anyone before him. But he was tapping into an ancient tradition. Arkady Ostrovsky notes that Putin manages to project power so effectively because "Russia is an idea-centric country, and the media play a disproportionately important role in it."[643]

As a former KGB officer, Putin knows how the Bolsheviks have consistently lied to gain power, to keep it, and to spread it. Information manipulation, along with terror, has been the oxygen that kept the dictatorship alive. For the past century, the KGB has been the party's tool. Putin, who wields it with impunity and great skill, understands that what seems is, ultimately, what is. Certainly in politics, reality is a function of belief, not fact.

Explains Ostrovsky:

As with any utopia, Communism disregarded reality, and as a pseudo-religion, it operated through words and images…. Lies and repression were the two main pillars that upheld the Soviet system. Words justified repression. Repression enforced the words. It worked like an arch. The mind dealt with the disconnection between signals and real life by developing doublethink – a condition described by George Orwell in *1984*. The Soviet Union expired not only because it ran out of money but also because it ran out of words. [644]

If not words, exactly, it did run out of plausible narratives. As the communication technology of the 1980s and early 1990s exploded, the lie-machine couldn't work fast enough; a new media-manipulation model would have to be found. By the time it was, the system would have to give way to a new version.

Eventually, that was done - thanks to highly trained propagandists, who took advantage of the opportunity to wield influence. By no means innocent victims of a ruthless dictator, Putin's idea-crafters, warns Ostrovsky, are no mere "helpless pawns in the hands of a despot. They are sophisticated and erudite men who started their careers during Gorbachev's perestroika and prospered in Yeltsin's 1990s but who now act as demiurges – creators of reality."[645] It is not an easy job; for unlike old-style Communism, as in North Korea, where genuine elections are inconceivable and information is trickled out by the regime at will. He has been remarkably successful, given that "for all his authoritarianism, Putin [has] derived his legitimacy from popular support, and while he did not believe in fair elections, he paid careful attention to public opinion."[646] Influencing public opinion is much harder than it used to be when censorship and fear more or less sufficed. What makes it easier, however, is the targets' willingness, if not eagerness, to be influenced.

Reminiscent of Nazi times, writes Ostrovsky, "the main reason propaganda works is that enough people want to believe it. … Opinion polls show that almost half the Russian population knows that the Kremlin is lying to the world about the absence of Russian troops in Ukraine, but it approves of these lies and sees them as a sign of strength. More than half think it is right for the media to distort information in the interest of the state. This propaganda feeds not so much on ignorance as on resentment, a mixture of jealousy and hostility."[647] A savvy manipulator will know how to transform it into a more full-blown ideology.

While circumstances have changed over time and space, human nature has not. Telling people what they want to hear continues to be effective; and Putin, with help from his media experts, does it confidently, as his subjects prefer and expect. Assuring them of his protection, "[h]e told his core, traditionalist electorate that the state was the only provider of public good and that it was surrounded by enemies. But he also had a message for the middle class: don't involve yourself in politics and enjoy life, while we, in the Kremlin, deal with the dark and uneducated plebs who have neither a desire nor the taste for Western democracy."[648] That resonates with the middle class, who now mistrust all political parties and organizations. To keep them in his corner, however, Putin has had to do more. Orienting himself toward the electoral majority, he has had to change the narrative, and in a manner that was minimally disruptive. Revolutionary rhetoric is always unwise in an autocracy; better to focus on a unifying theme.

So, shrewdly, "[at] this point Putin turned to anti-Americanism as the only ideological tenet that had survived the collapse of the Soviet Union."[649] TV journalist Maxim Shevchenko channeled Putin when he proclaimed that "Russia and the West are at war… There is a growing feeling that most Western people belong to a different humanoid group from us; that we are only superficially similar, but fundamentally different."[650] These are exceptionally dangerous words, reminiscent of Nazi characterization of Jews as cockroaches. And they resonate.

Xi Jinping's Mao-envy

If Putin has to keep in check a nation of some 143 million, China's is close to 1.4 billion. For most of its history, the enormous nation has been an enigma shrouded inside a mystery – and today is no different. Thus it is not a little refreshing to find a journalist admitting ignorance, in the pages of a widely-read publication no less, and about such an important geopolitical actor, about which everyone seems to have an opinion. Provocatively titled "Nobody Knows Anything About China," James Palmer only slightly mitigates the affront to his fellow Sinologists by adding, "including the Chinese government." So we are all in this together: "[w]e don't know China because, in ways that have generally not been acknowledged, virtually every piece of information issued from or about the country is unreliable, partial, or distorted." The reason? Simple:

"Official data is repeatedly smoothed for both propaganda purposes and individual career ambitions."[651]

What we don't know is quite a lot:

> real figures for GDP growth, for example. GDP growth has long been one of the main criteria used to judge officials' careers — as a result, the relevant data is warped at every level, since the folk reporting it are the same ones benefitting from it being high. If you add up the GDP figures issued by the provinces, the sum is 10 percent higher than the figure ultimately issued by the national government, which in itself is tweaked to hit politicized targets.[652]

And economic data may be more reliable than other putative facts.

Such as? Pretty much everything. The true size of the Chinese population, because of the reluctance to register unapproved second children or for the family planning bureau to report that it failed to control births. The real defense budget. The everyday conditions of the Chinese army, because the restrictions placed on military coverage and the ability of soldiers to talk are even more tightly limited than for civilians. Whether schools are good or bad; specifically, the extent of the collapse of rural education. The real literacy figures, not least because rural and urban literacy is measured by different standards, a common trick used for many statistics.

We certainly have no clue what people really think. After all, writes Palmer, "why would they tell pollsters they are more trusting of others than any other country in the world, when in practice paranoia about the intentions of others is so rampant that old people aren't helped on the streets for fear they're running a scam, and children like toddler Wang Yue are left to die after being hit by cars." And we know literally nothing about high-level Chinese politics, and how Zhongnanhai, the Chinese Kremlin, operates. We don't know either whether the officials targeted in the "anti-corruption" campaigns "were really unusually corrupt, lascivious, or treacherous — or whether they were just political opponents of Xi." They were, quite possibly, both.

But a few things we do know: most obviously, Xi Jinping's recent elevation to Mao-status, as President and party secretary of the Chinese Communist Party, for whatever counts as perpetuity under Communism, post- or otherwise. It didn't come as much of a shock. For as Dan Blumenthal points out, this was the next logical move for the Chinese strongman who has spent the last six years purging enemies, accumulating political power and recentralizing economic and national security policymaking. Xi is an ardent admirer of Russian President Vladimir Putin and is emulating many of Putin's political and national security strategies.[653]

Blumenthal calls it the "putinization" of China, which should be "a massive wake-up for America."

China's neighbors have already awakened: its new "Belt and Road" (BRI) diplomacy is giving them nightmares. And no wonder. Concludes a recent report by the Center for Strategic and International Studies:

> The BRI is the most ambitious geoeconomic vision in recent history. Spanning some 70 countries, it can claim to cover more than two-thirds of the world's population. It could include Chinese investments approaching $4 trillion. It intends to strengthen hard infrastructure with new roads and railways, soft infrastructure with trade and transportation agreements, and even cultural ties with university scholarships and other people-to-people exchanges.[654]

Robert Daly and Matthew Rojansky acknowledge that the BRI represents a very bold step for China. Like Putin, Xi invokes China's past glory, "confident that history proves the key to continental control lies in China."[655] In September 2013, for example, he told the Kazakhs that "more than 2,100 years ago … imperial envoy Zhang Qian was sent to Central Asia twice to open the door to friendly contacts between China and Central Asian countries as well as the transcontinental Silk Road linking East and West." That October, Xi echoed these sentiments in his address to the Indonesian parliament, claiming that "Southeast Asia has since ancient times been an important hub along the ancient Maritime Silk Road."

Actually, observe the authors, "the Silk Road was not Sinocentric, nor was it a road. Xi's mythologizing of the Silk Road also elides the fact that soldiers as well as salesmen moved along the storied routes." This hasn't stopped Communist Party operatives to praise him to high heaven, "reaching absurd heights" – at least to Western eyes. It isn't clear how the Chinese see it. Daly and Rojansky write, for example, that at a Beijing conference which they both attended in late 2017, "a Chinese foreignpolicy analyst claimed that Xi's vision could not only guide the peaceful development of the human race, but would benefit non-human animal species and plants as well." They speculate that "such fulsome nonsense, now as during the Mao era, serves to mask Chinese doubts about the wisdom of the BRI." On the other hand, doesn't this sound just like Putin's mouthpiece Maxim Shevchenko's statement of a "growing feeling that most Western people belong to a different humanoid group"? That too is nonsense, but the "different humanoid group" argument is a longstanding staple of illiberal parlance.

The two strongmen resort to the same political influence tactics for similar asymmetric warfare strategies. Writes Anne-Marie Brady, "[t]he key concept in Chinese foreign policy which links party and state organizations is the 'united front' (统一战线)."[656] Though adopted by the Chinese and adapted to their own strategic tradition, however, writes Brady,

> the united front is originally a Leninist tactic of strategic alliances. Lenin wrote in *"Left-Wing" Communism: an Infantile Disorder,* [t]he more powerful enemy can be vanquished only by exerting the utmost effort, and without fail, most thoroughly, carefully, attentively and skillfully using every, even the smallest, 'rift' among the enemies, of every antagonism of interest among the bourgeoisie of the various countries and among the various groups or types of bourgeoisie within the various countries, and also by taking advantage of every, even the smallest, opportunity of gaining a mass ally, even though this ally be temporary, vacillating, unstable, unreliable and conditional. Those who fail to understand this, fail to understand even a particle of Marxism, or of scientific, modern Socialism in general."[657]

"Xi," continues Brady, "has revived and revitalized many Mao era practices and institutions, lending them modern concerns and terminology. Like Mao, Xi stresses the importance of information control." Shades of Putin: "In the modernized information environment, this now means not only China's public sphere, but also how the international media and international academia comments on China and China-related issues. Thus the revitalized CCTV International, re-branded in 2016 as CGTV (China Global Television), provides the CCP line to the outside world (emphasizing business, not politics) via 24-hour satellite broadcasts and social media." It is but one of many public diplomacy efforts – and it is paying off.

But eventually, they ring alarm bells even in this nation's capital. Writes Josh Rogin:

> Washington is waking up to the huge scope and scale of Chinese Communist Party influence operations inside the United States, which permeate American institutions of all kinds. China's overriding goal is, at the least, to defend its authoritarian system from attack and at most to export it to the world at America's expense. The foreign influence campaign is part and parcel of China's larger campaign for global power, which includes military expansion, foreign direct investment, resource hoarding, and influencing international rules and norms. But this part of China's game plan is the most opaque and least understood. Beijing's strategy is first to cut off critical discussion of China's government, then to co-opt American influencers in order to promote China's narrative. [658]

Citing Andrew Nathan's counsel that "we need to recognize there really is a struggle over both ideology and values going on," Rogin adds: "All countries seek influence abroad, pursue soft power and spread propaganda. But the Chinese combination of technology, coercion, pressure, exclusion and economic incentives is beyond anything this country has faced before." The legitimacy of these concerns were confirmed by FBI director Chris Wray, who testified before the Senate in February, 2018, that China's

> use of non-traditional collectors, especially in the academic setting - whether it's professors, scientists, students—we see in almost every field office that the FBI has around the country… It's not just in major cities. It's in small ones as well, it's across basically every discipline…. [S]o one of the things we're trying to do is view the China threat as not just the whole of government threat, but a whole of society threat on their end and I think it's going to take a whole of society response by us. [659]

By "us" he means all Americans. But the Chinese threat must be taken seriously by everyone who is in the least concerned about the survival of liberal democratic values by any name, in any country. Citing Xi Jingping's famous declaration that having moved away from the "old road" – Communism – China should not now take the "evil road" (meaning, liberal democracy), Cheng Chen explains that it "of course has something to do with the continuing rule of the CCP [Chinese Communist Party], which severely limits opportunities for political contention, and the fact that embracing liberal democratic values would be tantamount to 'regime suicide.'"[660]

Slowly, surely, if stealthily, China's tentacles are spreading. Concludes Chen:

China's growing ambition to create a China-centric order regionally, if not yet globally, harken[s] back to the "all-under-heaven" system of ancient dynasties. Although it is too early to accurately gauge how successful these efforts will be in the long run, it is undeniable that China is already gaining a greater presence and having a deeper impact in many parts of the developing world, from Latin America to Africa to Asia. As China continues its rise internationally, its developmental strategy will only become more influential.[661]

Whatever "ism" it may be called (which isn't a trivial matter; we will return to that in the next chapter) the "all-under-heaven" model is not unique to China: it underlies every utopian ideology. That certainly includes – perhaps above all – Salafist-jihadism.

Jihad Weaves a World-wide Web

It all came as a huge surprise to the complacent Americans. When George W. Bush declared in 2002 that North Korea, Iran, and Iraq "and their terrorist allies constitute an axis of evil, aiming to threaten the peace of the world,"[662] people were taken aback. An axis, meaning straight line? Hadn't Iran and Iraq fought each other less than two decades ago? Some even recalled that the U.S. had taken Iraq's side. Also: what exactly did a Communist dictatorship have in common with a Shia theocracy and a secular Arab autocrat? Had Dubbya garbled something that his wonkish advisors had tried to tell him?

Here is how a perfectly-accented Will Farrell translated Bush a few weeks later, on *Saturday Night Live*: "America is presently at war. Not just a war on terrorism; but we are engaged in a deadly stand-off with an Axis of Evil. You know who I'm talking about - Iran, Iraq, and one of the Koreas. [Ouch.] But my Axis of Evil doesn't seem to interest the people out there. Some people just want to talk about the economy, and budgets, and Enron. I bet most of you out there don't even understand Enron. I sure as heck don't! It hurts my head to think about it." Then Farrell/Bush remembers he doesn't like Sen. Tom Daschle, so he is added to the Axis; same with France; and Germany, Italy, Japan. Oh yes, and Dick Cheney - to say nothing of Evel (pun intended? who knows...) Knievel. By the time his "Most Wanted" list is complete, the axis is not even funny.

We know the punchline: "So, you see, America? There's nothing to fear. Everything's fine."[663] If only this *non sequitur* were a joke. Bush had revealed the existence of a genuine international threat, but he first failed to elaborate and explain it, then lost whatever momentum had resulted from the attempt at mobilization by urging Americans to continue life as usual and "go shopping."[664] He didn't need SNL to miss his target.

The attempt was worse than a dud. Bush proved as bad at public diplomacy as Putin was good. Even conceding that Republican-bashing is a (for quite some time now, *the*) SNL staple, Ferrell's parody tells a bitter truth. The catchy phrase from Bush's address was clever enough, recalling our enemies in World War II, but it needed expanding, setting in context, educating the public. Unequal to the task, Bush dropped the phrase instead. Public diplomacy was no higher on his priorities list than it has been for most recent American presidents aside from Reagan.[665]

More than fifteen years later, in 2017, Aaron David Miller and Richard Sokolsky told CNN that "'the axis of evil' is back," as "Iran, North Korea and Syria (replacing Iraq) have joined ISIS [Islamic State in Iraq and Syria] as the administration's key bogeymen." They also venture a prediction: "More than likely, much as with Syria and North Korea, the administration is stuck pursuing an approach toward Iran that may contain some of its bad behavior in the region even while it continues to adhere to a nuclear accord it promised to scuttle. But the 'axis of evil' looks like it's here to stay."[666] Although the U.S. has since pulled out of the nuclear deal and ISIS has lost virtually all of its territory, much damage had already been done. Iran continues to vigorously sponsor terrorism, and ISIS has changed tactics but is hardly extinct – quite the contrary. In May 2019 it claimed credit for the murder of 257 innocents, mostly women and children, in Sri Lanka, while simultaneously waging an attack in Riyadh, Saudi Arabia. The Mullah's regime must never be underestimated.

In a 2017 report for the Center for a New American Security (CNAS), Nicholas Heras explains that "[i]n the three decades since the Islamic Revolution in Iran, the IRGC-QF has arguably developed the most competent gray zone doctrine of any Middle Eastern actor."[667] No mere bogeyman, writes Heras, this formidable regime is a complicated state actor with a millennia-old history as an empire; it is a nation that has generally had a coherent vision of how to engage pragmatically and to its own benefit in the affairs of the peoples in the areas surrounding it. Since 1979, Iran's Islamic Republic government has inherited this vision, and it added an ideological, revolutionary component to Iranian national security decisionmaking, which is the prerogative of the nation's supreme leader and the IRGC apparatus, which is charged with protecting and propagating the Islamic Revolution.[668] Iran's engagement in the current civil wars in Syria, Iraq, and Yemen is framed as part of a "sacred defense," which is meant to protect the Iranian homeland – fundamentally a narrative of resistance that allows Iran to cooperate with a range of proxies and partners throughout the MENA region.[669]

Iran is governed by a revolutionary utopian ideology that has slowly managed to weave a web of jihadist connections that cross sectarian and geopolitical lines to an unprecedented degree. The Syrian civil war, moreover, has provided Iran with a chance to increase its multinational network of proxy fighters, groups funded and controlled by Iran, with jihadists not only from Syria but also from Iraq, Afghanistan, Pakistan, Lebanon, as well as India. And while most of these are Shiia, governance vacuums throughout the region are ripe for jihadism. Heras continues:

Since 2011, tens of thousands of foreign fighters from North Africa and the trans-Sahara, particularly from Tunisia and Morocco, have traveled to Syria. These fighters have been joined by Sunni jihadists from other areas of the Middle East, Central Asia, Russia and the Caucasus, Europe, and (to a far lesser extent) Southeast Asia and North and South America, creating a truly global movement. Although many of the foreign fighters have returned home, thousands are believed to remain in al-Qaeda–dominated areas of north-Western Syria and the remaining territories held by ISIS in Syria and Iraq.[670]

Iran's connections, however, go far beyond the Middle East. They penetrate deep into Latin America, especially Venezuela. Emanuele Ottolenghi and John Hannah, for example, cite "Venezuela's long history of collaboration with Iran, including sanctions evasion, terror finance, and ideological subversion."[671] The self-described "Bolivarian republic," whose socialist policies have led to starvation and massive refugee flight, is helping Iranian proxy Hezbollah turn worthless currency into dollars, which gains it political leverage in America's hemisphere. The authors charge that

> Iran, as the key facilitator of the Venezuela-Hezbollah connection, favors the injection of billions of counterfeit greenbacks into the global economy because such a step is damaging to the U.S. financial system. The sanctioning of a Quds Force network producing counterfeited currency to fuel the Yemen civil war shows that in this area, as in many other illicit activities, Iran unscrupulously engages in rogue behavior to promote its proxies and tend to their financial needs.[672]

Iran's cooperation with North Korea on nuclear weapons development is also well known, and long-standing. According to a 2017 study by Israel's Lt. Col. Dr. Raphael Ofek and Lt. Col. Dr. Dany Shoham, "[f]rom the 1990s onward, dozens – perhaps hundreds – of North Korean scientists and technicians apparently worked in Iran in nuclear and ballistic facilities."[673] And since the so-called "Iran deal" negotiated by Barack Obama placed almost no limits on the enhancement of Tehran's military nuclear program outside Iran, North Korea [NK] is an ideal partner. Their

> strategic, military-technological collaboration is more than merely plausible. It is entirely possible, indeed likely, that such a collaboration is already underway. ... [They] have followed fairly similar nuclear and ballistic courses, with considerable, largely intended, reciprocal technological complementarity. The numerous technological common denominators that underlie the NW [nuclear weapons] and ballistic missile programs of Iran and NK cannot be regarded as coincidental. Rather, they likely indicate – in conjunction with geopolitical and economic drives –a much broader degree of undisclosed interaction between Tehran and Pyongyang.

And yes, of course, there is also a Syria-North Korea connection. On March 20, 2018, Israel at last admitted responsibility for bombing a Syrian nuclear reactor on September 6, 2007, and released intelligence documents to back up its claim that the reactor "was being constructed with help from North Korea and had been months away from activation." Israel was sending a clear warning to "Iran that it would not be allowed to develop nuclear weapons."[674] It has no choice, given the fact that Iran is able to destroy the Jewish state and has repeatedly threatened to do so.

Meanwhile, though the worldwide jihadist-totalitarian web is manifest, the West unwittingly plays the fly. One problem in articulating a clear foreign policy for the United States is the current culture of ideological confusion, made far worse by widespread ignorance, notwithstanding the accessibility of information. Take the labeling of China and Russia as both "capitalist." Even the addition of qualifiers like "authoritarian" and "crony" does not change the absurdity of considering any one-party regime as "capitalist," where rule of "law" is subject to the whims of a small cadre.[675] What China and Russia have is an economy at the mercy of elites, for whom states like the United States and many of its allies constitute a threat of apocalyptic proportions. No wonder that one of their principal tools of subversion is to confuse and demoralize our own populations. The least we can do is to understand what we stand for, while staying as well informed as possible and resist being swayed by cant.

III. BRAVE NEW WORLD ORDER

Into this neutral air
Where blind skyscrapers use
Their full height to proclaim
The strength of Collective Man,
Each language pours its vain
Competitive excuse:
But who can live for long
In an euphoric dream.

W. H. Auden (1940)

9:
Liberty, Equality and Property

Property and the Bible

The story goes that a traveler arrives in a Galician town, and orders trousers from a Jewish tailor; but when the traveler has to leave, they are not yet ready. Seven years later, he returns, and the tailor finally delivers. The customer remonstrates, "God made the world in seven days, yet you take seven years to make a pair of trousers!" "Yes, but look at the world," the tailor ruefully replies. "And," he beams, "look at my trousers."

The tailor is entitled to be proud of his handiwork. Having been ordered to master the earth, man's job was to make the best of it. But the tailor goes further, obliquely implying that creation itself could have used another metaphorical day or two, which comes perilously close to criticizing God! He doesn't quite go there: the tailor is whimsically praising his own handiwork. Not so the utopian who presumes to take over where God left off - whereupon the joke ceases to be funny. A little risqué chutzpa turns into lethal conceit.

Hubristic people are often afflicted with an atrophied sense of humor. But a far more disturbing disability is a delusional sense of infallibility. Not everyone is equally susceptible; these twin maladies disproportionately afflict members of the "ideocracy." A nifty composite suggesting rule by idea-mongers, an elite that believes itself entitled to decide for others due to its superior intellect, knowledge, and virtue, the term [676] was coined by Jaroslaw Pekalkevich and Alfred Wayne Penn, who argue: "The legitimacy of an ideocratic political system derives from the principles of its monistic ideology. It is assumed that the decision makers of the system have a strictly defined framework of reference that allows them an absolutely correct interpretation of events... [that] 'reality can be interpreted by a universally true and exhaustive set of ideas.'"[677] To put it plainly: as the elite know the Truth, why waste time arguing, competing, and experimenting?

In the place of the seemingly haphazard actions of random individuals, the ideocracy will design a plan predicated on distributing resources throughout society. Emphatically rejecting the slightest hint of self-interest, the ideocracy proclaims allegiance to nothing but the Greater Good.[678] Variously described as the "contemplative," "intellectual," or "epistemic" class, to differentiate its members from the mercenary politicians of the rapacious class, the ideocrats purport to be altruistic humanists. Karl Mannheim has described the self-appointed champions of putatively benevolent authoritarianism as "advocates whose mission is to safeguard the spiritual interests of humanity at large."[679] Humble they are not.

And they know it. Historically, this group has tended to be dissatisfied with its lot, feeling under-appreciated. Desperate to play a larger role in fashioning society, they appeal to the numerous and angry masses. Contemptuous of the moneyed "ruling classes," these secular prophets have consistently cast themselves in the role of social saviors. An anti-clerical priesthood which presumes to speak for the unenlightened by championing equality in the name of social justice, this refurbished clergy has merely substituted history and nature for God.

The goals are surely worthy. Helping the destitute and underprivileged is indeed a high ideal hailed by the "people of the Book."[680] The sacred writings of all three Abrahamic religions are replete with calls to charity and compassion. Throughout the Old Testament (e.g., *Exodus* 23:10-11; *Leviticus* 19:9-10; 23:22; *Deuteronomy* 24: 6-13, 19-22), God is said to expect kindness to the defenseless members of society, and display generosity, civility, and fellow-feeling. The poor are to be helped without condescension, and warmly included in sharing sacrificial meals. Special portions of the annual tithe were to be earmarked for the poor. In the touching, allegorical "A psalm of Asaph," (*Psalm* 82) God is said to admonish his alleged fellow-divinities to stop defending the unjust and the wicked, and start to "Defend the wretched and the orphan,/ Vindicate the lowly and the poor,/ Rescue the wretched and the needy;/ Save them from the hand of the wicked." The eponymous Asaph ends by beckoning the one true Yehovah: "Arise, O God, judge of the earth, for all the nations are Your possession." But the ideocracy goes one better, proposing a surefire plan for God to redistribute His possessions. The only thing that ends up being sure, however, is the fire.

The Biblical vision of all humanity - the healthy and the sick, handsome and homely, talented and mediocre, rich and poor - dwelling side by side before God, encouraged efforts to minimize suffering. But nowhere does this imply the total eradication of inequality, whatever that might even mean. "Without overturning the basic economic system which brought about the existence of rich and poor," writes Harry M. Orlinsky,

"Hebrew law sought to raise the needy from the deepest and most severe type of economic distress."[681] This did not necessitate stigmatizing the rich merely for being rich. For in fact, "it was not social inequality but social injustice which [Hebrew law] denounced, not the existence of rich and poor within the same society but the abuse of the poor by their richer brethren which they decried, not the creation of a new society but the infusion of the Israel they knew with a new spirit which they demanded."[682]

The Old Testament states that the world is God's possession: He created it, so it belongs to Him. Humans have no such prerogative; they must earn their property. "By the sweat of your brow shall you get bread to eat," God tells Adam. (*Genesis* 3:19). Property is to be acquired and consumed on the basis of individual labor. People should keep and enjoy the fruit of their labor and investment. (*Genesis* 31:38-42; *Proverbs* 13:11) They are not even to covet anyone else's property (*Exodus* 20:17), let alone take it outright. (*Exodus* 20:15).

The lawful acquisition of property in accordance with the commandments is very much a mark of divine favor. Thus the common greeting *shalom* conveys at once a wish for peace and for material welfare. True, sometimes the best people have bad luck, while very bad people do well. But people who prosper despite being wicked are assumed to get their comeuppance sooner or later, whether it is clear to us or not. Ill-gotten riches, whether obtained by cheating or coercion, are another matter altogether: here's where the rule of law comes into play.

This does not translate into trusting a Philosopher King. The Biblical God repeatedly admonishes men to refrain from elevating anyone above themselves as an ersatz deity. When the aging prophet Samuel conveys to God his Jewish subjects' plea for a king, for example, the Creator bemoans their weakness: "Like everything else they have done ever since I brought them out of Egypt to this day – forsaking Me and worshiping other gods – so they are doing to you. Heed their demand; but warn them solemnly and tell them about the practices of any king who will rule over them." (*Samuel* 8: 8-9)

Solomon does as he was instructed, cautioning the Jews against conferring too much power upon an excessively strong king. He warns them to beware, for he will surely seize their choice fields, vineyards, and olive groves for use by his courtiers, and do many other bad things just because he can. Without doubt, "the day will come when you cry out because of the king whom you yourselves have chosen; and the Lord will not answer you on that day." (*Samuel* 8:11-19) The people must always stay vigilant whenever they give too much authority to any one man. What the Old Testament means by undue inequality is excessive political power and ability to coerce. Inequality deemed undue is emphatically not merely the existence of disparate resources.

On the contrary. The Jewish tradition actually encourages economic success. Writes Rabbi Joseph Isaac Lifshitz:

> Wealth that is gained through hard work and honest means is, in Judaism, a positive expression of man's efforts as a godly being. "One who benefits from his own labor," says the Talmud, "is more worthy than one who fears heaven." This stunning assertion is not meant to denigrate the fear of heaven but rather to affirm the principle that one who turns his talents into achievements is greater than one who neglects his own capacity to strive and create in the world. [683]

In Rabbinic teaching, poverty is considered a form of pointless suffering. The statement "There shall be no needy among you" (*Deuteronomy* 15:4) is understood, writes Lifshits, "as an obligation on man to avoid becoming poor, not as a divine promise to negate poverty." [684]

At the same time, charity is central to Judaism: "Jewish legal codes have always placed the laws of charity among religious duties (*isur veheter*), rather than civil law (*dinei mamonot*), ... [but] both categories are equally binding on the Jew." [685] As poverty among the Jews in the diaspora rose, the Rabbis sought guidance from the old rules, and authorized the Jewish community to compel its members to fulfill their obligation to give ten percent of their earnings to the poor. It is worth noting, however, that such coercive authority is religious rather than civil.

The same is true of Christianity; at bottom, what matters is the quality of man's soul, his spiritual health, and devotion. Accordingly, charity demonstrates that material wealth is less important than generosity. And generosity is predicated on the freedom to give. Indeed, in the last paragraph of *Utopia*, More's namesake observes that quite a few of that island's institutions "seemed to me quite absurd" - above all, "the very point which is the principal foundation of their whole social structure, namely their common life and subsistence with no exchange of money. That one fact entirely undermines all nobility, magnificence, splendor, and majesty, which are (in the popular view) the true adornments and ornaments of a commonwealth." [686]

Unfortunately, unlike the Torah, the New Testament contains passages that warn against wealth as such. The Virgin Mary, for example, thanks God for having "pulled down the mighty from their thrones and exalted the lowly. He has filled the hungry with good things; and the rich has sent empty away." (*Luke* 1:53-54). Hostility to the rich seems to result primarily, if not exclusively, from their wealth. Thus Jesus urges a disciple: "sell whatsoever thou hast, and give to the poor, and thou shalt have treasure in heaven: and come, take up the cross, and follow me.... [I]t is easier for a camel to go through the eye of a needle than for a rich man to enter the kingdom of God." (*Matthew* 19:21-25) And again: "Blessed are you who are poor, for yours is the kingdom of God." (*Luke* 6:20) Consistent with this sentiment, often in protest against priestly cupidity, devout Christians throughout the ages have taken a vow of poverty.

The most extreme antipathy to riches is expressed by the Apostle Paul, captured most starkly in his startling declaration that "the love of money is a root of all kinds of evil" (*Timothy* 6:10). This attitude, writes Paul Kahan, eventually opened the floodgates to utopian egalitarianism. Thus "Chaucer would cite it frequently, and it has formed the basis for many a modern Christian Socialist sermon. The consequence drawn from this attitude was, logically enough, that the good life did not involve wealth.... On earth, indeed, one was called upon to distribute one's treasure to the poor."[687]

Taking it up a notch, the book of *Acts* describes a time when "all those whom faith had drawn together held everything in common: they would sell their property and possessions and make a general distribution as the need of each required." (*Acts* 2: 44-45) At last, "the congregation of believers was one in heart and soul. No one claimed that any of his possessions was his own, but they shared everything they owned." (*Acts* 4:32)

A radical vision indeed. Writes Kahan:

Christian charity was different in kind from the generosity praised in the classical tradition. In the New Testament, possessions ought to be sold and the money given to the poor – regardless of their citizenship. Wealth is to be given away. St. Paul does suggest a limit to this process, but he goes well beyond Cicero's suggestion that one should not give so much today that one cannot keep on giving tomorrow: "There is no question of relieving others at the cost of hardship to ourselves; it is a question of equality. At the moment your surplus meets their need, but one day your need may be met from their surplus. The aim is equality."[688]

But lost in the ideological shuffle is that Jesus and his apostles advocate parting with one's riches voluntarily. None suggests having them expropriated or redistributed or managed by the state, let alone snatched away forcibly through revolution. That would have been unthinkable for a gentle Son of God who advised "rendering unto Caesar the things that are Caesar's and unto God the things that are God's," (*Matthew* 22:21) implicitly separating the sacred as far as possible from the profane, and in no way promoting forcible expropriation or violence. In the early days of Christianity, the followers of Jesus wanted to do as little as possible with the state; but after Christ's death, the Roman Empire became the enemy incarnate, an instrument of Satan.

Pellicani notes that at the outset, "Christians led a kind of 'underground, non-violent war' against institutions: 'Nothing is more foreign to us than the State.' On the surface, they were good citizens of the empire; underneath, they refused its basic values because they considered them meaningless, or even negative, in light of the second coming of Christ."[689] Anticipating Judgment Day, which Christ had promised, the Church Fathers continued for some time to condemn private property beyond the bare minimum, and advocate communal ownership as an ideal. Saint Basil of Caesarea (329/330-379) and John Chrysostom, Archbishop of Constantinople (c. 349-407) likened the rich man to a thief and a robber, while Saint Jerome (347-420) maintained that wealth is always the product of theft. An undue regard for riches seemed not only misplaced but proof of faithlessness.

But once Christianity was promoted from persecuted heresy to the Roman Empire's official state religion after Emperor Constantine officially converted in 312, the clergy had to adapt to its newly acquired power and property. Explains Pellicano: "It is often claimed that the transformation of Christianity from religion of protest to religion of legitimation of the existing order occurred when the empire took the church under its protective wing.... The church could not continue to be a school of anarchy, radically hostile to anything tasting of order and hierarchy..."[690] Nor could it continue to oppose all riches. Richard Pipes notes that "a church based on the advocacy of self-denial grew before long into a huge temporal power with vast landed possessions and other forms of wealth which it needed to carry out its religious and secular responsibilities."[691] It would become increasingly difficult to defend both power and powerlessness, both fortunes and humble poverty.

Unfortunately, the conflict within Christianity between the ideal of poverty as originally promoted by Jesus and the defense of wealth by later disciples has led to considerable confusion. But it didn't have to happen. Explains Daniel Mahoney:

> Christians do indeed side with the poor, but not in any reductive ideological sense. All groups, all classes, suffer from inordinate self-regard and are prone to sin and selfishness. The poor in the modern world can be just as rapacious and power hungry as some of the rich. The poor as an ideological category, as privileged beneficiaries of transformative revolution (in any case, a hopelessly utopian concept) owe nothing to Christian revelation.[692]

A woeful misunderstanding ensued, whose reverberations continue to this day.

Equal Liberty

Liberty doesn't grow on trees, forbidden or otherwise, but is "the delicate fruit of a mature civilization."[693] So thought Lord John Emerich Edward Dalberg Acton (1834–1902), and for that reason warned against its misuse: "If hostile interests have wrought much injury, false ideas [about liberty] have wrought still more."[694] A proper definition is therefore indispensable; and Lord Acton was prepared to offer it: "By liberty I mean the assurance that every man shall be protected in doing his duty against the influence of authority and majorities, custom and opinion." Ideally, such an assurance should be provided to *every human being,* unqualifiedly. The ability to act according to his own beliefs which underpin what he believes to be his duties, which in turn must guide his actions, is what gives every man his dignity. But whether that assurance is effective depends on prudent statecraft. And yes, there is an objective test for it: "The most certain test by which we judge whether a country is really free is the amount of security enjoyed by minorities."[695] (He meant **all** minorities; the word had yet to exclude Jews or American-Asians with disproportionately high test scores.)

Lord Acton claims no novel insight. That liberty is a necessary condition for acting upon one's beliefs had been understood for centuries, the Abrahamic tradition being predicated on human agency and responsibility. In the Jewish tradition, this translated into self-rule in accordance with the commandments (*mitzvot*). Lord Acton specifically commends "the Chosen People [for providing] the first illustrations of a federated government, held together not on physical force, but on a voluntary covenant. The principle was carried out not only in each tribe, but in every group of at least 120 families; and there was neither privilege of rank nor inequality before the law."[696] From their example, Lord Acton extrapolates that

> the parallel lines on which all freedom has been won – the doctrine of national tradition and the doctrine of the higher law; the principle that a constitution grows from a root, by process of development, and not of essential change; and the principle that all political authority must be tested and reformed according to a code which was not made by man."[697]

Given that liberty depends on good government for enforcement, a political system that sacrifices liberty to any other goal is logically incapable of being good: "[L]iberty is not a means to a higher political end. It is itself the highest political end." By "end" Lord Acton means not "outcome," but a principle of common life. He goes on to explain: "It is not for the sake of a good public administration that it is required, but for security in the pursuit of the highest objects of civil society, and of private life."[698] The pursuit of private goals, within a robust civil society, requires liberty, which in turn may only be enforced by a government that is capable of reform as circumstances change, without compromising its end of securing human dignity. That end, in turn, presupposes liberty.

While great ancient Greek philosophers were no strangers to these insights, neither Plato nor Aristotle opposed the one institution that epitomized their repudiation: slavery. It was left to the Stoics to proclaim the revolutionary idea that "[b]efore God, there is neither Greek nor barbarian, neither rich nor poor, and the slave is as good as his master, for by birth all men are free... brethren of one family, and children of God."[699] Adding the principle that "the test of good government is its conformity to principles that can be traced to a higher legislator,"[700] the Stoics thus anticipated modern liberalism.

Their founder, Zeno (c.490-430 BCE), categorically denied that either conquest or purchase could make one man the property of another. Zeno's later Roman disciple, the dramatist, philosopher, and statesman Seneca (c.4 BCE-65 AD) added that "no one is a slave by nature."[701] In full agreement, the Jewish philosopher and Seneca's contemporary, Philo of Alexandria (c.20 BCE-50 AD) went a step further: He conceived the world itself as "a great city [which] has one constitution and one law, and this is the reason of nature, commanding what should be done and forbidding what should not be done." To be sure, those commands were routinely disobeyed, the result of sheer "greed and mutual lack of trust...."[702] But the conceptual soil was being prepared: natural law and natural rights were but a logical step away.

Seneca's fellow-statesman Marcus Tullius Cicero (106-43 BCE) also agreed with the Stoics that empathy is natural and virtually universal. Can anything be more natural than parental affection? (Rousseau excepted perhaps.) From just that inborn instinct there had to have "developed the sense of mutual attraction which unites human beings as such... The mere fact of their common humanity requires that one man should feel another man akin to him.... [S]o we are united and allied by nature in the common society of the state. Were this not so, there would be no room either for justice or benevolence. ... We are by nature fitted to form unions, societies, and states."[703] These ideas would later be rekindled and eventually implemented, however unevenly.

While the Stoics were stunningly modern in their thinking, the practical impact in their own day was negligible. And no wonder; at such an early stage, observes Lord Acton, "three things are [still] wanting - representative government, the emancipation of the slaves, and liberty of conscience."[704] Admittedly, self-government, as already mentioned, was not altogether unknown - the Sanhedrin courts of the Jews, established in biblical times, were not disbanded until 425, when the Roman Empire abolished the rabbinic patriarchate.[705] That said, the Sanhedrin judges constituted not a legislative but a judicial body. Popular "government by an elected Parliament," writes Lord Acton, "was even in theory a thing unknown."[706]

Liberty of conscience was also occasionally respected, as Greek, and later Roman, polytheism did "admit some measure of toleration," notes Lord Acton. In fact, the principle itself preceded even the Greeks, having first been proclaimed by the Buddhist king Asoka some two and a half centuries BCE in distant India.[707] Isolated exceptions aside, however, the risk to social and political interests usually prevented dissenting views from being heard. Fear of change trumped the less immediate benefits of dialogue.

Ultimately, it was not for lack of ideas that liberty failed to take root in antiquity. Concludes Lord Acton: "There is hardly a truth in politics or in the system of the rights of man that was not grasped by the wisest of the Gentiles and the Jews, or that they did not declare with a refinement of thought and a nobleness of expression that later writers could never surpass."[708] The proverbial devil was in the implementation. "The liberties of the ancient nations were crushed beneath a hopeless and inevitable despotism," which denied to large segments of the human species dominion over their bodies and minds. Clearly, concludes Lord Acton, "slavery has been, far more than intolerance, the perpetual curse and reproach of ancient civilization."[709]

Eventually, the Stoic perspective gained ground, as Christian "divines of the second century [came to] insist on liberty, and divines of the fourth century on equality." The one major political transformation necessary to translate concepts into practice, however, was still in the distant future: "Popular governments had existed, and also mixed and federal governments, but there had been no limited government, no State the circumference of whose authority had been defined by a force external to its own."[710] What finally opened the door to the notion that however supreme, the ruler of a state is not exempt from severe sanction if found guilty of tyranny, was the Christian notion that no secular king has absolute power over his subjects, that even a putative Father of his People must answer to a still higher authority. Limited government thus appeared to be the only moral option.

Among the first to take this to heart were members of the Guelph and Ghibelline factions in German and Italian principalities during the 13th and 14th centuries. Both groups believed that a king who is unfaithful to his duty may be deposed, having himself become "a rebel whom the nation has a right to put down. For this purpose, the whole nation ought to have a share in governing itself... No government has a right to levy taxes beyond the limit determined by the people. All political authority is derived from popular suffrage, and all laws must be made by the people or their representatives.'"[711]

Similarly, in the British Isles the principle of a law that transcends even kings would be enshrined in the Magna Carta of 1215. Revised in 2016, an admittedly less radical Carta became more Magna, as half a millennium later it sprouted the theory of universal individual rights, which in turn was practically and effectively implemented in the American republic.[712] The plucky colonists, who had sailed across treacherous waters to brave a new world that didn't suffer fools, appealed to what comes most naturally to Anglo-Saxons and their ilk: common sense.

Property and Freedom

Common sense *qua* wisdom of simple folk is the product of hard-won experience. For many of them, progress tends to be a double-edged sword. True, new knowledge and better tools increase efficiency – yet there is a price they often have trouble paying. Social arrangements shift, leading some people to benefit greatly while others are uprooted; not a few inevitably prove incapable of adjustment altogether. Throughout history, scientific progress has often been "combined with that suffering which is inseparable from extensive changes in the condition of the people," rues Lord Acton. Unfortunately, it is just such volatile events that prompt intellectuals, "men of speculative or imaginative genius," to make matters far worse, by imagining ideal societies, reminiscent of "the legends of the golden age."[713] And as if economic disruption were not painful enough, instead of exploring ways to mitigate the effects of dislocation, it is the right of property itself that comes under radical attack. Thomas More's **Utopia** was among the first of increasingly radical "protests against a state of things, which the experience of their authors taught them to condemn, and from the faults of which they took refuge in the opposite extremes"[714] – of which the notion of abolishing inequality of property altogether was the most drastic.

The alluring simplicity of this long-touted solution to all evil was tailor-made for demagoguery: "Only the attraction of an abstract idea, or of an ideal state, can unite, in a common action, multitudes who seek a universal cure for many special evils," observes Lord Acton. But in the process, they almost invariably succumb to "false principles" which, however effective in igniting revolt, "cannot serve as a basis for the reconstruction of civil society."[715]

Preeminent among such false principles are schemes that impugn the distribution of power, property, and territory - which he names, respectively, "the theories of equality, Communism, and nationality." True, while sharing "a common origin, opposing cognate evils, and connected by many links, these did not appear simultaneously."[716] That said, they are all variations on the same theme: an appeal to central control, along with repression of freedom. (Lord Acton later did add a caveat regarding "nationality," distinguishing proper from the improper, meaning authoritarian, variety. He was more right than even he knew.) Slyly manipulated by powerful elites, these false principles succeeded widely across all times and places. By the seventeenth century, the British stood nearly alone. Having developed over many centuries the political capacity to implement the necessary checks on government, Lord Acton commends his compatriots for appreciating that "a people averse to the institution of private property is without the first element of freedom."[717] And that required an understanding of equal, universal rights.

In pre-modern times, it had been the *duties* of men to their superiors that mattered most. Nobles had duties to the king, peasants to their landlords, and so on. This had gradually been changing throughout the Middle Ages, culminating in the philosophy of John Locke (1632-1704), widely acknowledged as the rightful Father of Liberalism.[718] Leo Strauss considers John Locke's most revolutionary contribution to political thought to be a "shift of emphasis from natural duties or obligations to natural rights." In Locke, writes Strauss, "the individual, the ego, had become the center and origin of the moral world, since man – as distinguished from man's end – had become that center or origin."[719] This idea would come to define the Age of the Enlightenment, also known as the Age of Reason, a label that contributed considerably to its being misunderstood.

In his *Second Treatise on Government* (1690), Locke had declared: "[T]he natural liberty of man is to be free from any superior power on earth, and not to be under the will or legislative authority of man... [while] the liberty of man in society is to be under no other legislative power but that established, by consent, in the commonwealth."(IV.22) Individual freedom, in other words, logically precedes the political state. In a so-called "state of nature" (which was meant as a theoretical construct rather than literally), human beings are equal in the sense that no one has a prior claim to authority over anyone else. Prior to any social arrangement, "all men are naturally in... a state of perfect freedom to order their actions, and dispose of their possessions and persons, as they think fit, within the bounds of the law of nature, without asking leave, or depending upon the will of any other man." (II. 4)

How does Locke justify this claim? He shares Cicero and the Stoics' belief in a "common humanity," and agrees that we are "by nature fitted to form unions, societies, and states." But unlike the Stoics, who attributed this propensity to "the sense of mutual attraction which unites human beings," a feeling of benevolence and sympathy, Locke thought it rather "grounded on [man's] having reason, which is able to instruct him in that law he is to govern himself by, and make him know how far he is left to the freedom of his own will." (VI. 63) In his view, it is common reason, not sentiment, that philosophically justifies equality of natural rights defined as life, liberty, and "estate," which all fall under the right of personal property, the fruit of one's labor. He did not disagree that sympathy is important, but reason sufficed to justify consensual rule.

The emphasis on reason held a special appeal to French luminaries of the Enlightenment. But while the latter thought an authoritarian enforcer of the General Will to be indispensable, Locke would have dismissed such a construct, as did his Scottish brethren in the next century. It is unfortunate that critics of "the Enlightenment" invariably lump together the French and the British varieties, including both English and Scottish. While all three share a belief in human emancipation, and admit some form of popular government. Himmelfarb notes that "the French themselves credited that venerable English trinity, [Francis] Bacon, Locke, and Newton, with the ideas that inspired their own Enlightenment." Yet the British, along with the Scottish, version "took a form very different from that of its counterpart on the continent."[720]

For while both the French and the English acknowledged that reason is common to all, it was the virtues of benevolence and sympathy "which, the British believed, naturally, instinctively, habitually bound people to each other. They did not deny reason; they were by no means irrationalists. But they gave reason a secondary, instrumental role."[721] This was even more true of the Scots. Where they agreed with Locke was on the centrality of the individual in political life, the universality of rights, and the need to protect the rule of law against illegitimate government power, no matter how putatively well intentioned. Ultimately the combined Anglo-Saxon contribution to the American experience is definitely greater than the French. Had it been otherwise, writes Himmelfarb, "Americans could have injected into their Revolution a larger utopian mission, rather than the pragmatic, cautious temper conspicuous in *The Federalist* and the Constitution."[722] Much misunderstanding could have been avoided had the complex legacy of the Enlightenment been better understood. This is particularly true of America's debt to the Scots, to whom we now turn.

The Scottish Enlightenment may be said to have been launched by Francis Hutcheson (1694-1746), an immensely popular philosophy professor at the University of Glasgow, possibly the first to teach in the vernacular rather than Latin, and who encouraged robust student discussions instead of straight lecturing. Though a preacher himself, Hutcheson's principal message, in keeping with his affable temperament, was that religion should not inspire fear; rather, it should encourage a disinterested affection for others. His listeners, writes historian Arthur Herman, would discover that the underlying principles of all human behavior were part of an "immense and connected" moral system governed by the dictates of natural law. That included "*oeconomicks*, or the laws and rights of the several members of a family," as well as "private rights, or the laws obtaining in natural liberty."[723]

In this context, economics is used in its Aristotelian sense of household management; that term would soon be expanded, thereby founding a whole new discipline, by the man who was to inherit Hutchenson's chair, his far better-known student, Adam Smith (1723–1790).

Hutcheson, to his everlasting glory, had indeed set the framework in his *System of Moral Philosophy*, stating that

'tis plain each one has a natural right to exert his powers, according to his own judgment and inclination, for purposes [of natural affections] in all such industry, labor, or amusements, as are not hurtful to others in their persons or goods, while no more public interests necessarily requires his labors, or requires that his actions should be under the direction of others. This right we call *natural liberty*.[724]

'Tis plain: which is to say, it's common sense. And being "natural," liberty is *ipso facto* universal.

Hutcheson's main accomplishment was to endorse much more than freedom of speech and religion: he condemned all forms of oppression against all human beings. Writes Herman: "Francis Hutcheson had created a new political and social vision...: the vision of a 'free society.' He is Europe's first liberal in the classic sense: a believer in maximizing personal liberty in the social, economic, and intellectual spheres, as well as the political."[725] Perhaps he and Locke could share the honor, notwithstanding their differences.

Thomas Jefferson agreed with Hutcheson that "man," as he wrote to his friend Peter Carr in 1787, "was destined for society... He was endowed with a sense of right and wrong merely relative to this. This sense is as much a part of his nature as the sense of hearing, seeing, feeling: it is the true foundation of morality."[726] While indebted to Locke, Jefferson had no trouble positing a "moral sense" as had Hutchenson:

The moral sense, or conscience, is as much a part of man as his leg or arm. It is given to all human beings in a stronger or weaker degree, as force of members is given them in a greater or less degree. It may be strengthened by exercise, as may any particular limb of the body. This sense is submitted indeed in some degree to the guidance of reason; but it is a small stock which is required for this: even a less one than what we call Common sense. State a moral case to a ploughman and a professor. The former will decide it as well, and often better than the latter, because he has not been led astray by artificial rules.[727]

It is on this basis that Jefferson and the other Founders supported the principles of the Declaration,[728] summarized in the one phrase that has since galvanized the world: "We hold these truths to be self-evident, that all men are created equal, that they are endowed by their Creator with certain unalienable[729] Rights, that among these are Life, Liberty and the pursuit of Happiness. That to secure these rights, Governments are instituted among Men, deriving their just powers from the consent of the governed." He later explained in a letter that by "self-evident" he had meant merely "to place before mankind the common sense of the subject, in terms so plain and firm as to command their assent, and to justify ourselves in the independent stand we are compelled to take."[730] These truths were deemed self-evident, because it was the common understanding of the subject, certainly in America. That made them also "sacred and undeniable" – which had been the original wording.[731]

When the Declaration signers substituted "pursuit of Happiness" for "property" in Locke's original trinity of unalienable rights, they were not disagreeing about the significance of property rights as against happiness. Jefferson was here echoing Hutcheson and other Scots, notably Thomas Reid, who all wrote of "the natural, the unalienable right of judging for ourselves" how to pursue our own happiness, in no way implying that property was up for grabs. At bottom, the object of the American Revolution was to set up a government whose powers are strictly limited by the requirement to protect that basic unalienable right which spawned an infinity of others. These powers were potentially infinite; for the Ninth Amendment in the Bill of Rights pointedly noting that their "enumeration in the Constitution of certain rights shall not be construed to deny or disparage others retained by the people." *Ergo*, what Congress is not specifically delegated to do, it has no power to do. Conversely, there is no logical reason to protect against encroachment any rights that the government has no power to encroach upon in the first place.

It was this crucial principle that made the American system truly unique, indeed exceptional.

Substituting "the pursuit of happiness" for "property" among man's unalienable rights, far from minimizing the latter's importance, in reality expands it, for property provides the means to pursue happiness. It was a truth that Adam Smith, who opposed England's obsolete restrictions on inheritance and trade left over from feudalism, fully understood. But as Robert Curry explains,

> [even m]ore important was the fact that Americans also created conditions favoring the transfer of property among ordinary citizens. That is what [Peruvian economist Hernando] de Soto found when he examined American economic history in order to find out what had set America apart from the rest of the world. He found the answer in strong property rights grounded in clear titles to property. [732]

It was no mere stroke of good luck that landed future U.S. President James Madison at Princeton University, where he came under the powerful influence of Hutcheson's student, Reverend John Witherspoon (1723-1794). The only clergyman and only college president to sign the Declaration of Independence, Witherspoon had deliberately sought out students from throughout the colonies, and Madison was luckily among them. From Witherspoon, the brilliant young Virginian learned that a common, natural moral sense, along with the ability to reason, rendered all human beings equal, with none entitled to decide for another without consent. But the most powerful impact on Madison was made by the Scotsman who considered both moral sense and reason ultimately subordinate to self-interest: Adam Smith.

Smith did not deny that reason was universal but argued that its main function was to promote personal interest. Which was fine so long as no one could encroach on anyone else's right to do the same; thereby limited, healthy competition would result in the most efficient and prosperous outcome no matter how minimal the sense of empathy. The same could apply to politics: if every power center, branch of government, agency, or provincial entity pursues its own interests, pitting different constituencies against one another, the result would be far preferable to allowing any one power center to prevail over others. That went even for the chief executive, whose actions would be subject to judicial review.

Smith believed that competition itself is a system of checks and balances that, as if by an invisible hand, leads to an optimum state of affairs both in practical and moral terms. Madison agreed, adapting the reasoning to the political sphere. The result is certainly no perfection, either in the market or the public square, but it is better than any alternative: the operative word is "optimum," in stark contrast to "utopian." In *An Inquiry into the Nature and Causes of the Wealth of Nations*, published in the year of Hume's death and the colonists' Declaration, Smith explained why allowing people to pursue their own goals as they see fit leads to the greatest prosperity of the whole. Equally, if not more important, was that such an arrangement permits the greatest degree of individual freedom without prejudice as to social distinctions. Hence democracy was the best form of government. Explains Joseph Cropsey: Unlike those among "[t]he ancient moralists [who] coldly concentrated upon the distinction between the politically weighty people and the entire populace that dwelt within the frontiers... democracy [alone] has the merit of making possible the effacement of that distinction." [733]

A regime that minimizes the distinction between men was the ultimate aim of Smith's philosophy, often referred to as capitalism, free enterprise, or laissez-faire. Smith of course never used those terms. What he proposed to defend was "the natural system of perfect liberty and justice," or more briefly, "the system of natural liberty" [734] But he didn't think himself an innovator: "[L]iberty," explains Cropsey, meant to Smith the same thing that "it had meant to Locke, to Aristotle, and to the long tradition of political philosophy: the condition of men under lawful governors who respect the persons and property of the governed, the latter having to consent to the arrangement in one way or another." [735] The term "capitalism" came from Marx, hence the nearly inescapable pejorative connotation.

Liberty meant the same to the Founders as it did to Smith. The result was a superbly calibrated federal system outlined in an elegantly concise federal Constitution, synchronized with state constitutions, based on the immutable principle that all power rests with the people. No wonder that Alexander de Tocqueville (1805-1859), in a speech before the French Constituent Assembly on September 12th, 1848, declared plainly that America was the one nation that both defined and implemented the idea of liberty as nowhere else on earth.

The issue before the Assembly that day concerned the possibility of solving the unemployment problem plaguing the new – second – French republic following the overthrow of King Louis Philippe I, by setting up government work projects, guaranteeing employment at a fixed wage. In this extraordinary speech,[736] Tocqueville confronted his fellow lawmakers bluntly: the real issue at hand was "socialism." And he wasn't having it.

Acknowledging that several systems could qualify as socialist, he proposes examining only their common characteristics, which he identifies as follows: First, "an incessant, vigorous and extreme appeal to the material passions of man;" second, "an attack, either direct or indirect, on the principle of private property;" and third, "a profound opposition to personal liberty and scorn for individual reason, a complete contempt for the individual." In a word, socialism is quite "simply a new system of serfdom."

He goes on to charge that the Old Regime, the monarchy, was actually far less distant from socialism than it seemed, as both "held that wisdom lay only in the State and that the citizens were weak and feeble beings who must forever be guided by the hand." Yet what he calls socialism "pretended to be the legitimate continuation of democracy," which he finds ludicrous. Tocqueville then turns from theory to hard evidence: "I look for democracy where I have seen it, in the only country on earth where it exists, where it could possibly have been established as something durable in the modern world – in America." He specifies:

> There you will find a society where social conditions are even more equal than among us; where the social order, the customs, the laws are all democratic; where all varieties of people have entered, and where each individual still has complete independence, more freedom than has been known in any other time or place; a country essentially democratic, the only completely democratic republic the world has ever known. And in these republics you will search in vain for socialism.

Democracy and socialism, Tocqueville contends, are

> not only different but opposing philosophies.... Democracy extends the sphere of personal independence, socialism confines it. Democracy values each man an agent, an instrument, a number. Democracy and socialism have but one thing in common - equality. But note well the difference. Democracy aims at equality in liberty. Socialism desires equality in constraint and in servitude.

His contemporary Frederic Bastiat (1801-1850) shared his fellow-countryman's opposition to what they both called "socialism." "The parallels between the two men are numerous," writes George Roche III. Though the former has sometimes been labeled a conservative and the latter a libertarian,

> there was much of the conservative in Bastiat, much of the libertarian in Tocqueville. Neither Bastiat nor Tocqueville would have hesitated to identify the enemy as the centralizing power of big government. It is highly unlikely that they would have allowed any mere difference in labels to cause them to turn upon one another while forgetting the identity of the real enemy. [737]

Perhaps more generous than Tocqueville, Bastiat sought no quarrel with any of his ideological opponents: "The sincerity of those who advocate protectionism, socialism, and Communism is not here questioned," he wrote in the posthumously published "The Law."[738] He continues, however, mincing no words, that the three "isms" "are basically the same plant in three different stages of its growth. All that can be said is that legal plunder is more visible in Communism because it is complete plunder; and in protectionism because the plunder is limited to specific groups and industries." That said, he hastens to "assure the socialists that we repudiate only forced organization, not natural organization," and categorically rejects being willfully and erroneously attacked for having in mind different ends: "[E]very time we object to a thing being done by government, the socialists conclude that we object to its being done at all."[739] The kibbutz would have been fine by him. The problem was not utopianism as a *personal* choice but the coerced, hubristic variety, particularly the kind that sought justification in millenarian terms.

Bastiat welcomes his fellow political scientists coming up with different types of social combinations, trying them out and advertising them, but he does "dispute their right to impose these plans upon us by law – by force – and to compel us to pay for them with our taxes."[740] Recognizing socialism as "the most popular fallacy of our times," he fully appreciates its "seductive lure," yet he also accuses its proponents of wanting to play God. They are, he charges, afflicted by "a fatal desire – learned from the teachings of antiquity... to set themselves up above mankind in order to arrange, organize, and regulate it according to their fancy."[741] Though passionate, Bastiat's fulminations are expressed with uncompromising clarity:

The mission of the law is not to oppress persons and plunder them of their property, even though the law may be acting in a philanthropic spirit. Its mission is to protect persons and property. ... [I]f you attempt to make the law religious, fraternal, equalizing, philanthropic, industrial, literary, or artistic – you will then be lost in an uncharted territory, in vagueness and uncertainty, in a forced utopia or, even worse, in a multitude of utopias, each striving to seize the law and impose it upon you.[742]

It is not a little ironic that the one nation where Bastiat's ideas most resonated, the United States, at that very time continued to consider slaves as property that the government should protect. Bastiat abhorred such a notion: "It is sad to think that the science of law as we know it in the nineteenth century is still based on principles formulated in antiquity to justify slavery," he wrote in "Property and Law."[743]

Sad it was indeed that the nearly ideal new democracy across the Atlantic would soon lose close to one million citizens in one of history's bloodiest civil wars to right that egregious wrong. Though no one could have anticipated the magnitude of the carnage, the event was anything but a complete surprise. The constitutional provision that each state could count the number of slaves within its jurisdiction as three-fifths of the number of its white inhabitants (for census purposes only; slaves were obviously prohibited from voting) had always contradicted the lofty principles of the Declaration. No one knew that better than its authors, especially Thomas Jefferson.

For among the grievances against King George meant to justify the colonists' severing of ties with the Mother Country, listed in his (original) draft of the Declaration but omitted in the final version, was the accusation that "he has waged cruel war against human nature itself, violating it's [sic] most sacred rights of life & liberty in the persons of a distant people who never offended him, captivating & carrying them into slavery in another hemisphere, or to incur miserable death in their transportation thither."[744] These words could not have been included in the official draft: the political and economic realities made it quite impossible.

It fell to Abraham Lincoln to explain, on June 26, 1857, that the Founders had

simply meant to declare the right [to freedom], so that the enforcement of it might follow as fast as circumstances would permit. They meant to set up a standard maxim for a free society, which should be familiar to all, and revered by all;...constantly labored for, and even though never perfectly attained, constantly approximated and thereby constantly spreading and deepening its influence, and augmenting the happiness and value of life to all people of all colors everywhere. The assertion that "all men are created equal" was of no practical use to our effecting our separation from Great Britain; and it was placed in the Declaration, not for that, but for future use.[745]

Once those circumstances did allow it, the Thirteenth amendment to the Constitution freed all enslaved people; the Fourteenth gave them full citizenship; and the Fifteenth granted black men the right to vote. It would take decades more of legal and cultural reforms to undo an evil that, in the final analysis, can never be set right altogether, let alone obliterated.

Eventually, women too were awarded this ultimate prize, fulfilling Abigail Adams's hope and rightful request. So at last political equality seemed more or less guaranteed. But if political rights were eventually recognized, property rights have fared much less well. Explains Roger Pilon:

When the post-Civil War Framers revised our original federalism, they did it the right way, by amending the Constitution to make it consistent with its underlying moral and political principles. The New Deal politicians, having less regard for the Constitution and its underlying principles, rejected that course, choosing instead to browbeat the Court into effectively rewriting the Constitution, undermining its moral and political principles in the process. But don't take my word for it. Here is Franklin Roosevelt, writing to the chairman of the House Ways and Means Committee: "I hope your committee will not permit doubts as to constitutionality, however reasonable, to block the suggested legislation." And here is Rexford Tugwell, one of the principal architects of the New Deal, reflecting on his handiwork some 30 years later: "To the extent that these [New Deal policies] developed, they were tortured interpretations of a document intended to prevent them." They knew exactly what they were doing. They were turning the Constitution on its head.[746]

Morality and Equality: Ends and Means

Smith was not engaged in a polemic designed to defend any system as ideal; that's the job of delusional "men of 'system,'" the utopians whom he loathed. Smith had no illusions: men were imperfect, both emotionally and intellectually, and the world was complicated and unpredictable. He saw man "as being by nature [simultaneously] altruistic and egoistic – a species-member moved by [both] love of self and fellow feeling with others,"[747] writes Joseph Cropsey. But Smith subscribed to the Golden Rule, which he held common to Christianity, and formed the basis of natural law: "As to love our neighbor as we love ourselves is the great law of Christianity," writes Smith, "so it is the great precept of nature to love ourselves only as we love our neighbor, or ... as our neighbor is found capable of loving us."[748]

Since the moral law is thus "natural," religious justification for its observance is extremely important, even if not strictly necessary. It helps that in addition to the bonds of immediate sense and feeling, man is also tied to his brethren by calculation or reason, since this compensates for the deficiency in empathy so commonly observed even (not to say especially) among the self-styled altruists among us. But neither pure reason nor beneficence, however necessary, suffices to insure observance of the Golden Rule. He sought to base freedom on a more realistic footing.

Smith was interested in how men are in reality, rather than what *man* is, in the abstract. Individual humans are preoccupied with self-preservation; and commerce allows for the most efficient satisfaction of personal needs, since no one can supply everything alone. "Every man thus lives by exchanging, or becomes in some measure a merchant, and the society itself grows to be what is properly a commercial society," wrote Smith in *The Wealth of Nations*.[749] It is easy to see how this can be misunderstood and infer that Smith reduced everything to commerce and money. In fact, that is exactly wrong.

In his earlier (1759) though far less well-known treatise, *The Theory of Moral Sentiments*, Smith states "that to feel much for others and little for ourselves, that to restrain our selfish, and to indulge our benevolent affections, constitutes the perfection of human nature."[750] But above all, the wisest and most virtuous man is he whose "whole mind... is deeply impressed, his whole behavior and deportment are distinctly stamped with the character of real modesty" – that is, "humility."[751] Some people are better than others in various respects, but no one is without flaw.Smith did not see men as cold, rational, mercenary creatures. Writes

Arthur Herman: "Contrary to popular misunderstanding, Adam Smith never supposed that everyone is driven solely by self-interest in a material sense. He knew that many of us, perhaps most, are not. "[752] Rather, he observed a felicitous impetus to improve our circumstances that may incidentally also profit others, even in the absence of a deliberate altruistic motive. Experience teaches that reaching out to others, offering them something that they want or need, is more often than not consistent with our self-interest. "It is not from the benevolence of the butcher, the brewer, or the baker, that we expect our dinner, but from their regard to their own interest."[753] Far from being self-sufficient, humans could never survive alone. Unlike animals in the wild, "man has almost constant occasion for the help of his brethren, and it is in vain for him to expect it from their benevolence only. He will be more likely to prevail if he can interest their self-love in his favor and shew them that it is for their own advantage to do for him what he requires of them."[754]

So despite being neither especially benevolent nor always rational, ordinary human beings muddle along. Somehow it all works out in the end: to an outside observer, it might even seem as if everyone were being directed by an invisible hand. Smith does not insinuate that the hand is divine, just very effective. For, writes Herman, Smith's "real point was not that a market-based order was perfect or even perfectible. Rather, it was more beneficial, and ultimately more rational, than ones put together by politicians or rulers, who are themselves creatures of their own passions and whims."[755] Note: *more*.... Not perfect, not utopia. Just better.

Its disingenuous opponents notwithstanding, far from being correlated with egoism and heartlessness, the free market boosts philanthropy as a result of higher prosperity. No wonder that "America has been named as the world's most generous nation in the world, where its citizens give the most to charity, according to a new report," followed by New Zealand and Canada.[756] Charity is incompatible with free, capitalist societies only if one assumes them to be populated by ruthlessly self-interested, i.e., selfish, individualistic money-lovers. Some surely are; but not all.

Economist Deirdre McCloskey, who shares the socialists' professed concern for the poor, the disadvantaged, the vulnerable, categorically disagrees with the alleged heartlessness of capitalists: not only is the free market compatible with these values, it is actually indispensable to their pursuit. McCloskey argues that all such worthy "leaps into the modern world – more democracy, the liberation of women, improved life expectancy, greater education, spiritual growth, artistic explosion – are firmly attached to the Great Fact [of the Industrial Revolution], [which is] the increase by 2,900% in food and education and travel."[757]

There is a vast amount of empirical evidence demonstrating the economic superiority of limited regulation and unfettered trade. The poor in a democratic capitalist, i.e., free-market, nation are still far better off than most people residing in a centrally-controlled state, which is invariably authoritarian. The website www.humanprogress.org, launched in 2013 by Marian L. Tupy, posts comparative information on a variety of categories, such as food, health, housing, education, energy, environment, and violence. Categories such as the average caloric intake and infant mortality, both worldwide and in particular countries, are duly sourced and listed, then correlated. The results speak for themselves: indices of well-being are intimately connected with absence of regulation and personal constraint.

The Cato Institute's *2017 Human Freedom Index* (HFI), edited by Ian Vasquez and Tanja Porcnik, comes to a similar conclusion.[758] The authors note "that human freedom and material human progress are related. To give just one example, countries in the top quartile of freedom enjoy a significantly higher average per capita income ($38,871) than those in other quartiles. The average per capita income in the least-free quartile is $10,346. The HFI also finds a strong relationship between human freedom and democracy."[759]

The Index uses 79 distinct indicators of personal and economic freedom in areas such as rule of law, security and safety, movement, religion, expression and information, identity and relationships, size of government, legal system and property rights, access to sound money, and freedom to trade internationally. Also included are freedom of association, assembly, and civil society, and regulation of credit, labor, and business.[760] The pattern is straightforward: personal and economic freedom go hand in hand.[761]

That nonmaterial goods such as better education, artistic accomplishment, women's participation in all areas of society, are the direct result of an increase in available goods is a simple correlation. But McCloskey goes a step further. Rejecting the old conventional wisdom that the Industrial Revolution "came from material causes, from investment or theft, from higher saving rates or from imperialism,"[762] she claims that the "Revolution was sparked instead by changes in the way people *thought*, and especially by how they thought about each other." Attitudes came first; success followed. People started liking change, admired entrepreneurs, and "the middle class started to be viewed as *good*, and started to be allowed to do good, and to do well."[763] Thus "it was ideas, or 'rhetoric,' that caused our enrichment, and with it our modern liberties."[764]

A common reaction to the claim that freedom works best is to drudge up alternative facts. The presumption that free markets cause the rich to get richer and the poor poorer is widely accepted as gospel truth. And how can it be otherwise, when evidence used to bolster it comes from Oxfam, whose annual report is dutifully disseminated by the BBC, National Public Radio, and other media outlets. Its fifth such report, released on January 2, 2018, for example, claims once again that the gap between the superrich and the rest of the world widened – "82 percent of all wealth created in the last year went to the top 1 percent, while the bottom 50 percent saw no increase at all."[765] This is an "unacceptable and unsustainable" situation,[766] the solution being that"[g]overnments must create a more equal society by prioritizing ordinary workers and small-scale food producers instead of the rich and powerful." What makes a system "crony," then, is whether or not it puts the finger on the economic scales as progressives wish.

But what if the result is the opposite of that (allegedly) intended? James Pethokoukis, responding to virtually the same conclusions reached by Oxfam's 2014 report, asks rhetorically: "[D]oes Oxfam's simplistic narrative of crony capitalism tell the economic story of the past three decades better than the 80 percent decline in extreme poverty? And why exactly are there 250 million fewer extremely poor people in the world today?"[767] The answer is: not redistribution but lower barriers to freedom of trade, thought, and expression, accounting for unprecedented innovation and communication.

Equally unconvinced, Sam Dumitriu has looked into the methodology used by Oxfam reports to uncover what rendered them so misleading. His efforts were amply rewarded: it turns out that the reports arrive at poverty figures by counting as someone's putative "wealth" only the value of assets such as property and land, minus debts, while inexplicably excluding wages or income, both current and anticipated. This would put a medical student with high debts into the "poor" category, notwithstanding the high probability of future earnings.[768]

The report's claim that "two-thirds of billionaires' wealth is the product of inheritance [19 percent], monopoly and cronyism [65 percent]" is similarly based on shady statistics. Thus Dumitriu found that Oxfam counted as "product of inheritance" the wealth of individuals "regardless of whether that wealth has grown substantially since the inheritance." This ignores any extra wealth generated by that inheritance. So for example, a $1-billion fortune all counts as "inherited," even if the original sum amounted to a mere $1,000, disregarding altogether the wise investment and hard work that accounted for its growth.

"The cronyism figure is more speculative still," writes Ryan Bourne: "It includes 'wealth mainly acquired in a corruption-prone country and state-dependent industry (high presumption of cronyism)' or 'wealth mainly acquired in the mining, oil and gas industry.'"[769] How is that justified? Surely natural resources do not *all* end up in "crony" hands. They do in autocracies such as Russia, Venezuela, Iran, Saudi Arabia, and Kazakhstan, but not in the United States, Israel, or Canada.

Whatever the merits or demerits of inequality, the facts should not be skewed to fit an ideology. When Barack Obama claims that income inequality is the "defining challenge of our time," he is reflecting the widespread assumption that it has increased in recent years in the United States. Yet according to Diana Furthtgott-Roth, "[p]ublished government spending data by income quintile show that the ratio of spending between the top and bottom 20 percent has essentially not changed between 1987 and 2012. In terms of total spending, inequality is at the same level as 1987."[770] The data show "if anything, a narrowing rather than an expansion of inequality."

The practical or utilitarian defense of individual freedom as the organizing principle of government aside, there are crucial moral questions to consider. First, how can charity be considered truly moral if it is made compulsory? Also, isn't obliging someone to perform an action because it is deemed required by "public values" still compulsion? Would a doctor required by law to treat everyone who needs his services not become a virtual slave? Would he be obliged to serve anyone and everyone who needs him, whenever he is needed? At what cost? To whom? As for the alleged altruism of the do-gooder: how can any people imagine *they* are being unselfish when they advocate demanding that *other* people do something? "We are neither entitled to be unselfish at someone else's expense nor is there any merit in being unselfish if we have no choice,"[771] writes F. A. Hayek. Morality and human dignity are predicated on free action.

"Responsibility, not to a superior, but to one's conscience, the awareness of a duty not exacted by compulsion, the necessity to decide which of the things one values are to be sacrificed to others, and to bear the consequences of one's own decision, are the very essence of any morals which deserve the name,"[772] argues Hayek. When utopian ends are used to justify any means, morality succumbs to ideology. "That in this sphere of individual conduct," observes Hayek sadly, "the effect of collectivism has been almost entirely destructive is both inevitable and undeniable. A movement whose main promise is the relief from responsibility cannot but be antimoral in its effect, however lofty the ideals to which it owes its birth."[773] Morality itself has to be redefined, or rather, abandoned.

The assumption of the hubristic utopian is that given the undeniable purity of the end, whatever it takes to reach it, including violence, is automatically considered moral. Compulsion to march to history's drumbeat is purifying. As material (income, health, food, clothing, etc.) equality is considered to be absolutely Good, whatever produces such equality is deemed by implication to be legitimate, in the name of Progress. Writes Samuel P. Huntington: "All the common ideational ideologies of modern Western society approach existing institutions with an 'ought demand' that the institutions be reshaped to embody the values of the ideology. In this sense all ideational theories involve some degree of radicalism, i.e., criticism of existing institutions."[774] Not all ideational ideologies are egalitarian; some embrace values other than income equality. They may prefer black supremacy, as does the Nation of Islam, the New Black Panthers, the Israelite School of Universal Practical Knowledge. Or white supremacy, as did the late Afrikaner National Party of South Africa, neo-Nazis the world over, and the Ku Klux Klan, among others. What all these lunatics share is that none would subscribe to the system of natural liberty.

But, you ask, how can socialism be even compared with supremacist ideologies of any stripe? Isn't protecting the vulnerable the very epitome of morality, the opposite of any form of racism? Yes, of course. But if that protection is to be achieved through redistribution of "public resources," *someone* must decide how such reallocation is to be carried out. That means, in practice, government officials. Their actions in turn are justified, at least in a democracy, by electoral means; and economists who study public choice have amply confirmed[775] what common sense intuits, which is that "reallocation" invariably benefits one influential faction or another. It is what the Founders had hoped to avoid. Explains Richard Epstein:

As Madison recognized, factions come in all shapes and sizes, which is why either "a majority or a minority of the whole" can be the dominant, i.e., prevailing, faction…. In the absence of any strong social or institutional constraints, a dominant faction could use its voting power or political clout to confiscate the wealth of the political losers, or more subtly, to hobble their economic activities with legal restrictions. Nor will the propertied classes, often a minority in number, necessarily come out on top, especially if the vast majority of the population is allowed to vote transfer payments to itself from, as they are now called, the top 1 percent. [776]

That is predictably what happened with the rise of the administrative state, which empowers unelected bureaucrats to create rules designed to favor special interest groups. These include labor and agricultural cartels, which are routinely exempt from antitrust legislation that seeks to break up corporate monopolies. Zonings and rent control statues are also paradigmatic examples of influence-peddling by local real estate markets. [777] Since government power has traditionally been used for various ends that profit some at the expense of others, the best we can hope for is to pit these groups against one another and pay attention to what works best in which circumstances. Sometimes federal legislation is more effective, but not always. Observes Epstein: "[U]niform national laws work better for trade, but local governments are better able to respond to variations in local conditions, as with land-use regulation. In the end, no single strategy can deal with this hydra-headed problem. Redundancy and multiple safeguards are needed at all levels of government, and the Constitution provides them." [778]

It is certainly possible to express the ideals of free market individualism, traditionally called liberalism, in terms that are nearly utopian: no one's negative rights would be violated; private property would be respected; all decisions made by directly-elected representatives would faithfully represent the electors' wishes and interests; and government would be practically nonexistent except for enforcing rights; associations would always be based on mutual consent, not "nationality" or religion; and peace would become the norm. But men are neither perfectly rational, nor are they angels. As James Madison wrote in "Federalist 51":

If men were angels, no government would be necessary. If angels were to govern men, neither external nor internal controls on government would be necessary. In forming a government which is to be administered by men over men, the great difficulty lies in this: you must first enable government to control the governed; and in the next place oblige it to control itself.[779]

As men are neither completely good nor completely rational, ultimately what matters is that, to the largest extent possible, no one be prevented from following his own conscience, along with everyone else. After all, what reason is there to believe that government interference makes matters better rather than worse? Explains Hayek: "the [classical, or true] liberal feels that no respect for established [or any other] values can justify the resort to privilege or monopoly or any other coercive power of the state." But that, of course, flies in the face of the utopian elitist's lethal hubris that he knows what is best for everyone, that he embodies the collective Good.

The constitutional system that still exists to a large extent in the United States provides reasonably effective safeguards against that menace, to which democracy is anything but immune. Democracy left unchecked is surely no panacea: Hayek pointedly does "not regard majority rule as an end but merely as a means, or perhaps even as the least evil of those forms of government from which we have to choose." He has no doubt that "[t]he chief evil is unlimited government, and nobody is qualified to wield unlimited power. The powers which modern democracy possesses would be even more intolerable in the hands of some small elite."[780]

It should be clear by now that a political system based on the principle of equal freedom is agnostic as to what constitutes a better world. Some prefer a wide variety of restaurants, avant-garde music, and abstract art, while others swear by McDonald's burgers, can't stand anything written after Brahms, and consider virtually the entire Modern Art Museum collection an insult to good taste. Someone who wishes to protect such a system "is very much aware that we do not know all the answers and that he is not sure that the answers he has are certainly the rights ones or even that we can find all the answers. He also does not disdain to seek assistance from whatever non-rational institutions or habits have proved their worth."[781] This does not mean that all choices are equally good. Relativism is not the obverse of absolutism. Reasonable people may have reasonably different tastes, without implying that they are on a par. But musical preferences, for example, are on an entirely different plane than bartering child brides or burning widows. The latter practices are not a matter of taste; they are inhumane.

Similarly, empirical truths, such as rise in temperature, are not a matter of preference or taste. So when someone utters "world climate has been steadily warming," there are metrics to prove or disprove it. Denial or affirmation should not be taken as proof of either heresy or piety. Unfortunately, observes Rebecca Newberger Goldstein, "[i]n today's political discourse, we have taken to repurposing certain propositions so that pronouncing them is not so much an assertion of truth as a pledge of allegiance to our political tribe." This is nothing new; but the explosion of electronic data has heightened a false sense of omniscience while social media has reinforced our biases. Her assessment that "our readiness today to proudly defy evidence is very troubling" is seriously understated. But casting all blame on the post-modernists whom no one understands them anyway is to put the proverbial cart before the visceral, hubristic horse: "I would say instead that the downgrading of truth, both within the academy and without, shares a common cause - namely, the promotion of political ends above all else. We have lost the capacity to limit the reach of our ideologies and the identities that go with them."[782] Forget euphemisms; political ends spells *power*.

A 2016 study has documented "a large and consequential bias in how Americans perceive the major political parties,"[783] with serious repercussions in voting behavior. The good news is that "when provided information about the actual composition of the out-party, partisans come to see its supporters as less extreme and feel less socially distant from them." But seldom is accurate information provided, let alone sought, to correct misperceptions. Too often, ideologies drive information - and though some have the impression that they win, which perhaps in the short run they do in a way, on a fundamental level everyone loses. Factions, tribes, and interest groups are inevitable; they represent the flip side of a cooperative instinct. People join together to pursue common goals, as they must. But unless everyone's right to do the same is respected, civil society degenerates, and the rule of law is sacrificed to the highest bidder.

Some people are more materialistic than others. Some value travel more than leisure, fancy cars more than fine art, hard liquor over books, greasy food over longevity. Not all pursuits are equally commendable, any more than all art is good or food healthy. But values are one thing, the freedom to pursue them another. People may use their freedom well or badly, to hurt themselves or to improve their lot and that of others. But if freedom is not an unmitigated good, its absence is an unmitigated evil.

A capitalist society – or as Smith called it, "a system of natural liberty" – cannot guarantee that everyone will pursue the highest ends. It provides no more than the necessary conditions for such a pursuit and is by no means sufficient. Ultimately, as Joseph Cropsey points out, "Smith advocated capitalism because it makes freedom possible – not because it *is* freedom." Freedom must be protected by a political and economic system devoted to its preservation from all potential enemies, foreign and domestic. That system may be called capitalist, but Smith's criticism of materialism, selfishness, and hubris "antedate Left, Right, and capitalism alike."[784] These categories have all been distorted for partisan ends. The reasons are disturbing, but hardly mysterious.

10:
Capitalism's Discontents

Antiamericanisme

Anti-Americanism captures what James Ceaser identifies as "the political religion of our times."[785] But what is Americanism, exactly? It depends whom you ask. How about "Americanism signifies the virtues of courage, honor, justice, truth, sincerity and strength"? Unless spoken at a Tea Party or MAGA (Make America Great Again) rally, this is a bit over-the-top. Even a century ago, when Theodore Roosevelt uttered these words without a trace of irony,[786] the hyperbole risked ridicule, and not only on college campuses.

Since the end of World War II, but especially in the last few decades, anti-Americanism has proliferated like crabgrass. The term applies to a spectrum of animosity ranging from the merely vicious to the homicidal. What the sentiment lacks in logic it makes up in toxicity - a fact 9/11 has rendered beyond dispute.

Scholars have been trying to make sense of the phenomenon with limited success. Brendan O'Connor, editor of the four-volume *Anti-Americanism: History, Causes, Themes*, concedes as much, but defends the critical importance of studying it. For even if it were merely "another form of prejudice" (like, say, against Italians, or vegans), it absolutely "should be challenged and confronted."[787] After all, America matters not merely because of its size, power, and influence, but because of what it stands for. And no, this isn't prejudice in just "another form" – though it is that too; anti-Americanism reflects a war of ideas that, whether recognized or not, continues unabated.

Fortunately, thanks to the English tradition of adopting foreign words (unlike, say, the French, who still guard the purity of their vocabulary with a ferocity once reserved to preserving a maiden's honor), we can dispense with another neologism. That deceptively euphonic word is *antiamericanisme*. It refers to a specific kind of hostility against the creed of America's founding - the protection of individual freedom.

Not that France is America's congenital enemy. At the outset, the ragged colonial soldiers could never have gained their embryonic nation's independence from Britain without help from Versailles. And we are members of NATO together (more or less). Yet traces of Gallic animosity antedate our Revolutionary War, the New World having met with general skepticism – at least, until the arrival of Benjamin Franklin, America's envoy and genius extraordinaire, who brilliantly elucidated the geopolitical opportunities presented by the colonies' war against Louis XVI's arch-enemy across the English Channel. Not to mention his persuasive work with the ladies, whose diplomatic assistance was hardly negligible. Yet with the notable exception of enlightened and brave men like the Marquis de Lafayette, who would be wounded while fighting alongside American soldiers, French assistance in those halcyon days was more strategic than sentimental.

Things deteriorated rapidly after Bastille. Philippe Roger explains that as "[t]he Revolution became more radical... advocates of the American model and the men who symbolized the Franco-American alliance left the public sphere or lost their lives."[788] The latter's liberal sympathies were not shared by the utopianist crowd. Throughout the nineteenth and well into the 20th century, changed circumstances may have temporarily mitigated, but never entirely extinguished, the now deeply entrenched animosity. *Antiamericanisme* had taken hold long before the word was coined.

The sentiment, alas, seemed irreversible. Neither America's interventions that saved France in both world wars, nor the generous Marshall Plan, could prevent increased resentment against this boorish, uncultured upstart. It is hard not to notice how easily it re-erupts at the slightest policy difference, "triggering anti-Americanism again and again and setting off the infernal machine of a nearly Pavlovian hostility."[789] But that hostility, however deeply felt, is no mere irrational emotion. Rather, explains Roger, its appeal is the result of a consistent, deep-seated narrative, which "need not necessarily be linked to any felt animosity."

Antiamericanisme is an ideology, barely concealing a revulsion of cataclysmic proportions. Its English equivalent, as defined in Webster's *American Dictionary of the English Language,* takes it to mean "opposed to America, or to the true interests or government of the United States; opposed to the revolution in America."[790] But interests vary with circumstances, and various administrations have at times disappointed their own citizens; the real, ultimate target of America's opponents is the nation's founding principles, the impetus behind the Revolution itself.

That at least is Webster's take; it behooved the term's Gallic users to explain their intent. Only that took a while. Having entered ordinary political language in France in the nineteenth century,[791] the term was not permitted to grace the hallowed pages of *Le Petit Robert* dictionary until 1968. The spectacle of Russian tanks rumbling on the streets of Prague shook the French radicals to the core. "[I]t would not be going out on a limb to suggest that the term spread as a counterpoint to 'anti-Sovietism,'"[792] writes Roger, as it allowed Communists and socialists to oppose liberal capitalism without necessarily implying that they were pro-Soviet. It managed to recalibrate the war of narratives and focus on attacking the Antichrist of capitalism.[793]

The notion of a *narrative*, increasingly popular in recent years, is easier to grasp than its close relative, *ideology* (defined in this book's Introduction as a system of ideas and ideals which include economic or political theories, however inchoate). While they both refer to a set of interrelated ideas united by a certain consistency, some descriptive (factual) and others normative (evaluative), *narrative* connotes a story, a more or less coherent picture which evokes particular feelings.

Paul Hollander, for example, uses the term anti-Americanism, to describe "a deep seated, emotional predisposition that perceives the United States as an unmitigated and uniquely evil entity and the source of all, or most, other evils in the world."[794] Intimately related to fear of modernity and expanding economic as well as cultural globalization, this predisposition, writes Hollander, is also a result of "the belief that big corporations (capitalism) are in the process of extending their influence and power around the world, and that the United States, as the major capitalist country, plays a prime role in this undesirable process."[795] Ready-made for balmy-weather Occupy Wall Street sit-outs, this narrative is easily accessible to the even minimally indoctrinated, if maximally impressionable, revolutionary-in-training.

As it happens, the most numerous proponents of this creed are also among the most educated, or rather, the most credentialed. Caesar observes that "on every continent, large contingents of intellectuals, backed by significant numbers in the political class, organize their political thinking on the basis of anti-Americanism."[796] Whether in part the result of envy, resentment, and fear, as the only superpower - now designated "hyperpower" and thereby deemed "hegemonic" - America is hard to love.

Thus Jean Baudrillard, commenting on world reaction to September 11, admitted to thinking "how all the world without exception dreamt of this event, for no one can avoid dreaming of the destruction of a power that has become hegemonic.... It is they who acted, but we who wanted the deed."[797] Even allowing that "all the world without exception" is mostly rhetorical overkill (no pun intended), Baudrillard's confession of having "wanted the deed" is deeply shocking - the "we" hardly exculpatory.

Those who make words and ideas their business are generally adept at rationalizing their hatred of material success, and the individual freedom that enhances it, in esoteric jargon. Writes Ceasar: "America has become a symbol for something to be despised on philosophical grounds."[798] Yet the animosity that comes from resentment is still essentially pathological, meriting to be called Americanophobia on the level of, say, arachnophobia (fear of spiders) or agoraphobia (fear of crowds). And just as petting an arachnoid does nothing to endear him, so the effect of facts on a seductive narrative has been essentially negligible.

No one quite understands what first prompted it. Observes Denis Lacome:

> The story of French Americanophobia is an old one, going back to the beginnings of the trans-Atlantic relationship. It was best expressed in Cornelius de Pauw's virulent thesis of American degeneracy. In his *Recherches Philosophiques sur les Américains*, published in 1768, the primary concern of this Dutch priest who wrote in French and worked at the court of Frederick the Great, was to serve the interests of his master. Realizing that the prince wished to discourage German emigration to North America, and inspired by Buffon and some French explorers, de Pauw argued that, in America, all natural forms, whether vegetal, animal or human, had degenerated to the point of having a shrunken appearance.[799]

When politics is at stake, manufactured facts are among the most effective and least expensive weapons.

America's Founders could not afford to ignore such drivel, however absurd. John Adams, Thomas Jefferson, and James Madison, alongside Franklin, all sought assiduously to refute it. Two centuries later, the grounds for hatred may have changed, but not the sentiment: "[I]t was now the excess of American civilization, American hyper-modernity, that nourished anti-American sentiment." Americanophobe Roger Vailland tries to mix humor and irony, "in a denunciation of that hilarious new gadget, the refrigerator" (the punchline must have become lost in translation), but in all seriousness, "Americanophobia today expresses itself in a morbid desire for the military defeat of America, or even for the destruction of America."[800]

Notwithstanding American help in the Great War, "in a grand *elan* heralding the anti-capitalist utopia of the thirties,"[801] Robert Aron and Arnaud Dandlieu deflected attention from Hitler's imminent rise by issuing a warning against *Le Cancer Americain*, which they accused of infecting civilization itself. "America is a method, a technique, a sickness of the mind,"[802] they charged. No garden-variety antipathy, the poison continues to afflict the likes of Baudrillard who, far from regretting his murderous thoughts on 9/11, seems to have grown only more contemptuous with time. He loathes America, a vast despotism that practices a "consensual integrism (of Enlightenment, or rights of man, ... of sentimental humanism) that is just as ferocious as that of any tribal region or primitive society."[803] No sentimental humanism for this choleric philosopher.

The opprobrium against America extends to its alliances, including NATO, that alleged tool of capitalist terror. Daniel Bensaid, for example, sees no difference between the Serbian policy of ethnic cleansing and Western foreign policy: "Milosevic and NATO are twin contemporary forms of modern barbarism."[804] Emmanuel Mounier similarly defines Americanism as the "barbarism which threatens the entire human edifice," whose success would result in the "extermination of all individual life forms" – a veritable "idolatrous mechanism" that mandates mankind's awakening "to save the future of mankind, whatever it might hold."[805] Such secular eschatology eerily resembles its theological kin in blood-curdling menace.

James Ceaser is entitled to conclude that hatred of America is a cold-blooded attack on the idea of the West, however difficult that may be to define. "Theoretical anti-Americanism is the Trojan horse that has been introduced to destroy Western civilization."[806] What makes this Trojan horse pathologically unique, however, is its being built by the Trojans themselves.

The Rage of the Anticapitalist Vanguard

Speculation about underlying psychological forces behind the adoption of any particular idea or ideas is always risky. This has not stopped Lewis S. Feuer from suggesting that "the emotional need for an ideology is the primary theme in the history of intellectuals; it is their longing for a generational myth of a mission."[807]   And since every ideology includes "a conception of an elite, a historically chosen class, and an emerging higher society," the intellectual – broadly understood as someone whose work involves ideas [808] - believes himself chosen for just such a task. Considering, moreover, that nothing is quite as potent an amphetamine as violence, the smell of blood seduces with unsurprising success. Writes Feuer:

> [C]entral to ideology is the notion of the revolutionary myth.... [And] ideology is the mode of thought which... speaks the language of "Revolution"; more than the social changes themselves it seeks the experience of the violent expression of energies and the exhilaration of mastery over and humiliation of the traditional authority. [809]

The promise of a utopian "higher society" inebriates its proponents, who embrace the new political religion with pious devotion.

This religion too has its prophets not unlike their putative Hebrew predecessors, who, argues Feuer, "as ideologists, claimed to know the plan of God in history and His long-term purposes." But with ironic pathology, their self-aggrandizement resulted in an equally hubristic form of self-flagellation. The argument goes as follows: Since God could do no wrong, whatever calamities fell on Israel must have been due to something *his disciples* did to anger Him. So "since the Hebrews dared not question God, they had to accuse themselves. The prophetic achievement was to introduce self-hatred, masochism, into the Jewish ethic." [810] Ultimately, utopianism trumped altruism: the prophets' presumption of divine insight, writes Feuer, was to them more important than the harm they may have been causing to the society in which they lived. And in an increasingly secular age, where political religion replaced its theocratic predecessors, the intellectuals took on the prophets' mantle along with its masochism.

Feuer saw their role as having evolved, over the course of the past five centuries, in several stages. "At first, ... the intellectuals wrote Utopias... [which] almost always shared one trait – they have been described as ruled by an elite of intellectuals.... Then came the second stage, when the intellectuals found their class ally, their 'mass base,' their social carrier force; the peasantry, proletariat, nation or Third World was assigned the historical role for providing the physical force which would bring the intellectuals to the status of the governing elite." [811]

He goes on to describe the third stage as "more self-consciously irrational," even "mythological." But even while seemingly under "a compulsion to see the existing system in its entirety as doomed," the intellectuals tacitly expect to play the role of "redeemers fashioning the new society."[812] Feuer's own attraction to the Marxism of his youth, which vanished after revelations of Soviet atrocities, may have fueled his later fury at the refusal of so many fellow intellectuals to undergo a similar change of heart.

He believes that a significant motivating factor for secular utopianism is a passionate desire for moral purpose here and now. Citing an unpublished autobiography by the leading intellectual of the British Labor Party, Harold Laski, documenting self-doubt about his Jewish heritage yet his need to love "the Jewish nation," Feuer notes that "within a few years the proletarian was to be substituted for the Jews, and a Marxist ideological equivalent for Judaism." But whatever the nature of Laski's personal odyssey, ideology is not merely a replacement-religion for most of its adherents, it also provides a lofty political mission: building the City of Man. Thus "the religious vacuum is most keenly felt by intellectuals because they require a charter that will validate their new messianism."[813]

The publication of Feuer's controversial study in 1975 was followed in 1981 by Paul Hollander's *Political Pilgrims*, which tackles a similar topic. For almost half a century until his death in 2019, Hollander would patiently study how intellectuals originally seduced by totalitarian regimes reacted to revelations about atrocities committed with impunity. Seeking to understand the underlying mindset of the intelligentsia without undue psychologizing, Hollander's conclusions are more nuanced, as he observes different reactions ranging from revelation to denial.[814] Yet he fundamentally agrees with Feuer that many intellectuals are blinded by a lust for power to which, secretly and not-so-secretly, they feel entitled.

Hollander also cites approvingly Joseph Schumpeter's belief that "capitalism creates a critical frame of mind, which, after having destroyed the moral authority of so many other institutions, in the end turns against its own." Schumpeter adds: "[T]he bourgeois finds to his amazement that the rationalist attitude does not stop at the credentials of kings and popes but goes on to attack private property and the whole scheme of bourgeois values."[815] The intellectuals' crusade against the very system that maintains them ultimately destroys the edifice: the vanguard falls victim to its own logic run amuck. Babel buries all of its inhabitants when it crumbles, including its own architects.

"The utopian susceptibilities of contemporary Western intellectuals," writes Hollander, "are part of a long-standing tradition of seeking heaven on earth… [which] is not to say that utopian and religious designs are antithetical, but that the utopian ones often feed on and derive from religious impulses." These utopian ideals tend to have much in common: they are in principle applicable to all mankind, and must be radically, categorically different from present circumstances. But here is by far the most important element:

> [Utopians] lean toward the belief that most people do not know what is good for them, that the individual pursuit of happiness is inefficient and often leads to the collision of the desires of different individuals (which could be averted in the utopian framework proposed). It follows from the compelling character of many utopian schemes that those intent on their realization cannot, in good conscience, exclude the use of force to bring it about and to maintain it.[816]

Indeed, the use of force is often a kind of aphrodisiac. For this reason, *From Benito Mussolini to Hugo Chavez: Intellectuals and a Century of Political Hero Worship*, Hollander's last book, includes not only Mussolini but also Hitler and the Baathist neo-Nazi Saddam Hussein alongside the usual Communist suspects. These are all ruthless men of uncommon charisma, criminals shrewd enough to use the rhetoric of equality. Hollander does not mince words: "[T]he dictatorships which appealed to many Western intellectuals in the twentieth century were not ordinary authoritarian regimes but, as a rule, totalitarian ones, which proclaimed commitment to secular-religious beliefs and the sweeping transformation of social institutions and even human nature."[817] The more radical, it seems, the better for the ideocrats: Apocalypse now.

Hans Borkenau also found common religious overtones in totalitarian utopian thinking: "The essence of these revolutionary creeds is the belief that the final day of salvation has come, that the millennium on this earth is near… that complete virtue, simplicity and happiness can be brought about by violence."[818] Violence is supposed to be a means to bring about its own eventual end, forever. But while the justification for endorsing it is made in lofty terms like virtue and happiness, the fuel is simple hatred of individual freedom, call it what you will, capitalism or modernity or Americanism. In his extensive discussion of the intellectuals' fascination with Mussolini, Hollander notes that *Il Duce's* admirers shared with their "left-wing" colleagues "a profound distaste for capitalism and that their anti-capitalism and aversion to modernity were closely linked." For what both Nazism and Italian fascism ultimately "had in common with Communist systems and their ideologies [was] a pervasive collectivism."[819] *Non pluribus; unum.*

By way of example, Hollander mentions George Bernard Shaw, who admired both Mussolini and Lenin, along with Stalin, because of "the inadequacy of democracy. Dictatorship, [Shaw] claimed, was more efficient and more of the people. 'Italy is governed by a man of the people,'"[820] was he not? *Il Duce* had said so himself. Similarly, Lincoln Steffens's trip to the Soviet Union prompted this infamous inscription on his wife's Ella Winter's 1933 book *Red Virtue:*[821] "I have seen the future, and it works." (His death three years later came too soon for remorse - assuming he would have harbored any, which seems unlikely.) Writes Hollander: "For Steffens and countless other liberals [meaning here, progressives], Mussolini, Lenin and Stalin were all doing the same thing: transforming corrupt, outdated societies."[822] History must march on to eutopia, even if it turns out to be no-where.

Thomas Sowell agrees that collectivism appeals to Western intellectuals, especially since they expect to constitute the vanguard. But

> preferences for collective, surrogate decision-making from the top down are not all that the democratic left has shared with the original Italian Fascists and with the National Socialists (Nazis) of Germany. In addition to political intervention in economic markets, the democratic left shared with the Fascists and the Nazis the underlying assumption of a vast gap in understanding between ordinary people and elites like themselves. Although both the totalitarian left – that is, the Fascists, Communists and Nazis – and the democratic left have widely used in a positive sense such terms as "the people," "the workers" and the "masses," these are the ostensible beneficiaries of their policies, but *not* autonomous decision-makers.... it has long been clear that decision-making has been seen as something reserved for the anointed in these visions.[823]

And what stands in the way? Why, America – both the actual country and, more insidiously, the abstract idea. What especially irks the egalitarian elite is what they perceive as American materialism, a vulgar propensity which Friederich Nietzsche (1844-1900) despised for "spreading a spiritual emptiness [*Geistlosigkeit*] over the continent." Admired by Nazis and self-described Marxists alike, Nietzsche worried that "the faith of the Americans is becoming the faith of the European as well."[824]

Heaven forbid: if there is one thing Europeans never want to become is "Americanized." In his decades-long research on European anti-Americanism, Andrei S. Markovitz has found hostility to America embedded in "a deep-seated prejudicial structure in contemporary West European discourse, with a massive historical lineage."[825] The conceptual framework for this structure owes a great deal to the prominent Nietzsche-disciple and Nazi party member Martin Heidegger (1889-1976). Heidegger, who deplored Americanism as "soulless," inspired acolytes across the borders to France and the self-hating Europhile intellectuals across the Atlantic.

Although Heidegger's former student and lover, Hannah Arendt, who made her home in America after barely escaping the Nazis, as a Jew, repudiated his impression of Americans on both empirical and theoretical grounds. She understood that Americanophobia was the seed which "may well become the beginning of a new pan-European nationalism." [826] It seemed clear to Arendt that Europeans were prepared to "consider the establishment of a European government an act of emancipation from America."[827]

If Moscow had originally viewed the European integration process with suspicion during the 1970s, by the end of the 1980s, as we now know thanks to the ineffable Vladimir Bukovsky, who uncovered the relevant documents, Politburo chief Mikhail Gorbachev realized its anti-capitalist potential from the outset: "Until 1984 the head of the intelligence administration of the KGB, [Vladimir] Kryuchkov, instructed his residents in Europe to increase efforts at penetrating all the structures of the EC [European Commission] and oppose its further integration" at first. But "the more the socialists and social democrats gained the upper hand in the structures of the EC, the more benignly it was viewed by Moscow. By 1989 the creation of a 'common European home' became their battle-cry, although naturally enough none of them admitted openly that this 'home' was to be a socialist one. The plan was approved at a meeting of the Politburo on 26 March 1987 (24 March 1987, Pb, SA)."[828] The text of that meeting is worth reading in full, but Gorbachev's message is simple and clear: "We have more active contacts with social circles in the USA than in Europe... We need to plan our work with Europe with great care. Create a regrouping of scientific forces. ... we need to do a lot of work to support propaganda."[829]

In 1993, the EC became the European Union (EU), but this was far more than a name-change, as Vaclav Klaus, former Minister of Finance, Prime Minister, and then President of the Czech Republic, told the Center for Financial Studies on March 13, 2019: The treaties that established the EU brought about significant changes to the original arrangement.

They transformed the original concept of integration into something else, into unification.

> They pushed the heterogeneous community of sovereign European states into a union of subordinated regions and provinces (Länder in German terminology). They substantially augmented the power of the bureaucratic central agency in Brussels. They suppressed democracy and turned it into a post-democracy (misleadingly called liberal democracy). I agree with John Laughland that these treaties created "a mechanism which allows governments to pass laws for which they would prefer not to argue in public, safely away from the glare of democratic scrutiny and parliamentary opposition."[830] ...It hasn't been accidental. We live in the era of a new authoritarianism of illiberal elites, of neomarxists of the Frankfurter School, of so-called "experts," of bureaucrats of international organizations, of IT protagonists and lobbyists, of loud and noisy exponents of political NGOs.[831]

The name itself, European *Union*, moreover, mirrors more explicitly that of its rival/ally counterpart across the ocean. Calling it so, however, hardly makes it so: EU "patriotism" is seldom witnessed outside the occasional soccer game against an evenly-matched, say, Brazilian team. Observes Markovitz: "While at the moment it remains unclear what positive sentiments and identifications unites Swedes and Greeks, it is quite clear what negative dimension does: that of *not* being American. Today, one is primarily European by dint of not being American."[832] Defining an identity negatively, as against a common enemy, is the simplest solution to internecine division, and Americanophobia famously fits the bill. The addition to the EU of countries largely sympathetic to the U.S. has not helped. But having just escaped from the clutches of another anti-nationalist neo-empire with a serious democracy-deficit, their attitude is understandable.

Esprit-de-corps or not, the vision of the EU follows the script, "repeated endlessly in European publications, proclamations, and conferences: the belief in the European ideal of peace, harmony, and universal law; the rejection of nationalism in all its forms" etc etc etc, as

John Fonte points out.[833] But Fonte is inclined to suspect more material and interest-based motivations, citing Karen Alter's findings that the European court system, to mention but "financial, prestige or political power"[834] to lawyers and legal examples, gave financial but one of countless examples. Fonte calls the EU's bureaucracy, along with the international governing elite throughout the UN system, members of the "Global Governance Party."

That elite, unfortunately, tend to set the tone for their fellow countrymen. Thus, according to a survey conducted by the Pew Research Center in 2017, a sharp decline in America's favorability rating "has been particularly notable in several European countries. In 2016 a median of 61 percent held a favorable opinion across France, Germany, Poland, Spain and the UK, compared with 26 percent who had an unfavorable assessment. In 2017 the medians among these countries are 46 percent positive, 52 percent negative."[835] (Poland helped keep up the positive percentages, at a consistently high approval rating of 73 percent.)

Homegrown Anti-Amerikanism

If a sense of alienation is the intellectual's occupational hazard, a visceral hatred of one's own society need not be. Yet in the America of the 1960s and '70s, it became *de rigueur*. Roger Kimball explains in his seminal analysis of the era:

> As the 1950s wore on, anti-Americanism became a necessary badge of authenticity for writers and intellectuals; more and more, the cultural establishment demanded the pose of anti-establishment animus. Among those railing against the evils of America – or "Amerika," as it was often spelled in the 1960s – the novelist Norman Mailer occupies a special place.[836]

Mailer became *l'enfant terrible* of his day. In a bizarre article published in 1957 titled "The White Negro" - which he praises (ambiguously) as "one of the best things I've ever done"[837] - Mailer lionizes what he calls "the hipster" who, finding himself "trapped in the totalitarian tissues of American society,"[838] becomes a "philosophical psychopath." Ever the iconoclast, Mailer means that as an honorific. The "drama" of the much-misunderstood psychopath, which might elude lesser mortals, is that he searches for love – or, rather, sex. "But in his search," muses the precocious novelist, "the psychopath becomes an embodiment of the extreme contradictions of the society which formed his character.... It is therefore no accident that psychopathy is most prevalent with the

Negro." (May we assume that when Mailer uses the word it's not politically incorrect?)

Mailer means this too as a compliment, commending the alleged prototypical "Negro" for having chosen to move "in that other direction where all situations are equally valid." "[T]he Negro," continues the rant, "discovered and elaborated a morality of the bottom, an ethical differentiation between the good and the bad in every human activity from the go-getter pimp (as opposed to the lazy one) to the relatively dependable pusher or prostitute." Mailer rails against "the anti-sexual foundation of every organized power in America, and brings into the air such animosities, antipathies, and new conflicts of interest that the mean empty hypocrisies of mass conformity will no longer work. A time of violence, new hysteria, confusion and rebellion will then be likely to replace the time of conformity."

He ends with another incoherent, possibly acid-induced, tirade, anticipating a time when Marx would be idolized mainly for denouncing sexual repression as one of the major "social cruelties" of capitalism. He yearns for

> some gigantic synthesis of human action where the body of Marxist thought, and particularly the epic grandeur of *Das Kapital* (that first of the major *psychologies* to approach the mystery of social cruelty so simply and practically as to say that we are a collective body of humans whose life-energy is wasted, displaced, and procedurally stolen as it passes from one of us to another) would find its place in an even more Godlike view of human justice and injustice, in some more excruciating vision of those intimate and institutional processes which lead to our creations and disasters, our growth, our attrition, and our rebellion.[839]

If Mailer was smoking something, he must have shared it with his editor.

Aptly dubbed "the marriage of Marx and Freud" by Kimball, that unsavory nuptial also inspired Norman O. Brown, whose hugely popular *Life Against Death*, first published in 1959, presumed to outline "The Psychoanalytic Meaning of History." Brown's great gift, writes Kimball, "was infusing mystical pronouncements with a radical, antibourgeois animus and a febrile erotic charge.... Brown offered his readers a little of everything: the rhetoric of Christian eschatology and neo-Marxist radicalism and polymorphous sexuality."[840] *Life Against Death*, though centered on Freud, is replete with erudite classical references – notably to Baruch Spinoza, Plato, and William Blake – which give it just the requisite scholarly veneer. Exhibit A:

> Both the Platonic Eros and the Christian Agape, at their highest point of mystic exaltation, transcend their own limitations and their mutual differences and become a positive challenge requiring an extension and development of the Freudian doctrine of narcissism. In Plato's *Symposium*, after Eros has satisfied its own want by coming to possess the essence of Beauty, it passes on to a further stage, not grounded in the original definition, which Plato calls "giving birth in beauty" as if the satisfied Eros must overflow, out of its own abundance, into creativity. And in Luther, the perfect Agape of God is a *quellende Liebe*, a love overflowing into creativity. These images suggest that the self-activity and self-enjoyment of the narcissistic Eros must consist in an overflow outward into the world.[841]

One cannot help wondering whether that editor high on something too. In plain English, narcissism is fine. The "mystic exaltation" common to the pagan Plato and to Christianity, particularly Luther, is, in all candor, mostly euphemism. Brown cites Blake: "Exuberance is Beauty... The cistern contains, the fountain overflows..." His own prose akin to a biblical flood, its message uneasily recalls *The Book of Revelation.*

Amerikanism, then, is code-word for repression, for work as against pleasure, the capitalist "social cruelties" as against Rousseau's "natural" man who is "born free and everywhere is in chains." Amerika is the enemy; socialism spells salvation. Private property makes men greedy; communal living is groovy. The Flower Children of the sixties got high on slogans, yet the rampant hedonism proved but the gateway drug to a far deadlier potion, which led to violence, conveniently (and by no means accidentally) playing right into the hands of the nation's enemies.

It all exploded with the Vietnam war. Writes Kimball: "More than any other event, it legitimated anti-Americanism and helped insinuate radical feeling into the mainstream of cultural life.... [In brief,] the war helped to 'normalize' a spectrum of radical sentiments."[842] Especially unfortunate was "the transformation of the civil-rights movement from a non-violent crusade for equal rights into an agitation for black power,...[amounting to] not only a new segregationism but also a blueprint for the 'victim politics' and demands for political correctness that have so disfigured American culture in the 1980s and 1990s,"[843] on to today. (Whether the self-absorbed radicals responsible for this change were in the least concerned about its actual effects on the African-American community itself, the evidence suggests otherwise.[844])

The war could not have come at a better time for a generation itching to overthrow something, preferably their own country. That goal proved harder to reach than expected. The U.S. Constitution being inconveniently saddled with an explicit Bill of Rights, dissent did not bring instant celebrity. Instead of being sent to Siberia, wannabe revolutionaries, many of them trust-fund babies, found that they would have to break laws to succeed being imprisoned; and even then, over-solicitous parents or friends bailed them out with inconvenient rapidity. Alexander Bickel, writing in the 1970s, understood that "to be revolutionary, in a society like ours, is to be a totalitarian, or not to know what one is doing"[845] – more often both. The utopian impulse afflicted the power-hungry and the clueless in equal measure.

The impulse to overthrow society for egalitarian ends is bicephalic - one head nodding, credulously, toward an impossible ideal of perfection unattainable on earth, while the other, enraged, prepares for Armageddon. Explains Kimball:

> The French Revolution, honing its guillotines with a rhetoric of virtue derived from Rousseau, dramatizes this as surely as have many grisly efforts to instantiate the tenets of Marxism, Fascism, and other utopian schemes in the course of this unhappy century. Leszek Kołakowski summed it up neatly in his essay 'The Death of Utopia Reconsidered' (1983): "Utopians, once they attempt to convert their visions into practical proposals, come up with the most malignant project ever devised: they want to institutionalize fraternity, which is the surest way to totalitarian despotism."[846]

Did the Vietnam-era *enrages* grasp this? Unapologetic about the sweeping scope of their ire, they could scarcely plead innocent. Susan Sontag admits that "Vietnam offered the key to a systematic criticism of America"[847] Radical student leader Jerry Rubin, who called himself "a child of Amerika," went one better in his 1970 book *Do It! Scenarios of the Revolution*: "If there had been no Vietnam war, we would have invented one. If the Vietnam war ends, we'll find another war."[848] In the introduction, Eldredge Cleaver, former presidential nominee of the Peace and Freedom Party with Rubin as his Vice President, predicts that "if everybody carried out Jerry's program-there would be immediate peace in the world. Amerika, for one, would cease to bleed."

The "program," explained Cleaver, "unite[s] around hatred of pig judges, around hatred of capitalism, around the total desire to smash what is now the social order in the United States of Amerika. Around the dream of building something new and free upon the ruins."[849] Cleaver was writing from Algeria, reminiscing about the time, in 1966, when he and a handful of other leading radicals were staring, stoned, at a wall poster of the Cuban Communist Che Guevarra, with his "farseeing eyes, staring fiercely and fearlessly into the revolutionary future."[850] The same poster would soon be found throughout America's college dorms. (I spotted his face a few weeks ago on the t-shirt worn by a fellow suburban gym-member, who was also sporting Che's look. So cool. Woke.)

This is how Rubin describes his (romantically illegal) meeting with Che, along with 83 other American students, in 1964: "As Che rapped on for four hours, we fantasized taking up rifles. Growing beards. Going into the hills as guerrillas. Joining Che to create revolutions throughout Latin America. None of us looked forward to returning home to the political bullshit in the United States."[851] And what had Che said to so entrance the fantasizing students? "You North Amerikans [sic] are very lucky. You live in the middle of the beast. You are fighting the most important fight of all, in the center of the battle. If I had my wish, I would go back with you to North Amerika to fight there."[852]

But who, exactly, was this Ernesto "Che" Guevarra? A photogenic pathologically ruthless killer. It boggles the mind of self-described leftist Daniel Benveniste, author of *The Venezuelan Revolution: A Critique from the Left*, how members of his beloved counterculture, who had preached peace and love, "could turn around and celebrate Che Guevara, who personally executed and oversaw the execution of about five hundred people... [and who] spoke of 'hatred as an element of struggle; unbending hatred for the enemy, which pushes a human being beyond his natural limitations, making him into an effective, violent, selective, cold-blooded killing machine.'"[853] Except it wasn't a turnaround – at least, not for the leadership.

And certainly not after 1968. Writes Bryan Burrough:

For the hard core... 1968 bore signs of the Apocalypse. For these activists, who might be called apocalyptic revolutionaries, there was a vivid and growing sense that the world was on the brink of historic, irreversible change and that the morally corrupt American government, murdering the Vietnamese, unleashing dogs on Southern blacks, and beating its protesters, was poised for imminent collapse... This was a powerful idea, at once outlandish and intoxicating, providing a rush of intellectual adrenaline as strong as any drug.[854]

Heroin for heroics? cocaine for kooks? A new low in highs. It seemed that nothing short of a revolution would do. Continues Burrough:

Apocalyptic revolutionaries represented a strident new voice in the [radical] Movement, but they were able to draw from a wellspring of ideas that were not entirely new... They studied Lenin and Mao and Ho Chi Minh – it went without saying that revolutionaries were almost always Communists – but their favorite blueprint was the Cuban Revolution, their icon Ernesto "Che" Guevara, Castro's swashbuckling right-hand man.[855]

Perhaps the most charismatic of the student radicals, the telegenic Mark Rudd, leader of the Columbia University's radical Students for a Democratic Society (SDS) chapter, became the face of "the Movement" by 1968. But he was soon joined by another, no less attractive but more intelligent colleague, John Jacobs, known as JJ, judged by Burrough to be "surely the purest voice of the apocalyptic revolutionary." For he "popularized the parallels between Columbia and the Cuban Revolution, [and] preached that a select group of hard-core rebels could, as Castro and Guevara had with Cuba, lead America into revolution."[856]

His inspiration came from Regis Debray, a friend of Che's who taught philosophy in Havana. Convinced that "advanced" members of the proletariat could draw the masses into revolution, dubbed "vanguardism," Debray argued that guerilla warfare (which he called *foco* – fire) of the kind commanded by Che could overthrow a regime. Such ideas "were catnip to budding revolutionaries like JJ, many of whom had no problem imagining themselves as American Ches," writes Burrough. He adds, parenthetically, that "their ardor was undiminished by their hero's inability to make the *foco* theory work in Bolivia, where soldiers had captured and executed Guevara in 1967."[857] But death by gunfire is a good career move for aspiring messiahs.

So is adherence to prophesies of the Apocalypse, extermination of Antichrists, and filial love of humanity in the abstract rather than affection for individual people.[858] Che's adulation of combat as "the greatest joy of the guerilla's life" prompts Hollander to comment: "[T]his was precisely the type of mystified, romantic veneration of violence that would warm the hearts of Mailer and Sartre, a veneration that also animated the elite troops of Nazi Germany."[859] All these radicals were cold and selfish, but also victims of the millenarian seduction. Continues Hollander:

> Guevara's cult offers a superb illustration of the religious, or secular-religious, wellspring of all these cults and the hero worship they entail. Mark Rudd, a 1960s radical activist who visited Cuba in 1968 inspired by Guevara, confessed in his autobiography: "Like a Christian seeking to emulate the life of Christ, I passionately wanted to be a revolutionary like Che, no matter what the price." Michael Casey wrote, "In dying, Che rounds out his myth. We are left with a life similar to that of the prophets of the mainstream religions."[860]

No wonder the "Movement" could not be satisfied with mere sit-ins, however popular with the sizeable student body that gleefully exchanged love-ins for oh-so-boring study-ins. But they inevitably turned criminal. Notes retired FBI agent Frank Noel: "People have completely forgotten that in 1972 [alone] we had over nineteen hundred domestic bombings in the United States.... One bombing now and everyone gets excited. In 1972? It was every day. Buildings getting bombed, policemen getting killed. It was common place."[861] Fortunately, the technology was inferior compared to today. Writes Burrough: "During an eighteen-months period in 1971 and 1972, the FBI reported more than 2,500 bombings on U.S. soil, nearly 5 a day. Yet less than 1 percent of the 1970s-era bombings led to a fatality; the single deadliest radical-underground attack of the decade killed four people. Most bombings were followed by communiques denouncing some aspect of the American condition; bombs basically functioned as exploding press releases."[862] Before long, explosions gave way to cultural sabotage and historical amnesia.

Few among the under-60 remember SDS, the terrorist Weather Underground (WU), and their radical colleagues, let alone realize that they are still very much with us. On his last day in office, January 20, 2001, then-president Bill Clinton pardoned Linda Evans and Susan Rosenberg, both WU members who had been convicted for weapons and explosives charges. In addition, Rosenberg drove the getaway-car in a robbery where two police officers and an armored-car guard were killed.[863] Besides WU, she also joined the May 19th Communist Organization, which worked in support of the Black Liberation Army.

After her release, she taught literature at John Jay College of Criminal Justice, and was even offered a position to teach a course at Hamilton College on "Resistance Memoirs: Writing, Identity and Change," though after protest by some parents and alumni, and even some professors, she declined the offer. It is not clear whether there would be similar protests from the faculty today, considering the latest developments there.[864]

She shares a Hamilton College connection with Angela Davis, winner of the 1979 Lenin Peace Prize, who delivered that institution's commencement address in 1996 and again in 2016. There, "she encouraged the audience to reach for the world we wish to live in. That is, a world 'that has no need to rely on policing and imprisonment,' a world with 'free education, free health care, affordable housing.' In order to reach these goals, she sees an 'end to policing and incarceration as we know it' and acceptance of 'socialist principles,' which are fundamentally based on ideas of equality and tolerance."[865] Her earlier membership in the Che-Lumumba Club, an all-black branch of the Communist Party USA, and her support for the Soledad Brothers, three inmates who had killed a prison guard at Soledad Prison, were an obvious badge of honor.[866]

So was being placed on the FBI's Ten Most Wanted List in 1970 for having purchased firearms used in an armed takeover of a Marin County, California, courtroom in 1970, where a judge and three black men were killed. She is now a professor emerita at the University of California, Santa Cruz and former director of its Feminist Studies department. In 2017, Davis was a featured speaker and made honorary co-chair at the Women's March on Washington after Donald Trump's inauguration and is idolized by Rep. Ilhan Omar, the most radical member of Congress today. From underground to high ground, the sixties live on.

In a 2013 article titled "How 1960s Radicals Ended Up Teaching Your Kids," Michael Moynihan notes that "Kathy Boudin, a professor at Columbia University, was named the 2013 Sheinberg Scholar-in-Residence at NYU Law School. In 1984, Boudin, a member of the Weather Underground, a violent, oafish association of upper-class 'revolutionaries,' pled guilty to second-degree murder in association with the infamous 1981 Brinks armored car robbery in Nyack, New York. Babbling in the language of anti-racism and anti-imperialism, Boudin assisted in ending the life of three people, including Waverly Brown, the first black police officer on the Nyack police force, and left nine children fatherless."[867] Her Columbia University biography doesn't mention this.

There are more. A former leader of the radical Black Panther, Ericka Huggins was brought to trial in 1970 on charges of "aiding and abetting" the murder of Alex Rackley (having boiled the water used in his torture).[868] Having taught women's studies at California State University, she is now Professor of Sociology at Laney College and at Berkeley City College. She has also lectured at Stanford, Cornell, and the UCLA.

The latest WU member to be released is Judith Clark, who was serving a 75-year-to-life murder sentence. On April 23, 2019, she was granted clemency by New York governor Andrew Cuomo. This notwithstanding that she has never expressed remorse – anymore than has WU founder Bill Ayers, who wrote in his memoir "I don't regret setting bombs," while another colleague (still in prison) titled his book *No Surrender*. Patrick Dunleavy, former Deputy Inspector General for New York, brings us up to date: "In recent years, their radicalization has taken a new turn, embracing radical anti-Israel movements…[seeing] solidarity between 'former prisoners in Palestine and former U.S.-held political prisoners."

Bill Ayers, along with his wife and fellow-WU founder Bernardine Dohrn, "have both participated in the Viva Palestina movement, led by the U.K.'s George Galloway. Money raised by Viva Palestina was openly given to Hamas…. [They] were also involved in helping to organize the Free Gaza Movement shipments sent from Turkey."[869] So too, the photogenic Mark Rudd, who fled indictment and went "underground," after years of hiding at last turned himself in 1977 and was sentenced to two years' probation. He later taught at Central New Mexico Community College. To mention but a few. Anti-capitalism lives.[870]

It adapts with the times. And why not be a utopian? Proud of it, proclaims Erik Olin Wright. A Marxist professor who has been offering advice on "How to Be an Anticapitalist Today" in the increasingly fashionable magazine *Jacobin*, Wright acknowledges that capitalism has brought us fantastic technical innovations, astounding increases in productivity, longer life expectancy, and incredible medical advances. "And while it's true that income is unequally distributed in capitalist economies, it is also true that the array of consumption goods available and affordable for the average person, and even for the poor, has increased dramatically almost everywhere. Just compare the United States in the half century between 1965 and 2015,"[871] and you can understand why many people are skeptical of anti-capitalism.

But here's the rub: it isn't perfect. "Capitalism has generated massive increases in productivity and extravagant wealth for some, yet many people still struggle to make ends meet. Capitalism is an inequality-enhancing machine as well as a growth machine. Not to mention that it is becoming clearer that capitalism, driven by the relentless search for profits, is destroying the environment." The bottom line is this: "The pivotal issue is not whether material conditions on average have improved in the long run within capitalist economies, but rather whether, looking forward from this point in history, things would be better for most people in an alternative kind of economy." That alternative is, and he doesn't mind admitting it, "real utopias."

Unlike its prototype in 1516, however, Wright's version is not just "a fantasy of perfection;" rather, real utopias "transform the no-where of utopia into the now-here of creating emancipatory alternatives of the world as it could be in the world as it is," guided by the three "emancipatory ideals [which] are equality, democracy, and solidarity. All of these are obstructed in capitalist firms, where power is concentrated in the hands of owners and their surrogates, internal resources and opportunities are distributed in a grossly unequal manner, and competition continually undermines solidarity."

A specific example of real utopianism is UBI which, should any readers happen to be unwoke, stands for *unconditional basic income*. Wright explains:

> A UBI simply gives everyone, without conditions, a flow of income sufficient to cover basic needs. It provides for a modest, but culturally respectable, no-frills standard of living. In doing so it also solves the problem of hunger among the poor, but does so in ways that puts in place a building block of an emancipatory alternative. UBI directly tames one of the harms of capitalism — poverty in the midst of plenty. But it also expands the potential for a long-term erosion of the dominance of capitalism by channeling resources towards noncapitalist forms of economic activity.

What makes an economic activity capitalist is – what else? – money and profit. But unlike the radical utopianists, Wright does not think violent revolution is necessary; instead, he prefers a gradual subversion of the free enterprise system. To that end, he has established a project at the University of Wisconsin called *Real Utopias*, which "explores a wide range of proposals and models for radical social change," collected in a Real Utopias Project Series by the London-based Verso publishers. Thus eager to prompt action, his own book *A Rough Guide to Utopia* (2010) has been described as "not so much a manifesto as a handbook for contemporary socialists."

Many will still find it too tame, warns radical economist Tom Cutterham: "[I]t will be an uncomfortable read for activists whose instinct is to fight reactionaries at any opportunity." But don't write him off too quickly, for "Wright makes his commitment to a larger overall change tough to ignore. The key words that appear in different combinations on almost every page—radical, democratic, egalitarian, social, emancipatory—serve to keep these guiding ideals constantly in mind."[872]

To oppose these ideals makes you seem heartless, mean, selfish, the list of evils goes on. What do you mean "we" cannot afford – fill in the blank. Do you mean you are against – fill in the blank again. The problem with utopian thinking, as we have seen throughout this book, is twofold: cognitive and moral. The first leads to inaccurate predictions; the second presumes that some people are entitled to impose their vision of the Common Good. Writes economist and theologian Paul Heyne:

> Justice requires impartial rules in any society so large that tasks and benefits cannot be fairly allocated on the basis of the principle: from each according to ability, to each according to need and merit. That's the principle we use in families. It works effectively and fairly in families, for the most part, because the people involved are few enough and close enough to care for each other in a personal way. In societies significantly larger than families, the members simply cannot know enough to assign tasks and benefits on the basis of personal circumstances and still do it fairly. The problem is knowledge; it is not simply goodwill. Goodwill by itself will not enable us to determine one another's abilities, needs, or merit in a society as large as two hundred people, much less one of two hundred million people. Any attempt to do so is bound to produce arbitrary and hence unfair results.[873]

This rather obvious truth appears to be too hard for some people to accept, so they turn to old habits that tempt each generation anew.

Hubristic demagogues emerge to incite the majority to attack the Antichrist-*du-jour*, resulting in what George Will describes as "socialism now: From each faction according to its vulnerability, to each faction according to its ability to confiscate."[874] But this is not merely about money; it is ultimately about truth.

Post-truth

The Oxford Dictionaries reacted to the surprising election of Donald Trump as President of the United States on November 8, 2016, by announcing its choice as "official Word of the Year the increasingly ubiquitous 'post-truth.'"[875] An approximately 2,000 percent increase in frequency over 2015 undoubtedly qualifies as record-breaking, a feat that should alone have guaranteed the choice. In addition, however, it was deemed especially apt for having best captured "the ethos, mood, or preoccupations of that particular year," which is that truth is increasingly considered as irrelevant. The importance of actual facts is supplanted by appeals to emotion and personal prejudices in influencing public opinion.

It appears to have first been used in this sense by Steve Tesich who had lamented, in a 1992 article published by *The Nation*, that "we, as a free people, have freely decided that we want to live in some post-truth world." The term was popularized by Ralph Keyes, whose 2004 book *The Post-truth Era* described a political ethos based more on personal prejudices than objective fact. Synonymous with "enhanced truth," Keyes argued, post-truth could also be called neo-truth, soft truth, truth lite, in short, "ambiguous statements that are not exactly the truth but fall just short of a lie."[876] Deceivers have always existed, as has the willingness to be deceived, but politically motivated deception has reached such massive proportions that *post-truth* now describe an Era.

If *post-truth* won the day in 2016, however, the runaway favorite runner-up was "adulting," which is "associated especially with millennials, known for their ambivalent relationship with the trappings of adulthood."[877] And no wonder, since the principal such trapping is a respect for truth. If childhood is a state of pre-truth, growing up is defined by the courage to accept difficult realities. Refusing to grow up is dangerous to the individual; when it infects an entire society, a common side-effect of abundance, the inability to face even minor obstacles threatens its collapse.

No mere figure of speech, maturity-deficiency is actually being diagnosed. Dr. Humbelina Robles Ortega, for example, has found that "an increasingly larger number of adults are presenting emotionally immature

behaviors in Western society." What she calls "the Peter Pan Syndrome...
usually affects dependent people who have been overprotected by their
families and haven't developed the necessary skills to confront life." The
Peter Pans of present society, argues Dr. Ortega, "see the adult world as
very problematic and glorify adolescence, which is why they want to stay
in that state of privilege."[878]

David C. Stolinsky endorses her observations and explains their
political manifestations:

> These victims of arrested emotional development seem to
> confuse good motives with good results.... They kind-heartedly
> want a "more equal distribution of wealth"; so they fantasize that
> they can maneuver it without penalizing and discouraging the
> productive members of society, while rewarding and
> encouraging the unproductive ones. Yet this is exactly what has
> happened wherever there distribution of wealth was tried.[879]

He finds that many people suffer from this syndrome. These adult
children, "like Peter Pan, wish to live in Neverland – a place that, in the
real world, does not exist." *I.e.,* utopia.

Notwithstanding its logical connection with the Peter Pan
syndrome, fewer people seem to be aware of the Oxford Dictionaries'
Word of the Year 2017, perhaps with good reason: for as *Fortune*
magazine admits, it "sounds made up, but it's not." That word is
youthquake, meaning "a significant cultural, political, or social change
arising from the actions or influence of young people," and its selection
reflects a fivefold increase in usage over the previous year. But the main
reason for its choice is its presumed political significance: the press release
thus cites *The Guardian*'s having credited "youthquake" for the Labor
Party's June 2017 election surge "that divides generations."[880]   The
division falls not along chronological so much as ideological lines: the
youngsters seem enthralled with septuagenarian party leader Jeremy
Corbyn, an erstwhile leader in the Campaign for Nuclear Disarmament, a
zealous anti-Zionist who numbers Hamas and Hezbollah members among
his friends, and supports Venezuela's Nicolás Maduro.

Though all the rage now in the United Kingdom, youthquake was
born in America in the days (this author remembers all too well) when
"Don't Trust Anyone Over Thirty" became a popular campus slogan. In
keeping with the times, the patrician *Vogue* editor-in-chief Diana Vreeland
gushed on the pages of her magazine in January, 1965, over how "youth,

... gay as a kitten yet self-sufficient as James Bond, is surprising countries east and west with a sense of assurance serene beyond all years." Obsequiously praising their "exuberant tremor ... coursing through America – which practically invented this century's youth in the first place," she heralded the dawn of a new era: "Here. Now. Youthquake 1965."

It is unclear whether she was aware of the century's earlier youthful fashionistas – sporting brown shirts in Berlin and red kerchiefs in Moscow – who were similarly smug in their conviction that the ideological tremors they precipitated had been "invented" in their respective capitals: their exuberance had certainly sent reverberations coursing throughout the world. Ms. Vreeland was flattering her magazine's readers, confirming their self-image as "self-sufficient," in emulation of Hollywood's promiscuous self-absorbed secret agent. The Oxford Dictionaries' press release comments that "Vreeland coined *youthquake* – based on the pattern of 'earthquake' – to describe the youth-led fashion and music movement of the Swinging Sixties, which saw baby boomers reject the traditional values of their parents."[881] But an advertiser's slogan may mask sinister realities, as rejecting traditional values has the potential of becoming politically explosive.

Not everyone, however, takes the implications seriously. For proof that 2017 saw the United Kingdom "at the heart of the youthquake," the press release seamlessly transitions from its role in the success of the Labor Party to "'the London Look' of boutique street-style individualism taking the high fashion houses of Paris, Milan, and New York by storm to inform a mass-produced, ready-to-wear fashion directive worldwide." The Dictionaries' President himself, Casper Grathwohl, is next quoted as believing that it was high time for a word "we can all rally behind."

The feline narcissists are also responsible for the second most popular word of 2017: Antifa. Described as a "controversial brand of radical leftism, ... [t]he US in particular has been a crucible for the rise of this word and associated politics, with reportedly over 200 independent groups now active across the country, united by a drive to oppose fascism through direct action – though interpretations of this mission statement vary drastically." Definition is superfluous: "fascist" is just the standard epithet that Antifa members hurl at anyone who disagrees with any part of their radical agenda. Other things routinely being hurled at perceived enemies are weightier: for instance, on the morning of Inauguration Day 2017, rocks and bottles were thrown at police officers, chunks of pavement at windows of random businesses, and a limousine was set on fire. (It seems unlikely that the limo's owner, who happened to be a Muslim immigrant by the name of Muhammad Ashraf, would describe himself as a "fascist" – but no matter.)

In February, Antifa set fires at UCLA to prevent the British journalist-provocateur Milo Yiannopoulos from speaking to a group of students. It next threatened violence against Fox News contributor and author Ann Coulter, who rejected her invitation after the university and law enforcement refused to find a secure location for her to speak. When economist Heather Mac Donald of the free-market-oriented Manhattan Institute was prevented from speaking at Claremont McKenna College in California in April 2017, a group of students from another of the Claremont consortium colleges, Pomona, hastened to label Dr. Mac Donald "a fascist, a white supremacist, a warhawk, a transphobe, a queerphobe, a classist, and ignorant of interlocking systems of domination that produce the lethal conditions under which oppressed peoples are forced to live."[882] In brief, she was accused of having challenged "the right of Black people to exist."

Had any of the protesters actually read her research, they would have found that according to the evidence, the reluctance to police minority communities has disproportionately affected those same communities: it turns out that more young black men were being killed by St. Louis police department's hands-off approach than were being killed by "proactive policing." But who cares about evidence? The point is whose "narrative" it advances. As attorney K-Sue Park wrote in a *New York Times* article in 2017: "Sometimes standing on the wrong side of history in defense of a cause you think is right is still just standing on the wrong side of history."[883] Conversely, if you think you are on the right side of history, all bets are off.

While thuggish assaults on speakers gain disproportionate media attention, free speech has long been eroding on the nation's campuses in more insidious ways, ever since the Woodrow Wilson administration began a "reversal of academic freedom ... by stoking nationalistic extremism in order to enter and win World War I."[884] Pre-dating the infamous McCarthy era by three or four decades, "all over the nation, patriotic zealots on boards of trustees, in the community, and on the faculties themselves, harassed those college teachers whose passion for fighting the war was somewhat less flaming than their own," wrote Walter P. Metzger in 1955.[885]

Things only got worse. Reports Jay Schalin:

Until the 1960s, academic freedom differences had largely been administrators and faculty against trustees and politicians, or faculty against administrators. But in that decade, radical students took the foreground, pushing hard against all other interests.... [T]he New Left's "extensive array of tactics of confrontation and disruption ... to prevent the rational use of "evidence and logic,"... [has since become] "a serious threat to reasoned discourse,"[886] according to New York University professor Sidney Hook.[887]

Reasoned discourse has given way to revolutionary angst, or a close facsimile. The current assault on free speech on campuses is but one more, albeit the most alarming, manifestation of the post-truth malady which the Rand Corporation calls *Truth Decay*. Defined as a "shift away from facts and data in political debate and policy decisions,"[888] a report released in August 2018, explains it in terms of four related trends:

1. increasing disagreement about facts and analytical interpretations of facts and data;

2. a blurring of the line between opinion and fact;

3. the increasing relative volume, and resulting influence, of opinion and personal experience over fact; and

4. declining trust in formerly respected sources of factual information.[889]

The effects of this nefarious combination are understated by the authors, who opine only that "policy decisions made primarily on the basis of opinion or anecdote can have deleterious effects on American democracy and might impose significant costs on the public."[890] Not can, not might: it does. Truth decay, moreover, is among the principal causes of civilizational putrefaction.

Ecocalypse

But it is the literal kind of decay, which at its most extreme spells Armageddon, that has taken center stage after the Soviet empire disintegrated. After the sublime exhilaration in Berlin when the Wall succumbed to curses and hammers, its demise the most eloquent refutation of an argument based on putrid premises, came the morning-after. And a morning after that. The hard-core anti-capitalists, whose revolution had anything but ended, had to recalibrate. Fortunately, the solution had been there all along: Ecological doomsday scenarios provided the perfect narrative for channeling the new angst. Long convinced that nuclear energy was synonymous with world cataclysm, radical critics had little trouble fomenting ever greater anxiety concerning the future of the entire benighted planet. The apparent victory of unbridled capitalism when the Iron Curtain melted could be no more than a temporary setback, a clarion call to the crusaders for social justice to adopt a smarter strategy for the march of History and synchronize their steps.

And so the vanguard mobilized. In 1992, the USSR having just collapsed, mathematician Michel Serres noted in *The Natural Contract*: "[T]he recent conferences on the environment in Toronto, Paris, London, and The Hague testify to an anxiety that is beginning to spread. It suddenly resembles a general mobilization!"[891] It's nothing short of a war, or even worse, warns Serres: "Air raid warning! Not a danger coming in from space, but the risk run on earth by the atmosphere: by the weather or climate understood as global systems and as general conditions of survival."[892]

In all fairness, not everyone felt this way, beyond the organizers and attendees of those conferences, acolytes in tow. Rupert Darwall detected all the signs of a new revolutionary cause being recycled for Western consumption, to replace the recently failed version. The recipe is similar, even if the ingredients have been slightly altered: "Viewed as an ideology, environmentalism took the Marxist conception of the alienation of the working class from the means of production and applied it to the rich man's alienation from nature."[893]

Pascal Bruckner agrees, adding this breathtaking overview of the latest in the series of millenarian transmutations, in *The Fanaticism of the Apocalypse: Save the Earth, Punish Human Beings*, published in 2011:

> For the past half-century, we have in fact been witnessing a slide from one scapegoat to another: Marxism designated capitalism as responsible for human misery. Third-Worldism, upset by the bourgeoisification of the working classes, substituted the West for capitalism as the great criminal in History and the 'inventor' of slavery, colonialism, and imperialism.... With ecologism, we move up a notch: the guilty party is humanity itself, in its will to dominate the planet, to "challenge it" (*harausfordern*), to use Heidegger's terminology. Here there is a return to the fundamentals of Christianity: evil is the pride of the creatures who are in revolt against their Creator and who exceed their prerogatives.... That is why so many old Bolsheviks are converting to ecologism in order to broaden their palette of

accusations. This amounts to recycling anti-capitalist clichés as one recycles waste water: ecologism adds a supplementary layer of reprobation, claiming to be the culmination of all earlier critiques.[894]

True, the new cataclysm is not quite the same as the old: unlike the millenarian version, which is supposed to herald a new beginning, this one would end everything. No universal salvation to follow, game over. Unchanged is the usual culprit - greed, materialism, selfishness. In the name of profit, goes the narrative, money-hungry Adam has now stooped to sacrificing Nature itself. Created by God to cherish the Earth, improve it with his labor and populate it with his grateful offspring, ingrate Adam repays his Maker by annihilating all His work, sparing not even himself. Ecologism proclaims suicide by geocide.

Bruckner sees ecologism as applying to all existence, modes of production, and ways of life. Visuals work well, as Al Gore demonstrated in his 2016 movie *An Inconvenient Sequel*, an update to *An Inconvenient Truth* released a decade earlier. *The New Republic*'s Emily Atkin gives a snapshot:

> In an emotional scene, he shows the impact of 2013's Typhoon Haiyan. A young Filipino cries as he recalls almost dying; another describes breaking through the ceiling of his home to escape drowning. At another point, Gore narrates over helicopter shots of sweeping, devastating wildfires, "Every night on the evening news is like a nature hike through the Book of Revelation."[895]

Apocalyptic crises call for apocalyptic solutions. Imagine the anxiety, given the stakes: "[t]here's a profound fear among many activists that time is running out, that we have only a few more years to take the necessary actions to solve the climate crisis." Lest there be any doubt, Gore assures his movie audience of his sincerity: "'I feel very deeply about what the right thing is. I'm not confused about it at all.'"[896] His certainty sounds theological, grounded in a dialectical-cosmic determinism that motivates believers to action (the "will-thus-should" fallacy again). Explains Bruckner: "In a strange mixture of fatalism and activism to which Marxism had already accustomed us, a certain kind of ecologism describes the death of the planet as inexorable while at the same time exhorting us to delay it as much as we can."[897] From contradiction emerges utopia. It is up to the vanguard to show the way, and the Way is Good.

But first, notes Hans Jonas, the German disciple of Heidegger and the Green Party's guru, "ethics had to be reformulated to take into account a new responsibility to the natural world."[898] Ecologism, like all ideologies, is normative: it defines good and bad. The responsibility "to the natural world" justifies taking up the same old fight. The dualist antinomy of the millenarian is easily recycled: rich vs. poor, selfish vs. selfless, greedy vs. altruist, individualist vs. communitarian, climate destroyers vs. climate saviors, CO_2 addicts vs. hikers.

Thus in 2010, the aptly named French monthly *La Decroissance* (The Decline), launched in 2004 to combat "the ideology of consumption" (*L'idéologie de consummation*), identified the root of all evil in familiar terms: "The enemies of life are found not only among the industrialists, but also those who do not believe in the catastrophe." Infidels, priests of Mammon, beware, for thou shalt be liquidated. Thoroughly secular in practical intent, the underlying theme is nonetheless biblical, writes Brucker:

> [T]he matrix of the whole environmentalist discourse is the story of the Fall in Genesis: in the beginning there was the earthly paradise, but humans ate of the fruit of tree of knowledge, and God drove them out. At the same time that Europe denies its Christian roots, it manifests them in its slightest references: our thinking takes place more than ever in the light of the Bible, whose lexicon and structure continue to be at work in our everyday life. We all date the damnation in our own ways.

In a bizarre use of the meme of class struggle, "the globe becomes the new proletarian that has to be saved from exploitation."[899]

But if many modern-day environmental utopians are openly Marxist, few recognize their movement's roots in the racist pseudo-science that was Progressive-era eugenics. The German geneticist Fritz Lenz, for example, had good reasons to claim, in 1933, that his 1917 essay *Race as the Principle of Value: On a Renewal of Ethics* "contained all the main features of the National Socialist worldview." (As it happens, an offprint of the essay was found in Hitler's library.[900]) In 1934, Ernst Lehmann described National Socialism as "political-applied biology," explaining: "This striving towards connectedness with the totality of life, with nature itself, a nature into which we are born, this is the deepest meaning and essence of National Socialist thought."[901] To be sure, hostility to urban civilization was widespread among people of varied convictions. But that specific mixture of hatred against technology, money, and greed with a romantic adoration of pristine Nature was peculiar to the Nazis. Who blamed it all on the Jews.

Thus even as the Nazi leadership tolerated the help of bankers and industrialists for short-term financial reasons, under no circumstances could it have made common cause with capitalists in the long run. Writes Darwall: "Hitler's hatred of Jews led him to reject accommodation with a global economic order dominated by…Wall Street Jewry and the Jewish media" and advocated instead a back-to-nature model with totalitarian control. Hitler's and the rest of

> [t]he Nazis' profound hostility to capitalism and their identification with nature-politics led them to advocate green policies half a century before any other political party. … [I]t might come as a shock but should not surprise that Hitler and the Nazis were the first to advocate large-scale renewable energy programs.[902]

Thus in 1932, on the eve of the general election, an article published in the Nazi newspaper *Völkischer Beobachter* (People's Observer) headlined "National Energy Policy," claimed that wind power could transform the economy and provide "green jobs" to millions of Germans. That same year, Nazi economic spokesman Frank Lawaczeck, who extolled the corporatist state in his *Technology and the Economy*, praised Stalin's Five-Year Plans along with denouncing egoistic-liberal-Jewish capitalism. He argued against using coal for energy, claiming that hydro and wind power were natural and "at hand to use, free of cost, but Man has weighed them down to an incredibly high degree with monetary interest."[903]

The resurgence of eco-socialism (a term Darwall favors over "ecologism"), jump-started in Sweden during the 1960s with Germany close behind, was yet hardly the mass movement the utopians were craving. To the rescue came the old scapegoat, providing the most powerful catalyst for the Red–Black–Green merger, which would catapult them into the mainstream. The Six-Day War was a propaganda god-send; immediately, "the New Left 'discovered' the Palestinians," writes Paul Hockenos.[904] Paul Berman agrees: "[T]he New Left's vision of a lingering Nazism of modern life was suddenly re-configured, with Israel in a leading role." The anti-Western forces were galvanized, argues Darwall, as "deeds followed words. In the final weeks of 1969, the 21-year-old [Joshka]

Fischer [who would later become Vice Chancellor and foreign minister of Germany, from 1998–2005] formed part of a five-person SDS [the left-wing *Sozialistische Deutsche Studentenbud*] delegation to a Palestine Liberation Organization (PLO) solidarity congress in Algiers."[905] The ideologies were finally synchronized, thanks once again to the Jews.

Fisher had had a powerful ally in Bruno Kreisky (1911-1990), an Austrian Jew who had survived the Holocaust by hiding in Sweden. A life-long Marxist, he became Chancellor of Austria in 1970, leading "the Socialists to victory for the first time [in this Catholic country] in their history."[906] As for many of his Austrian contemporaries, writes Robert Wistrich, socialism had been for Kreisky "a secular religion defining a moral commitment to serve the cause of the proletariat. It held out the universalist promise of a new world and a classless society in which mankind would be redeemed irrespective of race, religion, and nationality."[907] That year Austria also became the first Western country to recognize the PLO. He then turned to air-brushing Austria's Nazi past, by proclaiming "that he intended to ignore the Nazi background of all persons who had been reintegrated into postwar Austrian society." The result was bizarre: "The first Socialist of Jewish ancestry to head an Austrian government was presiding over the only cabinet in Europe which included such a high number of ex-Nazis."[908] His constituents were ecstatic.

The totalitarian ideology had come full circle precisely three decades after the start of World War II. Laments Paul Berman: "[I]t became obvious that the New Left in its more radical or revolutionary version was not, as everyone had imagined, an anti-Nazi movement. On the contrary."[909] In the early '70s, the left-wing Revolutionary Cells started collaborating with the Popular Front for the Liberation of Palestine (PFLP) in hijacking airplanes, killings, and kidnappings. Simultaneously, anti-Zionist venom was escalating exponentially. Explains Wistrich: "Anti-Zionism in the 1970s and 1980s increasingly began to look like the leftist functional equivalent of what classical antisemitism had once represented (in the interwar period) for the fascist Right... [thus] steadily emerging as the lowest common denominator between sections of the Left, the Right, and Islamist circles."[910]

The revolutionaries adapted with agility. An excellent political opportunity arose in 1980, when German Chancellor Helmut Schmidt, in response to the OPEC oil crisis of the mid-seventies, naively decided to build more nuclear power stations, merely because it made economic and ecological sense. The move was deeply unpopular. Fischer and his comrades soon realized the political potency of energy ideology, and the Green Party was duly formed in the first months of 1980.

The party "attracted the ecological old guard—ex-Nazis, neo-Nazis, and other far-right nationalists. One of these was August Haussleiter and his AUD (Commonwealth of Independent German Action) party. Founded in 1965, the AUD developed elements of Nazi ideology, notably its environmentalism anticonsumerism and promise of a Third Way between Communism and capitalism."[911] After Haussleiter was elected Green Party spokesman, the AUD dissolved, but Darwall sees here a seamless ideological progression: "From the discussion of nuclear power it was a short step to considering the fragility of the whole eco-system and the possibilities of alternative sources of energy," wrote Haussleiter in 1988. Concludes Darwall: "The New Left shared the nihilism and antihumanism of the Nazis, which made it highly susceptible to adopting similar positions as the Nazis—and not just once, with its anti-Semitic violence, but a second time, when its leaders became born again Greens."[912]

What happened next was a deep penetration of West Germany by East German agents, and the creation of a Soviet-financed peace movement. By 1981, 70 percent of active supporters of the Peace Movement were also supporters of the Greens, with Communist Party members among its most active organizers. Germany was gradually but irrevocably being "greened" - and the same could be said of other European countries. The United States eventually followed suit. When interviewed by Jeffrey Goldberg in 2016, President Barack Obama denied that ISIS was an existential threat to the US, while insisting that "climate change is a potential existential threat to the entire world."[913] In his mind, this justified bypassing the US Congress in signing the Paris Agreement on Climate Change by executive fiat, knowing it would fail public scrutiny. Leaving such important matters to the vagaries of public opinion would be irresponsible. What, after all, are vanguards for, if not to protect the people from themselves?

But the anti-capitalist intellectuals in charge of providing the ideological veneer are not always the disinterested idealists they claim, and are routinely portrayed, to be. Members of what Darwall calls the Climate Industrial Complex (CIC) include: well-paid staff of the Environmental Protection Agency (EPA); a sizeable army of climatologists in academia who receive private (foundation, corporate, and personal) as well as government monies; vocal European activists and environmental non-governmental organizations (NGOs) in concert with the infamously politicized United Nations; and, most critically, the gullible and not-so-gullible media. They constitute "an amalgam of American money and European ideas."[914] And in fact, some of that money ends up, however surreptitiously at times, outright subsidizing "green industries."

Some benefits of eco-radicalism, however, are not immediately visible to the innocent eye. Tom Steyer, for example, became one of the CIC's most vocal proponents of fighting climate change after earning billions from investment in coal mines and power plants through investments made by his company, Farallon Capital. Steyer finally had to sell his shares in Farallon after massive protests and public embarrassment. But that was not until late 2012; by then, his billions had already been made, and plenty of folks fooled. The *New York Times* wrote in 2014 that "even after his highly public divestment, the coal-related projects his firm bankrolled will generate tens of millions of tons of carbon pollution for years, if not decades, to come. Over the past 15 years... Farallon... has pumped hundreds of millions of dollars into companies that operate coal mines and coal-fired power plants from Indonesia to China, records and interviews show." But don't be too hard on the man: "the investment was financially irresistible."[915]

Other climate change enthusiasts are making billions in unrelated industries, in Silicon Valley and Seattle, perhaps to deflect attention. Multi-billionaire Mark Zuckerberg's signature low-carbon-imprint t-shirt and eco-friendly logos adorning heftily-insured and endowed bosoms are *de rigueur*, as is the designer price-available-upon-demand gear sported by the chic woke. "Climate change is ethics for the wealthy," suggests Darwall: "it legitimizes great accumulations of wealth. Pledging to combat it immunizes climate-friendly corporate leaders and billionaires from being targeted as members of the top one-tenth of the top one percent."[916]

What they share is a stake in the "youthquake" that includes a loudly proclaimed antipathy to materialism and a loudly proclaimed, virtue-signaling "green" attitude toward some of the unfashionable accoutrements of wealth associated with the less-*nouveau riches*. Solar is in, oil and coal are out – and have been for some time. Ultimately, writes Darwall, "the man-made climate crisis isn't about climate; it is and always has been about energy." Though claiming to fight climate change caused by man-made carbon emissions, most of the activists' real purpose is "the replacement of hydrocarbon energy with wind and solar."[917]

The most inconvenient truth is that wind and solar energy hit the poor hardest. In the US, for example, after Congress strengthened the ethanol mandate in 2007, the price of corn rose from $2.50 a bushel to nearly $8 a bushel, currently accounting for 40 percent of the US corn crop. Developing nations are hard-pressed to pay the high prices of renewables when much cheaper alternatives are at hand. Nigeria, for example, over half of whose 190 million citizens lack access to electricity, has an estimated 2 billion tons of coal reserves which would provide a huge boost to its economy. Writing in the *Wall Street Journal* on September 3, 2018, Neanda Salvaterra reports that "coal plants are attractive because they are less expensive to build than renewable energy facilities. The cost of constructing a renewables plant is roughly double the outlay of a fossil-fuel facility, experts say." Other developing countries are following suit. "Bangladesh plans to use coal to generate 50% of the country's power by 2030, up from 2% today. Like many countries in the region, it is funding its expansion with loans and technological help from China and Japan."[918]

The wealthy may be able to afford the higher prices, but even they would rather not, if they can get away with it. Unsurprisingly, they often don't. The Program Director of the radical Greenpeace International, for example, was exposed in 2014 as having commuted the 250 miles between Luxembourg and Amsterdam by plane since 2012. Not only did each trip cost Greenpeace a great deal of money, it also would have generated 313 pounds of carbon dioxide emissions.[919] Al Gore has come under similar criticism for living in an energy-gobbling house quite at odds with his professed views. On February 26, 2007, ABC News cited the assessment by the Tennessee Center for Policy Research that Gore's 20-room home and pool house consumed more than 20 times the national average during 2006.[920]

The Sierra Club also received millions of dollars from a consortium of the largest transnational oil companies that constitute the Oil and Gas Climate Initiative (OGCI) in 2014. And after some Club members objected, the OGCI entered into partnership with the Environmental Defense Fund (EDF) to create EDF+Business, to the tune of a few billion dollars. Writes David Wojick: "EDF is clearly getting a lot of money for this. They say they get none directly from the companies, rather that they get it from unspecified 'philanthropies.' Where these philanthropies get it may be a different story.[921] They could easily be laundering Big Oil money. It may be telling that OGCI does not issue a financial report." EDF admits that one "element that makes EDF unique is its ability to form unlikely partnerships around common goals. When looking specifically at EDF+Business, the common goal is finding the opportunities where both business and the planet can thrive." For their part, big oil companies "have good commercial reasons, which are killing coal and making natural gas more 'climate friendly.' After all, Big Oil is also Big Gas."[922] And it helps EDF's bottom line, which grew 41%, from $158 million in 2017 to $223 in 2018, with the largest boost coming from "foundations and other institutional giving."[923]

But even if many who advance ecologism are hypocritical, its general appeal, which stretches far beyond the elite insiders of the CIC, cannot be overestimated. For the picture it paints of the Antichrist *du jour* is tailor-made for the times. The ecologist narrative offers satisfying confirmation for the worldview of the post-truth generation that gets its "facts," such as they are, from a vanguard whose ideological GPS points to a Neverland of windmill-operated smartphones.

Each era has its own truth, wrote Max Horkheimer in 1935; truth is whatever fosters social change in the direction of a "rational" society.[924] But aside from being the opposite of "irrational," the positive content of such an arrangement eludes the reader. Horkheimer was Director of the Frankfurt School of Critical Theory, a Marxist think-tank founded in 1923 to address the problem of influencing culture in an anti-capitalist direction. But "critical theory" did little beyond criticizing and offered little by way of positive vision of what such a "rational" society might look like beyond the usual pablum.

The best that the most influential of the Frankfurt School philosophers, Herbert Marcuse, could propose just before his death, in 1979, was to reiterate his fellow-Marxist Ernst Bloch's vision of a "concrete utopia, [which] refers to a society where human beings no longer have to live their lives as means for earning a living in alienated performances. Concrete utopia: 'utopia because such a society is a real possibility."[925] True to its Marxist pedigree, the vision is self-contradictory. A fantasy fit for Peter Pans.

11:
On Earth, Not Heaven

The Weaponized Narrative

"The first thing a man will do for his ideals is lie," observed Joseph A. Schumpeter, to which Thomas Sowell has added: "As history has also shown, especially in the twentieth century, one of the first things an ideologue will do after achieving absolute power is kill." Lying does not always lead to violence, but the converse rarely holds, for violence invariably seeks refuge behind a cloak of deception. Upon receiving the Nobel Prize for literature in 1970, Alexander Solzhenitsyn exhorted his audience not to "forget that violence does not live alone and is not capable of living alone: it is necessarily interwoven with falsehood. Between them lies the most intimate, the deepest of natural bonds."[926] An ideological system such as that of the USSR, which had to both preserve and validate the raw exercise of power, must institutionalize the lie. As a result, "it is not simply crude power that triumphs," explained the former Gulag inmate, "but its exultant justification."

As the instruments of violence have become increasingly deadly, so too have the tools of deception and psychological warfare. Solzhenitsyn went on:

> Our world is rent asunder by those same old cave-age emotions of greed, envy, lack of control, mutual hostility which have picked up in passing respectable pseudonyms like class struggle, racial conflict, struggle of the masses, trade-union disputes. The primeval refusal to accept a compromise has been turned into a theoretical principle and is considered the virtue of orthodoxy.[927]

A refusal to compromise, so frequently deplored nowadays but hardly novel, naturally reflects the model of an indissoluble dialectic: the thesis-antithesis of opposing forces presumes that for progress to take place, destruction is indispensable. Philosophers obligingly provide the needed euphemisms: how conveniently does calling the aftermath of an Apocalypse a "synthesis" whitewash the blood and gore, a deceptively antiseptic logic serving as alibi. The orthodoxy of radical progress shrouds envy and fear with lofty names; meanwhile, evil is "crawling across the whole world in front of our very eyes, infesting countries where they could not have been dreamed of; and by means of the hijackings, kidnappings, explosions and fires of recent years they are announcing their determination to shake and destroy civilization! And they may well succeed." These words were spoken three decades prior to 9/11; Solzhenitsyn is now gone, as is the USSR, but what Sowell has called "the tyranny of visions"[928] persists, the utopian narrative elastic enough to accommodate jihadism along with anti-zionism and *chavismo*-style Communism.

Students of rhetoric have long acknowledged the power of narrative as the key aspect of rationality, defining "the nature of persons as narrative beings," based on the observation that "humans are essentially storytellers."[929] But a narrative is not only, or even primarily, a string of factual events ordered around a plot. Make no mistake: "[W]here, in any account of reality, narrativity is present, we can be sure that morality or a moral impulse is present too," writes Hayden White.[930] Stories teach lessons - whence we have *the moral* of a tale. They have an inner coherence and fall into patterns that make sense of a complex and dangerous world. Both the desire for simplicity and for moral justification may be satisfied by a narrative that is in line with traditional ways of thinking as well as personal inclinations.

Which is why, despite its ambiguity, the term has recently gained notoriety even in military circles. The Defense Department[931] at least attempts to engage in strategic communication (alternately referred to as information warfare, information operations, psychological operations, public diplomacy, political warfare and peacefare[932]), while the State Department, the U.S. Agency for International Development, the U.S. Agency for Global Media, and many other organizations, wholly or partly taxpayer-funded, are floundering with insufficient resources, analytical depth, strategic guidance, or public appreciation of the vital task at hand.

Prompting the unusual focus on communication by the military have been two glaringly costly wars whose missions, never quite articulated, have been hard to consider accomplished. It turns out that what drops out of the strategic picture are "the social and political dimensions of conflict when conflict is conceptualized in a purely force-on -force manner,"[933] with disastrous results. Yet "force-on-force" conceptualization has been the norm in the United States for at least a century. In an attempt to address this problem, the U.S. Army Special

Operations Command has conducted and recently released a study of *Narratives and Competing Messages*. It is a commendable and encouraging effort.

Eager to "better understand how narratives shape political behavior," the study avoids generalizations and value judgments, recognizing that "[a]ny political landscape is full of competing actors, motivations, and goals. [But n]arratives are especially important tools for turning these disparate parts into comprehensible stories."[934] Among these, the most influential narratives have a deep psychological origin. Specifically:

> Unresolved tension or conflict in the narrative fosters a desire for action that can only be sated when the conflict itself is resolved. The classic example is Adolf Hitler's manifesto, *Mein Kampf* (My Struggle). Hitler's story created an unresolved desire for a German utopia. The story invited its readers to take to action to satiate the desire, namely the elimination of the Jews.[935]

The study candidly acknowledges the limitations of this approach – inevitable, given the subject matter. After all, how does one measure the "desire" for genocide? And should such a desire be taken as a given, like the need for food or sex? What about the moral dilemmas? But such intractable queries aside, the Special Forces Operators (SFOs) seek to learn how effectively "resistance movements" use narratives. Whether it is psychology, or anthropology, or any other social science that comes up with a workable model, the SFOs themselves do not look under the proverbial hood - perhaps no one is able to do so. The authors concede that "researchers have not yet progressed to reliably identifying causal relationships between narrative elements and changes in behavior. Part of the challenge … is measuring the effectiveness of narratives."[936]But challenges are there to be faced.

The military is right to take a hard-nosed, quantitative approach to the study of narrative, although a more comprehensive analysis would doubtless also benefit strategists. Equally admirable is the establishment of a new center at Arizona State University (ASU) named the Weaponized Narrative Initiative, as part of the Center on the Future of War which was launched by ASU in cooperation with the New America Foundation. The Initiative's co-directors, Brad Allenby and Joel Garreau, declare that the "Weaponized Narrative Is the New Battlespace:"

In the hands of professionals, the powerful emotions of anger and fear can be used to control adversaries, limit their options, and disrupt their functional capabilities. This is a unique form of soft power. In such campaigns, facts are not necessary because – contrary to the old memes of the Enlightenment – truth does not necessarily prevail. It can be overwhelmed with constantly repeated and replenished falsehood. Especially powerful are falsehoods or simplifications that the target cohort has been primed to believe by the underlying narratives with which they are also being supplied.[937]

And the most central of these narratives is none other than apocalyptic utopianism, whose chameleonic adaptability is exceeded only by the ability of a hubristic "professional" elite ability to seduce the gullible into submission. Write Allenby and Garreau:

> Narrative is basic to what it means to be human. What's new is the extraordinary power of today's *weaponized* narrative. It attacks our group identity – our sense of who we are, our privilege of not being identified as "other." The rise of the Connected Age allows attacks that tear down old identities that have bound us together. But it also allows the creation of narratives that define the new differences between "us" and "them" that are worth fighting for.... The emotionally satisfying decision to accept a weaponized narrative - to believe, to have faith - inoculates cultures, institutions, and individuals against counterarguments and inconvenient facts.... [while] media tools and messages ... reinforce the narrative — crucially, by demonizing outsiders.

The elite bears the brunt of the blame for the ensuing calamities. Whether labeled "right" or "left," observes Robert Conquest, "there is a great similarity, a real continuity, among minds closed to tolerance and pluralism.... The essential is, and was, hatred of the open society."[938] The first Western historian to chronicle Stalin's use of famine to decimate Ukraine's population in the 1930s, Conquest agrees with Zhelyu Zhelev, a Bulgarian dissident who ascended to his country's presidency after the fall of the Soviet Union, about the essential similarities between "left" and "right" totalitarianisms:[939] They both oppose pluralism, and inevitably resort to murder.

Conquest frequently cites George Orwell's comment that the man in the street is at once too sane and too stupid to fall for the fads of the intelligentsia, adding: "We might note that the opposite of sane and stupid is insane and intelligent. But insanity itself is a denial of intelligence." The self-styled elite may not be unintelligent by the usual standards. "The crux," writes Conquest, "is less intelligence than a failure to confront that intelligence with reality – and even a drive to use that intelligence to deny or pervert reality."[940] The propensity for self-deception is exacerbated by the illusion of knowledge that the academy fosters. Referring to the current situation in the West, Conquest observes: "[W]e have an educated class which has historically misunderstood and misevaluated history."[941] To the ranks of the academic ideocracy, add the bureaucracy and the rest of the secular clerisy among "the holders of certain opinions [that] at a certain level of conviction, are both argument-proof and fact-proof,"[942] and the result is at best intellectual sclerosis. With hubris, it becomes a slow-growing cancer of the soul.

What helps the idea-mongers succeed in perpetrating their chosen narrative is a deeply entrenched bias against material self-interest, which persuades the gullible "who, often without knowing it, become apologists and finally accomplices of the closing of society. They often start by imagining that people who have no monetary interest in a political stance, who urge changes apparently of no benefit to themselves, are hereby proved to be of pure motive, and their cause a deserving one." Meanwhile, they "forget the attractions of power, of revenge, of all the nonprofit nastinesses that have afflicted the world."[943] And yet it is those very vices that account, at least as much as monetary greed, for injuring other human beings, for violating their natural rights - whether by curtailing their freedom of expression or by expropriating their goods, in the name of the putative sacred "common good" of society by allegedly redressing the myriad inequalities that separate each one of us from others. The ensuing utopia is sometimes deemed synonymous with "justice," or rather, to use an ideologically less imprecise concept, "cosmic justice."

The term was coined by Thomas Sowell to mean "putting particular segments of society in the position that they would have been in but for some undeserved misfortune." Such substantive "justice," alone deemed "fair," is attained when everyone possesses roughly the same amount of "good" as everyone else: the good of all must also be the good of each. But this cannot be. For "[t]his conception of fairness requires that third parties must wield the power to control outcomes, over-riding rules, standards, or the preferences of other people."[944] Though some adjustments may be minor, as happens in (small) democratic communities where judiciously calibrated safety nets for its most unfortunate citizens are provided by consensual agreement, the spectrum of coercive interventions ranges from the minor to the totalitarian. The body can stand a little bloodletting with few or no serious repercussions; but there are limits.

Everyone agrees that inequalities abound in every society, including the most prosperous. The question before a policymaker is not "the abstract desirability of equality" which, writes Sowell, "like the abstract desirability of immortality, is beside the point when choosing what practical course of action to follow. What matters is what we are prepared to do, to risk, or to sacrifice, in pursuit of what can turn out to be a mirage. Processes designed to create greater equality cannot be judged by that goal but must be examined in terms of the processes created in pursuit of that goal."[945] If those processes, no matter how well-intentioned, end up causing more harm than good, they should be abandoned. But this requires respect for empirical evidence, not mere wishful thinking. Some means are more effective than others in producing a desired goal.

Equally significant is the preference of the citizens themselves. Proclaiming that "a more equal society is a better society even if its citizens prefer inequality," as does Ronald Dworkin, is quintessentially hubristic, profoundly contemptuous of the very constituency he and his likeminded philosopher-kings purport to protect. Writes Sowell:

> How little the well-being of the ostensible beneficiaries really matters is shown by how little attention is usually shown to testing theories logically beforehand or empirically afterwards, as compared to the unremitting efforts put into propagandizing or into demonizing those with alternative views. [946]

People, moreover, might agree that a goal is desirable in principle, yet not agree on how much they want to pay for it. Priorities can differ widely.

What characterizes elite hubris is that it's all about *them*: "The arrogant vision of an anointed elite comes not from the simple fact that it is a vision, but from the sense of themselves as morally anointed among those who hold this particular vision."[947] Little has changed since Sowell wrote these words in 1999. A decade later, in his *Intellectuals and Society*, a long list of accusations demonstrates the many ways that intellectuals have managed to undermine American principles of self-reliance, philanthropy, and individual freedom: "Above all, they exalt themselves by denigrating the society in which they live and turning its members against each other."[948] The outcome weakens the nation from within. The weaponized narratives of the elite do more harm to their own society than even they realize. Words are powerful tools of mass distraction, insidious WMDs invisible to mere physical radar, designed to explode soundlessly inside a nation's soul.

Write Allenby and Garreau: "[I]t is certainly a reasonable hypothesis that the Enlightenment age of the individual - the core to any democratic system – is clearly ending. Unprecedented complexity, and information volumes and velocities, simply mean that individual cognitive capabilities – no matter how brilliant – are overwhelmed."[949] And so we take refuge in simplistic patterns, familiar yet misleading narratives that mix varying amounts of truth with lies and emotionally effective memes, as "[p]ower shifts towards those who understand and deploy narrative, be they large states, large corporations, or religious and cultural communities" - above all, one may add, the media and the academy. But just because knowledge is difficult, and reliable expertise is sometimes hard to sort out when specialization is inevitable in an increasingly complex world, the notion of truth itself cannot be abandoned: it constitutes the rock upon which civilization as we know it must stand.

The Art of War and Peace

How should a non-utopian form of government that respects individual freedom, sometimes ambiguously called "liberal," deal with attacks on its integrity and freedom? Are pacificism and non-interventionism the most effective ways of preventing war? Samuel P. Huntington, worried that "liberal thinking has been largely concerned with economics and economic welfare and has opposed large military forces, balance of power diplomacy, and military alliances,"[950] considers "liberal" states ill-equipped for war, adding that "liberalism is generally hostile to armaments and standing armies." This was indeed true of Thomas Jefferson, along with many of his likeminded fellow Republicans, at least until he became president. At that point, fed up with having to pay ransom to the Barbary pirates who had been hijacking American ships for decades, he came to recognize at least the benefits of at least a standing navy. He had his inveterate Federalist foe Alexander Hamilton to thank for the brave vessels that resisted those law-despising thugs of the sea, however ineffectually at first. [951]

Although no less a defender of the self-evident rights to life, liberty, and the pursuit of happiness (through property) than his Republican fellow Founders, Hamilton had argued in "Federalist 8" that "safety from external danger is the most powerful director of national conduct. Even the ardent love of liberty will, after a time, give way to its dictates."[952] Surely external danger, military attack, was what the fledgling United States had to worry about most. Security will always come first, since liberty and happiness cannot very well be pursued without… life.

Overemphasis on security can obviously undermine liberty, and Hamilton knew that. "The violent destruction of life and property incident to war, the continual effort and alarm attendant on a state of continual danger, will compel nations the most attached to liberty to resort for repose and security to institutions which have a tendency to destroy their civil and political rights."[953] It is precisely to avoid having to resort to such institutions that Hamilton argued in favor of a standing army and building a navy. Noting that thanks to America's salutary geographic situation, "extensive military establishments cannot be necessary to our security,"[954] these should not be feared unduly. He, along with the other Founders, would surely have recognized that our geographic situation no longer protects us much in the days of long-range nuclear missiles, to say nothing of cybercrime. But that is not a matter of ideology; it is reality.

Huntington is not unique in failing to differentiate between the formal principles of individual freedom and the practical foreign policy measures consistent with those principles. Empirical evidence must guide those measures; whatever protects the citizens of a nation is what must be implemented. Even Adam Smith conceded that

> [i]f any particular manufacture was necessary, indeed, for the defence of the society, it might not always be prudent to depend upon our neighbours for the supply; and if such manufacture could not otherways be supported at home, it might not be unreasonable that all the other branches of industry should be taxed in order to support it. The bounties upon the exportation of British-made sail-cloth, and British-made gun-powder, may, perhaps, both be vindicated upon this principle.[955]

Note the "perhaps:" this is not the language of an ideologue. "It might not always be prudent" to depend on others for an item deemed critical for self-defense. That self-defense is one of the most important functions of government is a given.

Another misunderstood defender of individual freedom is Immanuel Kant (1724–1804), whose essay with the admittedly unfortunate utopian title "Perpetual Peace" has invariably been interpreted as prophetic rather than, as had been his intention, merely theoretical. The concept did indeed refer to a state of mutual respect among nations; but Kant thought such a condition unattainable by human powers. Rather, it was Nature that miraculously seems to strive toward a kind of order: "The guarantee of perpetual peace is nothing less than that great artist, Nature," he wrote; though one would never guess it by observing actual human beings: "In her mechanical course we see that her aim is to produce a harmony among men, against their will and indeed through their discord."[956] Like Adam Smith, he did not deny men's benevolence, but saw its limits. That did not mean peace was impossible; both thought it could be attained if human beings at least did not violate one another's rights. Peace was not logically impossible, even if highly unlikely.

It is not a little ironic that some of Kant's detractors use the term "perpetual peace" to mock his allegedly utopian, presumably anti-realist position. This is especially deplorable when in fact Kant himself was fully aware of its absurdity. In the preamble to his essay, for example, Kant reports having spotted the phrase "perpetual peace," which he deems little more than a "satirical inscription, on a Dutch innkeeper's sign upon which a burial ground was painted." He adds whimsically that whether "its object [was] all mankind in general or the rulers of states in particular, who are insatiable of war, or merely the philosophers who dream this sweet dream, it is not for us to decide."[957] So much for Kant being a naïve utopian! Even if he never did leave his little Prussian hometown of Konigsberg, he was no fool.

Kant was simply engaging in philosophical discourse, admittedly very dense – for which German syntax must be at least partially be blamed. His preamble continues: if "the practical politician assumes the attitude of looking down with great self-satisfaction on the political theorist as a pedant whose empty ideas in no way threaten the security of the state, inasmuch as the state must proceed on empirical principles," Kant asks the politician to "not suspect some danger to the state in the political theorist's opinions."[958] The irony was not entirely disingenuous; he wasn't writing for politicians. (Nor, one imagines, would he have objected to being described as a pedant: the upright burghers of Konigsberg were said to have set their watches by his precisely timed daily walks.)

What Kant did provide, however, is a useful definition of a state as "a society of men whom no one else has any right to command or to dispose except the state itself. It is a trunk with its own roots. But to incorporate it into another state, like a graft, is to destroy its existence as a moral person, reducing it to a thing."[959] America's Founders added a corollary: when new roots give rise to a new trunk, it in turn must live separately, lest it be destroyed. To be sure, those roots had to prove they could sustain the trunk; but the Founders were intent on proving that their own tree would not only survive but become the sturdiest that ever grew on this earth.

They were convinced that the experiment they had commenced, upon the metaphorical hill across the Atlantic from the Old World, represented the success or failure of humanity itself. If this constituted exceptionalism, it did not amount to boasting, at least not yet: the jury was still very much out whether Americans would prove equal to the challenge; the Founders knew that better than anyone. That said, extrapolating from this sense of specialness to any one foreign policy mindset - whether expansionist or isolationist - is unwarranted. James Ceaser notes with discomfort the "attempts by some historians to connect the founders' idea [of a special mission with global relevance] to a particular kind of policy, whether exemplary or by use of more forceful means.... [because that] serves only to confuse the meaning of the mission."[960]

The Founders did not fit any of the ideologies that later political theorists would try to pin on American foreign policy. That in itself actually constituted a notably underestimated strength. Ceaser cites Walter McDougall[961] as a prime example of a historian who links the Founders' alleged view, "which he then defines as exceptionalism - to a foreign policy of restraint, contrasting it to the views found in the politics of manifest destiny and imperialism."[962] Others agree, while many hold the opposite view.

Scholars have often sought to claim justification for their preferred theory by tracing it to America's early years. The temptation to rewrite history to buttress political preferences is a seemingly irresistible affliction to which an antidote has yet to be discovered. The reality, to the extent that documents allow us to glimpse it, is rather less dramatic, though more profound: Notwithstanding the Founders commitment to the ideal of freedom, most of them were pragmatists, in foreign as well as domestic matters – i.e., they knew the difference between what may or may not be achieved. No doubt, Americans believed that they had a mission, which inspired and energized them. Ceaser notes, however, that it was meant in a practical rather than a messianic and utopian sense. Specifically, the Federalists "appeal[ed] to Americans' reason and understanding of the situation," which requires prudence and factual evidence. Accordingly, "by the nature of the case, prudential judgments cannot be fixed in advance but must be determined by considering America's power and resources and the conditions prevailing in the world."[963]

In other words, America could ill afford to ignore how the world works. Experience, as Hamilton said many times in *The Federalist*, is the best teacher. Realism was not an option but an imperative. Had the Founders not been as well educated, principled, yet strategically versatile and capable of recalibrating in the face of changing circumstances, astutely securing support from all the nations and individuals willing to help for whatever motive, America would never have gained independence, let alone kept it and attain the highest level of prosperity and power in the world. It bears recalling and studying anew.

Those who argue that the Founders were really, deep down, expansionists, whether or not they acknowledged it (even to themselves), are as mistaken as those on the opposite side who interpret outgoing President George Washington's warning against "entangling alliances" as a sure sign of what would later be called isolationism. Obviously, as a fledgling nation that was creating itself while busy fighting for its birth, the United States could ill afford to do more than survive as best it could, by its wits and strategic acumen, bolstered by every tool at its disposal and every friend it could find, while fending off formidable foes. From the outset, however, the aim was for the nation to become strong enough to seek peace on its own terms - looking forward to a time, to quote Washington, "when we may choose peace or war, as our interest guided by justice shall Counsel."[964]

While admittedly "revolutionary" for having declared independence from England and establishing a republic, the Founders steered clear of justifying forcible regime change in other lands. And this was not simply because at the time they lacked the military prowess. Alexander Hamilton, who opposed promoting regime change abroad, no matter what the purpose of such action, was by no means alone. Whether or not it may have been entitled to "afford assistance" to another people that has long been oppressed, argued Hamilton, a nation should always refrain from encouraging and fomenting insurrection and revolution, let alone undertaking it itself.

> When a nation has actually come to a resolution to throw off a yoke, under which it may have groaned, and to assert its liberties, it is justifiable and meritorious in another, to afford assistance to the one which has been oppressed, and is in the act of liberating itself; but it is not warrantable for any nation

beforehand, to hold out a general invitation to insurrection and revolution, by promising to assist every people who may wish to recover their liberty, and to defend those citizens, of every country. [965]

Implicit in the last statement is that "promising to assist every people who may wish to recover their liberty" is quite absurd.

The Founders had no use for vain utopias; they fully appreciated the real-world limits on what could and could not be done. The Constitution did not provide for "foreign aid" - on the contrary, the enumerated powers of Congress barely justified a modicum of taxation. But there was never a question of what America stood for, and what message it was to send to the world. In a letter to his friend Samuel Cooper on May 1, 1777, Benjamin Franklin reported from France that

all Europe is on our side of the Question [of independence], as far as Applause and good Wishes can carry them. Those who live under arbitrary Power do never the less approve of Liberty, and wish for it. They almost despair of recovering it in Europe . . .'Tis [indeed] a Common Observation here that our Cause is the Cause of all Mankind; and that we are fighting for their Liberty in defending our own. 'Tis a glorious Task assign'd us by Providence; which has I trust given us Spirit and Virtue equal to it, and will at last crown it with Success. [966]

That said, the federalist republican system conceived by Madison and eventually adopted by the delegates at the Constitutional Convention, while reserving considerable power to the states, had conferred upon the central government the all-important role of defending the collective security of all the American people. In the aftermath of the Revolutionary war, most (though not all) Founders quickly recognized that providing for the common defense, which involved a number of related functions, could only be performed by a firm Union that needed to be established with the greatest urgency. To that end, the Constitution created a single-person executive as well as an agency to conduct foreign policy. It also tasked Congress, rather than the states, to "regulate Commerce with foreign Nations, and among the several States, and with the Indian Tribes," and conferred upon it also the (strictly limited) power to lay and collect taxes, duties, imposts, and excises.

The Federalist was published in 1787 and 1788 to garner support for the new Constitution. Their and the Constitution's basic premise, writes Walter LaFeber, was that Americans "could survive as a people only if they could effectively fight the other great world empires. The United States has never been isolated or outside the world's political struggles. It was born in the middle of those conflicts, and its great problem was—and has always been—how to survive those struggles while maintaining individual liberty at home."[967] Even if it had wanted to be "isolated," America had no choice but to engage. Realistically, this mandated the establishment of an effective commander-in-chief. Though Jefferson and Madison, along with other Republicans, had always dreaded a creeping quasi-monarchy almost as much as, or maybe even more, than they feared foreign powers, no one doubted that the president of the new nation had to be empowered to make decisions in the national interest. It helped that the first president would be the eminently practical General Washington, who had no monarchical ambitions, and whose strategic acumen had been amply demonstrated during the Revolutionary War, as he nimbly adapted to the changing circumstances on the ground.

Dave Richard Palmer commends Washington's uncanny ability to calibrate his tactics to all four distinct phases of the war, especially during the final two years, when "the war was fought mainly in theaters other than the United States, including the negotiating arenas in Europe."[968] Audacity being needed at the outset, Washington was audacious; when, next, serious setbacks required caution, he proved cautious; as decisive victory became possible, he turned decisive; and after the critical victory at Yorktown, when steadfastness was key, "he became the nation's solid anchor."[969] Malleable as circumstances demanded, he nevertheless did not lose sight of the ultimate goal: "From first to last, he never added or subtracted from the vision of a United States free of Europe and supreme in North America."[970]

No Napoleon, Washington had assumed his office with trepidation, leery of the hugely complex dangers threatening the fledgling nation. He knew that he was walking in uncharted territory. Though the Constitution's framers had finally agreed to endow the central government with sufficient powers to act in the common interest, the question still remained how to wield it effectively. True, the commander-in-chief had the authority to act; now all he needed was the wisdom to know when, where, and how. The international storms, meanwhile, were gathering; indeed, there had hardly been a cloudless moment all along.

Some policies seemed to have been adopted almost by default. Given the nation's military unpreparedness, for instance, Congress seemed to have little choice but to start engaging in some form of economic warfare - which it promptly did, rather too precipitously. Among the first moves by the newly established U.S. Congress was to temporarily forget about Adam Smith and indulge in punitive protectionism – passing bills levying tonnage duties eight times higher on foreign vessels than on U.S. ships in American ports, as well as levying taxes on foreign goods entering the country. Notes LaFeber: "Americans wanted freer trade, but they were prepared to play rough mercantilist trading games if necessary."[971]

As Alexander Hamilton soberly pointed out, however, before Americans could properly engage in economic warfare (or economic diplomacy, if you will), they had to put the nation's own fiscal house in order. The financial genius thus proceeded to put together a program that promised to do just that, including a plan to pay the quite sizeable national debt, without which credit to borrow from other nations would not be forthcoming, and to create a national bank. Unsurprisingly, this – as indeed any other - plan was heavily dependent on British funds.

Unfortunately, the influential Thomas Jefferson, along with James Madison, opposed this approach. He regretted his role in the compromise that allowed Hamilton to get his financial scheme through – the compromise that established Washington as the nation's capital. Most, even if not all, Republicans were viscerally hostile to the British and sympathetic to the French, who had, after all, helped the colonies during the war of independence. Those sympathies not only continued after the collapse of the monarchy on July 14, 1789, they escalated, as the American Francophiles assumed a philosophical kinship with the Parisian mob. But how could they reconcile both the need for British credit and waging economic war against the Mother Island?

President Washington soon felt overwhelmed. Though prepared to do whatever his country required of him, the task was Herculean. Hardest was figuring out how to respond to the increasingly belligerent developments in 1792 and 1793, as France, Britain, and Spain scrambled for advantage and territory. Unsure of what course to take, Washington sought advice from[972] his cabinet members. His Secretary of State Thomas Jefferson and Secretary of Treasury Alexander Hamilton, unsurprisingly, offered divergent views. With characteristic intemperance, Jefferson responded bluntly that were Britain to send troops to Canada against the French or attack the Spanish in New Orleans, or both, the United States should declare war against the British Empire.

What Jefferson, in his zeal, neglected to indicate, however, was just what sort of preparations, exactly, should be made for such an eventuality. Indeed, far from recognizing, at last, that the United States would profit from having a robust military capability, Jefferson paradoxically continued to decry, as he always had, the absence from the Constitution of an outright prohibition against standing armies. Writes Forrest MacDonald: "Jefferson inverted Theodore Roosevelt's maxim: he spoke loudly and self-righteously and carried no stick at all."[973]

But how could war be declared against Britain? It sounded bizarre. Hamilton, by contrast, offered his commander-in-chief practical reasons why belligerence might be unwise. Not only was it strategically inadvisable to have a powerful and hostile neighbor, he argued, but Great Britain was the primary market for American exports. That said, he suggested that if Washington decided, for whatever reason, to choose to play hardball, loud talk wouldn't suffice. In the event that the President saw any prospect of fighting, he had to be prepared to support his stand "if necessary by sword." In addition to obtaining effective—and plentiful—swords, added Hamilton, it would behoove Washington to call a special session of Congress, so as to insure popular support. In other words, he intimated that declaring war on Britain would be sheer madness. The times called for nuance. Washington agreed. No war.

Rather more inclined toward idealism, even if not utopia, Jefferson had expressed enthusiasm for the French Revolution even long after its abuses had become hard to ignore. His sympathy was rooted in the widespread belief that America's example should, and perhaps would, strike a sympathetic chord throughout the globe; France was only the first of an expected set of dominos. Jefferson's vision, a kind of pre-Hegelian progressivism, was tempered by wisdom. Hamilton's hard childhood, by contrast, had inoculated him against such ideology. While he too believed that a republican government was best, Hamilton exhibited an unabiding respect for context and circumstance, and for allowing each society to choose for itself the specific manner in which it exercises self-government.

This did not imply any lesser enthusiasm on Hamilton's part for self-government as necessary for freedom. Nonetheless, he believed that the practical means of attaining that ideal could not be settled a priori, and the timing of political evolution differed from case to case. That does not, however, justify Henry Kissinger's contemptuous assessment of early America's approach to the world: "In a nutshell, the foreign policy of the United States was not to have a foreign policy."[974] The Founders deserve better. Kissinger seems to have misread Washington's admonition against "permanent alliances" to imply a rejection of all alliances "for any cause whatsoever."[975] Careful neither to overcommit abroad nor ignore the new nation's own need for support, Washington, along with his occasional ghost-writer-cum-de-facto-prime-minister Hamilton, had gone on to add that temporary alliances, at least, would sometimes be eminently prudent, depending on changing circumstances, as circumstances are wont to be. Notes Franz-Friedrich Walling: "Though the idea of no alliances of any kind quickly became an American dogma that lasted until World War I, Hamilton had deliberately built exceptions into the rule to allow for a significant degree of strategic flexibility."[976] This caveat should not have escaped the brilliant Kissinger; however unpopular, alliances had never been ruled out by the Founders.

It was Hamilton's fellow-Federalist (if, unfortunately, and quite unnecessarily, personal enemy) John Adams who put this most clearly: "It is obvious that all the powers of Europe will be continually maneuvering with us, to work us into their real or imaginary balances of power. ... I think it ought to be our rule not to meddle, and that of all the powers of Europe not to desire us, or perhaps even to permit us, to interfere, if they can help it."[977] Adams had no illusions that America would be obliged to live in the real world and could not afford to put its head in the sand. Not meddling is not the same as staying aloof and detached; not succumbing to the desire of European powers that America interfere on their continent did not imply closing our eyes and ears to the world.

Adams was among the many Founders who came close to idealizing the power of free trade to spread benevolence on an international scale, quite in line with the Baron de Montesquieu's conviction that "[p]eace is the natural effect of trade. Two nations who traffic with each other become reciprocally dependent; for if one has an interest in buying, the other has an interest in selling; and thus their union is founded on their mutual necessities."[978] Indeed, an exaggerated trust in the power of free trade to advance simultaneously the cause of American independence and world peace was so deeply entrenched that it required repeated encounters with reality to diminish. That trust, alas, was utopian, but the result was not to abandon free trade so much as to temper the hope of its emulation by societies or elites less willing or able to implement it.

No one grasped as clearly as did the consistently realistic Alexander Hamilton the naivety of assuming that economic interests would trump the hunger for conquest and glory. In *Federalist* number 6, he had dismissed the silly illusions of those "visionary or designing men who stand ready to advocate the paradox of perpetual peace between the States" on the ground that "the genius of republics (they say) is pacific; the spirit of commerce has a tendency to soften the manners of men, and to extinguish those inflammable humors which have so often kindled into wars." The rhetorical question asked by Hamilton (writing as "Publius") contains its own response: "Is not the love of wealth as domineering a passion as that of power or glory?"[979]

But that did not diminish either his or his fellow Founders' devotion to ideals they considered deeply moral as well as practical. They understood the importance of generosity, kindness, empathy. Most, if not quite all, the colonists had been deeply religious. And even the most secular were idealistic defenders of freedom, for which they were prepared to risk everything. They knew there was a steep road ahead and were prepared to climb it. "The American war is over; but this is far from being the case with the American revolution. On the contrary, nothing but the first act of the drama is closed. It remains yet to establish and perfect our new forms of government, and to prepare the principles, morals, and manners of our citizens for these forms of government after they are established and brought to perfection."[980] So spoke Dr. Benjamin Rush to the people of Philadelphia on a cold January day in 1787.

Although some, notably Jefferson, thought that "a nation as a society forms a moral person,"[981] most Founders thought it was the other way around: the nation could not continue free unless its citizens were virtuous. In the words of Benjamin Franklin: "Only a virtuous people are capable of freedom. As nations become more corrupt and vicious, they have more need of masters."[982] Such masters may help the nation survive, but at the expense of freedom.

The citizens of a free society certainly have the opportunity to be virtuous, since the legal framework does not put any obstacles to the full exercise of their ingenuity, imagination, and benevolence. But by the same token, they are free to squander it. Benjamin Franklin advised against it in his celebrated collection of homespun wisdom, *Poor Richard's Almanack,* published in 1738: ""Sell not virtue to purchase wealth, nor Liberty to purchase power."[983] Freedom does not come with built-in guarantees. The University of Pennsylvania enshrined Franklin's beliefs in its Ciceronian motto: "*Leges sine moribus vanae*" (Laws without morals are in vain.)[984]

Eager to establish a society based on individual freedom and set up the institutional means for securing property rights and free trade, the Founders were nevertheless keenly aware of the need for active and tireless promotion of what were then called virtues. And while today the term itself has a quaint archaic ring, the traits of character to which it refers continue to be as critically important as ever. They are enshrined, for example, in the Girl Scout Law, which every girl promises to uphold: "I will do my best to be honest and fair, friendly and helpful, considerate and caring, courageous and strong, and responsible for what I say and do, and to respect myself and others, respect authority, use resources wisely, make the world a better place, and be a sister to every Girl Scout."[985] It is nearly identical to the Boy Scout Law: "On my honor, I will do my best, to do my duty to God and my country and to obey the Scout Law; to help other people at all times; to keep myself physically strong, mentally awake and morally straight."[986] (That the latter does not refer to sexual orientation has in fact been recently clarified.[987])

But not everyone becomes a scout; and not everyone takes these pledges seriously upon growing up. It is possible to go through life without violating anyone else's life yet failing to live a fulfilled life. As Leon and Amy Kass, along with Diana Schaub, note in their anthology of *What So Proudly We Hail*, "while commerce and prosperity contribute to our freedom, this freedom can be put solely in the service of the accumulation of wealth – the means becoming the end." That doesn't suffice to make most people happy. True, "thanks to technological progress and democratic capitalism, the average American worker today enjoys a higher standard of living and a longer, healthier life than did dukes and duchesses but a century ago."[988] But expectations have also risen, as has discontent with the system's flaws. Of which, to be sure, there are plenty; the point however is to distinguish between the problems encountered by any human community trying to please disparate factions as against fatal threats to the fundamental principles that constitute its very essence.

The anthology selects the following character traits to illustrate the chapter that deals with "The Virtues of Civic Life," dividing them into five sets: first, the *individual virtues* of self-command and self-respect, without which neither personal nor fruitful civic engagement is possible; second, the *elementary civic virtues* of lawabidingness and justice; third, *virtues for critical times*, not only in battle but in other difficult situations as well, courage and self-sacrifice; fourth, virtues required toward our neighbors, such as civility, tolerance and compassion; and finally, virtues related to the nation and mankind, notably public-spiritedness, charity, and reverence.[989] This last need not imply allegiance to any particular religion, but it does suggest an appreciation for the spiritual that gives meaning to our existence beyond mere survival.

By far the most important of all the virtues, however, was identified by the oldest, most versatile, and certainly the funniest of the Founders – who else but Benjamin Franklin. In his *Autobiography*, he first describes how he would keep track of his progress practicing good behavior while shunning the bad, by painstakingly noting, on a calendar, his daily success in fixing each of his moral infirmities - one at a time. The entries are amusing yet in deadly earnest. He recounts that at first he didn't realize he needed to add one more item to his list: humility. "I cannot boast of much Success in acquiring the Reality of this Virtue," he confesses; "but I had a good deal with regard to the Appearance of it." At least he did try.

His final reflections on the matter capture best what distinguishes the mindset of a proponent of liberty from that of a utopian: "In reality there is perhaps no one of our natural Passions so hard to subdue as Pride. Disguise it, struggle with it, beat it down, stifle it, mortify it as much as one pleases, it is still alive, and will every now and then peep out and show itself. You will see it perhaps often in this History. For even if I could conceive that I had completely overcome it, I should probably be proud of my Humility."[990] As well he could have been.

Is Capitalism Dead Yet? What About Antisemitism?

The results are in from SurveyMonkey, as of January 2019: "Most people in the U.S. are still proponents of capitalism, but a majority also believe that the economic system we have is inherently unfair. 58 percent of people say that 'unfairness in the economic system that favors the wealthy' is a bigger problem than 'over-regulation of the free market that interferes with growth and prosperity' (39 percent). Among 18-24 year-olds, that gap is a chasm: 76 to 21 percent."[991] Other surveys, though not quite as dire, are still worrisome: Gallup finds that of 18- to 29-year-olds, 51 percent had more positive views of socialism than of capitalism, with only 45 percent preferring the latter.[992] But that is not quite the whole story. The Victims of Communism Foundation dug a little deeper, and what it discovered will surprise no one. It turns out that "despite Millennials' enthusiasm for socialism and [even] Communism, they do not, in fact, know what those words mean. Our study indicates that the attraction of socialism for Millennials has less to do with their familiarity with the ideology and more to do with their discontent with the current economic system, the flaws of which they blame on free-market capitalism."[993]

If many millennials don't know much about history or biology, as goes Sam Cooke's great song from 1960, they obviously know even less about economics. A famous remake of that catchy song, by Linda Ronstadt and Aaron Neville, in 1989, ran second on the charts that year just behind "Another Day in Paradise," an ironic salvo to inaugurate a generation hooked on virtual reality. How could they possibly remember what happened before their birth, or know what "socialism" even means?

Which doesn't stop them from having opinions about it. Used to pithy one-liners meant to be shared on social media with all the other woke people of all genders, it's a vulnerable demographic, hooked on glibness. They are ready prey for the likes of Chapo Traphouse, a podcast specifically targeting their age-set. Its ethos is captured by this excerpt from a book authored by a Chapo host: "Capitalism, and the politics it spawns, is not working for anyone under 30 who is not a sociopath."[994] LOL (translation, for the benefit of ancient readers untutored in Twitter lingo: laugh out loud.) OK, so maybe it's not quite hilarious.

Not everyone has the same sense of humor. Consider, for example, Waleed Shahid, communications director of the Justice Democrats, a group of Bernie Sanders campaign alumni recruiting progressive candidates to Congress, whose one-liner runs: "My joke is that unlike Barack Obama, I am a Muslim socialist." (The reader may be excused for wondering which of the possible punchlines is supposed to be funny.) According to *538*, a blog of opinion poll analysis founded in 2008, he and several others are among

> a cadre of young left activists whose voices have grown louder in the years following Hillary Clinton's loss to Trump. Many came of political age in the decade following the financial crash of 2008, and many are disillusioned by a Democratic Party they think has been ideologically hollowed out. They've organized outside the traditional party apparatus — the Democratic Socialists of America, the Justice Democrats — and worked to get representation in Congress, pushing figures like newly minted congresswomen Alexandria Ocasio-Cortez and Ayanna Pressley. Now they find themselves holding greater purchase than ever before in the formal Washington political process. For a few years now, Democratic voters have shown they're primed for a leftward shift, and this rising group of activists and politicians wants to push them even further. At the heart of the young left's project is a discomfort with the free market capitalist system under which we live. It's a system deeply ingrained in many Americans' identities, though increasingly less so: 2016 was the first year since Gallup started tracking the

question that it found Democrats had a more positive view of socialism than they did of capitalism. [995]

Considering its tenuous hold on empirical facts, the anticapitalist wave is alarmingly successful. Writes the *Economist* on February 14, 2019: "[W]hat might be called 'millennial socialism' is having something of a cultural moment." [996] Whether the exact nature of that "moment" is particularly new, the word itself certainly isn't. Marxist activist Chris Harman, writing for the journal *International Socialism*, for example, reports that

[t]he mass media discovered a new phrase in 1999 – "anti-capitalism". It first entered British headlines with the protests against financial institutions of the City of London on 18 June. It flashed across the world, on a much bigger scale, with the protest against the World Trade Organisation in Seattle on 30 November. They were painfully discovering something very real. Ten years after the supposed final triumph of market capitalism ... a growing number of people were rejecting their system. [997]

While the circulation of *International Socialism* is presumably negligible, Harman's article also appeared on a bilingual German-English site that includes it among several readings under the rubric "The Anti-Capitalist Movement. Called both REDS [sic] and, in German, *Die Roten*, the site's builders candidly admit: "Originally we intended to start our site later, but while researching the current events in the Middle East, particularly the conflict between the Israelis and the Palestinians, it came to our attention that there are very few resources presenting an analysis based on the classical Marxist tradition." That text had last been updated on November 3, 2001, as the world was still shaken by the 9/11 tragedy. Evidently, the millenarian utopianists lost no time in framing the narrative. Anyone who bothers to pays attention cannot fail to notice that anti-capitalism and anti-zionism are Siamese twins, and the website builders saw to it that they are thus perceived. For the two isms together constitute a far more powerful apocalyptic tool than either could be alone. Though by no means is the calculus merely political; the ideology had been ready-made for decades, indeed centuries, as this book sought to demonstrate.

That dark, sunny September morning when the towering symbols of man's technological success exploded, incinerating thousands, was ready-made for countless scenarios meant to validate "the international conspiracy" mantra consistent with the narrative propagated by *The Protocols of the Elders of Zion*. Most Muslims throughout the world refused to believe that the perpetrators were fellow-Muslims; some blamed the CIA for wanting to stoke Islamophobia.[998] Just as strange is the theory that the Israelis conspired with the United States.[999]

It will surprise no one that the lunatic fringe feeds on such fodder. But how many people are aware that Nation of Islam (NOI) leader Louis Farrakhan shares the same sentiments? He certainly has not kept those views private, having told parishioners in Chicago on NOI's Savior's Day, on March 1, 2015: "We now know that the crime they say is at the root of terrorism was not committed by Arabs or Muslims at all. It is now becoming apparent that there were many Israelis and Zionist Jews in key roles in the 9/11 attacks."[1000] He continued, according to CBS: "We're dealing with thieves and liars and murderers. ...We know that the World Trade Center was insured by its owner Larry Silverstein right before the attack.... We know that many Jews received a text message not to come to work on September 11th. Who sent that message that kept them from showing up? Within minutes of the attacks, Ehud Barak, the founder and master of the Israeli military's covert operation force, was in a London studio of the BBC blaming Osama bin Laden and calling for a war on terror." There you have it. Could it be more obvious?

Three years later, in 2018, Farrakhan was once again preaching in Chicago on Savior's Day, and again he railed against Jews for being "the mother and father of apartheid," declaring that "the Jews have control over those agencies of government," and suggesting that Jews have chemically induced homosexuality in black men through marijuana." Sitting in the audience, listening in silence, was the national co-chair of the Women's March, Tamika Mallory.[1001] She was later surprised that her presence caused a furor among Democrats. After all, she'd been going to the annual Nation of Islam function for years; her parents were activists in the movement. A few days later, she held a conference call where, according to Women's March Washington state chapter President Angie Beem, Mallory "went on to defend Farrakhan to over 40 women on the call. And she wasn't alone. [Carmen] Perez and [Bob] Bland [two other co-chairs] jumped in to defend him as well."[1002] So what was the big deal.

There was more. For as Leah McSweeney and Jacob Siegel of the online magazine *Tablet* reported in December 2018, according to several people present at an organizational meeting with Mallory and Carmen Perez, the two expressed the view "that Jewish people bore a special collective responsibility as exploiters of black and brown people" and "claimed that Jews were proven to have been leaders of the American slave trade." In addition, the fourth co-chair of the 2016 Women's March, the Palestinian American activist Linda Sarsour famous for her 2012 tweet that "nothing is creepier than Zionism," had long been an avowed anti-Semite. It was all a bit much for many of the Democratic women who were less comfortable with this attitude. In the end, the 2019 March lost most of its original participants. But the forces behind it are hardly weakened; they are only recalibrating.

Certainly, the more woke among Jews of the self-described political left—the National Council of Jewish Women, Jews for Racial and Economic Justice, If Not Now, and other groups—know perfectly well what the four co-chairs believe. But continuing to staunchly support the Women's March, they joined the Jewish Voice for Peace in condemning the uproar against the march as an "opportunistic attempt to break up a strong and growing cross-movement coalition by rehashing a painful conversation that has been happening in progressive spaces since Farrakhan first assumed leadership of Nation of Islam." No need for uproar; it's just a conversation.

Undaunted, Farrakhan is the unwelcome gift that keeps on giving. On February 17, 2019, for example, he blamed "wicked Jews" for trying to use him "to break up the women's movement," and then went on to defend Somali-American Rep. Ilhad Omar for this tweet: "It's all about the Benjamins baby," which has been widely condemned as antisemitic: "[Y]ou have nothing to apologize for," he told her. "Israel and AIPAC [the American Israel Political Action Committee] pays off senators and congressmen to do their bidding, so you're not lying."[1003] But if tweets are notoriously thoughtless, her connection to the radical Witness for Peace (WFP) organization clarifies her ideology. In 2017, Omar traveled to Honduras as part of a delegation sponsored by WFP, whose mission statement describes its members' commitment to oppose all forms of inequality. Specifically, it opposes "[t]he neoliberal free trade model [which] has created a 'race to the bottom' in terms of wages and working conditions."[1004] WFP focuses on Latin America, but several of its board members are active in rabidly anti-Israeli organizations.

WFP board member Atrayus O. Goode, for example, gave a sermon in 2017 after traveling to the Middle East, accusing Israel of "modern day apartheid." He has accused Israel of "stealing land and displacing Palestinians by any means necessary," and compared Israel to America as governments of "white supremacy." "If you change the word Israeli Jew to white and Palestinian to black, depending on the time period, you would think I was talking about America," he said. "America's sin was this country being founded as a white society on the stolen land of Native Americans and on the enslavement of Africans. It was whiteness being written into legislation in the late 1600s, it was all the subsequent laws and policies that reinforce white supremacy even up until this day."[1005] That more or less captures it: America's sin is the same as that of Israel. The two nations together constitute the bicephalic Antichrist.

Robert Wistrich fully understood the power of the narrative that gained enormous popularity during and after the Six-Day War of 1967, when harsh "anti-Israeli rhetoric soon emerged from both the Right and Left, which permitted the revival of what had been a temporarily dormant antisemitism in the early 1960s.… Zionism was vilified as a peculiarly pernicious, supremacist vision of the world and the lackey of American imperialism of the Middle East."[1006] Never mind that "contrary to the prevailing left-wing mythology about Israel's creation being a Western Zionist-imperialist conspiracy, official American support for Israel was comparatively lukewarm."[1007] Mythologies trump facts every time.

Zionism thus became "the historical heir of earlier antisemitism… which has become even more true today than it was several decades ago. In the current context anti-Zionism has indeed become a powerful point of connection between the latent anti-Americanism of many European intellectuals and the endemically anti-Western attitudes in the Arab Middle East."[1008] Hardly ever does one hear about the forced exodus of Jews from Arab lands in the Middle East after World War II. Writes Wistrich:

> Post-1945 Zionism is as much a Middle Eastern as a European phenomenon. Along with the Russian pogroms and the Nazi mass murder, the mob assaults of Arabs against "Oriental" Jews contributed a great deal to forging the "Zionist" consciousness of what is today half of the Israeli Jewish population. This is the deliberately suppressed reality that many liberals and leftists – with their guilt complex about Western colonialism and their ambivalence toward the Jews – are unable to deal with.

But insult has been added to injury: "The success of tiny Israel as a thriving Western-style democracy and high-tech economy in an ocean of brutal Arab dictatorships has plainly been intolerable to the radical Left. Arab 'socialism' produced only a grim blacklist of despicable tyrannies" – no wonder its ideological disciples are enraged. It provides sufficient justification for supporting "the pro-Palestinian narrative that Israel is solely to blame for the continuing conflict in the Middle East." Concludes Wistrich: "Anti-Zionism serves here as an *ersatz* – a substitute religion as well as a magnet for all the post-1989 Marxist debris – the orphaned causes of what Bernard-Henry Levy picturesquely described as 'all these dark little stars fallen from doctrinaire galaxies.'"[1009]

But do even a lot of dark little stars do not add up to a terminal black hole, argue the opponents of some crazy "Cold War redux."[1010] OK, so there are some undoubted strongmen out there; and yes, they do all kinds of nasty things, sometimes in cahoots with drug dealers, hackers, and terrorists. And yes, it's hard to deny that "tactically, disparate state and non-state actors do seem to be converging." OK, maybe even more than seeming. But tactical convergence is still "more about the nuts and bolts of domestic governance than some unified, global conspiracy." Conspiracy-talk is for assorted lunatics of the Right and Left. We need to all chill: "Assuming that authoritarians have a coherent ideology capable of replacing democratic capitalism gives their fragile beliefs far more credit than they deserve."

Whatever foreign threats there might be, the new "progressive foreign policy" being advanced by a vocal segment of the Democratic party represented by Bernie Sanders and Elizabeth Warren is "highly skeptical of military interventions" even if not necessarily unwilling to use force "when it is necessary."[1011] But above all, self-described progressives "believe that an equitable domestic economy is the foundation of national power," and its ultimate goal is "making a more equitable international economic system." But *equitable* – according to the progressive ideology - is just what capitalism is not.

Nor are progressives reluctant to invoke American "exceptionalism." For action along progressive lines "will obviously require American leadership. Progressive foreign policy advocates are showing the direction in which they will lead instead of spending time talking about decades-old buzzwords." Exceptionalism is one of them; same word, new meaning. A new hybrid, "authoritarian capitalism," describes an economy whose president is dedicated to the "basic realization of socialist modernization," and whose top priority is to "perpetuate CCP [Chinese Communist Party]." Except that according to the Defense Department's Annual Report to Congress assessing Chinese strategy, the regime "continues to operate as a centrally controlled, planned economy. China restricts inbound investment, limits other countries' exports, and pursues state-guided investment overseas, including in strategic sectors."[1012] It also partners with countries such as Russia, Iran, North Korea, and their ilk – all the while stealing Western technology and engaging in ideological sabotage.[1013]

Conspicuously absent from the progressive foreign policy blueprint is any mention of the threat of Islamism and terrorism. But to be fair, the 2018 National Security Strategy is also deficient on this issue; for it states explicitly: "Inter-state strategic competition, not terrorism, is now the primary concern in U.S. national security."[1014] If only we could convince ourselves that we can walk and chew gum at the same time.

Though evil can be traced on a conceptual axis, there is no need to assume an outright conspiracy. On the contrary: internecine warfare within the Islamic world, Chinese-Russian animosities, fear of Islamists, corruption that cuts all ways, constitute a protection of sorts for the U.S. and its allies – however dangerous and double-edged. In other ways, however, these centripetal forces do not prevent a pragmatic pooling of resources by rivals with otherwise contrasting purposes in order to advance a common cause: the demise of classical liberalism and Western civilization. While the enemies of freedom deserve no more credit for offering a realistic vision of utopia than they ever did, to imagine that our system of natural liberty is anything but fragile amounts to incalculably dangerous wishful thinking.

Freedom might end with an apocalypse, in which case everybody loses. Or less dramatically. In which case everybody still loses, whether they know it or not.

Epilogue

Though exactly one hundred years have gone by since the Irish poet W. B. Yeats composed his poem "Slouching Toward Bethlehem," its relevance today is uncanny. Here is how Yeats describes the malaise that followed the devastation of World War I:

> Turning and turning in the widening gyre
> The falcon cannot hear the falconer;
> Things fall apart; the center cannot hold;
> Mere anarchy is loosed upon the world,
> The blood-dimmed tide is loosed, and everywhere
> The ceremony of innocence is drowned;
> The best lack all conviction, while the worst
> Are full of passionate intensity.

Relativism both moral and epistemic, unbelief, loneliness, hypocrisy, cynicism; the soul yearns for some relief – the center cannot hold. "Surely some revelation is at hand;/ Surely the Second Coming is at hand." Or is it rather Armageddon?

> The Second Coming! Hardly are those words out
> When a vast image out of Spiritus Mundi
> Troubles my sight: a waste of desert sand;
> A shape with lion body and the head of a man,
> A gaze blank and pitiless as the sun,
> Is moving its slow thighs, while all about it
> Wind shadows of the indignant desert birds.
> The darkness drops again but now I know
> That twenty centuries of stony sleep
> Were vexed to nightmare by a rocking cradle,
> And what rough beast, its hour come round at last,
> Slouches towards Bethlehem to be born? [1015]

Commenting on this splendid poem in the *Paris Review*, Nick Tabor observes that "[t]he narrator suggests something like the Christian notion of a 'second coming' is about to occur, but rather than earthly peace, it will bring terror... A century later, we can see the beast in the atomic bomb, the Holocaust, the regimes of Stalin and Mao, and all manner of systematized atrocity."[1016] Beware of atrocities systematized at the behest of hubristic vanguards in the name of earthly peace, social justice, progress, or some other putative ideal: the beast may sport a human face but its gaze is blankly lethal. Don't be fooled by protestations of altruism, for it is at bottom pitiless, and a bottomless pit. Beware of those who refuse to debate, engage in dueling epithets devoid of factual content, and demonize those who might disagree with them - the stuff of what Gorman Beauchamp has called "ideological melodrama."

Mob thinking is a prelude to violence. Nothing is easier than making sweeping generalizations that enflame passions, fuel controversy, and push political agendas. Ideologists of all both "left" and "right" are wrong insofar as "neither deals with complex, multidimensional historical beings, but with abstractions."[1017] Alas, complexity and multidimensionality are bewildering. Human beings are infinitely more complicated than physical nature, which is daunting enough. Yet man yearns for simplicity and clarity, something meaningful that he can believe in deeply, with absolute conviction. He certainly wants to not be afraid – to the point that he is willing to deceive himself.

It takes myth and metaphor to portray such difficult feelings with any hope of accuracy, and it helps to have had direct experience of tragedy on an epic scale. Wislawa Szymborska, winner of the 1996 Nobel Prize in Poetry, had the fortune and misfortune of both. Born in 1923 in a small Polish town, she survived the war studying in underground classes and working as a railroad employee. Though at first sympathetic to the Communist regime, she became disenchanted after seeing it in action, and proceeded to establish contacts with dissidents both inside and outside Poland. She was able to publish her poems in samizdat (illegal press) and the Paris-based journal *Kultura*. In 1976, at the height of the Cold War, she wrote what would become the quintessential description of the utopian mentality. Its title was, obviously, "Utopia."

The poem describes an "[i]sland where all becomes clear./ Solid ground beneath your feet./ The only roads are those that offer access./ Bushes bend beneath the weight of proofs." It is an utterly comforting place, one might call it Paradise: "If any doubts arise, the wind dispels them instantly./ Echoes stir unsummoned/ and eagerly explain all the secrets of the worlds."

But there is a problem: "For all its charms, the island is uninhabited,/ and the faint footprints scattered on its beaches/ turn without exception to the sea./ As if all you can do here is leave/ and plunge, never to return, into the depths./ Into unfathomable life."[1018]

And as we plunge into the unfathomable life each of us has been miraculously granted, against immeasurable odds, it behooves us to be grateful, humble, and generous, remembering that God has created us in His ineffable image.

Notes

[1] https://is.muni.cz/el/1423/jaro2010/MVZ203/OBL___AQ__Fatwa_ 199 6.pdf

[2] Lawrence Wright, *The Looming Tower: Al-Qaeda and the Road to 9/11* (New York, NY: Doubleday, 2006), 235.

[3] https://fas.org/irp/world/para/docs/980223-fatwa.htm

[4] Francis Fukuyama, "The End of History," *The National Interest*, Summer 1989. https://www.embl.de/aboutus/science_society/discussion/discussio n_2006/ref1-22june06.pdf

[5] Francis Fukuyama, *The End of History and the Last Man* (New York, NY: Free Press, 1992), xvii.

[6] *Ibid.*, 383.

[7] In *Thus Spoke Zarathustra*, Nietzsche defines the idea in anti-religious terms: "The overman is the meaning of the earth... I beseech you, my brothers, *remain faithful to the earth,* and do not believe those who speak to you of otherworldly hopes!"

[8] Friedrich Nietzsche, *The Will to Power,* 48 (March-June 1888) https://ia800304.us.archive.org/25/items/TheWillToPower-Nietzsche/ will to power-nietzsche.pdf

[9] Luciano Pellicani, *Revolutionary Apocalypse: Ideological Roots of Terrorism* (New York, NY: Praeger, 2003), 271-272.

[10] Michael W. S. Ryan, *Decoding Al-Qaeda's Strategy: The Deep Battle Against America* (New York, NY: Columbia University Press, 2013), 87.

[11] Bruce Hoffman, Threat Assessment #Fail: Al-Qaida Quietly Growing, By Design," *The Cipher Brief,* Feb. 13, 2018, https://www.thecipherbrief.com/ article /exclusive / middle-east / threat-assessment-fail-al-qaida-quietly-growing-design

[12] Though "he" will be used generically throughout this book to refer to man in the sense of human being, the reasons are aesthetic ("he or she" is unnecessarily cumbersome) and grammatical ("he" is the commonly accepted neutral in English, which lacks the gendered nouns typical of Romance languages). Charges of misogyny should be dismissed not merely because of the author's gender, which she has never doubted, but because she has already addressed the topic at length in *Soulmates: Resurrecting Eve* (Piscataway, NJ: Transaction Publishers, 2013).

[13] John Dewey, *Liberalism and Social Action* (Amherst, N.Y.: Prometheus Books, 2000), 30.

[14] Milton Friedman spoke for a Cato Institute event on December 8, 1992, on "Why I am not a conservative;" that same year, Cato also published a paper by F.A. Hayek with a similar title was published in 1992, though it originally appeared as part of Hayek's 1960 book *The Constitution of Liberty.*

[15] Frank S. Meyer, *In Defense of Freedom: A Conservative Credo* (Chicago, IL: Henry Regnery Co.,, 1962).

[16] "Interview with Richard Epstein," *The Accidental Libertarian,* Septem ber 8, 2017 https://ricochet.com/podcast/the-accidental-libertarian /

[17] Jonah Goldberg, *Liberal Fascism: The Secret History of the American Left, From Mussolini to the Politics of Change* (New York, NY: Crown Forum, 2009)

[18] David Oshinsky, "Heil Woodrow!" *The New York Times*, Dec. 30, 2007. http://www.nytimes.com/2007/12/30/books/review/Oshinsky-t.html

[19] Peter S. Goodman, "Beyond Left and Right: It's About Reality*,"* *Huffington Post*, Feb. 10, 2011. https://www.huffingtonpost.com/2011/02/ 10/beyond-left-and-right-its-about-reality_n_821582.html

[20] Chrispin Sartwell, "The Left-Right Political Spectrum is Bogus," *The Atlantic*, June 20, 2014. https://www.theatlantic.com/politics/archive/ 2014/06/the-left-right-political-spectrum-is-bogus/373139/

[21] Meyer, *op. cit.,* 90-92.

[22] Shiraz Maher, *Salafi-Jihadism: The History of an Idea* (New York, NY: Penguin Books, 2016)

[23] William Dennis, *In Defense of Freedom and Related Essays,* by Frank S. Meyer (Indianapolis, IN: Liberty Fund, Inc., 1996), Foreword, xii. https://www.libertyfund.org/books/in-defense-of-freedom-and-related-essays

[24] Frank S. Meyer, *The Moulding of Communists: The Training of the Communist Cadre* (New York, NY: Harcourt, Brace, 1961), 47-57, 156-58.

[25] Transcribed by William Dennis from a speech delivered by Meyer in New York on Nov. 11, 1965. *Ibid.*, xv.

[26] Political scientist Cheng Chen offers a more limited definition of ideology as "any coherent and consistent system of ideas advanced officially by state elites to define and promote a regime identity and mission… that transcends individual leaders, parties, and political generations." The system sets out values and hopes alongside claims about its actual nature and specific outcomes. In other words, an "ideology includes not only a supposedly factual component about the regime's enduring characteristics but also a normative component that justifies and guides regime behavior." Cheng Chen, *The Return of Ideology: The Search for Regime Identities in PostCommunist Russia and* China (Ann Arbor, MI: University of Michigan Press, 2016), 4. There is no reason, however, not to apply this definition to any political group, whether in power or not.

[27] A. James Gregor, *Totalitarianism and Political Religion: An Intellectual History* (Stanford, CA: Stanford University Press, 2012)

[28] Arthur P. Mendel, *Vision and Violence*, edited by Richard Landes (Ann Arbor, MI: University of Michigan Press, 1999), vi.

[29] Vladimir Bukovsky, *Judgment in Moscow: Soviet Crimes and Western Complicity* (Los Angeles, CA: Ninth of November Press, 2019)

[30] Landes, *op. cit.,* 175.

[31] Robert S. Wistrich, "Judeophobia and Marxism," *Commentary*, December 1, 2014. https:// www.commentarymagazine.com / articles/ judeophobia – and - marxism/

[32] F. A. Hayek, *The Road to Serfdom* (Chicago, IL: The University of Chicago Press, 1994), 46.

[33] *Ibid.*, 153-154.

[34] Landes, *op.cit.*, 11-12.

[35] Dennis Prager and Joseph Telushkin, *Why the Jews?* (New York, NY: Touchstone, 2003), 193-4.

[36] Carus, Paul. *The History of the Devil and the Idea of Evil: From the Earliest Times to the Present Day* (Peaks Pine Publishing. Kindle Edition, 2016), 6.

[37] Frank E. Manuel and Fritzie P. Manuel, *Utopian Thought in the Western World* (Cambridge, MA: Belknap Press, 1982), 5.

[38] *Ibid.,* 11.

[39] Raymond Ruyer, *L'Utopie et les utopies* (Paris, France: Presses Universitaires de France, 1950), 9.

[40] *Utopian Thought*, 13.

[41] *Ibid.,* 14.

[42] "The psychological roots of the paradise myth and of millenarian hope, never to be divorced from the Apocalypse – with its dual prophecies of terror and salvation – are so profound that their existence may sometimes be taken for granted or overlooked." *Ibid.,* 33.

[43] Juliana Geran Pilon, *Soulmates: Resurrecting Eve*, (Piscataway, NJ: Transaction Publishers, 2013), 6.

[44] Northrop Frye, *The Great Code: The Bible as Literature* (Orlando, FL.: Harcourt Brace Jovanowich, 1983), 32-33.

[45] See Aaron Lynch*, Thought Contagion: How Belief Spreads Through Society* (New York, NY: Basic Books, 1999) and Susan J. Blackmore, The Meme Machine (Oxford: Oxford University Press, 1999).

[46] James C. Scott, *Domination and the Arts of Resistance* (New Haven, CT: Yale University Press, 1992), 38.

[47] Landes, *op. cit.*, 10. He cites here Lee Quinby*, Anti-Apocalypse: Exercises in Genealogical Criticism* (Minneapolis, MN: University of Minnesota Press, 1994).

[48] *Ibid.* 10-11. Landes cites Daniel C. Dennett, *Breaking the Spell: Religion as a Natural Phenomenon* (New York, NY: Viking, 2006).

[49] Sir James George Fraser, *The Golden Bough* (New York, NY: Macmillan Publishing Co., 1953), 303.

[50] *Ibid.,* 304-5.

[51] In Greek mythology, the Titans were gods who preceded the Olympian deities.

[52] Carus, *op. cit.*, 107.

[53] "When Azazel began to be neglected, Satan rose into existence. The belief in a God of Evil was replaced by the belief in all evil demon." Carus, *op. cit.,* 45.

[54] For links to different translations, see http://biblehub.com/genesis/11-1.htm

[55] Leon Kass, *The Beginning of Wisdom: Reading Genesis* (Chicago, IL: University of Chicago Press, 2003), 223.

[56] *Ibid.*, 231. Emphasis added.

[57] *Ibid.*, 233.

[58] *Ibid.*, 235-6.

[59] *Ibid.*, 237.

[60] *Ibid.*

[61] Franz Kafka, *Parables and Paradoxes* (New York, NY: Schocken Books, 1961), 35.

[62] Ronald Hendel, "Tower of Babel: The Hidden Transcript," *The Torah: A Historical and Contextual Approach,* Oct. 19, 2014 http://thetorah.com/ tower-of-babel-the-hidden-transcript/

[63] As reference for the concept of "hidden transcripts," Hendel cites James C. Scott: *Domination and the Arts of Resistance: Hidden Transcripts* (New Haven, CT: Yale University Press, 1990)

[64] *Ibid.*

[65] Though all Apocalypses unveil heavenly secrets, only some relate to the future. See Christopher Rowland, C. R. A. Morray-Jones, *The Mystery of God: Early Jewish Mysticism and the New Testament* (Leiden, the Netherlands: Brill, 2009), xvii.

[66] See Elaine Pagels, *Revelations: Visions, Prophecy, and Politics in the Book of Revelation* (New York, NY: Penguin Books, 2012)

[67] *Daniel,* 7: 13-14.

[68] For comments on differences between Daniel and John, see *The Mystery of God, op. cit.,* 90.

[69] "Daniel's beasts from the sea... become in John's vision a terrible epitome of all that is most oppressive on earth. This unique example in the early Christian literature of the apocalyptic genre is profoundly indebted to Jewish apocalyptic and mystical ideas." *Ibid.*, 65.

[70] The term "zealot," the common translation of the Hebrew kanai (קנאי, frequently used in plural form, קנאים, kana'im), means one who is zealous on behalf of God. The term derives from Greek ζηλωτής (zelotes), "emulator, zealous admirer or follower." As the Zealots advocated violence, the Talmud also refers to them as Biryonim (בריונים) meaning "boorish", "wild", or "ruffians."

[71] Paul Johnson, *A History of Christianity* (New York, NY: Simon & Schuster, 1976), 255-6.

[72] *Ibid.,* 256.

[73] Mendel, *op. cit.,* 43. Emphasis added.

[74] Or maybe resin. See R. Davidson, *The Cambridge Bible Commentary on the New English Bible: Genesis 1-11* (Cambridge, U.K.: Cambridge University Press, 1973), 31-35.

[75] "This giving of a name is an Old Testament way of declaring man's power over the rest of creation; it is the J parallel to the theme of man's dominion which is heard in the creation hymn in Gen. 1: 26-7." *Ibid.,* 37.

[76] For a detailed discussion of this concept, see Pilon, *Soulmates,* esp. part I.

[77] Clarence H. Miller, in Thomas More, *Utopia* (New Haven, CT.: Yale University Press, 2001), 1.

[78] Dominic Baker-Smith takes exception to that view: "In spite of the common tendency to interpret *Utopia* as a social blue-print, it seems more helpful to view it as a 'spiritual exercise': the imaginative engagement with a model which can modify our attitudes and even qualify our conduct." Dominic Baker-Smith, "Thomas More," Edward N. Zalta, ed., *The Stanford Encyclopedia of Philosophy* (Spring 2014 Edition), https://plato.stanford.edu/archives/spr2014/entries/thomas-more/

[79] Richard Marius, *Thomas More: A Biography* (New York, NY: Vintage Books, 1985), 77.

[80] In the teaching of the Roman Catholic Church, an indulgence is "a way to reduce the amount of punishment one has to undergo for sins." It may reduce the "temporal punishment for sin" after death (as opposed to the eternal punishment merited by mortal sin), in the state or process of purification called Purgatory. In 1517, Pope Leo X offered indulgences for those who gave alms to rebuild St. Peter's Basilica in Rome; the campaign was especially heavy-handed. See Edward Peters, *A Modern Guide to Indulgences: Rediscovering This Often Misinterpreted Teaching* (Chicago, IL: Liturgy Training Publications, 2008), 13.

[81] More, *op. cit.,* 46.

[82] *Ibid.,* 47.

[83] *Ibid.,* 44.

[84] Pieter Gillis (1486 -1533), also known as Peter Giles, was a humanist, printer, and secretary to the city of Antwerp in the early sixteenth century, friend of More and Erasmus.

[85] *Ibid.*

[86] More, *op. cit.,* 46-47. Marius cites Diogenes Laertius's report that "the Arcadians and Thebans, when they were founding Megalopolis, invited Plato to be their legislator; but... when he discovered that they were opposed to equality of possessions, he refused to go." *Ibid.,* 151.

[87] *Ibid.,* 82.

[88] *Ibid.,* 83-84

[89] R. W. Chambers, *Thomas More* (London, U.K.: Endeavor Press, 1935).

[90] *Ibid.*

[91] Historian Peter Garnsey shows that Aristotle had been the first to interpret Plato – incorrectly - as supporting equality of property in the Republic: "Plato was

credited, from Aristotle on, with a utopian regime involving a community-wide sharing of everything." Peter Garnsey, *Thinking About Property: From Antiquity to the Age of Revolution* (Cambridge, U.K.: Cambridge University Press, 2007), 25. He charges that More's *Utopia* not only continues that tradition but seems to have ushered in "a new phase in the manipulation of the political thought of Plato, which culminates in the modern period when Plato becomes a weapon, or a victim, in the ideological warfare between Left and Right." *Ibid.,* 58.

[92] Cited in Garnsey, *ibid.,* 56.

[93] More, *op. cit.,* 22.

[94] *Ibid.,* 67.

[95] Garnsey, *op. cit.,* 57.

[96] Marius, *op. cit.,* 160.

[97] *Ibid.,* 78.

[98] The celebrated film critic Roger Ebert called it "one of the greatest of all films, because it pushes beyond the others, into the dark places of the soul. It is not about war so much as about how war reveals truths we would be happy never to discover." Roger Ebert, "Apocalypse Now," *RogerEbert.com*, Nov. 28, 1999. https://www.rogerebert.com/reviews/ great-movie-Apocalypse-now-1979

[99] "The 10 Best Apocalypse Movies of All Time," *Esquire,* Feb. 20, 2017. https://www.esquire.com/uk/culture/news/a12998/10-best-Apocalypse-movies-of-all-time/

[100] Luciano Pellicani, *Revolutionary Apocalypse: Ideological Roots of Terrorism* (New York, NY: Praeger, 2003)

[101] Pipes, *op. cit.,* 17.

[102] Johnson, *op.cit.,* 256.

[103] Writes Pellicani: "There would be no authority, no money, no private property. In a *Tractatus contra errores* on the 'extermination of the evil,' by one of the intellectual leaders of the Taborite [radical Hussite] movement, the powerful and the rich are said to represent evil. There was no alternative but to annihilate the privileged, in order to restore the Kingdom of God. 'Whoever did not join them in 'liberating truth' and destroying sinners was himself a member of the hosts of Satan and Anti-Christ and therefore fit for annihilation.' This meant murdering whoever did not identify with the chosen charismatic community, regardless of social status. The logic of millenarianism and the imperatives of class war soon transformed the community into a theocratic society..." Pellicani, *op. cit.,* 16-17.

[104] Johnson, *op. cit.,* 260.

[105] Pellicani, *op. cit.,* 15.

[106] *Ibid.*

[107] Elizabeth L. Eisenstein, *The Printing Revolution in Early Modern Europe* (Cambridge, UK: University of Cambridge Press, 1983)

[108] Norman Kohn, *The Pursuit of the Millennium: Revolutionary Millenarians and Mystical Anarchists of the Middle Ages* (Oxford, U.K.: Oxford University Press, 1970), 284.

[109] *Ibid.,* 246.

[110] Roland H. Bainton, "Thomas Müntzer, Revolutionary Firebrand of the Reformation," *Sixteenth Century Journal,* vol. XII, No. 2, 1982, 6.

[111] *Ibid.,* 12.

[112] Kohn, *op. cit.,* 247.

[113] Müntzer to the Allstedter, cited in *ibid.,* 247-8.

[114] *Ibid.,* 248.

[115] Frank E. Manuel and Fritzie P. Manuel, *Utopian Thought in the Western World* (Cambridge, MA: Belknap Press, 1982), 201-203.

[116] *Ibid.,* 251.

[117] Marx cites Müntzer's pamphlet against Luther, in *Karl Marx: Early Writings,* translated and edited by T. B. Bottomore (New York, NY: McGraw-Hill, 1964), 37

[118] Cited in Kohn, *op. cit.,* 243-43.

[119] See https : // web.stanford.edu /~ jsabol / certainty / readings / Luther-ChristianNobility.pdf.

[120] For a splendid history of Germany see Christopher Clarck's *Iron Kingdom: The Rise and Downfall of Prussia, 1600-1947* (Cambridge, MA: Harvard University Press, 2006)

[121] Luther, Martin. *On the Jews and Their Lies,* cited in Robert Michael, *Holy Hatred: Christianity, Antisemitism, and the Holocaust* (New York, NY: Palgrave Macmillan, 2006): "In more than a dozen different contexts, Luther associated the Jews with the devil. Jews were 'the devil's people,' 'consigned by the wrath of God to the devil,' 'circumcised physically to the devil,' 'serpents and children of the devil.' Luther recommended that 'Wherever you see a genuine Jew, you may with a good conscience cross yourself and bluntly say: 'There goes a devil incarnate.'" 111.

[122] Michael, *ibid.*

[123] Michael, *ibid.,* 105.

[124] L. Steiman, *Paths to Genocide: Antisemitism in Western History* (New York, NY: Palgrave Macmillan, 1998), 54.

[125] Karl Popper, *The Poverty of Historicism* (New York, NY: Harper & Row, 1964), 85.

[126] "Utopia is a continuation of the humanist tradition forwarded by Erasmus, with the ultimate goal of reforming not only the Church, but Christian society as a whole, specifically England." Julia Nelson, "Sir Thomas More, Christian Humanism and Utopia," *Archive* 2004, 60. https://uwarchive.files.wordpress.com /2010/12/julia-nelson.pdf

[127] More, *op. cit.,* 81.

[128] Stephen Greenblatt, *The Swerve: How the World Became Modern* (New York, NY: W. W. Norton, 2011), 230.

[129] More, *ibid.,* 65-66.

[130] *Ibid.,* 81.

[131] *Ibid.*

[132] Greenblatt, *op. cit.*, 232.

[133] Michael Allen Gillespie, *The Theological Origins of Modernity* (Chicago, IL: University of Chicago Press, 2008) 34.

[134] *Ibid.,* 16-17.

[135] Wistrich, *A Lethal Obsession*, 94.

[136] Hannah Arendt, *On Revolution* (New York, NY: Penguin Books, 1963) 28.

[137] *Ibid.,* 26.

[138] Sandow Birk and Peter S. Hawkins, *Dante's Paradiso* (San Francisco, CA: Chronicle Books, 2005), ix.

[139] Gillespie, *The Theological Origins of Modernity*, 2.

[140] Manuel and Manuel, *op. cit.,* 2.

[141] *Ibid.*

[142] The term is notoriously ambiguous, and historians continue to debate it. A thorough analysis is beyond the scope of this book.

[143] "This is where Knox, and they [the Puritans] disagreed with the leaders in England. All were agreed about the changes in doctrine ... but the *differentia* of Puritanism is that it does not stop at a reformation of doctrine only, but insists that the reformation must be carried through also into the realm of practice." Martyn Lloyd Jones, *John Knox and the Reformation* (Edinburgh, UK: Banner of Truth, 2011), 52-56.

[144] Michael Walzer, *The Revolution of Saints* (New York, NY: Atheneum, 1969), 67.

[145] Pellicani, *op. cit.,* 20.

[146] *Ibid.*

[147] Walzer, *op. cit.* 42.

[148] Pellicani, *ibid.* He cites here Eric Vogelin, *The New Science of Politics* (Chicago, IL: University of Chicago Press, 1952).

[149] Leanda de Lisle reflects on the events in 1649: "Parliament had by then become a monster that devoured its own." *The White King* (New York, NY: Public Affairs, 2017). The most vivid and insightful descriptions of the social, economic, and religious complexities, and sundry personal motivations, fueling discord at the time are found in the superb novels of Walter Scott, notably *Waverley*.

[150] "He had pitted the power of central government against local government to the ultimate disservice of the nation.... He may not have wanted to become an absolute king, but he acted as if that were his intention." Peter Ackroyd, *Rebellion: The History of England from James I to the Glorious Revolution* (New York, NY: St. Martin Griffin, 2014), 470.

[151] The extensive impact of Epicureanism in post-Renaissance and eighteenth-century Europe, have been masterfully documented in the many books by Alan Charles Kors, most recently *Naturalism and Unbelief in France, 1650-1729* (Cambridge, UK: Cambridge University Press, 2016)

[152] Thomas Kuhn, *The Copernican Revolution: Planetary Astronomy in the Development of Western Thought* (Cambridge, MA: Harvard University Press, 1957), 1.

[153] *Ibid.* A fuller history of the Scientific Revolution is eminently worth exploring. It would include the names of the great Galileo Galilei, Johannes Kepler, and countless other giants. See the magnificent, timeless classic *The Mechanization of the World Picture*, by E. J. Dijksterhuis (Oxford: Oxford University Press, 1961)

[154] *Ibid.*, 261. Emphasis added.

[155] Cited in James H. Billington, *Fire in the Minds of Men: Origins of the Revolutionary Faith* (New York, NY: Basic Books, 1980), 18.

[156] *Ibid.*

[157] James Howell, *Parthonopoeia, or the History of the Most Noble and Renowned Kingdom of Naples,* 1654, discussed in Melvin J. Lasky, "The Birth of a Metaphor: On the Origins of Utopia and Revolution, *Encounter*, March 1970, 32.

[158] Billington, *op. cit.*, 19.

[159] *Ibid.*

[160] Jean-Jacques Rousseau, *Ideal Empires and Republics.* See *Rousseau's Social Contract, More's Utopia, Bacon's New Atlantis, Campanella's City of the Sun* (New York, NY: Wm. H. Wise & Co., 1901)

[161] Jean-Jacques Rousseau, *The Social Contract and Discourses*, translated with an introduction by G.D.H. Cole (New York, NY: E. P. Dutton, 1950), 135.

[162] *The Social Contract*, 140.

[163] *Ibid.*, 137.

[164] *Ibid.*, 23.

[165] Billington, *op. cit.*, 20.

[166] *Ibid.*

[167] Gertrude Himmelfarb, *The Roads to Modernity: The British, French, and American Enlightenments* (New York, NY: Vintage, 2007),170.

[168] Cited in Richard Pipes, *Property and Freedom* (New York, NY: Alfred A. Knopf, Inc., 1999), 39.

[169] *Ibid.*

[170] *Ibid.*, 251-2.

[171] *Ibid.*, 293.

[172] Garnsey, *op. cit.*, 165.

[173] *Social Contract*, 18.

[174] Arendt, *op. cit.*, 77.

[175] Denis Diderot, "Natural rights," *The Encyclopedia of Diderot & d'Alembert Collaborative Translation Project.* Translated by Stephen J. Gendzier (Ann Arbor, MI: Michigan Publishing, University of Michigan Library, 2009) http://hdl.handle.net/2027/spo.did2222.0001 Originally published as "Droit naturel," *Encyclopédie ou Dictionnaire raisonné des sciences, des arts et des métiers*, 5:115–116 (Paris, 1755).

[176] Pipes, *op. cit.*, 43.

[177] Alan Bloom, "Jean Jacques Rousseau," in Leo Strauss and Joseph Cropsey, eds., *History of Political Philosophy*, 3rd edition (Chicago, IL: University of Chicago Press, 1987), 570.

[178] Billington, *op. cit.*, 33.

[179] The Abbe Sieyes, a leading voice of the Third Estate, declared that "the printing press has changed the fate of Europe, it will change the fate of the world.... The press is for the immense spaces of today what the voice of the orator was on the public square in Athens and Rome." Billington, *op. cit.*, 33.

[180] Pellicani, *op. cit.*, 32.

[181] *Ibid.*

[182] *Ibid.*, 33.

[183] Cited in Himmelfarb, *op. cit.* 184.

[184] Michael L. Kennedy, *The Jacobin Clubs in the French Revolution, 1793-1795* (New York, NY: Berghahn Books, 2000), 64

[185] *Ibid.*, 65.

[186] Cited in Billington, *op. cit.*, 72.

[187] *Ibid.*

[188] Babeuf, "Manifeste des Plebeiens" and "Le Manifeste des Enrages, » cited in Billington, *ibid.*, 532, footnote 146.

[189] Cited in *Ibid.*, footnote 150.

[190] Billington, *Ibid.*, 72.

[191] Cited in *ibid.*, footnote #162.

[192] Pellicani, *op. cit.*, 40. He cites Babeuf's *Il Tribuno del Popolo* (Rome, Italy: Editori Riuniti, 1969), 252 and 241.

[193] Frank McLynn, *Napoleon: A Biography* (London, UK: Jonathan Cape, 1996), 666.

[194] Victor Davis Hanson, *Between War and Peace: Lessons from Afghanistan to Iraq* (New York, NY: Random House, 2004), 175.

[195] Alexander Grab, *Napoleon and the Transformation of Europe* (New York, NY: Palgrave, 2003) xii.

[196] Billington, *op. cit.*, 87.

[197] Gauchet, "Right and Left," in Pierre Nora, ed., *Realms of Memory: Conflicts and divisions*, vol. 1 (New York, NY: Columbia University Press, 1996), 241.

[198] *Ibid.*

[199] *Ibid.*

[200] *Ibid.*, 245

[201] Ronald Schechter, *Obstinate Hebrews: Representations of Jews in France, 1715-1815* (Berkeley and Los Angeles, CA: University of California Press, 2003), 150-193.

[202] *Ibid.*, 158.

[203] *Ibid.*, 162-163.

[204] Gauchet, *op. cit.*, 249.

[205] *Ibid.*, 253.

[206] *Ibid.,* 253 #51

[207] Robert Wistrich, *From Ambivalence to Betrayal*, 70.

[208] Voltaire, Theodore Besterman trans., *Philosophical Dictionary* (London, UK: Penguin Books, 1971), 144.

[209] Paul Johnson, "Marxism vs. Antisemitism," *Commentary*, April 1, 1984. https:// www.commentarymagazine.com / articles/marxism-vs-the-jews/

[210] *Ibid.*, 71.

[211] Michele Battini, *Socialism of Fools: Capitalism and Modern Anti-Semitism* (New York, NY: Columbia University Press, 2016), 3.

[212] *Ibid.*, 33.

[213] *Ibid.,* 72.

[214] Billington, *op. cit.*, 80.

[215] *Ibid.*, 81.

[216] Restif's first novel, published in 1769, that featured a foot fetish, was followed by a defense of prostitutes, complete with a plethora of sexual facts and fantasies, entitled *Le Pornographe*, published in 1779. His many ensuing descriptions of nightly adventures along the streets of Paris were likely no more edifying.

[217] *Karl Marx: Early Writings, op. cit.,* 174.

[218] *Ibid.*, 179.

[219] *Ibid.*, 193.

[220] Pellicani, *op. cit.*, 77.

[221] *Ibid.,* 93.

[222] Leszek Kolakowski, *Main Currents of Marxism: Its Rise, Growth, and Dissolution*, Volume I: *The Founders*, translated by P. S. Falla (Oxford, UK: Clarendon Press, 1978), 219.

[223] Kolakowski, *op. cit.*, 187.

[224] Lewis S. Feuer, ed., *Marx & Engels: Basic Writings on Politics & Philosophy*, (New York, NY: Doubleday Co., 1959), 3-4.

[225] *Ibid.,* 4.

[226] *Ibid.*

[227] Mendel, *op. cit.* 141.

[228] Cited in Mendel, *ibid.,* 145.

[229] *Ibid.*, 143.

[230] Marx and Engels were deeply influenced by Hegel, even if they thought of history not as an evolution of mere subjective "ideas" but rather of concrete, or presumably objective "material" events, which were further reduced to economic conditions. Explains historian O. D. Skelton: "The present conflict [according to Marx] is to be the last, the victorious proletariat will have no inferior to oppress, and will usher in a class-less commonwealth, where the wicked will cease from troubling and the fighters be at rest. This eschatological side of the Marxist theory is, in all probability, not so much a theological echo as yet another illustration of Hegelian influence, the final cessation of class struggle being a deduction from

the Hegelian postulate of the final reconcilement of the dialectic conflict in the attainment of an absolute synthesis. Only the teleological optimism of the Hegelian formula can explain Marx's assumption that the clash of classes would lead, not to chaos and relapse to lower levels, as has happened before in the world's history, but to the triumph of the oppressed and living happy ever after in classless Eden." O. D. Skelton, *Socialism: A Critical Analysis* (New York, NY: Houghton Mifflin Co., 1911), 113.

[231] Feuer, *op. cit.,* 20.

[232] *Ibid.,* 41.

[233] *Ibid.,* 29.

[234] Pellicani, *op. cit.,* 82. The letter from Marx is cited in Domenico Settembrini, *Il labirinto marxista* (Milan, Italy: Rizzoli, 1975), 333.

[235] *Ibid.*

[236] Ibid., 86. Domenico Settembrini, "Anarchismo, marxismo e cristianesimo" in *Socialismo e rivolutione dopo Marx* (Naples, Italy: Guida, 1974), 101.

[237] Andrei Sinyavsky, *Soviet Civilization: A Cultural History* (New York, NY: Arcade Publishing, 1988), 3-4.

[238] *Ibid.*

[239] *Ibid*, 7.

[240] Edmund Silberner, "Was Marx an Anti-Semite?" in Ezra Mendelsohn, ed., *Essential Papers on Jews and the Left* (New York, NY: New York University Press, 1997), 389. Michael Ezra notes that "[i]n a review of the recently published book, *Antisemitic Myths: A Historical and Contemporary Anthology,* edited by Marvin Perry and Frederick M. Schweitzer, David Hirsh has argued that it is a 'standard misreading' of Marx to say that 'Marx was an antisemite.' With this, he concurs with Robert Fine, who attempted to "explode the myth" of Marx's antisemitism. As far as Professor Fine is concerned, those who believe this 'myth' have an 'inability' to read Marx or comprehend Marx's 'ironic style' of writing." Ezra convincingly disagrees: "When considering Marx and his views towards Jews, one must go further than his infamous essay, his correspondence also needs to be considered. Marx used the Bambergers to borrow money but showed contempt for them. In a derogatory fashion he referred to the father and son as 'Jew Bamberger' or 'little Jew Bamberger.' Similarly, Spielmann, whose name appears frequently in correspondence between Marx and Engels was referred to as 'Jew Spielmann.' When on holiday in Ramsgate in 1879, Marx reported to Engels that the resort contained "many Jews and fleas." In an earlier letter to Engels, Marx referred to Ferdinand Lassalle as a 'Jewish nigger.' Professor Fine has not discussed this but I do not see such comments as 'witty' or 'ironic,' they are simply racist." "Karl Marx's Radical Antisemitism," *The Philosophers' Magazine*, March 23, 2015. https://www.philosophersmag.com/opinion/30-karl-marx-s-radical-antisemitism

[241] *Ibid.,* 394.

[242] Paul Johnson, "Marxism vs. Antisemitism," *op. cit.*

243 Bottomore, *op. cit.,* esp. pp. 36-40.

244 Johnson, *op. cit.*

245 Jerry Z. Muller, *Capitalism and the Jews* (Princeton, NJ: Princeton University Press, 2011) 42.

246 *Ibid.,* 41.

247 Battini, *op. cit.,* 43.

248 *Ibid.,* 50.

249 Pellicani, *op. cit.,* 101.

250 See Nial Fergusson's *The Ascent of Money: A Financial History* (New York, NY: Penguin Books, 2009), and *The House of Rothschild* (New York, NY: Penguin Books, 1999), both superb.

251 Michail Bakunin, "Rapports personnels avec Marx," cited in Robert S. Wistrich, *A Lethal Obsession: Antisemitism from Antiquity to the Global Jihad* (New York, NY: Random House, 2010) 12.

252 "Pogrom is a Russian word which, when directly translated, means "to wreak havoc." Pogroms typically describe violence by Russian authorities against Jewish people, particularly officially-mandated slaughter, though the word has been extended to the massacres of other groups as well." https://www.history.com/topics/russia/pogroms

253 Cited in Wistrich, *A Lethal Obsession,* 113.

254 Boris Sapir, "Jewish Socialists Around *Vpered*," in *International Review of Social History*, 1965, 383.

255 See Lucy Dawidowicz, *The Golden Tradition: Jewish Life and Thought in Eastern Europe* (New York, NY: Holt, Rinehart and Winston, 1967), 406.

256 Wistrich, *A Lethal Obsession*, 114.

257 Cited in Billington, *op. cit.*, 351.

258 *Ibid.,* 267.

259 Bottomore, *op. cit.,* 245.

260 Kolakowski, *op. cit.,* 375.

261 Sinyavsky, *op. cit.*, 43.

262 Lenin, *op. cit.,* 21.

263 *Ibid.*

264 Cited in Pellicani, *op. cit.*, 97.

265 Karl Marx, *What Is To Be Done?* (1902; Marxist Internet Archive), 15. https://www.marxists.org/archive/lenin/works/download/what-itd.pdf

266 Rosa Luxemburg, *Selected Political Writings* (London, UK: Cape, 1972), cited in Pellicani, *op. cit.*, 112.

267 Pellicani, *op. cit.*, 106.

268 Rett R. Ludwikowski, *The Crisis of Communism: Its Meaning, Origins, and Phases* (McLean, VA: Pergamon-Brassey's, 1986), 9.

269 Pellicani, *op. cit.*, 108.

270 Sean McMeekin, *The Russian Revolution: A New History* (New York, NY: Basic Books, 2017), xvi.

[271] *Ibid.*, 127.

[272] *Ibid.,* 128.

[273] *Ibid.*, 134.

[274] *Ibid.,* 346.

[275] Stéphane Courtois, "Introduction: The Crimes of Communism," in Jean-Louis Panne *et al.,* eds., *The Black Book of Communism: Crimes, Terror, Repression* (Cambridge, MA: Harvard University Press, 1999), 8.

[276] Paul Hollander *The October Revolution of 1917: Its Significance, Aftermath and Western Perceptions,* speech delivered on November 8, 2017, at the Victims of Communism conference commemorating the 100th anniversary of the Russian Revolution, Washington, DC.

[277] *Ibid.*

[278] *Ibid.,* 12

[279] *The Black Book of Communism, op. cit.,* 8.

[280] *Ibid.*, 13.

[281] *Ibid.*

[282] *Ibid.*, 15. Emphasis added.

[283] Pellicani, *op. cit.*, 247.

[284] Cited in *ibid.*

[285] Ibid., 248.

[286] Chang, *op. cit.*, 453.

[287] *Ibid.*

[288] John Gittings, "Reporting China since the 1960s," in Lionel Jensen & Timothy Weston, eds., *China in Transformation: the stories beyond the headlines* (Lanham, MD: Rowman & Littlefield, 2006) http://johngittings.tripod.com/id32. html

[289] *Ibid.*

[290] Chang, *op. cit.*, 559.

[291] Bukovsky, *op. cit.*, chapter 3, sec. 3.1.

[292] *Ibid.*

[293] For an insightful overview of Jewish conceptions of history, see Eric Mechoulan, "What Is the Meaning of Jewish History?" *Mosaic Magazine*, Aug. 6, 2018. https://mosaicmagazine.com / essay/2018 / 08 / what-is-the-meaning-of-jewish-history/

[294] See especially Mircea Eliade, *The Sacred and the Profane: The Nature of Religion* (Chicago, IL: University of Chicago Press, 1968), along with many other writings.

[295] Arthur P. Mendel, *op. cit.,* 102-103.

[296] Mircea Eliade, *Cosmos and History: The Myth of the Eternal Return* (New York, NY: Harper & Row, 1959), 145-149.

[297] Robert Nisbet, *History of the Idea of Progress* (New York, NY: Basic Books, 1980), 5. (Italics in original)

[298] Ronald J. Pestritto and William J. Atto, *American Progressivism* (Lanham, MD: Rowman & Littlefield,2008), 5. "This reflects a sea change that had occurred in American higher education in the second half of the nineteenth century.... By 1900, the faculties of American colleges and universities had become populated with European Ph.D.s, and the historical thinking that dominated Europe (especially Germany) in the nineteenth century came to permeate American higher education. Johns Hopkins University, founded in 1876, was established for the express reason of bringing the German educational model to the United States and produced several prominent progressives, including Wilson, Dewey, and Frederick Jackson Turner." 5-6.

[299] Woodrow Wilson, "Socialism and Democracy, August 22, 1887," *Papers of Woodrow Wilson*, Arthur S. Link, ed. (Princeton, NJ: Princeton University Press, 1966 – 1993), volume 5, p. 561.

[300] Commonly referring to 1890 -1920. https://www2.gwu.edu/ ~ erpapers /teachinger/glossary/progressive-era.cfm

[301] Jane Addams, "The Subjective Necessity for Social Settlements," in *American Progressivism, op. cit.,* 99-106.

[302] Georg Hegel, *Philosophy of History*, "The Embodiment Spirit Assumes," par. 41. https://www.marxists.org/reference/archive/hegel/ works/hi/history4.htm

[303] Walter Rauschenbusch, "Christianizing the Social Order," *ibid.*, 118.

[304] Edward Alsworth Ross, *Social Control* (New York, NY: Macmillan Co., 1901). Cited in Paul C Violas, "Progressive Social Philosophy: Charles Horton Cooley and Edward Alsworth Ross," in C.J. Karier, P. C. Violas, and J. Spring. eds., *Roots of Crisis: American Education in the 20th Century* (Chicago, IL: Rand McNally, 1973). 40–65.

[305] Murray N. Rothbard, *The Progressive Era and the Family*, in Joseph R. Peden and Fred R. Glahe, eds., *The American Family and the State* (San Francisco, CA: Pacific Research Institute, 1986), https://mises.org/library/ progressive-era-and-family

[306] *Ibid.*, 11.

[307] The word was coined by Pierre Teilhard de Chardin, in *The Phenomenon of Man* (New York, NY: Harper & Row, 1961).

[308] Herbert Croly, *Progressive Democracy* (New York, NY: The Macmillan Company, 1914), 167.

[309] Theodore Roosevelt, "The Right of the People to Rule," *ibid.*, 254.

[310] John Locke, *Second Treatise on Government*, VII.87.

[311] Roger Pilon, "The United States Constitution: From Limited Government to Leviathan," *Economic Education Bulletin*, Vol. XLV No. 12, Dec. 2005, 10. https://object.cato.org/sites/cato.org/files/articles/CT05 .pdf

[312] Theodore Roosevelt, "What is a Progressive?" in Pestritto and Atto, *op. cit.*, 44.

[313] *Ibid.*, 36.

[314] Peter Ackroyd, *Rebellion*, 435. The first British parties represented a mix of religious and secular positions.

[315] Richard Hofstadter, *The Idea of a Party System: The Rise of Legitimate Opposition in the United States, 1780-1840* (Chicago, IL: University of Chicago Press, 1970), 4.

[316] Lenin, *op. cit.*, 59.

[317] Woodrow Wilson, "The Study of Administration," in Pestritto and Atto, *op. cit.*, 197.

[318] Herbert Croly, "Progressive Democracy," *ibid.*, 267.

[319] "Progressive Party Platform, 1912," *ibid.*, 274.

[320] "Wilson and Roosevelt," *New Republic*, November 4, 1916; reprinted on June 24, 2002. https://newrepublic.com/article/92253/wilson-and-roosevelt

[321] TR confessed his fondness for this West African proverb in a letter to Henry L. Sprague, dated January 26, 1900. Its ambiguity is treacherous, lending itself to easy misinterpretation as implying a preference for the stick as against the soft speech.

[322] Henry Kissinger, *Diplomacy* (New York, NY: Touchstone Books, 1994), 49.

[323] *Ibid.*, 40.

[324] Woodrow Wilson, Annual Message to Congress, December 8, 1914, in Arthur S. Link, ed., *Papers of Woodrow Wilson* (Princeton, NJ: Princeton University Press, 1996 -) vol. 31, 423.

[325] John Maynard Keynes, *The Economic Consequences of the Peace* (New York, NY: Penguin Books, 1995), 44.

[326] *Ibid.*, 41.

[327] *American Progressivism, op. cit.*, 307.

[328] Margaret McMillan, *Paris 1919: Six Months that Changed the World* (New York, NY: Random House, 2002), 11. Emphasis added.

[329] *Ibid.*, 317-322.

[330] *Ibid.*, 14-15.

[331] Cited in David Fromkin, *A Peace to End All Peace: The Fall of the Ottoman Empire and the Creation of the Modern Middle East* (New York, NY: Henry Holt & Co, 1989), 262.

[332] *Ibid.*

[333] See for example Pieter M. Judson, *The Habsburg Empire: A New History* (Cambridge, MA: Belknap Harvard University Press, 2016)

[334] Woodrow Wilson, *The State* (Boston, MA: D. C. Heath and Co., 1889), 2-3. Cited in Ronald J. Pestritto, *Woodrow Wilson and the Roots of Modern Liberalism* (Lapham, MD: Rowman & Littlefield, 2005), 43.

[335] *Ibid.*, 44-45.

[336] Roosevelt, "The New Nationalism," in Pestrito and Atto, *American Progressivism*, 214-15.

[337] Ronald Pestritto, "Founding Liberalism, Progressive Liberalism, and the Rights of Property," *Social Philosophy & Policy*, Oxford, Vol. 28, Issue 2, Jul 2011, 56-73.

[338] Theodore Roosevelt, *The Strenuous Life: Essays and Addresses* (New York, 1900), 29. Cited in Eric L. Goldstein, "The Unstable Other: Locating the Jew in Progressive-Era American Racial Discourse," *American Jewish History*, Vol. 89, No. 4, The Jew as "Other" in America (December 2001), 391.

[339] *Ibid.*, 405.

[340] Thomas C. Leonard, "More Merciful and Not Less Effective: Eugenics and Progressive-Era American Economics," *History of Political Economy* 2003, 35(4), 709-34.

[341] Luca Fiorito and Cosma Orsi, "Anti-Semitism and Progressive Era Social Science: The Case of John R. Commons," *Quaderni Del Dipartimento De Economia Politica e Statistica*, n. 658, Oct. 2012.

[342] Usually referring to the period 1890 to 1920, but see John D. Buenker, John C. Burnham, and Robert M. Crunden, *Progressivism* (Cambridge, MA: Schenkman, 1977)

[343] *Buck v. Bell*, 274 US 200 (1927) https: // supreme.justia.com / cases / federal/us/274/200/case.html

[344] Adam Cohen, *Imbeciles: The Supreme Court, Eugenics, and the Sterilization of Carrie Buck* (New York, NY: 2016) offers a heartrending account of this tragic case, as well as a good overview of the eugenics movement.

[345] *Ibid.*, 16.

[346] *Ibid.*, 32.

[347] *Ibid.*, 55-56.

[348] *Ibid.*

[349] James W. Trent, Jr., *Inventing the Feeble Mind: A History of Mental Retardation in the United States* (Oxford: Oxford University Press, 2016), 166

[350] Theodore Roosevelt, "Twisted Eugenics," *The Outlook*, January 3, 1914, 31.

[351] *Ibid.*, 32.

[352] "Consider Popenoe and Johnson's very successful *Applied Eugenics* (1918), published as part of the Social Science textbook series edited by Richard T. Ely. Popenoe and Johnson argued for legislation that would abolish child labor and provide education for all children, quintessentially progressive policies. But compulsory education and child labor bans, for Popenoe and Johnson, were desirable because the unfit poor would be unable to put their children to work and thus would have fewer children, a eugenic goal. Indeed, Popenoe and Johnson opposed free school lunches and textbooks for the poor on the grounds that subsidies of books and lunches would lower the cost of child rearing and thereby increase the number of children born to the unfit." Thomas C. Leonard, "Eugenics and Economics in the Progressive Era," *Journal of Economic Perspectives,* Volume 19, Number 4, Fall 2005, 220.

[353] Art Carden and Steven Horwitz, "Eugenics: Progressivism's Ultimate Social Engineering," Foundation for Economic Education, Sept. 21, 2011 https://fee.org/articles/eugenics-progressivisms-ultimate-social-engineering/

[354] *Ibid.*

[355] *Ibid.* Sidney James Webb, 1st Baron Passfield (1859 – 1947) had been a British socialist and member of the Labor Party. He and his famous wife Beatrice never wavered in their support of the Soviet Union even long after its long list of crimes became common knowledge.

[356] Mendel, *op. cit.,* 117.

[357] Edwin Black, *War Against the Weak: Eugenics and America's Campaign to Create a Master Race* (New York, NY: Dialog Press, 2012), xvi.

[358] *Ibid.,* xviii.

[359] Garland E. Allen, "Was Nazi eugenics created in the US*?"* *European Molecular Biology Organization* (EMBO) reports, VCL 5, No. 5, 2004, 451-452.

[360] *Ibid.*

[361] Daniel Okrent, *The Guarded Gate: Bigotry, Eugenics and the Law That Kept Two Generations of Jews, Italians, and Other European Immigrants Out of America* (New York, NY: Scribner, 2019)

[362] *Ibid.,* 318.

[363] "The growth of fascism would not have been possible without the revolt against the Enlightenment and the French Revolution which swept across Europe at the end of the nineteenth century and the beginning of the twentieth." Zeev Sternhell with Mario Sznajder and Maia Asheri, *The Birth of Fascist Ideology: From Cultural Rebellion to Political Revolution* (Princeton, NY: Princeton University Press, 1994), 3.

[364] "The experience of World War I was the most decisive immediate precondition for fascism." Paxton, *op. cit.,* 28.

[365] Luciano Pellicani, "Fascism, capitalism, modernity," *European Journal of Political Theory* 11(4), 2012, 405.

[366] Franz Neumann, *Behemoth: The Structure and Practice of National Socialism, 1933-1944* (Oxford: Oxford University Press, 1944), 39.

[367] Robert O. Paxton, *The Anatomy of Fascism* (New York, NY: Vintage Books, 2005), 231.

[368] *Ibid.*

[369] George L. Mosse, *The Fascist Revolution: Toward a General Theory of Fascism* (New York, NY: Howard Fertig, 1999), 6.

[370] See Judson, *The Habsburg Empire.*

[371] Sternhell, *op. cit.,* 10.

[372] E. Corradini,"Il nazionalismo e I sindacati,"a speech given on 16 March 1919 at the Nationalist Congress in Rome, *Discorsi politici (1902–1923)* (Florence, Italy: Vallechi Editore, 1923), 421., cited in Sternhell, *op. cit.,* 11.

[373] *Ibid.*

[374] Mosse, *op. cit.,* 7.

[375] Georges Sorel, "For Lenin," *Soviet Russia,* Official Organ of The Russian Soviet Government Bureau Vol. II April 1920, (New York, NY: Official Organ of The Russian Soviet Government Bureau), 356.

[376] Jacob L. Talmon, *The Myth of the Nation and the Vision of Revolution: The Origins of Ideological Polarization in the 20th Century* (New York, NY: Routledge, 2017) 451. Sorel's March 1921 conversations with Jean James Variot, published in Variot's *Propos de Georges Sorel* (Paris: Gallimard, 1935).

[377] Reza Taghizadeh, "The Unlikely Partnership Of Venezuela And Iran," *RadioFreeEurope/Radio Liberty,* Oct. 18, 2010. https://www.rferl.org/a/The_Unlikely_Partnership_Of_Venezuela_And_Iran/2193900.html

[378] Georges Sorel, *Reflections on Violence,* transl. by T. E. Hulme (London: George Allen & Unwin, 1915) 33.

[379] *Ibid.*

[380] *Ibid.*

[381] *Ibid.*, 35.

[382] *Ibid.*

[383] *Ibid.*, 36. This is not to imply that Sorel endorses all violence, only the revolutionary kind.

[384] Concludes Sternhell: "From being a heavy, ossified, and powerless machine, Marxism, revised, improved, and completed by Sorel, had now become an impressive mobilizing force." *Op. cit.,* 64.

[385] *Ibid.*

[386] *Ibid.,* 30.

[387] Sternhell, *op. cit.* 239-40.

[388] *Ibid.*, 242.

[389] See R. J. B. Bosworth, *Mussolini* (London: Arnold Publishers, 2002), 70. Also Sternhell, *ibid.*, 34.

[390] Anthony James Gregor, *Young Mussolini and the Intellectual Origins of Fascism* (Berkeley and Los Angeles, CA: University of California Press, 1979), 46

[391] *Ibid.*, 41.

[392] Emilio Gentile, cited in Gregor, *Totalitarian Movements, op.cit.*, 326-375.

[393] *Ibid.*, 340.

[394] Charles Burdett, "Italian Fascism and utopia," *History of the Human Sciences,* Vol. 16, No. 1, 2003, 101.

[395] *Ibid.,* 94-95.

[396] Benito Mussolini, "The Doctrine of Fascism," *Fascism Doctrine and Institutions* (Rome: Ardita Publishers, 1935), Appendix, par. 22.

[397] *Ibid.*, par. 17

[398] *Ibid.*, par. 11.

[399] *Ibid.*, par. 7.

[400] *Ibid.,* par. 3.

[401] *Ibid.,* 18.

[402] *Ibid.*, 3.

[403] *Ibid.*, 11.

[404] *Ibid.*, 10.

[405] *Ibid.*, 3.

[406] Gentile, *op. cit.*, 356. For the apocalyptic interpretation of modernity as one of the characteristics typical of totalitarian movements after the First World War, see E. Gentile, "Un apocalisse nella modernità: La Grande Guerra e il Mito della Rigenerazione della politica," *Storia contemporanea* 26/5 (1995).733–87.

[407] Burdett, *op. cit.*, 95-96.

[408] For a brilliant study of the German context, see Christopher Clark, *Iron Kingdom: The Rise and Downfall of Prussia, 1600-1947* (Cambridge, MA: Harvard University Press, 2009)

[409] *Ibid.*, 11.

[410] Mosse, *The Fascist Revolution*, 10.

[411] Pellicani, *op. cit.*, 402.

[412] Robert S. Wistrich, *A Lethal Obsession, op.cit.*, 14.

[413] Bernard Lewis, "The New Antisemitism," *The American Scholar*, Vol. 75, No. 1, Winter 2006, 25-33.

[414] Wistrich, *op. cit.*, 19.

[415] Helen Fein, ed., *The Persisting Question: Sociological Perspectives and Social Contexts of Modern Antisemitism* (Berlin, Germany: Walter de Gruyter, 1987), 110.

[416] Wistrich, *op. cit.*, 19-20.

[417] Philippe Burrin, "Nazi Antisemitism: Animalization and Demonization," in Robert S. Wistrich, ed., *Demonizing the Other: Antisemitism, Racism, and Xenophobia* (Amsterdam, The Netherlands: Harwood Academic Publishers, 1999), 223-35.

[418] Wistrich, *op. cit.*, 20.

[419] Uriel Tal, *Religion, Politics, and Ideology in the Third Reich: Selected Essays* (London: Routledge, 2004), 33-35.

[420] See Isaac Eisenstein Barzilay, "The Jew in the Literature of the Enlightenment," *Jewish Social Studies* 18, no. 4, 1956, 243-61.

[421] First published in *Deutsch-Franzosische Jahrbucher* (1844) https://www.marxists.org/archive/marx/works/1844/df-jahrbucher/outlines.htm

[422] Jerry Z. Muller, *Capitalism and the Jews* 334.

[423] Karl Marx, "Theses on Feurbach," first published as an appendix to *Ludwig Feuerbach and the End of Classical German Philosophy* in 1888; https://www.marxists.org/archive/marx/works/1845/theses/theses. pdf

[424] Walter Zwi Bacharach, "Antisemitism and Racism in Nazi Ideology," in Michael Berenbaum, ed., *The Holocaust and History: The Known, the Unknown, the Disputed, and the Reexamined* (Bloomington, IN: Indiana University Press, 1998), 64-74.

[425] Muller cites Stefi Jersch-Wenzel, "Legal Status and Emancipation," in Michael Meyer, ed., *German-Jewish History in Modern Times*, vol. 2 (New York, NY: Columbia University Press, 1997), 31.

[426] Bacharach, *op. cit.*

[427] See David Nirenberg, *Anti-Judaism: The Western Tradition* (New York, NY: W. W. Norton, 2014), for a superb history of the concept of "judaism" as referring to ideas and habits independent of actual Jews.

[428] Adolf Hitler, *Mein Kampf*, James Murphy, trans. (CreateSpace Independent Publishing Platform, 2011), 61.

[429] *Ibid.*, 297.

[430] *Ibid.*

[431] *Ibid.*, 61,

[432] *Ibid.*, 369

[433] Eberhard Jäckel, *Hitler's Weltanschauung: A Blueprint for Power* (Cambridge, MA: Harvard University Press, 1981), 53.

[434] Bachrach, *op. cit.*

[435] Eugen Fischer, *Zeitschrift für Morphologie und Anthropologie* 24 (1933), cited in *ibid.*

[436] Mosse, *op. cit.*, 4.

[437] *Ibid.*, 34-35.

[438] *Ibid.*, 17.

[439] *Ibid.*, 36.

[440] Fritz Stern, *The Politics of Cultural Despair: A Study in the Rise of the Germanic Ideology* (Berkeley and Los Angeles, CA: University of California Press, 1961), 63.

[441] Mosse, *op. cit.*, 140.

[442] *Ibid.*, 9.

[443] https://www.marxists.org/archive/marx/works/1844/jewish-question/

[444] Pellicani, *"Fascism, capitalism, modernity," op. cit.*, 395,

[445] Ludwig von Mises, *Omnipotent Government: The Rise of Total State and Total War* (1944), chapter 7, reprinted by the Foundation for Economic Education, March 10, 2016 https://fee.org/resources/the-economic-policy-of-the-nazis/

[446] *Ibid.*

[447] *Ibid.*, 403.

[448] *Ibid.*, 404.

[449] Avraham Barkai, *Nazi Economics: Ideology, Theory, and Policy* (New Haven, CT: Yale University Press, 1990), 13.

[450] *Ibid.*, 10.

[451] *Ibid.*, 249.

[452] Adolf Hitler, "Why We Are Antisemites," speech delivered on August 15, 1920; original published in *Vierteljahrshefte für Zeitgeschichte*, 16. Jahrg., 4. H. (Oct., 1968), 390-420. Edited by Carolyn Yeager, 2013 https://carolynyeager.net/why-we-are-antisemites-text-adolf-hitlers-1920-speech-hofbr%C3%A4uhaus

[453] *Ibid.*

[454] *Ibid.*

[455] Otto Wagener, *Hitler – Memoirs of a Confidant* (New Haven, CT: Yale University Press, 1985), 17.

[456] Wegener, *Ibid.*

[457] Hitler, *ibid.*, 1920.

[458] Cited in Pellicani, *"Fascism, capitalism, modernity,"* op. cit., 397.

[459] William Reich, *The Mass Psychology of Fascism*, Teodore P. Wolfe, trans. (New York, NY: Orgone Institute Press, 1946) https://ia801409. us.archive.org/11/items/WILHELMREICHTheMassPsychologyOfFascism/WIL HELM%20REICH%20-%20The%20Mass%20Psychology%20of %20Fascism.pdf

[460] Michael Burleigh, *The Third Reich: A New History* (New York, NY: Hill and Wang, 2000), 481.

[461] *Why the Jews?* 193.

[462] For an excellent history, see Gavin I. Langmuir, *Toward a Definition of Antisemitism* (Berkeley and Los Angeles: University of California Press, 1990).

[463] Binjamin W. Segel, in Richard S. Levy, *A Lie and a Libel: The History of the Protocols of the Elders of Zion* (Lincoln, Nebraska: University of Nebraska Press, 1996), 55.

[464] Steven J. Zipperstein, *Pogrom: Kishinev and the Tilt of History* (New York, NY: W. W. Norton & Co., 2018), 146, 171-175.

[465] Indeed, "Krushevan himself would acknowledge this sloppiness...." *Ibid.*, 171.

[466] Cited by Levy, *ibid.*, 17. He credits Charles A. Ruud, "The Policy and the Jewish Question in Late Imperial Russia," paper delivered before the American Association for the Advancement of Slavic Studies, Honolulu, November 20, 1993.

[467] For a timeline that chronicles the publication and exposure of the forgery, see the Holocaust Encyclopedia, published by the U.S. Holocaust Museum. https://www.ushmm.org/wlc/en/article.php?ModuleId=10007244

[468] Nora Levin, *The holocaust: the destruction of European Jewry, 1933-1945* (New York, NY: T. Y. Crowell Co., 1968), 19.

[469] See Albert Lee, *Henry Ford and the Jews* (New York, NY: Stein and Day, 1980).

[470] Richard Landes, *Heaven on Earth: The Varieties of the Millennial Experience* (Oxford: Oxford University Press, 2011) 427.

[471] *Ibid.*, 430.

[472] *Ibid.*, 434.

[473] Shmuel Bar, *A Warrant for Terror: The Fatwas of Radical Islam and the Duty to Jihad* (Latham, MD: Rowman & Littlefield, 2006), xiv, 7, 99.

[474] *Ibid.*, 29-30

[475] Martin Kramer, *Islam Assembled: The Advent of the Muslim Congresses* (New York, NY: Columbia University Press, 1986), ix.

476 *Ibid.*, 179, note 37.

477 See Eugene Rogin, *The Fall of the Ottomans: The Great War in the Middle East* (New York, NY: Basic Books, 2015).

478 Henry Morgenthau Sr., *Ambassador Morgenthau's story* (New York, NY: Cosimo Inc., 2008), 111.

479 *Ibid.*, 113.

480 *Ibid.*, 115.

481 *Ibid.*, 118.

482 Barry Rubin & Wolfgang G. Schwanitz, *Nazis, Islamists, and the Making of the Modern Middle East* (New Haven, CT: Yale University Press, 2014), 32.

483 *Ibid.*

484 "I am conducting this war according to orders from the German General Staff." *Ibid.*, 35.

485 *Ibid.*, 36

486 Irving Louis Horowitz, *Taking Lives: Genocide and State Power* (New Brunswick, NJ: Transaction Publishers, 2002), 158.

487 Rubin & Schwanitz, *op. cit.*, 37.

488 Repeatedly disappointed in their efforts, many Jews decided to turn to Britain and the allies. The most remarkable of these were the brilliant botanist Aaron Aaronson, founder of the famous Nili spy ring, and his heroic sister Sara. Their riveting and important story is brilliantly told by Ronald Florence in *Lawrence and Aaronsohn: T. E. Lawrence, Aaron Aaronsohn, and the Seeds of the Arab-Israeli Conflict* (New York, NY: Penguin Books, 2008). I am grateful to Dr. Stephen A. Bryen for bringing it to my attention.

489 Rubin & Schwanitz, *op. cit.*, 37.

490 Although Rogin, *op. cit.*, cites several instances of genuine impact on increasing pan-Islamic sentiment.

491 *Ibid.*, 70.

492 Stephen Cohen describes Yevgeny Aleksandrovich Gnedin as Nicolai Bukharin's "family friend" and his colleague at Izvestiya in the 1930s, serving later in Berlin but arrested in 1939 by Stalin, and imprisoned in the Gulag. Introduction to *This I Cannot Forget: The Memoirs of Nikolai Bukharin's Widow*, by Anna Larina (New York, NY: W. W. Norton & Company, 1994), 26.

493 *Ibid.*, 71.

494 *Ibid.*

495 Laurent Murawiec, *The Mind of Jihad* (Cambridge, UK: Cambridge University Press, 2008), 203.

496 *Ibid.*, 207. Dr. Farooq's Study Resources Page, http://globalwebpost.com/farooqm/study_re/default.html.

497 *Manifesto*, pp. 167-177.

498 "… so immense that one delivery consisted of six hundred Kalashnikov submachine guns, fifty machine guns, thirty antitank RPG-7s, three thousand hand

grenades, two thousand mines and two tuns of explosives (10 October 1975, Pb 192/6). Bukovsky, *op. cit.*, Ch. 1, sec. 1.5.

[499] 9 February 1987, St 39/65, *ibid.*

[500] For a comprehensive analysis, see Jonathan Schneer, *The Balfour Declaration: The Origins of the Arab-Israeli Conflict* (New York, NY: Random House, 2010).

[501] Wistrich, *op. cit.*, 94.

[502] He mentions this in a draft of *Mein Kampf*, though omitted from the published version. Rubin, 77.

[503] Other spellings include: Hussain, Husein, Husayn, etc.

[504] Murawiec, *op. cit.*, 238-9.

[505] Walter Laqueur, *Communism and nationalism in the Middle East* (New York, NY: Routledge Kegan Paul, 1956), 236.

[506] Richard P. Mitchell, *The Society of the Muslim Brothers* (Oxford: Oxford University Press, 1969), 15. Cited in Murawiec, *op. cit.*, 33.

[507] Cited in Ivessa Lubben, "The Economic Ideology of Hasan Al-Banna and the Egyptian Muslim Brotherhood," in Hartmut Elsenhans, Rachid Ouaissa, Sebastian Schwecke, Mary Ann Tétreault, eds., *The Transformation of Politicised Religion: From Zealots into Leaders* (London: Ashgate Publishing, 2015), 81.

[508] Murawiec, *op. cit.*, 260.

[509] Cited in Lubben, 84.

[510] *Ibid.*, 86. For more on Al-Bahi al-Khuli, see also Nathan J. Citino, *Envisioning the Arab Future* (Cambridge, UK: Cambridge University Press, 2017), 40.

[511] What drew the definitive ire of Egyptian President Gamal Abdel Nasser (1918–1970), who had seized power through a military coup against the ruling King Farouk on July 23, 1952, was the Brotherhood's decision to support Nasser's Presidential rival in 1954. Ideology might be tolerated, but treachery, never. Following an attempt on his life by a Brotherhood member, Nasser banned the organization that year. Yet this was not a clash between secular and Islamic state models. It was personal.

[512] Malise Ruthven, *A Fury for God: The Islamist Attack on America* (New York, NY: Granta, 2002), 71.

[513] Karen Armstrong, *Islam: A Short History* (New York, NY: Random House, 2002), 170.

[514] Cited in Ruthven, *op. cit.*, 90-91.

[515] *Ibid.*, 91.

[516] *Ibid.*, 92-3.

[517] Ahmad S. Moussalli, *Radical Islamic Fundamentalism: The Ideological and Political Discourse of Sayyid Qutb* (Beirut, Lebanon: American University of Beirut, 1992) 200-203.

[518] Murawiec, *op. cit.* 257.

[519] Sayyid Abul Ala Maududi, *Jihad fi sabilillah (Jihad in Islam)*, Huda Khattab, ed., translated by Prof. Khushid Ahmad (London, UK: UKIM Dawah Center, n.d.)

[520] Cited in Michael W. S. Ryan, *Decoding Al-Qaeda's Strategy: The Deep Battle Against America* (New York, NY: Columbia University Press, 2013), 32.

[521] *Ibid.*

[522] *Ibid.,* 37.

[523] Amir Taheri, *The Persian Night: Iran under the Khomeinist Revolution* (New York, NY: Encounter Books, 2008), 78.

[524] Imam Khomeini, *Islam and Revolution: Writings and Declarations of Imam Khomeini (1941-1980),* (Mizan Press, 1981), 53-54.

[525] Shmuel Bar, *op. cit.,* 32.

[526] *Ibid.,* 52.

[527] See Christopher Hitchens, "Defending Islamofascism," *Slate,* Oct. 22, 2007. https://slate.com/news-and-politics/2007/10/defending-the-term-islamofascism.html

[528] Morteza Motahari, *Pyramoon Enqelab-e Iran dar Dow Harekat [Iran's Revolution in Two Moves]* (Tehran, Iran: 1984, n.d.), 84.

[529] Rubin, *op. cit.,* 182.

[530] "The director of the CIA, Mike Pompeo, has spoken about the 'open secret' regarding links between Iran and Al-Qaeda during the Obama administration. Pompeo criticised the Obama administration for downplaying the relationship. He said: 'It's an open secret and not classified information that there have been relationships, there are connections. There have been times the Iranians have worked alongside Qaeda.'" "Open Secret of Iran and Al-Qaeda," *Iran Focus,* Oct. 21, 2017. http://www.iranfocus.com/en/index.php?option=com_content&view=article&id=32120:open-secret-of-iran-and-Al qaeda&catid=9:terrorism&Itemid=114

[531] "After a first wave of Al-Qaeda wives and daughters, along with hundreds of low-level volunteers, came husbands and unmarried fighters who were escorted to Tehran... From there, the Quds Force gave them false travel documents that disguised them as Iraqi Shia refugees and flew them out to other countries, where they either settled or went on to join other conflicts." *Ibid.*

[532] Ryan, *op. cit.,* 64.

[533] *Ibid.,* 78-79.

[534] Cited in *ibid.,* 87

[535] *Ibid.,* 88.

[536] *Ibid.,* 90.

[537] *Ibid.,* 92.

[538] *Ibid.,* 94.

[539] *Ibid.,* 109.

[540] *Ibid.,* 193.

[541] *Ibid.,* 232.

[542] *Ibid.,* 246.

[543] *Ibid..,* 201.

[544] Michael Sharnoff, *A Peace to End All Peace: Egypt's Response to the 1967 War with Israel* (New York, NY: Routledge, 2017), 209.

[545] *Ibid.*

[546] *Ibid.*

[547] There is a mountain of data on this largely neglected exodus. See for example Shmuel Trigano's "The Expulsion of the Jews from Muslim Countries, 1920-1970: A History of Ongoing Cruelty and Discrimination," Jerusalem Center for Public Affairs, Nov. 4, 2010. http://jcpa.org/ article/ the-expulsion-of-the-jews-from - muslim – countries -1920-1970-a-history – of – ongoing - cruelty - and - discrimination/

[548] Rubin, *op. cit.,* 69.

[549] For an interesting perspective on the British rationale, see Christopher Simon Sykes, *The Man Who Created the Middle East: A Story of Empire, Conflict, and the Sykes-Picot Agreement* (New York, NY: Harper-Collins, 2016)

[550] As Robert Wistrich observes, "this culture of hatred lies at the very core of the Middle East conflict." *Op. cit.,* 53.

[551] *Ibid.,* 5.

[552] Bar, *op. cit.,* 33-34.

[553] *Ibid.,* 34. Fatwa: Yousuf Qaradawi, *"Mubasharat fi Intisar al-Islam"* (Portents for the victory of Islam), April 1, 2002.

[554] https://www.investigativeproject.org/profile/167/yusuf-Al-qaradawi# ftnref.

[555] "Leading Egyptian cleric Qaradawi contests Interpol warrant," *Middle East Eye*, Dec. 8, 2014. https://www.middleeasteye.net/news/muslim-brotherhood-s-qaradawi-contests-interpol-warrant-462922597

[556] http: // www.aljazeera.com / news/2017 /11/Al-qaradawi-calls-islamic-awakening-171107094013049.html

[557] Daniel Pipes, "Examining Qatar's Influence," Jan. 29, 2019. http://www.danielpipes.org/18699/qatar-influence

[558] Trygve Throntveit, *Power without Victory: Woodrow Wilson and the American Internationalist Experiment* (Chicago, IL: University of Chicago Press, 2017), 10.

[559] *Ibid.,* 9.

[560] *Ibid.,* 11.

[561] *Ibid.*

[562] Townsend Hoopes and Douglas Brinkley, *FDR and the Creation of the UN* (New Haven, CT: Yale University Press, 2000), 9-10.

[563] Icarus and his father Daedalus attempt to escape from Crete by means of wings that his father constructed from feathers and wax. Daedalus warns him first of complacency and then of hubris, asking that he fly neither too low nor too high, so the sea's dampness would not clog his wings or the sun's heat melt them. Icarus ignored his father's instructions not to fly too close to the sun; when the wax in his wings melted he tumbled out of the sky and fell into the sea where he drowned. See https://www.greeklegendsandmyths.com/icarus.html.

[564] Franklin D. Roosevelt, Donald Day, *My Own Story: From Private and Public Papers* (New York, NY: Routledge, 2017), 79.

[565] https: // www.loc.gov/law/help/us-treaties / bevans/m-ust000003-0697 .pdf

[566] "The source text is a copy made in the Department of state. A copy in the Hopkins Papers bears the initials of Hopkins as the drafter of the memorandum." *Foreign Relations of the United States, The Conferences at Washington, 1941-1942 and Casablanca, 1943* (Washington, DC: Government Printing Office, 1968) http://avalon.law.yale.edu/wwii/ washc014.asp#b1

[567] See Juliana Geran Pilon, *The Art of War: Engaging a Complex World* (New York, NY: Routledge, 2016).

[568] Pedro A. Sanjuan, *The UN Gang: A Memoir of Incompetence, Corruption* (New York, NY: Doubleday, 2005). Also, Juliana Geran Pilon and Ralph K. Bennett, *The UN: Assessing Soviet Abuses* (London, UK: Institute for European Defence & Strategic Studies, 1988).

[569] Sanjuan, *ibid.*

[570] Thomas G. Weiss, "What Happened to the Idea of World Government," *International Studies Quarterly* (2009), vol. 53, 253-271.

[571] *Ibid.*

[572] *Ibid.*

[573] Peter Singer, *One World: The Ethics of Globalization,* (New Haven, CT: Yale University Press, 2004).

[574] John Fonte, *Sovereignty or Submission: Will Americans Rule Themselves or Be Ruled by Others?* (New York, NY: Encounter Books, 2011), xx.

[575] French, meaning "well-thinking." It refers to the conventional, politically correct ideocracy.

[576] The term is defined as "a network of professionals with recognised expertise and competence in a particular domain and an authoritative claim to policy relevant knowledge within that domain or issue-area." Peter M. Hass, "Introduction: epistemic communities and international policy coordination". *International Organization,* special issue*: Knowledge, Power, and International Policy Coordination,* Cambridge Journals, Winter 1992, 46 (1): 1–35.

[577] Kenneth Anderson, "Secular Eschatologies and Class Interests of the Internationalized New Class," in Peter Juviler and Carrie Gustafson, eds., *Religion and Human Rights: Competing Claims* (New York, NY: M.E. Sharpe, 1998), 107-116.

[578] *Ibid.*

[579] Kenneth Anderson, "After Seattle: Public International Organizations, Non-Governmental Organizations (NGOs), and Democratic Sovereignty in an Era of Globalization - An Essay in Contested Legitimacy" Draft, Aug. 29, 2000, 179. https://papers.ssrn.com/sol3/papers.cfm?abstract_id= 310641 Anderson accuses this group of elite organizations putatively concerned with "human rights" of being served by "liberal internationalism's package deal of liberal global governance and the regulated global market." 180.

[580] *Ibid.,* 182. Note 427.

[581] See Daniel J. Whelan & Jack Donnelly, *The West, Economic and Social Rights, and the Global Human Rights Regime: Setting the Record Straight,* 29 HuM. RTS. Q. 908, 911 (2007) ("Other states certainly supported economic and social rights. None, however, did so with more genuine commitment or greater actual impact than the United States and Great Britain, the two leading Western powers.")

[582] Gillian MacNaughton and Mariah McGill, "Economic and Social Rights in the United States: Implementation Without Ratification," *Northeastern University Law Journal,* Vol. 4, No. 2, 2012, 365-406.

[583] Aaron Rhodes, *The Debasement of Human Rights* (New York, NY: Encounter Books, 2018), 41.

[584] Franklin D. Roosevelt, President of the United States, Address to the Congress of the United States (Jan. 11, 1944), in 90 Cong. Rec. 54, 57 (1944) http://www.presidency.ucsb.edu/ws/index.php?pid=16518

[585] Rhodes, *op. cit.,* 41.

[586] Isaiah Berlin, "Two Concepts of Liberty," in *Four Essays on Liberty* (Oxford: Oxford University Press, 1969), 18.

[587] Rhodes, *op. cit.,* 45.

[588] Isaiah Berlin, *Four Essays on Liberty* (Oxford: Oxford University Press, 1979).

[589] *Ibid.,* 22. Emphasis added.

[590] Rhodes, 36.

[591] *Ibid.,* 117.

[592] http: // www . jus . uio . no / lm/ un.universal.declaration.of.human.rights. 1948 / portrait a4.pdf

[593] https://treaties.un.org/doc/publication/ctc/uncharter.pdf

[594] The International Forum for Social Development, *Social Justice in an Open World - The Role of the United Nations,* UN Department of Economic and Social Affairs, Division for Social Policy and Development, 2006 http://www.un.org/esa/socdev/documents/ifsd/Social Justice.pdf, 52.

[595] http://www.ohchr.org/Documents/ProfessionalInterest/progress.pdf

[596] *Social Justice, op. cit.,* 53.

[597] *Ibid.,* 55.

[598] Rhodes, *op. cit.,* 99.

[599] *Ibid.*

[600] *Social Justice, op. cit.,* 23.

[601] *Ibid.,* 27.

[602] Rhodes, *op. cit.,* 237.

[603] *Ibid.,* 248.

[604] James Taranto, "The Weekend Interview with Aaron Rhodes – What Went Wrong With Human Rights," *The Wall Street Journal,* Aug. 18-19, 2018, A13.

[605] Three decades after its publication, still the best account of the Soviet espionage and propaganda apparatus is John J. Dziak's *Chekisty: A History of the KGB* (Lanham, MD: Lexington Books, 1988).

[606] "The Struggle against Anti-Israel Bias at the UN Commission on Human Rights," UN Watch in Geneva, 4 January 2006, Issue 138. https://web.archive. org/web/20131023035552/http://www.unwatch.org/site/apps/nl/content2.asp?c= bdKKISNqEmG&b=1314451&ct=1766305

[607] Interview, Trouw, March 31, 1977. Cited in Eric Rozenman, *Jews Make the Best Demons: 'Palestine' and the Jewish Question* (Nashville, TN: New English Review Press, 2018), 100.

[608] For a list of events on "The Question of Palestine" coordinated by the Division for Palestinian Rights, see https://unispal.un.org/DPA/DPR/ unispal.nsf/div.htm

[609] Rozenman, *op. cit.*, 239.

[610] Paul Hoffman, "Dramatic Session," *The New York Times*, Nov. 14, 1974, https://www.nytimes.com/1974/11/14/archives/dramatic-session-plo-head-says-he-bears-olive-branch-and-guerrilla.html

[611] United Nations E/CONF. 66/34 http://www.un-documents.net/mex-dec.htm

[612] United Nations A/RES/3379 (XXX) November 10, 1975. https://unispal. un.org/DPA/DPR/unispal.nsf/0/761C1063530766A7052566A2005B74D1

[613] Bob Blaisdell, *Great Speeches of the 20th Century* (New York, NY: Dover Publications, 2011), 158 – 166.

[614] Ion Mihai Pacepa with Ronald Rychlak, *Disinformation: Former Spy Chief Reveals Secret Strategies for Undermining Freedom, Attacking Religion, and Promoting Terrorism* (Washington, DC: WND Books, 2013), 96.

[615] *Ibid.*, 97

[616] Wistrich, 50. He finds it "highly significant that Islamic antisemitism has enthusiastically embraced the *Protocols* as the most authoritative road map for deciphering a world in chaos dominated by the Jews and their demonic activities." *A Lethal Obsession., op. cit.*, 75.

[617] Harris Okun Schoenberg, *A Mandate for Terror: The United Nations and the PLO* (New York, NY: Shapolsky Publishers, 1989), iv.

[618] Robert S. Wistrich, *A Lethal Obsession, op. cit.*, 53.

[619] Josef Joffe, "Nations We Love to Hate: Israel, America and the New Antisemitism," (Jerusalem: Vidal Sassoon International Center for the Study of Antisemitism, 2005), 1.

[620] Study, Compilation and Translation by Dr. Arnon Groiss and Dr. Ronni Shaked, "Schoolbooks of the Palestinian Authority (PA): The Attitude to the Jews, to Israel and to Peace," The Simon Wiesenthal Center and the Middle East Forum, Sept. 2017. http://israelbehindthenews.com/wp-content / uploads / 2017 / 09 / Schoolbooks - PalestinianAuthority2017. pdf Only on August 31, 2018, did the State Department finally stop funding for UNRWA, soon followed by Congressional reprogramming of its funds. See Jim Zanotti and Rhoda Margesson, "Decision to Stop U.S. Funding of UNRWA (for Palestinian Refugees)" CRS Insight, Sept. 7, 2018. https://fas.org/sgp/crs/mideast/IN10964. pdf

[621] *Ibid.*, 20.

[622] *Ibid.*, 36.

[623] *Ibid.*, 245

[624] *Ibid.*

[625] Robert Fine and Philip Spencer, *Antisemitism and the left: On the return of the Jewish question* (Manchester, UK: Manchester University Press, 2017), 116.

[626] *Ibid.*, 124

[627] Will England, "Red Century," *The Washington Post*, Oct. 26, 2017. https://www.washingtonpost.com / graphics / 2017 / world / 100-years-of-Communism/?utm_term=.f551ef625dc3

[628] *Ibid.*

[629] China is comfortably North Korea's most important economic partner, covering nearly 90pc of its exports going there, and nearly 90pc of its imports, figures from the BACI International Trade Database show." Sam Dean, "Why secretive North Korea is edging towards a new crisis," *The Telegraph*, Feb. 26, 2017. https://www.telegraph.co.uk/business/2017/02/ 26/secretive-north-korea-edging-towards-new-crisis/

[630] David Albright, Sarah Burkhard, Allison Lach, and Andrea Stricker, "Countries Involved in Violating UNSC Resolutions on North Korea," Institute for Science and International Security Report, Dec. 5, 2017. http://isis-online.org/uploads/isis reports/documents / Countries_Involved_ in Violating_ NK_UNSC_Resolutions 5Dec2017_Final.pdf

[631] Zeeshan Aleem, "Here's why North Korea's economy is able to survive sanction after sanction," *Vox*, Dec. 7, 2017. https://www.vox.com/world/ 2017/12 /7/16745692/north-korea-sanctions-nuclear-economy

[632] Evan Osnos, "The Risk of Nuclear War with North Korea," *The New Yorker,* Sept. 18, 2017. https://www.newyorker.com/magazine/2017/09 /18/the-risk-of-nuclear-war-with-north-korea

[633] "That's partially because North Korea lacks chemical fertilizer, and many farmers rely on human excrement to fertilize fields." Cleve R. Wootson Jr., "What the parasites in a defector's stomach tell us about North Korea," *The Washington Post,* Nov. 19, 2017. https://www.washingtonpost.com/news/worldviews/wp/ 2017/11/19/what-the-parasites-in-a-defectors-stomach-tell-us-about-north-korea/ ?utm_term=.dc3e74dc7c20

[634] Venezuela's President Hugo Chavez promoted Bolivarism "as a superior model of democracy and a populist strategy of political transformation using constitution making, heavy state intervention in the economy, and anti-imperialism." Carlos de la Torre, « Hugo Chávez and the diffusion of Bolivarianism, » *Democratization*, 24:7, 1271. https://www.tandfonline.com/doi/full/10.1080/13510347.2017.1307825

[635] *Freedom in the World 2017*, https://freedomhouse.org/report/freedom-world/2017/cuba

[636] Richard Rahn, "Putinism," *The Washington Times* - Sept 20, 2007 https://www.washingtontimes.com/news/2007/sep/20/putinism/

[637] See Lilia Shevtsova's astute analysis of "Shades of Pragmatism" in *The American Interest*, Jan. 22, 2016. https://www.the-american-interest.com/2016/01/22/how-the-west-misjudged-russia-part-3-shades-of-pragmatism/

[638] Richard C. Longworth, "Putinism: The New Russian Ideology," Chicago Council on Global Affairs, Oct. 11, 2016. https://www.thechicagocouncil.org/blog/global-insight/putinism-new-russian-ideology-0

[639] Masha Gessen," Putin: The Rule of the Family," *The New York Review of Books*, March 14, 2016. http://www.nybooks.com/daily/2016/03/14/ putin-mafia-state-lesin-killing/

[640] *Ibid.*

[641] Andre Illarionov, "Putin's Sicilian Way of Rule," *New Eastern Europe*, Oct. 15, 2015. http://neweasterneurope.eu/old_site/interviews/1744-putin-s-sicilian-way-of-rule

[642] Cited in Longworth, *op. cit.*

[643] Arkady Ostrovsky, *The Invention of Russia: The Rise of Putin and Fake News* (New York, NY: Penguin Books, 2017), 6.

[644] *Ibid.*, 6-7.

[645] *Ibid.*, 8.

[646] *Ibid.*, 307.

[647] *Ibid.*, 322.

[648] *Ibid.*, 307-308.

[649] *Ibid.*, 312.

[650] Maxim Shevchenko, "My ne Evropa? I slava bogu!" (We are not Europe? Thank God*!) Moskovskii komsomolnets*, Feb. 10, 2011, 3.

[651] James Palmer, "Nobody Knows Anything About China," *Foreign Policy*, March 21, 2018 http://foreignpolicy.com/2018/03/21/nobody-knows-anything-about-china/

[652] *Ibid.*

[653] Dan Blumenthal, "Xi's 'putinization' of China is a massive wake-up for America," *The Hill*, March 2, 2018. http://thehill.com/opinion/ international /376352-xi-jinpings-putinization-of-china-is-a-rude-awakening-for-washington

[654] Jonathan E. Hillman, "China's Belt and Road Initiative: Five Years Later," CSIS Report, Jan. 25, 2018. https://www.csis.org/analysis/chinas-belt-and-road-initiative-five-years-later-0

[655] Robert Daly and Matthew Rojansky, "China's Global Dreams Give Its Neighbors Nightmares," *Foreign Policy,* March 12, 2018. http://foreignpolicy.com/2018/03/12/chinas-global-dreams-are-giving-its-neighbors-nightmares/

[656] Zhao Pitao*, Waishi gaishuo* [Summary of Foreign Affairs], Shanghai shehui kexue chubanshe, 1995, 166. Cited in Brady, *op. cit.*

[657] Anne-Marie Brady, "Magic Weapons: China's political influence activities under Xi Jinping," Conference paper presented at the conference on "The corrosion of democracy under China's global influence," supported by the Taiwan Foundation for Democracy, and hosted in Arlington, Virginia, USA, September

16-17, 2017. https://www.wilsoncenter.org/sites/default/files/ magicweaponsa nne -mariebradyseptember162017.pdf Lenin's words are from V.I. Lenin, *"Left-wing" Communism, An Infantile Disorder,* Moscow: Foreign Languages Publishing House, 1950, 91.

[658] Josh Rogin, "China's foreign influence operations are causing alarm in Washington," *The Washington Post,* Dec. 10, 2017. https:// www. washingtonpost.com / opinions/global – opinions / chinas – foreign -influencers – are – causing – alarm-in-washington/2017/12/10/ 98227264-dc58-11e7-b859-fb0995360725_story.html?utm_term=.598ffff1a02d

[659] "Intelligence Chiefs Take Questions from Senate Intelligence Committee," *CNN Newsroom Transcripts,* Feb. 13, 2018. http:// transcripts.cnn.com/ TRANSCRIPTS/1802/13/cnr.04.html

[660] Cheng Chen, *The Return of Ideology: The Search for Regime Identities in PostCommunist Russia and China* (Ann Arbor, MI: University of Michigan Press, 2016) 131.

[661] *Ibid.,* 143.

[662] George W. Bush, State of the Union Address, Jan. 29, 2002. https://web.archive.org/web/20111011053416/http://millercenter.org/President/s peeches/detail/4540

[663] Saturday Night Live Transcripts, Season 27, Episode 13. http://snltran scripts.jt.org/01/01mbush.phtml

[664] Andrew J. Bacevich, "He Told Us to Go Shopping. Now the Bill Is Due," *The Washington Post,* Oct. 5, 2008. http://www. Washingtonpost .com/wp-dyn/content/article/2008/10/03/ AR2008100301977.html

[665] See Juliana Geran Pilon, *Why America is Such a Hard Sell: Beyond Pride and Prejudice* (Lanham, MD: Rowman & Littlefield, 2007)

[666] Aaron David Miller and Richard Sokolsky, "The 'axis of evil' is back," CNN April 26, 2017. https://www.cnn.com/2017/04/26/opinions/axis-of-evil-is-back-miller-sokolsky/index.html

[667] Nicholas Heras,"Gray Zones in the Middle East," CNAS Report, Sept. 18, 2017.

[668] Babak Rahimi, "Contentious Legacies of the Ayatollah," in *A Critical Introduction to Khomeini,* ed. Arshin Adib-Moghaddam, (Cambridge, UK: Cambridge University Press, 2014), 301; Maryam Panah, *The Islamic Republic and the World: Global Dimensions of the Iranian Revolution,* (London, UK: Pluto Press, 2007), 1-70; and Ray Takeyh, *Hidden Iran: Paradox and Power in the Islamic Republic,* (New York, NY: Henry Holt, 2006), 34. Cited in Heras, *op. cit.*

[669] "IRGC Commander Says Iran's Sacred Defense Model for Resistance Forces," Tasnim News Agency, October 3, 2016, https:// www.tasnimnews.com / en / news / 2016 / 10 / 03 / 1203587 / irgc-commander - says - iran-s-sacred-defense-model-for-resistance-forces; Karl Vick, "Iranian Commander Lets Slip That

Revolutionary Guard Is Fighting in Syria," *Time*, May 7, 2014, http://time. com/90807/iran-syria-revolutionary-guard/ Cited in Heras, *op. cit.*

[670] Suleiman Al-Khalidi, "Jihadist group cements control of Syria's Idlib province: rebels," Reuters, July 23, 2017, http://www.reuters. com/article/us-mideast-crisis-syria-rebels-idlib-idUSKBN1A80T1?il=0; Ian Bremmer, "The Top 5 Countries Where ISIS Gets Its Foreign Recruits," *Time*, April 13, 2017, http://time.com/4739488/isis-iraq-syria-tunisia-saudi-arabia-russia/; and Colin P. Clarke and Amarnath Amarasingam, "Where Do ISIS Fighters Go When the Caliphate Falls?" *The Atlantic*, March 6, 2017, https://www.theatlantic.com/ international / archive / 2017 / 03 / isis – foreign - fighter – jihad – syria - iraq/518313/ Cited in Heras, *op. cit.*

[671] Emanuele Ottolenghi and John Hannah, "Venezuela: Narco-State Meets Iran-Backed Terror," *InFocus*, Winter 2018. An earlier version appeared in *Foreign Policy*, March 23, 2017. *http:// foreignpolicy.com/ 2017/ 03/ 23/ in- venezuelas - toxic-brew-failed-narco -state-meets-iran-backed-terrorism/*

[672] *Ibid.*

[673] Lt. Col. (ret.) Dr. Refael Ofek and Lt. Col. (ret.) Dr. Dany Shoham, "Iran Is Progressing Towards Nuclear Weapons Via North Korea," The Begin-Sadat Center for Strategic Studies, BESA Center Perspectives Paper No. 415, February 28, 2017. https://besacenter.org/perspectives-papers/iran-progressing-nuclear-weapons-via-north-korea/

[674] Stephen Farrell, "Israel admits bombing suspected Syrian nuclear reactor in 2007, warns Iran," Reuters, March 20, 2018. https://www.reuters.com/article/us-israel-syria-nuclear/israel-admits-bombing-suspected-syrian-nuclear-reactor-in-2007-warns-iran-idUSKBN1GX09K

[675] Tarun Chhabra, "The China challenge, democracy, and U.S. grand strategy," Brookings Institute Report, Feb. 15, 2019. https:// www.brookings.edu / wp - content/uploads / 2019 / 02/FP _ 20190227 _ us_grand_strategy_chhabra.pdf

[676] See Jaroslaw Piekalkiewicz and Alfred Wayne Penn, *The Politics of Ideocracy* (Albany, NY: State University of New York Press, 1995)

[677] *Ibid.*, 26-27.

[678] The scholarly literature on utopianism is replete with attempts to better understand the motivations, thought patterns, and social impact of the groups held responsible for violent revolutionary upheavals. To mention but the most illustrious: Karl Mannheim, Lewis S. Feuer, Paul Johnson, Paul Hollander, Leszek Kolakowski, Irving Louis Horowitz, Thomas Sowell.

[679] Karl Mannheim, *Ideology and Utopia: An Introduction to the Sociology of Knowledge* (London: Routledge & Kegan Paul, 1960), p. 140.

[680] See John A. Battle, "Property Rights and Responsibilities in the Old Testament," *Western Reformed Seminary Journal* 15:1 (February 2008), 15-27.

[681] Hillel Gamoran, "The Biblical Law Against Loans on Interest," *Journal of Near Eastern Studies* 30:3 (April 1971), 130.

[682] Harry M. Orlinsky, Understanding the Bible through History and Archaeology (New York, NY: Ktav Publishing House, 1972), 259-260.

[683] Joseph Lifshitz, *Judaism, Law & The Free Market: An Analysis* (Grand Rapids, MI: Acton Institute, 2012), 15.

[684] *Ibid.*

[685] *Ibid.*, 18.

[686] More, op. cit., 134. In a footnote to this passage, Clarence H. Miller adds: "What 'More' says here is in keeping with earlier Aristotelian arguments against community of property.... But many readers get the impression that More lets the mask of the character 'More' slip to reveal a hint of irony. For a discussion of the critical disputes about this passage see Thomas I. White, '*Festivitas, utilitas, et opes:* The Concluding Irony and Philosophical Purpose of Thomas More's *Utopia,*' *Albion* 10 (1978): 135-50." *Ibid.*, 162.

[687] Alan S. Kahan, *Mind Vs. Money: The War Between Intellectuals and Capitalism* (New Brunswick, NJ: Transaction Publishers, 2010), 42-43.

[688] *Ibid.* The passage is from *The Second Letter from Paul to the Corinthians*, Ch. 8. (Emphasis added.) http://www.katapi.org.uk/katapiNSBunix/NEB/NEBTextByBC.php?B=308&C=8&BoldKFm=308008017&BoldKTo=308008024

[689] Pellicani, *Revolution and Utopia.*, 14.

[690] *Ibid.*, 15.

[691] Richard Pipes, *Property and Freedom* (New York, NY: Knopf, 1999), 14.

[692] Daniel Mahoney, *The Idol of Our Age: How the Religion of Humanity Subverts Christianity* (New York, NY: Encounter Books, 2018), 20-21.

[693] Lord Acton, "The History of Freedom in Antiquity," in *Essays on Freedom and Power* (New York, NY: Meridian, 1964), 53.

[694] *Ibid.*

[695] *Ibid.*, 55-56.

[696] *Ibid.*, 56.

[697] *Ibid.*, 56-57.

[698] *Ibid.*, 74.

[699] *Ibid.*, 76.

[700] According to the third century biographer Diogenes Laertius, the illustrious member of that school Chrysippus (c.27-c.206 BCE) had said "that justice, as well as law and right reason, exists by nature and not by convention." Another biographer, Plutarch, adds that Chrysippus denied it "possible to discover any principle or any beginning of justice other than from that of the gods and from the common nature." The rights of man should not depend on popular whim: nature and the gods constitute higher sources of authority. None of his works have survived except as fragments cited by later authors such as Plutarch, Cicero, Seneca, and others. Jason L. Saunders, *Greek and Roman Philosophy After Aristotle* (New York, NY: The Free Press, 1966), 124-125. Saunders uses J. von

Arnim's standard text, *Stoicorum veterum fragmenta* (SVF) (Leipzig, 1905-24), 4 vols. Diogenes' citation is from SVF III, 308; Plutarch's from SVF III, 326.

[701] *Ibid.*, 127. SVF 127.

[702] *Ibid.*, 124. SVF III, 323.

[703] *Ibid.*, 126-127. SVF III 340, 342, and 351.

[704] Lord Acton, *op.cit.*, 77.

[705] "The Great Sanhedrin was the supreme religious body in the Land of Israel during the time of the Holy Temple. There were also smaller religious Sanhedrins in every town in the Land of Israel, as well as a civil political-democratic Sanhedrin." Shira Schoenberg, "Ancient Jewish History: The Sanhedrin," Jewish Virtual Library, http://www.jewishvirtuallibrary.org/the-sanhedrin

[706] Acton, *Ibid.*

[707] *Ibid.*, 78.

[708] *Ibid.*, 79.

[709] *Ibid.*, 78.

[710] *Ibid.*, 80-81.

[711] Acton, "The History of Freedom in Christianity," in *Essays*, 88.

[712] See David Starkey, *Magna Carta: The Medieval Roots of Modern Politics* (New York, NY: Quercus, 2015), esp. 149-155. Also, Roger Pilon, "Magna Carta's Importance for America," *Cato's Letter*, Summer 2015, Vol. 13, No. 3.

[713] Acton, "Nationality," in *Essays*, 141.

[714] *Ibid.*, 167.

[715] *Ibid.*, 143.

[716] *Ibid.*, 144.

[717] *Ibid.*, 167.

[718] See, for example, Nancy J. Hirschmann, *Gender, Class, and Freedom in Modern Political Theory* (Princeton, NJ: Princeton University Press, 2009), 79; Urmila Sharma and S.K. Sharma, *Western Political Thought* (Washington, DC: Atlantic Publishers, 2006), 440; and W. Julian Korab-Karpowicz, *A History of Political Philosophy: From Thucydides to Locke* (New York, NY: Global Scholarly Publications, 2010), 291.

[719] Strauss, *History of Political Philosophy*, 248.

[720] Himmelfarb, *op. cit.*, 5.

[721] *Ibid.*, 6.

[722] *Ibid.*, 21.

[723] Arthur Herman, *How the Scots Invented the Modern World* (New York, NY: Three Rivers Press, 2001), 82.

[724] Francis Hutcheson, *A System Of Moral Philosophy: In Three Books:To which is Prefixed Some Account Of The Life, Writings, And Character Of The Author*, Vol. 1 (London: Millar, 1755) 294.

[725] Herman, *op. cit.*, 83.

[726] From Thomas Jefferson to Peter Carr, with Enclosure, 10 August 1787, Founders Online https://founders.archives.gov/documents/Jefferson/01-12-02-0021

[727] *Ibid.*

[728] This led historian Thomas West to observe: "One of the striking things about the leading men [of the American Founding] is how different they were in their particular preoccupations, and yet how much they agreed on principles." *Ibid.,* 24.

[729] Jefferson had written "inalienable" – it was John Adams who changed it, perhaps inadvertently. See Carl L Becker, *The Declaration of Independence a Study in the History of Political Ideas* (New York, NY: Vintage, 1942), 140.

[730] Thomas Jefferson letter to Henry Lee, May 8, 1825. http://constitutionreader.com/reader.engz?doc=constitution&chapter=OEBPS/Text/ch3.xhtml

[731] Becker observes that "the handwriting of 'self-evident' resembles Franklin's." *op. cit.,* 142.

[732] Curry, *op. cit.,* 65.

[733] Joseph Cropsey*, Polity and Economy: Further Thoughts Principles of Adam Smith* (South Bend, IN: St. Augustine Press, 2001), 137.

[734] WoN, Bk. IV, Ch. VII, Pt. III, and Bk. IV, Ch. IX. In Cropsey, *ibid.,* 2.

[735] Cropsey, *ibid.,* 143.

[736] *New Individualist Review*, editor-in-chief Ralph Raico, introduction by Milton Friedman (Indianapolis, IN: Liberty Fund, 1981). "Tocqueville on Socialism," http://oll.libertyfund.org/pages/tocqueville-s-critique-of-socialism-1848

[737] George Charles Roche III*, Frederic Bastiat: A Man Alone* (New Rochelle, NY: Arlington House, 1971), 186. Reprinted by the Ludwig von Mises Institute, 2011. https://mises-media.s3.amazonaws.com/Frederic%20Bastiat%20A%20Man%20Alone_2_2.pdf?file=1&type=document

[738] Frederic Bastiat, *The Law* (Irvington-on-Hudson, NY: Foundation for Economic Education, 1990), 27.

[739] *Ibid.,* 32-33.

[740] *Ibid.,* 63.

[741] *Ibid.,* 52.

[742] *Ibid.,* 68-69. Emphasis added.

[743] Frederic Bastiat, "Property and Law," in George B. de Huszar, *Selected Essays on Political Economy* (Irvington-on-Hudson, NY: Foundation for Economic Education, 1964), 101.

[744] It continues: "this piratical warfare, the opprobrium of infidel power, is the warfare of the Christian king of Great Britain. Determined to keep open a market where MEN should be bought & sold, he has prostituted his negative for suppressing every legislative attempt to prohibit or to restrain this execrable commerce..." *Ibid.,* 147.

[745] The Dred Scott Decision: Speech at Springfield, Illinois, June 26, 1857. Joseph R. Fornieri, ed., *The Language of Liberty: The Political Speeches and Writings of Abraham Lincoln* (Washington, DC: Regnery Publishing, 2009), 219.

[746] Roger Pilon, "American Constitutional Theory and History: Implications for European Constitutionalism, The Cato Journal," Fall 2018. https : // www . cato . org / cato – journal / fall – 2018 / american-constitutional-theory-history-implications-european See Tugwell, R. (1968) "A Center Report: Rewriting the Constitution." *The Center Magazine*1 (3): 18-20.

[747] Cropsey, in Strauss and Cropsey, *op. cit.,* 641.

[748] *Ibid.,* 639.

[749] Adam Smith, *An Inquiry into the Nature and Causes of the Wealth of Nations,* R. H. Campbell and A. S. Skinner, eds. (Indianapolis, IN: Liberty Classics, 1981), Bk. I, ch. IV

[750] *The Theory of Moral Sentiments,* Pt. I, Sec. I, ch. V

[751] *Ibid.,* Pt. VI, Sec. III.

[752] Arthur Herman, *op. cit.,* 214.

[753] Smith, *The Wealth of Nations, op. cit.,* I, ii.

[754] *Ibid.*

[755] Herman, *op. cit.,* 216.

[756] "The USA, New Zealand and Canada have the highest rate of charitable donations as a percentage of gross domestic product (GDP), the Charities Aid Foundation (CAF) found. The UK had the fourth highest rate of charitable donations in a study of 24 nations and topped all other EU countries that were looked at." Loulla-Mae Eleftheriou-Smith, "America, New Zealand and Canada top list of world's most generous nations," *The Independent,* Feb. 2, 2016. http://www.independent.co.uk/news/world/ americas / america – new – zealand - and -canada-top-list-of-world-s-most-generous-nations-a6849221.html

[757] Deirdre N. McCloskey, "Liberty and Dignity Explain the Modern World," in Tom Palmer, ed., *The Morality of Capitalism: What Your Professors Won't Tell You* (Ottawa, IL: Jameson Books, 2011), 30.

[758] Somewhat similar surveys include the *2018 Index of Economic Freedom* published annually by the Heritage Foundation; https://www.heritage.org/index/ and the Fraser Institute's Economic Freedom website, https://www.fraserinstitute .org/economic-freedom /map ? geozone = world&page=map & year=2015 For a useful critique of both studies, see Ed Dolan, The Way Economic Freedom Indexes Measure Regulation is Deeply Flawed," Niskanen Center, Dec. 4, 2017. https://niskanencenter.org/blog/elusive-regulatory-state/

[759] *Ibid.*

[760] Marian L. Tupy, An Update on the Global State of Human Freedom," *Human Progress Blog,* January 25, 2018. http://humanprogress.org/blog/ an-update-on-the-global-state-of-human-freedom

[761] Somewhat similar surveys include the *2018 Index of Economic Freedom* published annually by the Heritage Foundation; https://www.heritage.org/index/

and the Fraser Institute's Economic Freedom website, https://www.fraserinstitute. org/economic-freedom/ map?geozone=world&page = map & year = 2015 For a useful critique of both studies, see Ed Dolan, The Way Economic Freedom Indexes Measure Regulation is Deeply Flawed," Niskanen Center, Dec. 4, 2017. https://niskanencenter. org/blog/elusive-regulatory-state/

[762] *Ibid.,* 27.

[763] *Ibid.,* 28.

[764] *Ibid.,* 30.

[765] *Reward Work, not Wealth,* Oxfam, 2018. https://www.oxfam.org/sites /www.oxfam.org/files/file _ attachments / bp - reward - work – not -wealth-220118-summ-en.pdf

[766] Sophie Christie, "Forty-two people hold the same wealth as half the world, Oxfam says," The Telegraph, Jan. 22, 2018. https://www.telegraph.co.uk/ business/2018/01/22/forty-two-people-hold-wealth-half-world-oxfam-says/

[767] James Pethokoukis, "Why the much-hyped Oxfam study on global inequality is misleading," AEIdeas, Jan. 21, 2014. http://www.aei.org/publication/why-the-much-hyped-oxfam-study-on-global-inequality-is-misleading/

[768] Katie Hope, "'World's richest 1% get 82% of the wealth', says Oxfam," *BBC News,* Jan. 22, 2018. http://www.bbc.com/news/business-42745853

[769] Ryan Bourne, "Oxfam Is Entitled to Its Own Opinions but Not Its Own Facts," CAPX, January 23, 2018.
https://capx.co/oxfam-is-entitled-to-its-own-opinions-but-not-its-own-facts/

[770]Diana Furchtgott-Roth, "The Myth of Increasing Income Inequality," Manhattan Institute E21 Report, Dec. 16, 2013. https:// economics21.org/html/ myth-increasing-income-inequality-65.html

[771] Hayek, *The Road to Serfdom,* 231.

[772] *Ibid.*

[773] *Ibid.,* 232.

[774] Samuel P. Huntington, "Conservatism as an Ideology," *The American Political Science Review,* Vol. 51, No. 2, June 1957, 408. http://www.jstor.org/stable/ 1952202

[775] For a brilliant, concise overview see William F. Shughart II, "Public Choice," *The Library of Economics and Liberty,* https://www.econlib.org/library/Enc/ PublicChoice.html

[776] Richard A. Epstein, *The Classical Liberal Constitution: The Uncertain Quest for Limited Government* (Cambridge, MA: Harvard University Press, 2014), 21.

[777] Epstein notes that "the impulse [favoring progressive outcomes] covered a wide range of dubious trade practices, including, for example, a provision of the National Industrial Recovery Act (NIRA), struck down by the Supreme Court in A.L.A. Schechter Poultry Corp. v. United States, that required butchers to purchase entire runs of poultry, including sick chickens." *Ibid.,* 37.

[778] *Ibid.,* 23.

[779] James Madison, *The Federalist Papers*, http://www.let.rug.nl/usa/ documents/ 1786-1800/the-federalist-papers/the-federalist-51.php

[780] F. A. Hayek, "Why I Am Not a Conservative," *The Constitution of Liberty* (Chicago, IL: University of Chicago Press, 2011), pp. 517-33. http://press. uchicago.edu/books/excerpt/2011/hayek_constitution.html

[781] *Ibid.*

[782] Rebecca Newberger Goldstein, "Truth Isn't the Problem—We Are," *Wall Street Journal*, March 18, 2018. https://www.wsj.com/articles/truth-isnt-the-problemwe-are-1521124562?mod=searchresults&page=1&pos=3

[783] Cited by John Sides, "Democrats are gay, Republicans are rich: Our stereotypes of political parties are amazingly wrong," *Washington Post*, May 23, 2016. Study by Douglas J. Ahler and Gaurav Sood, "The Parties in our Heads: Misperceptions About Party Composition and Their Consequences," Sept. 15, 2016. http:// www.dougahler.com / uploads /2/4 / 6/9 / 24697799/ ahlersood_party composition.pdf

[784] Cropsey, *Polity and Economy*, xii.

[785] James Ceaser, "The Philosophical Origins of Anti-Americanism in Europe," in Paul Hollander, *Understanding Anti-Americanism: Its Orgins and Impact at Home and Abroad* (Chicago, IL: Ivan Dee, 2004), 49.

[786] Marie-France Toinet, "Does Anti-Americanism Exist?" in Denis Lacorne, Jacques Rupnik, and Marie-France Toinet, eds*., The Rise and Fall of Anti-Americanism* (New York, NY: Palgrave Macmillan, 1990), 219.

[787] Brendon O'Connor, ed., *Anti-Americanism: History, Causes, Themes* (New York, NY: Praeger Publishers, 2007), 21.

[788] Philippe Roger, *The American Enemy: The History of French Anti-Americanism* (Chicago, IL: University of Chicago Press, 2005), 29.

[789] Ibid., xi.

[790] *Webster's Revised Unabridged Dictionary* (1913 + 1828), https://web. archive.org/web/20120305190842/http://machaut.uchicago.edu/?resource=Webs ter%27s&word=antiamerican&use1913=on&use1828=on

[791] Toinet, cited in Lacorne *et al., op. cit.,* 269.

[792] Roger, *op. cit.,* xiv.

[793] *New Republic* contributor Paul Berman calls Paris "the intellectual capital of the worldwide Communist system," which explains the enormous impact of the anti-Soviet turn of the younger generation in the 1970s. But for most, this did not translate into pro-American sentiment. *A Tale of Two Utopias: The Political Journey of the Generation of 1968* (New York, N.Y.: W.W. Norton, 1996), 286.

[794] Hollander, *op. cit.,* 12.

[795] *Ibid.,* 19.

[796] *Ibid.,* 45.

[797] "Que nous ayons rêvé de cet événement, que tout le monde sans exception en ait rêvé, parce que nul ne peut ne pas rêver de la destruction de n'importe quelle puissance devenue à ce point hégémonique, cela est inacceptable pour la

conscience morale occidentale, mais c'est pourtant un fait, et qui se mesure justement à la violence pathétique de tous les discours qui veulent l'effacer. A la limite, c'est eux qui l'ont fait, mais c'est nous qui l'avons voulu." Jean Baudrillard, "L'esprit du terrorisme," *Le Monde,* Nov. 3, 2001. http://www.lemonde.fr/ disparitions / article /2007/03/06/l-esprit-du-terrorisme-par-jean-baudrillard_ 879 920_3382.html#zmyjKtmOZM067IHO.99

[798] Ceaser, *op. cit.* 47.

[799] Denis Lacorne. "Anti-Americanism and Americanophobia: A French Perspectives," March 2005. https://hal-sciencespo.archives-ouvertes.fr/ hal-01065572

[800] *Ibid.,* 15

[801] *Ibid.,* 17.

[802] Quoted in Jean-Louis Loubet del Bayle, *Les nonconformistes des années trente* (Paris: Seuil, 1969), 259.

[803] Cited in Ceasar, *op. cit.,* 60.

[804] *Ibid.,* 61.

[805] Emmanuel Mounier, "Revue de culture générale," October 1930, 14-21, quoted in Jean-Louis Loubet del Bayle, *op.cit.,* 258. On Mounier and America, Lacorne recommends Seth Armus, "The Eternal enemy: Emmanuel Mounier's Esprit and French Anti-Americanism," *French Historical Studies*, n° 2, Spring 2001, 271-303.

[806] *Ibid.,* 62.

[807] Lewis S. Feuer, *Ideology and the Ideologists* (New York, NY: Harper and Row, 1975), 79

[808] Thomas Sowell defines "'intellectuals' … [as] people whose occupations deal primarily with ideas," whether they are paid for it or not. Thomas Sowell, *Intellectuals and Society* (New York, NY: Basic Books, 2009), 7.

[809] *Ibid.,* 192.

[810] *Ibid.,* 199.

[811] *Ibid.,* 203.

[812] *Ibid.,* 205.

[813] *Ibid.,* 169.

[814] Paul Hollander, *The End of Commitment: Intellectuals, Revolutionaries, and Political Morality in the Twentieth Century* (Chicago, IL: Ivan Dee Publishers, 2006).

[815] Paul Hollander, *Political Pilgrims (*New Brunswick, NJ: Transaction, 1981), 53. See Joseph A. Schumpeter, "Capitalism, its Nature – and Demise!" http : // itech . fgcu . edu / faculty / bhobbs / Schumpeter % 20 Capitalism%20-%20Its%20Nature%20and%20Demise.pdf – an abridgement from his *Capitalism, Socialism and Democracy* (1942).

[816] *Political Pilgrims,* 30. Hollander references here Crane Brinton, "Utopia and Democracy," in Frank. E. Manuel, *Utopias and Utopian Thought* (Boston, MA: Houghton Mifflin Co., 1971), 50.

[817] Paul Hollander, *From Benito Mussolini to Hugo Chavez: Intellectuals and a Century of Political Hero Worship* (Cambridge: Cambridge University Press, 2017), 17.

[818] Hans Borkenau in Michael Burleigh, *Sacred Causes: The Clash of Religion and Politics, from the Great War to the War on Terror* (New York, NY: Harper Perennial, 2008), 121.

[819] *From Benito Mussolini to Hugo Chavez*, 58-9.

[820] Richard Griffiths, *Fellow Travellers of the Right: British Enthusiasts for Nazi Germany 1933-9* (London: Oxford University Press, 1980), 20. Cited in *ibid.*, 68.

[821] Ella Winter, *Red Virtue: Human Relationships in the New Russia* (London: Victor Gollancz LTD., 1933)

[822] *Ibid.*

[823] Sowell, *op.cit*, 97.

[824] Cited by Ceasar, *op. cit.*, 53.

[825] Andrei S. Markovitz, "Americanisation and Anti-Americanism," in O'Connor, *op. cit.*, 55

[826] Arendt commended Rousseau for having "presupposed the existence and relied upon the unifying power of the common national enemy." *On Revolution* (New York, NY: Penguin Classis, 2006), 77.

[827] Markovitz, *op. cit.*, 55.

[828] Bukovsky, *op. cit.*, Ch. 6, sec. 6.7: The "Common European Home."

[829] Gorbachev's words were "particularly pleasing to the Italian comrades, whose] General Secretary, Alessandro Natta," had been in close contact for years, and had advised: "We need to ally not only with parties, the Communist, socialist and social democratic ones, but the entire complex of movements, progressive forces with differing aims, including religious movements." (27 January 1986, SA). *Ibid.*

[830] John Laughland, "European Integration: A Marxist Utopia?" *The Monist*, No. 2, 2009. https://www.jstor.org/stable/27904119

[831] Václav Klaus, "EU is not Europe," *Vaclav Klaus Institute,* 13. 3. 2019 https://www.klaus.cz/clanky/4374

[832] Markovitz, *op. cit.,* 57.

[833] Fonte, *op. cit.*, 136.

[834] Karen Alter, "Explaining National Court Acceptance of European Court Jurisprudence: A Critical Evaluation of Theories of Legal Integration," in The European Court and the National Courts," Cited in Fonte, *ibid.*, 137.

[835] Richard Wike, Bruce Stokes, Jacob Poushter and Janell Fetterolf, "U.S. Image Suffers as Publics Around World Question Trump's Leadership," Pew Research Center, June 26, 2017, 23. http://www.pewglobal.org/2017/ 06 / 26 / u – simage – suffers – as – publics – around – world – question -trumps-leadership/

[836] Roger Kimball, *The Long March* (San Francisco, CA: Encounter Books, 2000), 28-9.

[837] Kimball, *op. cit.*, 30, cites Norman Mailer's *Advertisements for Myself* (Cambridge, UK: Cambridge University Press, 1992), 335.

[838] Norman Mailer, " The White Negro," 1957. https: // www. Dissentma gazine .org/online_articles/the-white-negro-fall-1957

[839] *Ibid.*

[840] Kimball, *op. cit.,* 163-4.

[841] *Ibid.*

[842] *Ibid.,* 31.

[843] *Ibid.,* 31-2.

[844] Thomas Sowell has written extensively and persuasively on this topic, especially in his books *The Economics and Politics of Race,* (1983*), Ethnic America* (1981), *Affirmative Action Around the World* (2004), and others.

[845] *Ibid.,* 128.

[846] *Ibid.*

[847] Susan Sontag, *Trip to Hanoi: Journey to a city at war* (New York, NY: HarperCollins, 1969), 87.

[848] Jerry Rubin, *Do It: Scenarios of the Revolution* (New York, NY: Simon and Schuster, 1970), 105. It may be worth noting that the inside cover urges "Read this book stoned!"

[849] *Ibid.,* 7-8.

[850] *Ibid.,* 11.

[851] *Ibid.,* 20.

[852] *Ibid.,*

[853] Daniel S. Benveniste, *The Venezuelan Revolution: A Critique from the Left* (North Charleston, SC: CreateSpace, 2015), 119. Cited in Hollander, *From Mussolini to Chavez,* 237.

[854] Bryan Burrough, *Days of Rage: America's Radical Underground, the FBI, and the Forgotten Age of Revolutionary Violence* (New York, NY: Penguin Books, 2016), 61.

[855] *Ibid.,* 63.

[856] *Ibid.,* 64.

[857] *Ibid.,* 65.

[858] Hollander cites Cabrera Infante: "Che, like Trotsky, advocated permanent revolution. But loving humanity, an abstract idea, he forgot all about people. He believed in the New Man but not in human beings, new or old." *From Mussolini to Chavez,* 241.

[859] *Ibid.*

[860] Hollander, *ibid..,* 238.

[861] Burrough, *op. cit.,* 5.

[862] *Ibid.*

[863] The pardon was condemned by police and New York elected officials. Eric Lipton, "Officials Criticize Clinton's Pardon of an Ex-Terrorist," *The New York Times,* Jan. 22, 2001. https://www.nytimes.com/2001/01/ 22/nyregion/officials-criticize-clinton-s-pardon-of-an-ex-terrorist.html.

[864] Robert L.Paquette, "What Worlds Have They to Conquer?: A Higher Ed Dystopia," Law & Liberty, Feb. 1, 2018. https://www.lawliberty.org/ liberty-forum/what-worlds-have-they-to-conquer-a-higher-ed-dystopia/

[865] "Angela Davis: Redefining American Attitudes," *Hamilton*, Feb. 29, 2016.

[866] Angela Davis, Biography, A&E Television Networks, https://www. Biography .com/activist/angela-davis

[867] Michael Moynihan, "1960s Radicals Ended Up Teaching Your Kids," *The Daily Beast*, Apr. 10, 2013. https://www.thedailybeast.com/how-1960s-radicals-ended-up-teaching-your-kids

[868] The sordid story is described by Paul Bass and Douglas W. Rae in *Murder in the Model City: The Black Panthers, Yale, And the Redemption of a Killer* (New York, NY: Basic Books, 2006)

[869] Patrick Dunleavy, "Another Terrorist Gets Early Prison Release," *IPT News*. April 23, 2019. https://www.investigativeproject.org/7895/another-terrorist-gets-early-prison-release

[870] See also Stanley Kurtz's meticulously researched *Radical-in-Chief: Barack Obama and the Untold Story of American Socialism* (New York, NY: Threshold, 2010).

[871] Erik Olin Wright, "How to Be an Anticapitalist Today," *Jacobin*, Dec. 2, 2015, https://www.jacobinmag.com/2015/12/erik-olin-wright-real-utopias-anticapitalism-democracy

[872] Tom Cutterham, A Rough Guide to Utopia, *The Oxonian* 11-1-2010 Issue 14.2 http://www.oxonianreview.org/wp/a-rough-guide-to-utopia/

[873] Online Library of Liberty: "Are Economists Basically Immoral?" and Other Essays on Economics, Ethics, and Religion, 47. http://lf-oll.s3.amazonaws. Com/titles/2228/Heyne_1472_EBk_v6.0.pdf

[874] George Will, "The New, Angrier Socialism," *NR* February 17, 2019 https://www.nationalreview.com/2019/02/socialism-more-praised-than-defined-by-proponents/

[875] " Word of the Year 2016 is…" Oxford Dictionaries, Dec. 11, 2016. https:// www.oxforddictionaries.com/press/news/2016/12/11/WOTY-16

[876] Ralph Keyes, "The Post-Truth Era: Dishonesty and Deception in Contemporary Life," *Phil Papers,* 2004. https://philpapers.org/rec/ KEYTPE

[877] *Ibid.*

[878] "Overprotecting Parents Can Lead Children to Develop 'Peter Pan Syndrome," *Science Daily*, May 3, 2007. https://www.sciencedaily.com/ releases/2007/05/070501112023.htm

[879] David C. Stolinsky, "Progressives: The Real World vs. Neverland," Gatestone Institute, Sept. 2, 2018. https://www.gatestoneinstitute.org/ 12732/progressives-reality

[880] "Word of the Year 2017 is…" *Oxford Dictionaries*, Dec. 15, 2017. https:// en.oxforddictionaries.com / word-of-the-year / word-of-the-year-2017

[881] *Ibid.*

[882] Douglas Murray, "The Death of Facts," Gatestone Institute, May 3, 2017. https://www.gatestoneinstitute.org/10300/death-of-facts

[883] K-Sue Park, "The A.C.L.U. Needs to Rethink Free Speech," *The New York Times*, Aug. 17, 2017. https://www.nytimes.com/2017/08/17/opinion /aclu-first-amendment-trump-charlottesville.html

[884] Jay Schalin, "Academic Freedom in the Age of Political Correctness," John William Pope Center for Higher Education Policy, Sept. 2016, 14. https://www.jamesgmartin.center/wp-content/uploads/2016/09/Academic FreedomintheAgeofPoliticalCorrectness-1.pdf

[885] Walter Metzger, "Academic Freedom in the Age of the University," from Richard Hofstadter and W.P. Metzger, *The Development of Academic Freedom in the United States* (New York, NY: Columbia University Press, 1955), 495.

[886] Cited in Neil Hamilton, *Zealotry and Academic Freedom: A Legal and Historical Perspective* (New Brunswick, NJ: Transaction Publishers, 1998), 37.

[887] Schalin, *op.cit.*, 15.

[888] Jennifer Kavanagh and Michael D. Rich, *Truth Decay: An Initial Exploration of the Diminishing Role of Facts and Analysis in American Public Life* (Santa Monica, CA: RAND Corporation, 2018), ix.

[889] *Ibid.*, x-xi.

[890] *Ibid.*, iii.

[891] Michel Serres, *The Natural Contract* (Ann Arbor, MI: The University of Michigan Press, 1995), 5.

[892] *Ibid.*, 6.

[893] Rupert Darwall, *The Age of Global Warming: A History* (London: Quartet Books Ltd., 2013), 4.

[894] Pascal Bruckner, *The Fanaticism of the Apocalypse: Save the Earth, Punish Human Beings*, (Cambridge, UK: Polity Press, 2013), 13-14.

[895] Emily Atkin, "The Troubling Return of Al Gore," *The New Republic*, July 24, 2017. https://newrepublic.com/article/143966/troubling-return-al-gore-profile-inconvenient-sequel

[896] *Ibid.*

[897] Bruckner, 18.

[898] Hans Jonas, *The Imperative of Responsibility: In Search of an Ethics for the Technological Age* (Chicago, IL: University of Chicago Press, 1985), cited in Bruckner, 20.

[899] Bruckner, 14.

[900] *Ibid.*, 31.

[901] See Peter Staudenmaier, "Fascist Ecology: The 'Green Wing' of the Nazi Party and Its Historical Antecedents," in Biehl and Staudenmaier, *op. cit.*, 4. Cited in Rupert Darwall, *Green Tyranny: Exposing the Totalitarian Roots of the Climate Industrial Complex* (New York, NY: Encounter Books, 2017), 30. See also my review of this book in *The Israel Journal of Foreign Affairs*, 2018. https://www.tandfonline.com/doi/full/10.1080/ 23739770.2018.1507075

[902] *Green Tyranny*, 32.

[903] Frank Lawaczeck, *Technik und Wirschaft im Dritten Reich: Ein Arbeitsbeschaffunsgsprogramm* (3rd ed., Nationalsozialistische Bibliotek, 1933), 47-49. Cited in *Green Tyranny, 33*.

[904] *Ibid.,* 93.

[905] *Ibid.*

[906] Wistrich, *From Ambivalence to Betrayal*, 488.

[907] *Ibid.,* 482.

[908] *Ibid.,* 489.

[909] *Green Tyranny,* 98.

[910] Wistrich, *From Ambivalence to Betrayal*, 519.

[911] *Ibid.,* 99.

[912] *Ibid.,* 98.

[913] *Ibid.,* 245.

[914] *Ibid.,* xii.

[915] Michael Barbaro and Coral Davenport, Aims of Donor Are Shadowed by Past in Coal, *The New York Times*, July 4, 2014. https://www.nytimes. com / 2014 / 07 / 05 / us / politics / prominent – environmentalist – helped – fund – coal - projects.html?_r=0

[916] *Ibid.,* 212.

[917] Darwall, *Green Tyranny*, ix.

[918] Neanda Salvaterra, "Coal Shows Resilience in Global Comeback, Wall Street Journal, Sept. 3, 2018. https://www.wsj.com/articles/why-coals-power-persists-1535976000?mod=searchresults&page=1&pos=1

[919] Richard Spillett, "Greenpeace condemned by its original founder as 'evil' and being guilty of 'losing its humanitarian roots'," *MailOnline,* Oct. 15, 2014. http://www.dailymail.co.uk/news/article-2794116/greenpeace-condemned-original-founder-evil-guilty-losing-humanitarian-roots.html

[920] Jake Tapper, "Al Gore's 'Inconvenient Truth'? -- A $30,000 Utility Bill," ABC News, Feb. 26, 2007. https://abcnews.go.com/Politics/Global Warming/story?id= 2906888&page=1

[921] Space News actually asked EDF about this funding but got stonewalled. Here is their report: "However, EDF has provided few details about how much MethaneSAT will cost or how it will be funded. The project received last year a grant from a new initiative called The Audacious Project, although the size of the award was not disclosed. An EDF spokesman did not respond to an inquiry about the financial status of the project." Jeff Foust, "Ball and SSL win study contracts for methane emission tracking satellite," *SpaceNews*, Jan. 11, 2019. https://spacenews.com/ball - and-ssl-win-study-contracts-for-methane-emission-tracking-satellite/

[922] David Wojick, "Big oil goes big green," CFACT May 1st, 2019 https:// www.cfact.org/2019/05/01/big-oil-goes-big-green/

[923] https://www.edf.org/finances

[924] Martin Jay, *The Dialectical Imagination: A History of the Frankfurt School and the Institute of Social Research 1932-1950* (London, 1973), 63. https://www.marxists.org/subject/frankfurt-school/jay/ch01.htm Cited in *Green Tyranny*, 45.

[925] Herbert Marcuse, "Ecology and the Critique of Modern Society," *Capital Nature Socialism: A Journal of Socialist Ecology*, March 1992, 33. https : // www . marcuse . org / herbert / pubs / posthumous / 79Marcuse EcologyCritiqueModern Society1992CapNatSoc.pdf

[926] Aleksandr Isayevich Solzhenitsyn, Nobel Lecture 1970, https://www. nobelprize.org/prizes/literature/1970/solzhenitsyn/lecture/

[927] *Ibid.*

[928] Thomas Sowell, *The Quest for Cosmic Justice* (New York, NY: The Free Press, 1999), 127.

[929] Walter R. Risher, "Narration as a Human Communication Paradigm: The Case of Public Moral Argument," in John Louis Lucaites, Celeste Michelle Condit, Sally Caudill, eds. *Contemporary Rhetorical Theory: A Reader* (New York, NY: Guilford Press, 1999), 272.

[930] Hayden White, "The Value of Narrativity in the Representation of Reality," *Critical Inquiry* 7, 1980, 5-27. http://digitalrhetoricandnet workedcomposition . web . unc . edu / files / 2016 / 01 / white-value-of-narrativity.pdf

[931] There have been many efforts to evaluate Defense Department information operations, notably by the Rand Corporation. See for example Christopher Paul, Jessica Yeats, Colin P. Clarke, and Miriam Matthews, "Assessing and Evaluating Department of Defense Efforts to Inform, Influence, and Persuade: Desk Reference," Santa Monica, Calif.: RAND Corporation, RR-809/1-OSD, 2014.

[932] See Juliana Geran Pilon, *The Art of Peace: Engaging a Complex World* (New York, NY: Routledge, 2016), esp. ch. 13.

[933] Paul J. Tompkins Jr., USASOC Project Lead; Summer D. Agan, Editor; Amy Haufler, W. Sam Lauber, Summer D. Agan, and Guillermo Pinczuk, Contributing Authors, "Assessing Revolutionary and Insurgent Strategies: Narratives and Competing Messages," (United States Army Special Operations Command and The Johns Hopkins University Applied Physics Laboratory's National Security Analysis Department, May 18, 2018), 3.

[934] *Ibid.*

[935] *Ibid.*, 9. The authors cite Kenneth Burke, "The Rhetoric of Hitler's 'Battle,'" from *Readings in Propaganda and Persuasion: New and Classic Essays*, ed. Garth S. Jowett and Victoria O'Donnell (Thousand Oaks, CA: Sage Publications, 2006), 149–168.

[936] *Narratives*, 52.

[937] Brad Allenby and Joel Garreau," Weaponized Narrative Is the New Battlespace," *DefenseOne*, Jan. 3, 2017. https://www.defenseone.com/ ideas/ 2017/01/weaponized-narrative-new-battlespace/134284/

[938] Robert Conquest, *The Dragons of Expectation: Reality and Delusion in the Course of History* (New York, NY: W.W. Norton, 2006), 8.

[939] *Ibid.*, 11.

[940] *Ibid.*, 47.

[941] *Ibid.*, 49

[942] *Ibid.*, 51.

[943] *Ibid.*, 29.

[944] Sowell, *op. cit.*, 12.

[945] *Ibid.*, 51.

[946] *Ibid.*, 139.

[947] *Ibid.*, 140.

[948] Sowell, *Intellectuals and Society*, 313.

[949] Allenby and Garreau, *op. cit.*

[950] Samuel P. Huntington, *The Soldier and the State: The Theory and Politics of Civil-military Relations* (Cambridge, MA: Harvard University Press, 1957), 90.

[951] Woefully insufficient for the task, the warships sent by Jefferson in 1801 met with disaster: one ship ran aground, and the crew was seized. Four years later, the Americans could hardly claim victory. Jefferson seems at last to have realized that his earlier opposition to building any sort of navy had been short-sighted. See Pilon, *The Art of Peace*, 134.

[952] Alexander Hamilton, James Madison, and John Jay, *The Federalist Papers*, with an introduction by Clinton Rossiter (New York, NY: The New American Library, 1961), "Federalist 8," 67.

[953] *Ibid.*, 71.

[954] *Ibid.*

[955] Smith, *The Wealth of Nations*, IV, v.a, 522-523.

[956] Immanuel Kant, *Perpetual Peace: A Philosophical Sketch, First Supplement*, "Of the Guarantee for Perpetual Peace," https://www. mtholyoke.edu/acad/intrel /kant/kant1.htm

[957] Cited by John Gittings, in *The Glorious Art of Peace: From the Iliad to Iraq* (Oxford: Oxford University Press, 2012), 128. Gittings, however, points out that "in fact, the title to Kant's essay comes not from an inn-sign but from the Abbe de Saint-Pierre's Project."

[958] Kant, *op. cit.*

[959] *Ibid.*, I.2.

[960] James Ceaser "The Origins and Character of American Exceptionalism," *American Political Thought: A Journal of Ideas, Institutions, and Culture*, Vol. 1, No. 1, Spring 2012, 14.

[961] Walter McDougall, *Promised Land, Crusader State* (Boston, MA: Houghton Mifflin, 1997).

[962] Ceaser, *ibid.*

[963] *Ibid.*

[964] Washington's Farewell Address, Sept. 19, 1796. First read in the House of Representatives on Feb. 22, 1862. https://www.senate.gov/ artandhistory/history/ resources/pdf/Washingtons_Farewell_Address.pdf

[965] Pacificus 2. *The Pacificus-Helvidius Debates of 1793–1794: Toward the Completion of the American Founding* [1793]. http://oll.liberty fund.org/titles/ hamilton-the-pacificus-helvidius-debates-of-1793-1794

[966] http://founders.archives.gov/documents/Franklin/01-24-02-0004

[967] Walter LaFeber, "The American Age: U.S. Foreign Policy At Home and Abroad – 1750 to the Present," *The American Age: U.S. Foreign Policy At Home and Abroad - 1750 to the Present*, 2nd ed. (New York, NY: W.W. Norton & Company, 1994), 20.

[968] Dave Richard Palmer, *The Way of the Fox: American Strategy in the War for America 1775–1783* (Westport, CT: Greenwood Press, 1975).

[969] Kenneth A. Daigler, *Spies, Patriots, and Traitors: American Intelligence in the Revolutionary War* (Washington, DC: Georgetown University Press, 2014), 15.

[970] George Washington to Robert Hunter Morris, January 5, 1766, in John Fitzpatrick, ed., *The Writings of George Washington,* vol. 1 (Washington, DC: Government Printing Office, 1931–44), 268.

[971] LaFeber, *op. cit.,* 45.

[972] Forrest McDonald, *Alexander Hamilton: A Biography* (New York, NY: W. W. Norton, 1982), 267. Letter from Hamilton to Washington, September 15, 1790.

[973] *Ibid.,* 269.

[974] Henry Kissinger, *Diplomacy* (New York, NY: Touchstone Books, 1994), 36.

[975] *Ibid.,* 32.

[976] Karl-Friedrich Walling, *Republican Empire: Alexander Hamilton on War and Free Government* (Lawrence, KS: University Press of Kansas, 1999), 235.

[977] David McCullough, *John Adams* (New York, NY: Simon & Schuster, 2001), 281.

[978] The Spirit of Laws, Book 20, Ch. 1. From Philip B. Kurkland and Ralph Lerner, eds., *The Founders' Constitution* (Chicago, IL: University of Chicago Press and the Liberty Fund, 1987). http://press-pubs.uchicago.edu/founders/documents/ v1ch4s2.html

[979] "Federalist 6," 56–57.

[980] http://teachingamericanhistory.org/library/document/address-to-the-people-of -the-united-states/

[981] Letter from Thomas Jefferson to George Hammond, 29 May 1792 https://founders.archives.gov/documents/Jefferson/01-23-02-0506

[982] Letter from Benjamin Franklin to the Abbes Chalut and Arnoux, 17 April 1787 (unpublished) http://franklinpapers.org/franklin/framed Volumes.jsp?vol=44& page=605

[983] http://franklinpapers.org/franklin/framedVolumes.jsp?vol=2&page=190f

[984] For a history of the motto, see http://www.archives.upenn.edu/histy/ features/vis_obj/heraldry/guide.html

[985] http://www.girlscouts.org/en/about-girl-scouts/who-we-are.html

[986] http://usscouts.org/advance/boyscout/bsoathlaw.asp

[987] "In recent years, the Boy Scouts of America have expanded rights for gay people. In 2013, the group ended its ban on openly gay youths participating in its activities. Two years later, the organization ended its ban on openly gay adult leaders." Niraj Chokshi, *The New York Times*, Jan. 30, 2017. https://www. nytimes.com/2017/01/30/us/boy-scouts-reversing-century-old-stance-will-allow-transgender-boys.html

[988] Amy A. Kass, Leon R. Kass, and Diana Schaub, *What So Proudly We Hail: The American Soul in Story, Speech, and Song* (Bryn Mawr, PA: Intercollegiate Studies Institute, 2013), xiv.

[989] *Ibid.*, xxi.

[990] Benjamin Franklin, *The Autobiography*, in *ibid.*, 192.

[991] "Axios/Survey Monkey Poll: 2019 World Economic Forum," Jan. 27, 2019 https://www.surveymonkey.com/curiosity/axios-davos-2019/

[992] Karlyn Bowman, "Embracing Socialism," *Forbes*, Oct. 24, 2018 https://www.forbes.com/sites/bowmanmarsico/2018/10/24/embracing-socialism/#5c08314165e5

[993] Marion Smith, "Forty-Four Percent of Millennials Prefer Socialism. Do They Know What It Means?" Victims of Communism, https://www. Victimsof Communism.org/ witnessblog/ 2018 / 4 / 19 / forty-four-percent-of-millennials-prefer-socialism-do-they-know-what-it-means

[994] Cited in Clare Malone, "The Young Left's Anti-Capitalist Manifesto," *FiveThirtyEight* Jan. 22, 2019. https://fivethirtyeight.com/features/the-young-lefts-anti-capitalist-manifesto/

[995] *Ibid.*

[996] "Millennial socialists want to shake up the economy and save the climate*,"* *The Economist*, Feb. 14, 2019. https://www.economist.com/ briefing/2019/02/14/ millennial-socialists-want-to-shake-up-the-economy-and-save-the-climate

[997] Chris Harman Anti-capitalism: theory and practice (Part 1), *International Socialism* 2:88, Autumn 2000. http://www.marxists.de/ anticap/theprax/part1.htm #int

[998] "When asked whether they think groups of Arabs carried out the 9/11 attacks on the U.S., most Muslims in the nations surveyed say they do not believe this. There is no Muslim public in which even 30% accept that Arabs conducted the attacks. Indeed, Muslims in Jordan, Egypt, and Turkey are less likely to accept this today than in 2006." "Muslim-Western Tensions Persist," Pew Research Center, July 21, 2011. http://www. pewglobal.org/2011/07/21/muslim-Western-tensions-persist/

[999] "Based on a *Jerusalem Post* article describing the Israeli government's attempts to account for its citizens in the area of the World Trade Center and the Pentagon when the attacks occurred, a conspiracy involving '4,000 Jews' was born. According to the adherents of this theory, the Mossad (Israeli intelligence

agency) forewarned these Jews about the attacks, and so they were able to escape harm. Such rumors again arose after the bombings in the London subway last year. It seems that whatever happens in the world, there are people who will lay the blame at the feet of the Jews." Cinnamon Stillwell, "The Truth About 9/11 Conspiracy Theories," *SFGate* April 19, 2006. https://www.sfgate.com/politics /article/The-Truth-About-9-11-Conspiracy-Theories-2520182.php

[1000] "Louis Farrakhan: 'Israelis and Zionist Jews' played key roles in 9/11 attacks," *CBS DC,* March 5, 2015. https://washington.cbslocal.com/ 2015/ 03/05 / farrakhan-israelis-and-zionist-jews-behind-911-terror-attacks/

[1001] Adam Serwer, "Why Tamika Mallory Won't Condemn Farrakhan," *The Atlantic,* Mar. 11, 2018. https://www.theatlantic.com/politics/archive /2018/03/ nation-of-islam/555332/

[1002] Leah McSweeney and Jacob Siegel, *The Tablet,* December 10, 2018, https://www.tabletmag.com/jewish-news-and-politics/276694/is-the-womens-march-melting-down#amendments

[1003] Cameron Cawthorne, "Farrakhan: The 'Wicked Jews' Use Me to Attack Women's Movement, March Leaders," *Washington Free Beacon,* Feb. 18, 2019. https://freebeacon.com/culture/farrakhan-the-wicked-jews-use-me-to-attack-womens-movement/

[1004] http://witnessforpeace.org/the-issues/labor-rights-economic-justice/

[1005] Elizabeth Harrington, "Hypnotizing the World: Omar Has Ties to Radical Anti-Israel, Anti-American Group," *Washington Free Beacon,* Feb. 19, 2019 https://freebeacon.com/politics/hypnotizing-the-world-omar-has-ties-to-radical-anti-israel-anti-american-group/ For full text, see Atrayus Goode's Notes for Sermon Presented at the Chapel in the Pines, Chapel Hill NC July 2, 2017. http://www.aimeproject.org/events/ Counterfeit%20Theology%20Notes.pdf

[1006] Wistrich, *From Ambivalence to Betrayal,* 510.

[1007] *Ibid,* 513.

[1008] *Ibid.,* 519.

[1009] *Ibid.,* 525-7.

[1010] Clay R. Fuller, "Strongmen are on the rise. Here's how to defeat them," AEI Ideas, Apr. 24, 2019

[1011] Ganesh Sitaraman, "The Emergence of Progressive Foreign Policy," *War on the Rocks,* April 15, 2019. https://warontherocks.com/2019/04/ the-emergence-of-progressive-foreign-policy/

[1012] *Annual Report to Congress: Military and Security Developments Involving the People's Republic of China* 2019, May 2, 2019. https:// media.defense.gov / 2019 / May/02 / 2002127082 / -1/-1/1/2019% 20CHINA%20MILITARY%20 POWER%20REPORT%20(1).PDF

[1013] Ibid., "Special Topic: Influence Operations."

[1014] Summary of the National Defense Strategy Sharpening the American Military's Competitive Edge, Department of Defense, 2018. https:// dod.defense.

Gov / Portals / 1 / Documents / pubs / 2018 – National - Defense - Strategy - Summary.pdf

[1015] Cited in Nick Tabor, "No Slouch," *The Paris Review*, April 7, 2015 https://www.theparisreview.org/blog/2015/04/07/no-slouch/

[1016] *Ibid.*

[1017] Gorman Beauchamp, "'The Legend of the Grand Inquisitor': The Utopian as Sadist," *Humanitas,* Volume XX, Nos. 1 and 2, 2007, 143.

[1018] Wislawa Szymborska, *View with a Grain of Sand: Selected Poems*, Translated by Stanislaw Baranczak and Clare Cavanagh, (New York, NY: Harvest/Harcourt Brace, 1995), 127.

Bibliography

Peter Ackroyd, *Rebellion: The History of England from James I to the Glorious Revolution* (New York, NY: St. Martin Griffin, 2014)

Lord Acton, *Essays on Freedom and Power* (New York, NY: Meridian, 1964)

Hannah Arendt, *On Revolution* (New York, NY: Penguin Books, 1963)

Karen Armstrong, *Islam: A Short History* (New York, NY: Random House, 2002)

Shmuel Bar, *A Warrant for Terror: The Fatwas of Radical Islam and the Duty to Jihad* (Latham, MD: Rowman & Littlefield, 2006)

Avraham Barkai, *Nazi Economics: Ideology, Theory, and Policy* (New Haven, CT: Yale University Press, 1990)

Frederic Bastiat, *The Law* (Irvington-on-Hudson, NY: The Foundation for Economic Education, Inc., 1990)

Michele Battini, *Socialism of Fools: Capitalism and Modern Anti-Semitism* (New York, NY: Columbia University Press, 2016)

Deborah Baumgold, *Three-Text Edition of Thomas Hobbes's Political Theory: The Elements of Law, De Cive and Leviathan* (Cambridge, UK: Cambridge University Press, 2017)

Carl L Becker, *The Declaration of Independence a Study in the History of Political Ideas* (New York, NY: Vintage, 1942)

Daniel S. Benveniste, *The Venezuelan Revolution: A Critique from the Left* (North Charleston, SC: Createspace, 2015)

Michael Berenbaum, ed., *The Holocaust and History: The Known, the Unknown, the Disputed, and the Reexamined* (Bloomington, IN: Indiana University Press, 1998)

Isaiah Berlin, "Two Concepts of Liberty," in *Four Essays on Liberty* (Oxford: Oxford University Press, 1969)

James H. Billington, *Fire in the Minds of Men: Origins of the Revolutionary Faith* (New York, NY: Basic Books, 1980)

Edwin Black, *War Against the Weak: Eugenics and America's Campaign to Create a Master Race* (New York, NY: Dialog Press, 2012)

Bob Blaisdell, *Great Speeches of the 20th Century* (New York, NY: Dover Publications, 2011)

R. J. B. Bosworth, *Mussolini* (London, UK: Arnold Publishers, 2002)

Pascal Bruckner, *The Fanaticism of the Apocalypse: Save the Earth, Punish Human Beings*, (Cambridge, UK: Polity Press, 2013)

Vladimir Bukovsky, *Judgment in Moscow: Soviet Crimes and Western Complicity* (Los Angeles, CA: Ninth of November Press, 2019)

Michael Burleigh, *The Third Reich: A New History* (New York, NY: Hill and Wang, 2000)

Michael Burleigh, *Sacred Causes: The Clash of Religion and Politics, from the Great War to the War on Terror* (New York, NY: Harper Perennial, 2008)

Michael Burleigh, *Blood and Rage: A Cultural History of Terrorism* (New York, NY: HarperCollins 2009)

Bryan Burrough, *Days of Rage: America's Radical Underground, the FBI, and the Forgotten Age of Revolutionary Violence* (New York, NY: Penguin Books, 2016)

Paul Carus, *The History of the Devil and the Idea of Evil: From the Earliest Times to the Present Day* (Peaks Pine Publishing. Kindle Edition, 2016)

R. W. Chambers, *Thomas More* (London, U.K.: Endeavor Press, 1935)

Jung Chang with Jon Halliday, *Mao: The Unknown Story* (New York, NY: Anchor, 2006)

Cheng Chen, *The Return of Ideology: The Search for Regime Identities in Postcommunist Russia and China* (Ann Arbor, MI: University of Michigan Press, 2016)

Christopher Clark, *Iron Kingdom: The Rise and Downfall of Prussia, 1600-1947* (Cambridge, MA: Harvard University Press, 2009)

Morgan Cloud, Martha Albertson Fineman, Anna Grear, eds., *Vulnerability: Reflections on a New Ethical Foundation for Law and Politics* (New York, NY: Routledge, 2016)

Adam Cohen, *Imbeciles: The Supreme Court, Eugenics, and the Sterilization of Carrie Buck* (New York, NY: 2016)

Robert Conquest, *The Dragons of Expectation: Reality and Delusion in the Course of History* (New York, NY: W.W. Norton, 2006)

Stéphane Courtois, Andrzej Paczkowski, Karel Bartosek eds., *The Black Book of Communism: Crimes, Terror, Repression* (Cambridge, MA: Harvard University Press, 1999)

Herbert Croly, *Progressive Democracy* (New York, NY: The Macmillan Company, 1914)

Joseph Cropsey, *Polity and Economy: Further Thoughts Principles of Adam Smith* (South Bend, IN: St. Augustine Press, 2001)

Robert Curry, *Common Sense Nation: Unlocking the Forgotten Power of the American Idea* (New York, NY: Encounter Books, 2015)

Kenneth A. Daigler, *Spies, Patriots, and Traitors: American Intelligence in the Revolutionary War* (Washington, DC: Georgetown University Press, 2014)

Rupert Darwall, *Green Tyranny: Exposing the Totalitarian Roots of the Climate Industrial Complex* (New York, NY: Encounter Books: 2018)

Lucy Dawidowicz, *The Golden Tradition: Jewish Life and Thought in Eastern Europe* (New York, NY: Holt, Rinehart and Winston, 1967)

William Dennis, *In Defense of Freedom and Related Essays,* by Frank S. Meyer (Indianapolis, IN: Liberty Fund, Inc., 1996)

John Dewey, *Liberalism and Social Action* (Amherst, N.Y.: Prometheus Books, 2000),

John J. Dziak, *Chekisty: A History of the KGB* (Lexington, MA: Lexington Books, 1988)

Elizabeth L. Eisenstein, *The Printing Revolution in Early Modern Europe* (Cambridge, UK: University of Cambridge Press, 1983)

Mircea Eliade, *The Sacred and the Profane: The Nature of Religion* (Chicago, IL: University of Chicago Press, 1968)

Mircea Eliade, *Cosmos and History: The Myth of the Eternal Return* (New York, NY: Harper & Row, 1959)

Hartmut Elsenhans, Rachid Ouaissa, Sebastian Schwecke, Mary Ann Tétreault, eds., *The Transformation of Politicised Religion: From Zealots into Leaders* (London: Ashgate Publishing, 2015)

Richard A. Epstein, *The Classical Liberal Constitution: The Uncertain Quest for Limited Government* (Cambridge, MA: Harvard University Press, 2014)

Nial Fergusson, *The House of Rothschild* (New York, NY: Penguin Books, 1999)

Nial Fergusson, *The Ascent of Money: A Financial History* (New York, NY: Penguin Books, 2009)

Lewis S. Feuer, ed., *Marx & Engels: Basic Writings on Politics & Philosophy*, (New York, NY: Doubleday Co., 1959)

Lewis S. Feuer, *Ideology and the Ideologists* (New York, NY: Harper and Row, 1975)

Helen Fein, ed., *The Persisting Question: Sociological Perspectives and Social Contexts of Modern Antisemitism* (Berlin: Walter de Gruyter, 1987)

Robert Fine and Philip Spencer, *Antisemitism and the left: On the return of the Jewish question* (Manchester, UK: Manchester University Press, 2017)

John Fitzpatrick, ed., *The Writings of George Washington,* vol. 1 (Washington, DC: Government Printing Office, 1931–44)

Ronald Florence, *Lawrence and Aaronsohn: T. E. Lawrence, Aaron Aaronsohn, and the Seeds of the Arab-Israeli Conflict* (New York, NY: Penguin Books, 2008)

John Fonte, *Sovereignty or Submission: Will Americans Rule Themselves or Be Ruled by Others?* (New York, NY: Encounter Books, 2011)

Joseph R. Fornieri, ed., *The Language of Liberty: The Political Speeches and Writings of Abraham Lincoln* (Washington, DC: Regnery Publishing, 2009)

James George Fraser, *The Golden Bough* (New York, NY: Macmillan Publishing Co., 1953)

David Fromkin, *A Peace to End All Peace: The Fall of the Ottoman Empire and the Creation of the Modern Middle East* (New York, NY: Henry Holt & Co, 1989)

Erich Fromm, *Escape from Freedom* (New York, NY: Avon Books, 1965)

Northrop Frye, *The Great Code: The Bible as Literature* (Orlando, FL.: Harcourt Brace Jovanowich, 1983)

Francis Fukuyama, *The End of History and the Last Man* (New York, NY: Free Press, 1992)

Diana Furchtgott-Roth, "The Myth of Increasing Income Inequality," Manhattan Institute E21 Report, Dec. 16, 2013

Hillel Gamoran, "The Biblical Law Against Loans on Interest," *Journal of Near Eastern Studies* 30:3 (April 1971)

Peter Garnsey, *Thinking about Property: From Antiquity to the Age of Revolution* (Cambridge, UK: Cambridge Press, 2009)

Michael Allen Gillespie, *The Theological Origins of Modernity* (Chicago, IL: University of Chicago Press, 2008)

John Gittings, *The Glorious Art of Peace: From the Iliad to Iraq* (Oxford: Oxford University Press, 2012)

Jonah Goldberg, *Liberal Fascism: The Secret History of the American Left, From Mussolini to the Politics of Change* (New York, NY: Crown Forum, 2009).

Alexander Grab, *Napoleon and the Transformation of Europe* (New York, NY: Palgrave, 2003)

Stephen Greenblatt, *The Swerve: How the World Became Modern* (New York, NY: W. W. Norton, 2011)

Anthony James Gregor, *Young Mussolini and the Intellectual Origins of Fascism* (Berkeley, CA: University of California Press, 1979)

Anthony James Gregor, *Totalitarianism and Political Religion: An Intellectual History* (Stanford, CA: Stanford University Press, 2012)

Richard Griffiths, *Fellow Travelers of the Right: British Enthusiasts for Nazi Germany 1933-9* (London: Oxford University Press, 1980)

Pierre Hadot, *The Veil of Isis: An Essay on the History of the Idea of Nature* (Cambridge, MA: Harvard University Press, 2006)

John R. Hall, *Apocalypse: From Antiquity to the Empire of Modernity* (Cambridge, UK: Polity Press, 2009)

Alexander Hamilton, James Madison, and John Jay, *The Federalist Papers*, with an introduction by Clinton Rossiter (New York, NY: The New American Library, 1961)

Alexander Hamilton, *The Pacificus-Helvidius Debates of 1793–1794: Toward the Completion of the American Founding* [1793]

Victor Davis Hanson, *Between War and Peace: Lessons from Afghanistan to Iraq* (New York, NY: Random House, 2004)

Paul G. Harris, *International Equity and Global Environmental Politics* (London: Routledge, 2001)

Paul G. Harris, *World ethics and climate change from international to global justice* (Edinburgh, UK: Edinburgh University Press, 2010)

Peter M. Hass, "Introduction: epistemic communities and international policy coordination". *International Organization*, special issue: *Knowledge, Power, and International Policy Coordination*, Cambridge Journals, Winter 1992, 46 (1)

F. A. Hayek, "Why I Am Not a Conservative," *The Constitution of Liberty* (Chicago, IL: University of Chicago Press, 2011)

F. A. Hayek, *The Road to Serfdom* (Chicago, IL: The University of Chicago Press, 1994)

F. A. Hayek, *The Fatal Conceit: The Errors of Socialism* (Chicago, ILL: University of Chicago Press, 2018)

Arthur Herman, *How the Scots Invented the Modern World* (New York, NY: Three Rivers Press, 2001)

Denis Caulfield Heron, *An Introduction to the History of Jurisprudence* (London: J. W. Parker, 1860)

Gertrude Himmelfarb, *The Roads to Modernity: The British, French, and American Enlightenments* (New York, NY: Vintage, 2007)

Adolf Hitler, *Mein Kampf*, James Vincent Murphy, trans. (CreateSpace, 2011)

Eric Hobsbawm, *The Age of Extremes: A History of the World, 1914-1991* (New York, NY: Random House, 1994)

Richard Hofstadter, *The Idea of a Party System: The Rise of Legitimate Opposition in the United States, 1780-1840* (Chicago: University of Chicago Press, 1970)

Richard Hofstadter and W.P. Metzger, *The Development of Academic Freedom in the United States* (New York, NY: Columbia University Press, 1955)

Paul Hollander, *Understanding Anti-Americanism: Its Origins and Impact at Home and Abroad* (Chicago, IL: Ivan Dee, 2004)

Paul Hollander, *The End of Commitment: Intellectuals, Revolutionaries, and Political Morality in the Twentieth Century* (Chicago, IL: Ivan Dee Publishers, 2006)

Paul Hollander, *Political Pilgrims* (New Brunswick, NJ: Transaction, 1981)

Paul Hollander, *From Benito Mussolini to Hugo Chavez: Intellectuals and a Century of Political Hero Worship* (Cambridge, UK: Cambridge University Press, 2017)

Townsend Hoopes and Douglas Brinkley, *FDR and the Creation of the U.N.* (New Haven, CT: Yale University Press, 2000)

Irving Louis Horowitz, *Taking Lives: Genocide and State Power* (New Brunswick, NJ: Transaction Publishers, 2002)

Irving Louis Horowitz, *Ideology and Utopia in the United States, 1956-76* (Oxford: Oxford   University Press, 1977)

Samuel P. Huntington, *The Soldier and the State: The Theory and Politics of Civil-military Relations* (Cambridge, MA: Harvard University Press, 1957)

Samuel P. Huntington, *The Clash of Civilizations and the Remaking of World Order* (New York, NY: Simon & Schuster, 2011)

Francis Hutcheson, *A System of Moral Philosophy: In Three Books - To which is Prefixed Some Account Of The Life, Writings, And Character Of The Author,* Vol. 1 (London: Millar, 1755)

The International Forum for Social Development, *Social Justice in an Open World - The Role of the United Nations*, U.N. Department of Economic and Social Affairs, Division for Social Policy and Development, 2006.

Eberhard Jäckel, *Hitler's Weltanschauung: A Blueprint for Power* (Cambridge, MA: Harvard University Press, 1981)

Martin Jay, *The Dialectical Imagination: A History of the Frankfurt School and the Institute of Social Research 1932-1950*) (Berkeley, CA: University of California Press, 1996)

Lionel Jensen & Timothy Weston, eds., *China in Transformation: the stories beyond the headlines* (Lanham, MD: Rowman & Littlefield, 2006)

Josef Joffe, "Nations We Love to Hate: Israel, America and the New Antisemitism," (Jerusalem: Vidal Sassoon International Center for the Study of Antisemitism, 2005)

Paul Johnson, *A History of Christianity* (New York, NY: Simon & Schuster, 1976)

Hans Jonas, *The Imperative of Responsibility: In Search of an Ethics for the Technological Age* (Chicago: University of Chicago Press, 1985)

Garth S. Jowett and Victoria O'Donnell, eds., *Readings in Propaganda and Persuasion: New and Classic Essays* (Thousand Oaks, CA: Sage Publications, 2006)

Pieter M. Judson, *The Habsburg Empire: A New History* (Cambridge, MA: Belknap Harvard University Press, 2016)

Peter Juviler and Carrie Gustafson, eds., *Religion and Human Rights: Competing Claims* (New York: M.E. Sharpe, 1998)

Alan S. Kahan, *Mind Vs. Money: The War Between Intellectuals and Capitalism* (New Brunswick, NJ: Transaction Publishers, 2010)

Franz Kafka, *Parables and Paradoxes* (New York, NY: Schocken Books, 1961)

Alan S. Kahan, *Mind Vs. Money: The War Between Intellectuals and Capitalism* (New Brunswick, NJ: Transaction Publishers, 2010)

Immanuel Kant, *Perpetual Peace: A Philosophical Sketch, First Supplement*, "Of the Guarantee for Perpetual Peace" (EBook #50922 Project Gutenberg: Jan. 14, 2016)

C.J. Karier, P. C. Violas, and J. Spring. eds., *Roots of Crisis: American Education in the 20th Century* (Chicago, IL: Rand MCTally, 1973)

Leon Kass, *The Beginning of Wisdom: Reading Genesis* (Chicago, IL: University of Chicago Press, 2003)

Amy A. Kass, Leon R. Kass, and Diana Schaub, *What So Proudly We Hail: The American Soul in Story, Speech, and Song* (Bryn Mawr, PA: Intercollegiate Studies Institute, 2013)

Jennifer Kavanagh and Michael D. Rich, *Truth Decay: An Initial Exploration of the Diminishing Role of Facts and Analysis in American Public Life* (Santa Monica, CA: RAND Corporation, 2018)

Michael L. Kennedy, *The Jacobin Clubs in the French Revolution, 1793-1795* (New York, NY: Berghahn Books, 2000)

John Maynard Keynes, *The Economic Consequences of the Peace* (New York, NY: Penguin Books, 1995)

Roger Kimball, *The Long March* (San Francisco, CA: Encounter Books, 2000)

Henry Kissinger, *Diplomacy* (New York, NY: Touchstone Books, 1994)

Norman Kohn, *The Pursuit of the Millennium: Revolutionary Millenarians and Mystical Anarchists of the Middle Ages* (Oxford, U.K.: Oxford University Press, 1970)

Leszek Kołakowski, *Main Currents of Marxism: Its Rise, Growth, and Dissolution*, Volume I: *The Founders*, (Oxford, UK: Clarendon Press, 1978)

Alan Charles Kors, *Naturalism and Unbelief in France, 1650-1729* (Cambridge, UK: Cambridge University Press, 2016)

Martin Kramer, *Islam Assembled: The Advent of the Muslim Congresses* (New York, NY: Columbia University Press, 1986)

Thomas Kuhn, *The Copernican Revolution: Planetary Astronomy in the Development of Western Thought* (Cambridge, MA: Harvard University Press, 1957)

Thomas Kuhn, *The Structure of Scientific Revolution* (Chicago, IL: University of Chicago Press, 1962)

Philip B. Kurkland and Ralph Lerner, eds., *The Founders' Constitution* (Chicago, IL: University of Chicago Press and the Liberty Fund, 1987)

Stanley Kurtz, *Radical-in-Chief: Barack Obama and the Untold Story of American Socialism* (New York, NY: Simon & Schuster, 2010).

Denis Lacorne, Jacques Rupnik, and Marie-France Toinet, eds., *The Rise and Fall of Anti-Americanism* (New York, NY: Palgrave Macmillan, 1990)

Walter LaFeber, "The American Age: U.S. Foreign Policy At Home and Abroad – 1750 to the Present," *The American Age: U.S. Foreign Policy At Home and Abroad - 1750 to the Present*, 2nd ed. (New York, NY: W.W. Norton & Company, 1994)

Richard Landes, *Heaven on Earth: The Varieties of the Millennial Experience* (Oxford: Oxford University Press, 2011)

Gavin I. Langmuir, *Toward a Definition of Antisemitism* (Berkeley and Los Angeles: University of California Press, 1990).

Walter Laqueur, *Communism and nationalism in the Middle East* (New York, NY: Routledge Kegan Paul, 1956)

Joseph LeDoux, *Anxious: Using the Brain to Understand and Treat Fear and Anxiety* (New York, NY: Penguin Books, 2015)

Albert Lee, *Henry Ford and the Jews* (New York, NY: Stein and Day, 1980)

V.I. Lenin, *"Left-wing" Communism, An Infantile Disorder* (Moscow: Foreign Languages Publishing House, 1950)

Nora Levin, *The Holocaust: The Destruction of European Jewry, 1933-1945* (New York, NY: T. Y. Crowell Co., 1968)

Richard S. Levy, *A Lie and a Libel: The History of the Protocols of the Elders of Zion* (Lincoln, Nebraska: University of Nebraska Press, 1996)

Joseph Lifshitz, *Judaism, Law & The Free Market: An Analysis* (Grand Rapids, MI: Acton Institute, 2012)

Jean-Louis Loubet del Bayle, *Les nonconformistes des années trente* (Paris: Seuil, 1969)

John Louis Lucaites, Celeste Michelle Condit, Sally Caudill, eds. *Contemporary Rhetorical Theory: A Reader* (New York, NY: Guilford Press, 1999)

Rett R. Ludwikowski, *The Crisis of Communism: Its Meaning, Origins, and Phases* (McLean, VA: Pergamon-Brassey's 1986)

Rosa Luxemburg, *Selected Political Writings* (London: Cape, 1972)

Shiraz Maher, *Salafi-Jihadism: The History of an Idea* (New York, NY: Penguin Books, 2016)

Daniel Mahoney, *The Idol of Our Age: How the Religion of Humanity Subverts Christianity* (New York, NY: Encounter Books, 2018)

Karl Manheim, *Ideology and Utopia: An Introduction to the Sociology of Knowledge* (London: Routledge & Kegan Paul, 1960)

Frank E. Manuel and Fritzie P. Manuel, *Utopian Thought in the Western World* (Cambridge, MA: Belknap Press, 1982)

Frank. E. Manuel, *Utopias and Utopian Thought* (Boston, MA: Houghton Mifflin Co., 1971)

Richard Marius, *Thomas More: A Biography* (New York, NY: Vintage Books, 1985)

Karl Marx: Early Writings, translated and edited by T. B. Bottomore (New York, NY: McGraw Hill Co., 1963)

Karl Marx, *What Is To Be Done?* (1902; Marxist Internet Archive)

Sayyid Abul Al Maududi, *Jihad fi sabilillah (Jihad in Islam)*, Huda Khattab, ed., translated by Prof. Khushid Ahmad (London: UKIM Dawah Center, n.d.)

David McCullough, *John Adams* (New York: Simon & Schuster, 2001)

Forrest McDonald, *Alexander Hamilton: A Biography* (New York, NY: W. W. Norton, 1982)

Frank McLynn, *Napoleon: A Biography* (London, UK: Jonathan Cape, 1996)

Sean McMeekin, *The Russian Revolution: A New History* (New York, NY: Basic Books, 2017)

Margaret McMillan, *Paris 1919: Six Months that Changed the World* (New York, NY: Random House, 2002)

Arthur M. Mendel. *Vision and Violence,* Richard Landes, ed. (Ann Arbor, MI: University of Michigan Press, 1999)

Frank S. Meyer, *The Molding of Communists: The Training of the Communist Cadre* (New York: Harcourt, Brace, 1961)

Frank S. Meyer, *In Defense of Freedom: A Conservative Credo* (Chicago, IL.: Henry Regnery Company, 1962)

Michael Meyer, ed., *German-Jewish History in Modern Times*, vol. 2 (New York, NY: Columbia University Press, 1997)

Robert Michael, *Holy Hatred: Christianity, Antisemitism, and the Holocaust* (New York, NY: Palgrave Macmillan, 2006)

Terry Miller, Anthony B. Kim, and James M. Roberts, *The 2018 Index of Economic Freedom*, (Washington, DC: The Heritage Foundation, 2018)

Ludwig von Mises, *Omnipotent Government: The Rise of Total State and Total War* (1944), chapter 7, reprinted by the Foundation for Economic Education, March 10, 2016

Richard P. Mitchell, *The Society of the Muslim Brothers* (Oxford: Oxford University Press, 1969)

Henry Morgenthau Sr., *Ambassador Morgenthau's story* (New York, NY: Cosimo Inc., 2008)

George L. Mosse, *The Fascist Revolution: Toward a General Theory of Fascism* (New York, NY: Howard Fertig, 1999)

Morteza Motahari, *Pyramoon Enqelab-e Iran Dow Harekat* [Iran's Revolution in Two Moves] (Tehran, 1984, n.d.)

Jerry Z. Muller, *Capitalism and the Jews* (Princeton, NJ: Princeton University Press, 2011)

Laurent Murawiec, *The Mind of Jihad* (Cambridge: Cambridge University Press, 2008)

Benito Mussolini, "The Doctrine of Fascism," *Fascism Doctrine and Institutions* (Rome: Ardita Publishers, 1935)

Waller R. Newell, *Tyrants: A History of Power, Injustice & Terror* (Cambridge, UK: University of Cambridge Press, 2016)

David Nirenberg, *Anti-Judaism: The Western Tradition* (New York, NY: W. W. Norton, 2014)

Robert Nisbet, *History of the Idea of Progress* (New York, NY: Basic Books, 1980)

Pierre Nora, ed., *Realms of Memory: Conflicts and divisions*, vol. 1 (New York, NY: Columbia University Press, 1996)

Brendon O'Connor, ed., *Anti-Americanism: History, Causes, Themes* (New York, NY, Praeger, 2007)

Daniel Okrent, *The Guarded Gate: Bigotry, Eugenics and the Law That Kept Two Generations of Jews, Italians, and Other European Immigrants Out of America* (New York, NY: Scribner, 2019)

Harry M. Orlinsky, *Understanding the Bible through History and Archaeology* (New York, NY: Ktav Publishing House, 1972)

Arkady Ostrovsky, *The Invention of Russia: The Rise of Putin and Fake News* (New York, NY: Penguin Books, 2017)

Ion Mihai Pacepa, with Ronald Rychlak, *Disinformation: Former Spy Chief Reveals Secret Strategies for Undermining Freedom, Attacking Religion, and Promoting Terrorism* (Washington, WND Books, 2013)

Edward Peters, *A Modern Guide to Indulgences: Rediscovering This Often Misinterpreted Teaching* (Chicago, IL: Liturgy Training Publications, 2008)

Anthony Pagden, *Worlds at War: The 2,500-Year Struggle Between East and West* (New York, NY: Random House, 2009)

Elaine Pagels, *Revelations: Visions, Prophecy, and Politics in the Book of Revelation* (New York: Penguin Books, 2012)

Dave Richard Palmer, *The Way of the Fox: American Strategy in the War for America 1775–1783* (Westport, CT: Greenwood Press, 1975)

Tom Palmer, ed., *The Morality of Capitalism: What Your Professors Won't Tell You* (Ottawa, IL: Jameson Books, 2011)

Maryam Panah, *The Islamic Republic and the World: Global Dimensions of the Iranian Revolution*, (London: Pluto Press, 2007)

Robert O. Paxton, *The Anatomy of Fascism* (New York, NY: Vintage Books, 2005)

Joseph R. Peden and Fred R. Glahe, eds., *The American Family and the State* (San Francisco, CA: Pacific Research Institute, 1986)

Luciano Pellicani, *Revolutionary Apocalypse: Ideological Roots of Terrorism* (New York, NY: Praeger, 2003)

Ronald J. Pestritto, *Woodrow Wilson and the Roots of Modern Liberalism* (Lapham, MD: Rowman & Littlefield, 2005)

Ronald J. Pestritto and William J. Atto, *American Progressivism* (Lanham, MD: Rowman & Littlefield, 2008)

Jaroslaw Piekalkiewicz and Alfred Wayne Penn, *The Politics of Ideocracy* (Albany, NY: State University of New York Press, 1995)

Juliana Geran Pilon, *Why America is Such a Hard Sell: Beyond Pride and Prejudice* (Lanham, MD: Rowman & Littlefield, 2007)

Juliana Geran Pilon, *Soulmates: Resurrecting Eve* (Piscataway, NJ: Transaction Publishers, 2012)

Juliana Geran Pilon, *The Art of Peace: Engaging a Complex World* (New York, NY: Routledge, 2016)

Juliana Geran Pilon and Ralph K. Bennett, *The U.N.: Assessing Soviet Abuses* (London: Institute for European Defence & Strategic Studies, 1988)

Richard Pipes, *Property and Freedom* (New York, NY: Borzoi Books, Knopf, 1999)

Karl Popper, *Conjectures and Refutations: The Growth of Scientific Knowledge* (New York, NY: Basic Books, 1962)

Karl Popper, *The Poverty of Historicism* (New York, NY: Harper & Row, 1964)

Dennis Prager and Joseph Telushkin, *Why the Jews?* (New York, NY: Touchstone, 2003)

Babak Rahimi, "Contentious Legacies of the Ayatollah," in *A Critical Introduction to Khomeini*, ed. Arshin Adib-Moghaddam, (Cambridge, UK: Cambridge University Press, 2014)

Ralph Raico, editor-in-chief, *New Individualist Review*, introduction by Milton Friedman (Indianapolis: Liberty Fund, 1981)

William Reich, *The Mass Psychology of Fascism*, (New York, NY: Orgone Institute Press, 1946)

Aaron Rhodes, *The Debasement of Human Rights* (New York, NY: Encounter Books, 2018)

Philippe Roger, *The American Enemy: The History of French Anti-Americanism* (Chicago, IL: University of Chicago Press, 2005)

Eugene Rogin, *The Fall of the Ottomans: The Great War in the Middle East* (New York, NY: Basic Books, 2015)

Franklin D. Roosevelt, Donald Day, *My Own Story: From Private and Public Papers* (New York, NY: Routledge, 2017)

Edward Alsworth Ross, *Social Control* (New York, NY: Macmillan Co., 1901)

Jean-Jacques Rousseau, *Rousseau's Social Contract, More's Utopia, Bacon's New Atlantis, Campanella's City of the Sun*, (Washington, DC: M. Walter Dunne, 1901)

Jean-Jacques Rousseau, *The Social Contract and Discourses*, translated with an introduction by G.D.H. Cole (New York, NY: E. P. Dutton, 1950)

Christopher Rowland, C. R. A. Morray-Jones, *The Mystery of God: Early Jewish Mysticism and the New Testament* (Leiden, the Netherlands: Brill, 2009)

Eric Rozenman, *Jews Make the Best Demons: "Palestine" and the Jewish Question* (Nashville, TN: New English Review Press, 2018)

Barry Rubin & Wolfgang G. Schwanitz, *Nazis, Islamists, and the Making of the Modern Middle East* (New Haven, CT: Yale University Press, 2014)

Jerry Rubin, *Do It: Scenarios of the Revolution* (New York, NY: Simon and Schuster, 1970)

Malise Ruthven, *A Fury for God: The Islamist Attack on America* (New York, NY: Granta, 2002)

Raymond Ruyer, *L'Utopie et les Utopies* (Paris: Presses Universitaires de France, 1950)

Michael W. S. Ryan, *Decoding Al-Qaeda's Strategy: The Deep Battle Against America* (New York, NY: Columbia University Press, 2013)

Pedro A. Sanjuan, *The UN Gang: A Memoir of Incompetence, Corruption* (New York, NY: Doubleday, 2005)

Jason L. Saunders, *Greek and Roman Philosophy After Aristotle* (New York, NY: The Free Press, 1966)

Ronald Schechter, *Obstinate Hebrews: Representations of Jews in France, 1715-1815* (Berkeley and Los Angeles, CA: University of California Press, 2003)

James C. Scott, *Domination and the Arts of Resistance* (New Haven, CT: Yale University Press, 1992)

Michael Sharnoff, *A Peace to End All Peace Egypt's Response to the 1967 War with Israel* (New York, NY: Routledge, 2017)

Ronald Schechter, *Obstinate Hebrews: Representations of Jews in France, 1715-1815* (Berkeley and Los Angeles, CA: University of California Press, 2003)

Jonathan Schneer, *The Balfour Declaration: The Origins of the Arab-Israeli Conflict* (New York, NY: Random House, 2010)

Harris Okun Schoenberg, *A Mandate for Terror: The United Nations and the PLO* (New York, NY: Shapolsky Publishers, 1989)

Binjamin W. Segel, in Richard S. Levy, *A Lie and a Libel: The History of the Protocols of the Elders of Zion* (Lincoln, NE: University of Nebraska Press, 1996)

Michael Sharnoff, *A Peace to End All Peace: Egypt's Response to the 1967 War with Israel* (New York, NY: Routledge, 2017)

Edmund Silberner, "Was Marx an Anti-Semite?" in Ezra Mendelsohn, ed., *Essential Papers on Jews and the Left* (New York, NY: New York University Press, 1997)

Peter Singer, *One World: The Ethics of Globalization*, (New Haven, CT: Yale University Press, 2004)

Andrei Sinyavsky, *Soviet Civilization: A Cultural History* (New York, NY: Arcade Publishing, 1988)

O. D. Skelton, *Socialism: A Critical Analysis* (New York, NY: Houghton Mifflin Co., 1911)

Adam Smith, *An Inquiry into the Nature and Causes of the Wealth of Nations*, R. H. Campbell and A. S. Skinner, eds. (Indianapolis, IN: Liberty Classics, 1981)

Susan Sontag, *Trip to Hanoi: Journey to a city at war* (New York, NY: HarperCollins, 1969)

Georges Sorel, "For Lenin," *Soviet Russia*, Official Organ of The Russian Soviet Government Bureau Vol. II April 1920 (New York, NY: Official Organ of The Russian Soviet Government Bureau)

Georges Sorel, *Reflections on Violence* (London: George Allen & Unwin, 1915)

Thomas Sowell, *The Quest for Cosmic Justice* (New York, NY: The Free Press, 1999)

Thomas Sowell, *Intellectuals and Society* (New York, NY: Basic Books, 2009)

David Starkey, *Magna Carta: The Medieval Roots of Modern Politics* (New York, NY: Quercus, 2015)

L. Steiman, Paths to Genocide: Antisemitism in Western History (New York, NY: Springer, 1997)

Fritz Stern, *The Politics of Cultural Despair: A Study in the Rise of the Germanic Ideology* (Berkeley, CA: University of California Press, 1961)

Zeev Sternhell with Mario Sznajder and Maia Asheri, *The Birth of Fascist Ideology: From Cultural Rebellion to Political Revolution* (Princeton, NJ: Princeton University Press, 1994)

Leo Strauss and Joseph Cropsey, eds., *History of Political Philosophy*, 3rd edition (Chicago, IL: University of Chicago Press, 1987)

Wislawa Szymborska, *View with a Grain of Sand: Selected Poems*, Translated by Stanislaw Baranczak and Clare Cavanagh, (New York, NY: Harvest/Harcourt Brace, 1995)

Amir Taheri, *The Persian Night: Iran under the Khomeinist Revolution* (New York, NY: Encounter Books, 2008)

Uriel Tal, *Religion, Politics, and Ideology in the Third Reich: Selected Essays* (London: Routledge, 2004)

Ray Takeyh, *Hidden Iran: Paradox and Power in the Islamic Republic*, (New York, NY: Henry Holt, 2006)

Jacob L. Talmon, *The Myth of the Nation and the Vision of Revolution: The Origins of Ideological Polarization in the 20th Century* (New York, NY: Routledge, 2017)

Pierre Teilhard de Chardin, *The Phenomenon of Man* (New York, NY: Harper & Row, 1961).

Trygve Throntveit, *Power without Victory: Woodrow Wilson and the American Internationalist Experiment* (Chicago, IL: University of Chicago Press, 2017)

James W. Trent, Jr., *Inventing the Feeble Mind: A History of Mental Retardation in the United States* (Oxford: Oxford University Press, 2016)

Eric Voegelin, *From Enlightenment to Revolution* (Durham, NC: Duke University Press, 1975)

Eric Voegelin, *Modernity Without Restraint, The Collected Works of Eric Voegelin*, Vol. 5 (Columbia, MO: University of Missouri Press, 2000)

Voltaire, *Philosophical Dictionary* (London: Penguin Books, 1971)

Otto Wagener, *Hitler – Memoirs of a Confidant* (New Haven, CT: Yale University Press, 1985)

Karl-Friedrich Walling, *Republican Empire: Alexander Hamilton on War and Free Government* (Lawrence, KS: University Press of Kansas, 1999)

Michael Walzer, *The Revolution of Saints* (New York, NY: Atheneum, 1969)

Woodrow Wilson, *Papers of Woodrow Wilson* (Princeton, NJ: Princeton University Press, 1996)

Ella Winter, *Red Virtue: Human Relationships in the New Russia* (London: Victor Gollancz LTD., 1933)

Robert S. Wistrich, ed., *Demonizing the Other: Antisemitism, Racism, and Xenophobia* (Amsterdam: Harwood Academic Publishers, 1999)

Robert S. Wistrich, *A Lethal Obsession: Antisemitism from Antiquity to the Global Jihad* (New York, NY: Random House, 2010)

Robert S. Wistrich, *From Ambivalence to Betrayal: The Left, the Jews, and Israel* (Lincoln, NE: University of Nebraska Press, 2012)

Gordon S. Wood, *The Creation of the American Republic 1776-1787* (Chapel Hill, NC: University of North Carolina Press, 1998)

Lawrence Wright, *The Looming Tower: Al-Qaeda and the Road to 9/11* (New York, NY: Doubleday, 2006)

Theodore Ziolkowski, *Modes of Faith: Secular Surrogates for Lost Religious Belief* (Chicago, IL: University of Chicago Press, 2007)

Steven J. Zipperstein, *Pogrom: Kishinev and the Tilt of History* (New York, NY: W. W. Norton & Co., 2018)

Index

Acknowledgments

My father of blessed memory used to say, whenever I praised his modesty – for he really was a very humble man, considering how many languages he spoke, how widely he read, and how many people he'd helped without batting an eyelash - "Well, I have a lot to be modest about." Then he would chuckle, for he loved a *bon mot*. But he meant it: sometimes he confessed to me that he regretted not having continued his education. (Having to leave college in Paris to return home to his family in Romania after Hitler started World War II seemed insufficiently exculpatory.) Surviving Nazi occupation and forced labor, then later refusing to join the Communist Party and celebrating Passover surreptitiously, were all done with grace. Although I can never measure up to his all-but-impossible standards, I too have a lot to be modest about. Research for this book has only reconfirmed that Socrates's "I know nothing" is the apogee of wisdom, for the more I learn, it seems the less I know. My hope is to help disabuse the reader of some bits of illusory knowledge, and perhaps offer a few facts to encourage additional humility.

Any author must confess to at least some hubris, and I am no exception. Indeed, having taken on a topic of such breadth as here presupposes an uncommon excess of that noxious bile; and it is only thanks to incredibly supportive friends, family, and colleagues that I allowed myself to succumb to it at all, though not so far as to forget that the perfect is the enemy of the good. Living in Washington, moreover, has taught me one more truth, which might horrify the Platonic idealist – which is that the good is the enemy of the good-enough. I trust that a reader who has tolerated my occasional attempts at humor and general indifference to political correctness, not to mention all those footnotes, may forgive whatever flaws remain. My only excuse, though no justification, is that I have tried to be as faithful as possible to the evidence, and I welcome any corrections with gratitude. There would have been more flaws, without doubt, had it not been for all the support I have received from people who generously encouraged, nudged, and sometimes corrected my efforts, always with love and enthusiasm.

How do I count the ways I have been helped? To begin, I have a home at the Alexander Hamilton Institute for the Study of Western Civilization, whose mission is "to help cultivate a genuinely free marketplace of ideas and promote excellence in scholarship through the study of freedom, democracy and capitalism." Could a bookworm with three degrees in philosophy from the hallowed home of the Great Books, the University of Chicago, ever wish for more? I have benefited immeasurably from conversations about America's Founders with AHI's president and co-founder Robert Paquette, professor emeritus and former holder of the Publius Virgilius Rogers Chair in American History at Hamilton College, a consummate scholar and man of great integrity, who read and commented on my final draft. So too did Daniel J. Mahoney, professor of political science and holder of the Augustinian Boulanger Chair at Assumption College, whose encyclopedic knowledge of Christian theology and Russian, French, and British intellectual history (the list goes on) pales in comparison to the breadth of his soul and spiritual insight.

A very special thanks must go to the eminent student of ideology and the intellectuals, and human rights under communism worldwide, the late Paul Hollander. Professor emeritus of sociology at Amherst College, Paul hailed from my neck of the woods in East-Central Europe. Although he miraculously survived the Holocaust while I was born afterward, we both lived through enough of communism never to forget it, and to appreciate the insidious attraction yet ultimate lethality of what appears otherwise benign: the allure of substantive equality. What is more, we both spoke Hungarian. Well, he did; I tried, with uneven success. My accent was fine, but not so my spelling, which provided him with endless amusement. So it was that during the last year of his life, as I was writing my book, we exchanged regular emails. We recommended readings to one another; he was writing on the image of evil in Soviet literature, a book left unfinished when he was suddenly struck down by cancer. I never had a chance to thank him properly for his detailed comments on my book's original outline, which truly set me on the right track. He was a thoughtful scholar and a sweet man; I miss him.

Another invaluable supporter, my good friend Eric Rozenman, who for many years directed the Washington office of the Committee for Accuracy in Middle East Reporting and Analysis (CAMERA), read the book in its entirety with a journalist's magnifying glass. But he also provided much encouragement when the magnitude of my subject seemed too daunting. So too did Mary Curtis Horowitz, president of the famed Transaction Publishers, the brainchild of her late husband, Irving Louis Horowitz, a brilliant sociologist in the grand tradition, with a heart to match. Without Mary's sharp eye for the essential, the simple and direct, to temper my intellectual meanderings, this book would not have been possible. She has been my rock.

So many others have contributed to the ideas contained in this book, I can mention them only in passing. But I must single out Alan Charles Kors, the Henry Charles Lea Professor Emeritus of History at the University of Pennsylvania, whose superb studies on the Enlightenment helped me better understand that complex era. Equally important have been his insights on the Nazi-Communist axis. And most of all, I cherish his personal warmth.

I also cannot fail to thank my friend, Professor Tom Merrill, associate director of the Political Theory Institute and associate professor of government at American University. A stellar student of David Hume's political thought, he has provided me an opportunity to teach a course at AU and, in addition, to take on the sponsorship of the AU chapter of the Alexander Hamilton Society. Though separate from the AHI, AHS also promotes dialogue and debate, albeit with a focus on foreign policy and national security. That happens to coincide with the evolution of my own odyssey: for after post-graduate studies in international affairs at Stanford University's Hoover Institution, destiny took me in an unexpected direction, into the vortex of history. Who knew that I would witness Hungary's dismantling of its 150-mile-long border fence with Austria, on May 2, 1989, on-site?

Physical dismantling, yes. But the persistence of ideology was appreciated by very few. The courageous Vladimir Bukovsky was one who understood; Jack Dziak was another. The first director of the Masters Degree Program in Strategic Intelligence in what is now National Intelligence University, Jack is this country's foremost expert on the Russian secret police. I am honored that he took time from writing his book on the counterintelligence state to write this book's Foreword.

Finally, I must thank my husband Roger. I am hardly alone in acknowledging his expertise on the U.S. Constitution and the epistemological foundations of the theory of rights, about which he speaks and writes lucidly, passionately, eloquently. And my son Alex could always be depended on to offer sober advice on my prose, from a layman's perspective. A very smart layman, I hasten to add, second only to his sister Danielle, though only chronologically: they are both the best children, and they are the future. May it be bright, and may they live in freedom.

www.ingramcontent.com/pod-product-compliance
Lightning Source LLC
Chambersburg PA
CBHW051432270326
41935CB00018B/1803